Jones and Bartlett's Fund Raising Series for the 21st Century
Edited by James P. Gelatt, PhD, CFRE

Donor Focused Strategies for Annual Giving

Jones and Bartlett's Fund Raising Series for the 21st Century
Edited by James P. Gelatt, PhD, CFRE

Jones and Bartlett's Fund Raising Series for the 21st Century
Edited by James P. Gelatt, PhD, CFRE

Donor Focused Strategies for Annual Giving

Karla A. Williams, ACFRE
Principal
The Williams Group
St. Paul, Minnesota
Charlotte, North Carolina

JONES AND BARTLETT PUBLISHERS
Sudbury, Massachusetts
BOSTON   TORONTO   LONDON   SINGAPORE

World Headquarters

Jones and Bartlett Publishers
40 Tall Pine Drive
Sudbury, MA 01776
978-443-5000
info@jbpub.com
www.jbpub.com

Jones and Bartlett Publishers
Canada
2406 Nikanna Road
Mississauga, ON L5C 2W6
CANADA

Jones and Bartlett Publishers
International
Barb House, Barb Mews
London W6 7PA
UK

This publication is designed to provide accurate and authoritative information in regard to the Subject Matter covered. It is sold with the understanding that the publisher is not engaged in rendering legal, accounting, or other professional service. If legal advice or other expert assistance is required, the service of a competent professional person should be sought. *(From a Declaration of Principles jointly adopted by a Committee of the American Bar Association and a Committee of Publishers and Associations.)*

Library of Congress Cataloging-in-Publication Data

Williams, Karla A.
Donor focused strategies for annual giving / Karla A. Williams.
p. cm.
Includes bibliographical references and index.
ISBN 0-7637-2505-6 (pbk.)
1. Fund raising. 2. Charities—Finance. I. Title. II. Series.
HV41.2.W53 1997
361.'068'1—dc21   97-14433
CIP

Production Credits
Production Manager: Amy Rose
Associate Production Editor: Renée Sekerak
Production Assistant: Jenny L. McIsaac
Associate Marketing Manager: Joy Stark-Vancs
Manufacturing Buyer: Amy Bacus
Printing and Binding: PA Hutchison
Cover Printing: PA Hutchison

Printed in the United States of America
07 06 05 04   10 9 8 7 6 5 4 3 2

I dedicate this book to my family, who have always believed in me, encouraged me, and accepted me unconditionally. In particular, to my father who taught me to live life with intention, and to never get up in the morning to do anything other than what I loved to do. To my daughters, Allyson and Lindsey, who not only make my life rich and rewarding, but for whom motherhood is my greatest source of pride and joy.

Table of Contents

Preface

The genesis of this book on annual giving comes out of a perceived need to bring fund-raising practices into sync with our dynamic and ever-changing environment, and from a belief that a more donor-focused approach will lead to stronger relationships and mutually beneficial results for the long term.

As an emerging profession, fund raising has been defined primarily by experiential practice rather than researched theory offered through academic education. Nowhere is the absence of fund-raising research or theoretical underpinnings more obvious than in the area of annual gift giving, commonly referred to as the *annual fund*. Although there are numerous workshops and book chapters on the subject of the annual fund, nearly all strategies are based on how to implement the various annual methodologies and techniques which originated many years ago. Thus, for many practitioners, the annual fund practice is viewed as dull, repetitive, and mechanical—for some, a mathematical mandate. As a methodology that raises annual operating support for an institution, its very nature forces the focus to be more one-sided than balanced—almost exclusively on the meeting the institution's needs, as opposed as the donor's needs or interests.

This book promotes the application of an *annual integrated development process* that is designed to be more donor-sensitive, complex and comprehensive, virtually seamless, and an effective strategy for sustainable philanthropy. This new *annual integrated development process* relies on the tried and true practices of the past, while incorporating the latest innovations used by contemporary fund raisers. These newest approaches are designed to:

- better understand donors, their motivations, and their interests through research
- segment donors into similar, discrete constituencies
- select and communicate specific needs to different donor segments by way of an exchange
- select different fund-raising vehicles based on the donor's characteristics
- provide a form of case management for each donor, allowing him or her to move more naturally into a relationship of giving and receiving
- provide a higher level of donor communications, recognition, and stewardship

The rationale, then, for this book is to demonstrate that annual giving is the core of an integrated development program, and that its success depends on the extent to which fund raisers treat their donors as individuals with distinct needs and interests, rather than mass marketing their organizational cause. The book provides a review of the time-honored fund-raising principles, with all their variations. It recommends the use of marketing theory as the most natural donor-focused approach to build a sustainable, integrated development program. It offers a summary of the current research on internal donor motivations and external motivating factors. The book uncovers working case examples where new approaches are being successfully implemented. And it shows that annual giving in its contemporary version has greater richness, variety, complexity, and opportunity for innovation than any other aspect of fund raising.

The information used in the book is derived from the author's 25 years of practical fund raising experience, knowledge gained through active teaching and learning from other practitioners, and research gained from the writing of a 1995/6 master's thesis in philanthropy, titled "The Importance of Donor Research and Segmentation to Advance Annual Fund Practice and Theory."

Acknowledgments

To be a facilitator of the philanthropic process is a privilege of the highest order. It is, I am sure, what I was destined to do. I believe this privilege comes with a responsibility to nurture the philanthropy spirit, tradition, and sector by advancing its meaning and its acceptance within the world we live in. This may best be accomplished by learning from others, and about all there is to know, and then by passing it on to others who will contribute to its further advancement.

Like you, I am the accumulation of my genetic disposition, my cultural anthropology, and my life's circumstances, events, and experiences. As a person with passion for what is right, and a compassion for what is wrong, I have chosen to be a volunteer, a professional fund raiser, an organizational consultant, a teacher, and a writer. If I am the least bit successful in these endeavors it is because of those individuals who have taught me, challenged me, counseled me, encouraged me, and touched my heart and soul— personally, professionally, emotionally, and intellectually. I want to publicly acknowledge the following people.

Edward A. Ellis, CFRE, for being my philanthropic soul mate, for challenging me to find my own truth, and for doing what is not expected.

Robert L. Payton, PhD, for helping me to understand the meaning of inquiry, for stimulating questions that may not have answers, and for inspiring so many of us to pass it on.

Henry A. Rosso, CFRE retired, for showing me how to transfer the love of the practice into a laboratory of learning, teaching, and consulting.

Robert W. Toogood, MSW, for demonstrating how an executive director can inspire an organization and its volunteers to places only imagined, always centered on mission.

Roger S. Williams, for giving me the bedrock to reach beyond my limitations, for providing the safety net to fail now and again, and to keep on going.

To my colleagues, students, and clients: thank you for teaching me—you have made me a life-long learner. I can only hope that I give you as much inspiration in return.

Chapter 1

Organized Philanthropy and Fund-Raising History and Practices

Organized Philanthropy in America: A Conscious Reflective Effort to Eliminate Difficult Challenges Facing the Community

A contemporary book on fund raising cannot ignore the historical, sociological, philosophical, ethical, theoretical, or practical roots of the philanthropic process. Although these aspects are covered adequately in many other books, and in some cases covered as an area of focused study, we—as students of philanthropy—must be continuously reminded of our *rationale* for fund raising. Keeping the rationale in mind will ensure that we contemporary fund raisers pursue our work with as much vigor as those who preceded us and put all that we do in a proper, balanced perspective. When we understand our historic roots, and why certain practices evolved, we are better able to examine our current strategies, and to advance philanthropic fund raising with more clarity, creativity, and commitment.

As a field of study, philanthropy encompasses 3,700 years of historic evidence, beginning with the Egyptian Book of the Dead, proceeding through the Old Testament, into ancient Greece and Rome, through the emergence of Christian tithing, into the Middle Ages with all its hierarchical alms giving systems, past the famous Elizabethan "Poor Laws," followed by

Alexis de Toqueville's observation of the habits of generosity in post-colonial times, to what we know today as the spirit of American democracy, expressed through philanthropic acts by a multitude of differing peoples.

Because of the profusion of writing on the subject of philanthropy, the scope of this fund-raising book is limited to philanthropy's organized period and its contemporary posture, and, in this chapter, to the evolution of fund raising within the philanthropic system and process.

The Definition of Philanthropy Today

Over the years, scholars have attempted to define the word *philanthropy*, uncovering a multitude of interpretations. As philanthropy expands in dimension and dynamics, it takes on new meaning, shaped by cultural heritage and values.

Although Alexis de Toqueville did not use the word philanthropy, he had a great deal to say about the ways in which Americans performed and justified acts of helpfulness to one another. His observations painted vivid images of philanthropy in action. John D. Rockefeller, an early leader in the philanthropic movement, contemplated its meaning as a noun; he defined philanthropy as the main support mechanism for the nonprofit sector—what people did, rather than what they hoped to accomplish. Others suggest that philanthropy is much more than the act of giving or raising money; it is the *outcome* that philanthropy facilitates—a persuasive action. Fund raisers, in particular, use the words *philanthropy* and *fund raising* interchangeably. Of late, development professionals refer to their work as *philanthropic* to emphasize that it is mission-focused, in contrast to an exclusively money-raising endeavor (and in part to distinguish themselves from political fund raisers and paid solicitors who are engaged in telephone scams).

As an expression, philanthropy is the democratic spirit that keeps America strong and free. As an action, it is the free-will contribution of dollars and time. As an intention, it separates moral and ethical actions from "simply doing."

> *Charity:* An act of mercy or compassion, a spontaneous response to the less fortunate.
>
> *Philanthropy:* A conscious effort to eliminate difficult challenges facing the community.
>
> *Yusef Mgeni*

Often philanthropy is defined by contrasting it to *charity*, a concept viewed as more limited and less sophisticated. Yusef Mgeni, a lifelong student of philanthropy and leadership, points out the differences: *charity* is "an act of mercy or compassion, a spontaneous response to the less fortunate," whereas *philanthropy* is "a conscious reflective effort to eliminate difficult challenges facing the community" (Yusef Mgeni, personal communication). Historian and author Robert H. Bremner concurs that philanthropy is one of the principal methods of social advance—it is broader than charity given that it covers more than the problems of the poor. Its purpose is to "promote the welfare, happiness, and culture of mankind" (Bremner 1988, 3).

The National Society of Fund Raising Executives (NSFRE) describes philanthropy according to the Greek roots of the word—*love of humankind*. Michael Downes, of the World Fundraising Council, offers a more personal and poetic version: "Philanthropy is not a whim or a fancy; it is a commitment to life itself" (NSFRE 1989).

Although semantic differences exist, these definitions are certainly more accurate than those yielded from man-on-the-street interviews in Minneapolis several years ago. In that exercise, participants defined philanthropy as "the study of monkeys," "a scary disease," and "a new kind of ocean fish."

The most commonly accepted definition of philanthropy in the contemporary context is one advanced by Robert L. Payton (1988). His definition, stated in the title of his book, *Voluntary Action for the Public Good*, is succinct and deceptively simple; a reminder that concern for others is paramount in the nonprofit sector.

Philanthropy is not exclusively American, but in America it is part and parcel of our democratic voice. Nearly every major social movement in our nation's history started in the nonprofit sector. Because the sector cannot operate without consensus, it has been indispensable to our democratic traditions. As George Kirstein said, "Apart from the ballot box, philanthropy presents the one opportunity the individual has to express his meaningful choice over the direction in which our society will progress" (Lord 1987). Or as Gurin and Van Til (1990) point out, philanthropy is our tradition, our spirit, as well as being a sector of society.

Philanthropy as a Tradition: The Way We Do Things

Traditions are formed as a result of actions valued and passed on from people to people, generation to generation. Traditions by their nature are socially ingrained, part of a cultural trust. Momentum alone cannot ensure their vitality or endurance. They must be nurtured and reaffirmed as they travel through time.

Philanthropy is a **rich tradition** in America, having come out of the earliest response to human issues too critical to ignore or social advances too important to leave to chance. As a tradition, American "organized" philanthropy is an **institutional process** used to build and maintain a civil society.

Since America's founding, foreign visitors have commented on the uncommon persistence of Americans in forming voluntary organizations to address community problems. Our tradition of philanthropy is expressed in our response to acute social needs and problems and our impulse to nurture social justice and advance the quality of life. But it is the **action** that follows, which makes American philanthropy the unique tradition that it is.

In the beginning, the tradition manifested itself quite simply. People enlisted others in benevolent enterprises and provided opportunities for self-help and mutual improvement. Not to be confused with charitable alms giving or be-nevolent poor relief, the philanthropic tradition of the New World was the freedom to **pioneer**— to develop experimental programs, enrich cultural life, and improve self-help for all individuals and families at any and every income level. It was the freedom to do what individuals could not do alone and what governments could not or would not do.

The American philanthropic tradition has flourished since our nation's founding, and along the way it has been nurtured, cultivated, enhanced, and advanced. What makes it uniquely an American way of life are all its parts:

- the volunteer gathering of like-minded people
- who together create a formal or informal voluntary association
- in order to develop a solution or a strategy that will collectively address the chosen issue
- and to garner whatever voluntary means are available (time, talent, and treasure)
- to accomplish the established mission.

This tradition forms the fabric of healthy, diverse, and democratic communities—voluntary action through voluntary association, fueled by a philanthropic impulse.

Community building and strengthening are the underlying theme of the American philanthropic tradition. Out of this impulse have come an incredible variety of responses: child welfare, women's rights, prison reform, treatment of the emotionally and physically disabled, foreign aid, social work, public safety, support for refugees and immigrants, and medical research. An endless number of American institutions have emerged from this tradition: libraries, museums, civic organizations, universities, hospitals, arts and cultural institutions, and charitable coalitions like the United Way.

The tradition of voluntary action through voluntary association has provided the nonprofit sector with its infrastructure; its socialization, problem solving, and leadership; its quality of life; and its public power and community "self" (Van Til 1990, 26).

The collective, action-oriented response that is indicative of our philanthropic fabric is the combination of many caring acts—the **family** traditions of volunteering time with favorite charities, the **church** traditions of reaching out to developing countries, the **school** traditions of collecting pennies during the holiday season, and the **individual** traditions of remembering loved ones through memorial gifts. Giving, serving, caring, and gathering are the American way, nurtured by our families, our churches, our schools, our community organizations, and even our governments.

How dominant are these philanthropic traditions? The collective gathering of time, talent, and treasure cannot be measured precisely or adequately, but we can ascertain its impact by the dollars given and the hours volunteered. According to Independent Sector's *Giving and Volunteering in the United States* (1996), philanthropic giving in 1995 topped $143 billion, an increase of 9.2 percent over the previous year. This was the first significant increase since 1990, an indicator of public responsibility-taking along with the dismantling of government-sponsored social programs. Another measure of the vitality of the philanthropy tradition is the amount of time that people volunteer every year. In 1995, 48.8 percent of the population volunteered time valued at $201 billion, an all-time high. Perhaps this increase in giving and volunteering is the American way of keeping the philanthropic tradition alive and well or, as always, a way of expressing both sentiment (for something) and skepticism (against something). As Payton writes, "The philanthropic tradition is not just acts of benevolence; it is also a powerful lever of social change. It is the voice of discontent and dissatisfaction as well as the expression of nurture and encouragement" (Van Til 1990, 139).

Philanthropy as a Spirit: Why We Do Things

If the American philanthropic *tradition* is based upon a **sense of community**, the philanthropic *spirit* is based on **human compassion**. Such words as values and virtues come to mind when the spirit of philanthropy is examined. Other words abound: benevolence, stewardship, conscience, catalyst, advocate, innovator, and, more commonly, "doing good." Our motivations are very personal, confirming that philanthropy is the litmus test for the community's concerns, interests, and values.

Philanthropy was already part and parcel of the New World landscape when the settlers arrived; it was a prevalent theme in the Native Americans' way of life. Meeting Columbus at his first landfall in the New World, Indians were reported to be "ingenuous and free," willing to give anything asked of them "with as much love as if their hearts went with it" (Bremner 1988, 5).

American immigrants were of the same mind and spirit, albeit one that was more theologically rooted. The foundation of their philanthropic spirit was decidedly Christian, a code of conduct for those who came to create communities that would be better than those they left. The doctrine of stewardship was the literal belief in the brotherhood of man as children of God.

Several contemporary studies have identified behavioral characteristics that highlight the strong ties between religious affiliation and giving. Because 70 percent of Americans belong to a church, temple, or other religious institution and 40 percent report attending services every week or almost every week, religion has a major impact on the nation's *spiritual* culture. The intriguing fact that over half of individual's charitable dollars today go to religious organizations and causes year after year is thus understandable (Mixer 1993, 7).

Beyond the notion of the Golden Rule and the obligation of inherited religious ideologies, the spirit of philanthropy was also an attempt to bring competing and conflicting interests in society into harmony (Bremner 1988, 12–13).

> **Philanthropy is a rich tradition in America, having come out of the earliest response to human issues too critical to ignore.**

"Pious example, moral leadership, voluntary effort, and private charity" were not only sound policy, they were "a mild but effective instrument of social control" (13).

The notion of doing good had no socioeconomic basis; it was and continues to be a broadly shared, genuinely popular avocation of Americans—its spirit protects the environment, prevents disease, improves education, enhances the arts, preserves historical landmarks, and sustains the needs of charity.

A review of literature on **why** people give provides a good picture of the motivations that support the spirit of philanthropy. The 1992 Independent Sector studies offer a concise view of the multiple reasons for people's charitable behavior, ranging from functional altruism to highly pragmatic benefits (Exhibit 1–1).

As a *spirit*—derived from beliefs, values, and desires—philanthropy is not mere money giving or money raising. It is our country's conscience and its catalyst. It is the initiative that occurs when people see need that exists and the response they give when a change is in order. It is our fundamental human impulse to say how life should be and could be.

> **The notion of doing good had no socioeconomic basis; it was and continues to be a broadly shared, genuinely popular avocation of Americans.**

Exhibit 1–1 Reasons for Giving and Volunteering

Reasons for Giving and Volunteering

- Those with more should help those with less.

- Gain a feeling of personal satisfaction.

- Religious beliefs or commitments.

- Giving back to society some benefits derived from it.

- Being asked to contribute or volunteer by a personal friend or business associate.

- Ensure the continuation of activities or institutions that they benefit from.

- Serve as an example to others.

- Fulfill a business or community obligation.

- Create a remembrance of oneself or one's family.

- Obtain tax considerations and deductions.

- Encouraged by an employer.

Source: Data from V.A. Hodgkinson et al., Giving and Volunteering in the United States: Findings from a National Survey, 1992, *Independent Sector*.

Philanthropy as a Sector: How and What We Do

The central benefit of the philanthropic *sector* lies in the value-added dimension it brings to the other two sectors—the government and marketplace sectors. The philanthropic sector does things **differently**: it fills the gaps, experiments with new ideas, serves controversial constituencies, provides a forum for public policy, remains free from economic influences, and speaks for and against issues.

The smallest of America's three sectors, the philanthropic or independent sector has at times been one of the loudest, most diverse, and influential voices in our nation's acculturation. The growth of the nonprofit sector during the past 60 years is staggering. A 1996–1997 Independent Sector study reports that the nonprofit sector is today the fastest growing sector in the United States. Consider these statistics (Hodgkinson et al. 1996):

- From 1977 to 1994, the national income of nonprofits, including the value of volunteer time, grew at an annual rate of 3.7 percent, compared with 2.1 percent for business, 2.3 percent for government, and 2.2 percent for all sectors.
- In 1994, the nonprofit sector had revenues of $354 billion, and accounted for 6.3 percent of national income, up from 5.8 percent seven years earlier.
- Current operating expenditures of nonprofits as a percentage of the national economy more than doubled to 7.9 percent in 1993 from 3.6 percent in 1977.
- From 1987 to 1995, the total number of charitable organizations in the United States increased 47.9 percent from 389,415 to 576,133, at an annual rate of 5 percent.
- The number of private foundations totaled 37,571 in 1993, up from 22,088 in 1980.
- In 1994, the nonprofit sector employed 15.1 million people. Paid employees and volunteers represented nearly 11 percent of total U.S. employment in 1992, up from 8.5 percent in 1977.

With recent shifts of responsibility for social services from government to communities, the nonprofit sector will undoubtedly play an even larger role—as it has in every other historic time of need.

Philanthropy as a Dynamic Process

Philanthropy operates as an interactive, dynamic **process**, as an assembly of parts that together comprise the whole "subject"—the noun and the adjective. The process includes the person who is giving and his or her motivation for giving, the person through whom the gift is made, the institution through which the gift will be processed, the person who delivers or provides the service, and the person who is the recipient or beneficiary of the gift.

Underlying this **process** are several assumptions:

- People have interests, preferences, and convictions—and an inherent desire to give.
- Community problems and needs exist that cannot be met by government or private enterprise.
- The nonprofit sector endures as society's pursuit of pluralism and innovation and a desire to advance socially.
- Nonprofit organizations are often best equipped to deliver services that meet critical and emerging needs, serving as a conduit between resources and recipients.
- Central to the philanthropic process is the social exchange of private resources (philanthropic expressions) with unfilled needs (services with beneficial outcomes) (Ostrander and Schervish 1990, 67–68).

In this context, the philanthropic process focuses on the **human dimension**, with emphasis placed on **people** as givers and receivers who are supported by people who facilitate the ex-

> The philanthropic process focuses on the human dimension, with emphasis placed on people as givers and receivers.

change and people who deliver the service. The philanthropic process gives thoughtful attention, and precedence, to the values/interests of philanthropists **and** the anticipated positive outcomes for recipients. The organization then is defined by its vision, its stewardship, and its measurable impact. The organization, and the people who are employed by it, are philanthropic processors and guardians of the mission. As such, organizations have no needs—they serve the critical role of conduit between donative interests and the advancement of communities and individuals.

In summary, the process of philanthropy is a multifaceted five-part dynamic aimed at advancing the public good. See Exhibit 1–2.

When the philanthropic process is organized around the values of reciprocity, cooperation, mutual respect, accountability, and commitment, we are all beneficiaries.

The Evolution of Fund Raising: Experiential Practices and Tensions

Experiential Learning: Transformed by Theory

As an emerging profession, fund raising has until recently been defined primarily by experiential practice, rather than researched theory offered through academic education. Since the beginning of organized fund raising in the 1900s, senior-level fund raisers and consultants have traditionally passed on the learned fund-raising skills to those entering the field and have served as inspirational mentors for the profession. The preferred training/teaching sites for the first few generations of fund raisers were their home institutions, augmented by fund-raising workshops.

Fund raising is no longer the same unexplored, experiential field that our predecessors forged. It remains true that many fund raisers continue to learn their craft on the job, but gone is the day of having to invent a fund-raising strategy or activity from scratch. In its place are solid, time-honored core principles that have been invented, altered, expanded, enhanced, and passed down through four generations. For today's inquisitive fund raisers, an abundance of continuing education classes and workshops are offered through professional associations and academic institutions and are taught by practitioners who learned the hard way, by trial and error. Scholarly research and theory development are on the horizon. Books on the subject of fund raising have proliferated in recent years, focusing on core fundamentals with the latest practice iterations. Scholars are engaged in research studies that challenge and substantiate the rationale for fund raising. Articles are being published on "why, when, and how" certain dynamics are more effective than others. For the reflective practitioner, more field information is available than ever before.

Nevertheless, several problems exist with the transference of information that is gathered experientially. First, most fund-raising practices are passed on by oral tradition. Few fund raisers document or publish their strategies or measure their outcomes (except for their own use) in ways that could be analyzed and compared to that of other practitioners. Even after four generations of experiential learning, there is an absence of concrete, well-documented evidence on best practices, particularly on the subject of the annual fund. Even more challenging, what works in one setting may not work in another.

Second, fund-raising practices that have become embedded over time may become insular. If they remain in their original form, unchallenged by scholars and others outside the fund-raising practice, who is to say they are effective or merely an imitation of someone else's experience?

Third, because some fund-raising techniques are borrowed from other professions, such as

Exhibit 1-2 Dynamics of the Philanthropic Process

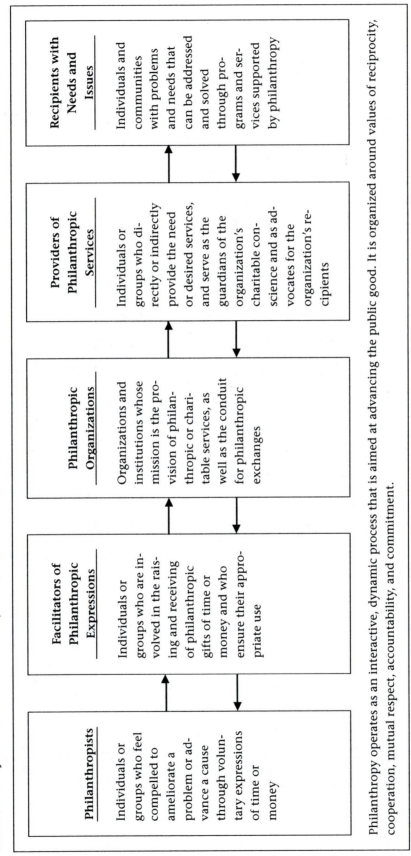

Philanthropists	Facilitators of Philanthropic Expressions	Philanthropic Organizations	Providers of Philanthropic Services	Recipients with Needs and Issues
Individuals or groups who feel compelled to ameliorate a problem or advance a cause through voluntary expressions of time or money	Individuals or groups who are involved in the raising and receiving of philanthropic gifts of time or money and who ensure their appropriate use	Organizations and institutions whose mission is the provision of philanthropic or charitable services, as well as the conduit for philanthropic exchanges	Individuals or groups who directly or indirectly provide the need or desired services, and serve as the guardians of the organization's charitable conscience and as advocates for the organization's recipients	Individuals and communities with problems and needs that can be addressed and solved through programs and services supported by philanthropy

Philanthropy operates as an interactive, dynamic process that is aimed at advancing the public good. It is organized around values of reciprocity, cooperation, mutual respect, accountability, and commitment.

business and communications, they are said to "skate on thinner intellectual ice than is prudent" (Payton et al. 1991, 277).

Fourth, fund raisers tend to focus more on learning the techniques and the methodologies of the profession, rather than the rationale for them. Unless experience is augmented by theory, the status quo will not be challenged.

On the other hand, all these issues present a welcome challenge for reflective practitioners who want to contribute to the advancement of the profession and its theory for now they can be an integral part of the industry's effort to professionalize the work through scholarly study, research, and education. They can borrow the old and help shape the new.

Four Generations of Fund Raising

In addition to understanding the history of organized philanthropy in America, it is extremely useful for the contemporary fund raiser to be aware of the **evolution** of fund raising—as described earlier, fund raising is but one of five component parts within the philanthropic process. An examination of experiential fund-raising practices and principles, passed down from generation to generation, demonstrates how fund raising has grown and changed or, in some cases, remained the same. By looking back, one can almost see anthropology at work: practices being initiated and sometimes inculcated, philosophies being shaped and sometimes challenged, theories emerging and sometimes tested.

As with every emerging profession, fund raising has its tensions. It has its zealots and its critics. Because fund raising is often misunderstood by observers and professionals alike, it is important to examine some persistent questions: Is fund raising a *career* or a *calling*? Is fund raising a discipline that is original in form, or is it an extrapolation of other disciplines? Is it a form of *communications or public relations* or a *managed, integrated business approach*? Does fund raising exist to serve the *needs of the organization* or to respond to the *interests of donors*? How does the fund raiser balance the multitude of existing tensions? Beyond the raising of funds, what is the fund raiser's role?

This section puts the evolution of fund raising into a contemporary perspective and reports on those ever-present tensions over money and mission. Because of the sparse literature on the subject, I have taken the liberty of arbitrarily segmenting fund raising/fund raisers into four generational groups, thereby providing a sequential order to show how fund raising evolved from its pioneer years into a professional stance (Exhibit 1–3).

The historic information for this section is derived primarily from Scott Cutlip's *Fund Raising in the United States: Its Role in American Philanthropy* (1965); Jeanne Harrah-Conforth's and Borsos' article, "The Evolution of Professional Fund Raising: 1890–1990," in *Taking Fund Raising Seriously* (1991); Thomas E. Broce's *Fund Raising: The Guide to Raising Money from Private Sources* (1986); and Robert H. Bremner's *American Philanthropy* (1988).

Generation One—The Pioneers: 1900–1930

Several historians and writers date fund raising to the year 1641 when Harvard University sent three clergy to England to raise funds to "educate the heathen Indian" (Van Til 1990, 13). Soon after, Yale University and The College of William and Mary sought and were awarded grants by their provincial governments, which helped spur contributions from individual donors in America. Records show that George Whitefield, a young English evangelist, traveled the country in 1739 taking up collections for poor debtors, disaster victims, and orphanages and to underwrite books and financial assistance for hard-pressed colleges. More notably, Benjamin Franklin was inspired to raise funds for several of his charitable interests, giving credence to the task of fund raising. He was particularly thoughtful and organized in his approach, recommending this to others

> In the first place, I advise you to apply to all those whom you know will give something; next, to those whom

Exhibit 1–3 Four Generations of Fund Raising

GENERATION ONE—THE PIONEERS: 1900–1930

- Some of the first codified fund raising techniques were developed.
- Moral and business ideologies were coalesced.
- Served as the initial training ground for future fund raisers.
- The first professional fund-raising firms were established.
- Campaign and federated fund drive innovations emerged.

GENERATION TWO—THE CAMPAIGNERS: 1930–1960

- Consultants were in high demand for resident campaigns and professional consultation.
- In-house fund-raising positions were created.
- Communications became an important component within fund raising, with the goal of educating and informing the public.
- Multi-million-dollar campaigns flourished, growing in size and scope.
- The *annual fund* and *legacy society* were developed as methods to raise funds for the general operating budget.
- Challenge grants, initiated by foundations, served as incentives for matched contributions from others.

GENERATION THREE—THE INNOVATORS: 1960–1980

- Fund raisers were widely recruited for many kinds of positions, in all types of nonprofit organizations.
- Professional societies established standards of practice, fund-raising benchmarks, and the first industry-approved code of ethical principles.
- Fund raising became a high-profile activity, stimulated by major public events and commercial activities.
- The most innovative fund-raising techniques in the history of fund raising were assembled, shaped and fine tuned.
- Volunteer opportunities multiplied with the rise in fund-raising events.
- The implementation of advanced technology reinforced fund raising as a business strategy, gaining access to more donors.
- Women entered the profession in large numbers, altering its profile and culture.
- Higher salaries reflected the growing level of professionalism.

GENERATION FOUR—THE PROFESSIONALS: 1980–2000

- Credentialing, ethical principles, advanced learning, and scholarly involvement were pursued as ways to achieve professional standing.
- Multiple job opportunities were available, ranging from generalist to specialist in direct mail, special events, prospect research, major gifts, planned giving, and campaign management.
- Continuing education opportunities promoted skill development and encouraged theory design.
- Greater emphasis was placed on the management of the integrated development program, reducing the number and variety of grassroots special events.
- Sophisticated donors demanded a more advanced level of communications and relationship building, and more accountability.

you are uncertain whether they will give anything or not, and show them the list of those who have given; and lastly, do not neglect those whom you are sure will give nothing, for in some of them you may be mistaken (Van Til 1990, 14).

Except for these few examples, fund raising in the 18th and 19th centuries was pretty much limited to the personal solicitation of wealthy benefactors and the passing of the church plate. There were but a few social service agencies—the YMCA, Salvation Army, and Hull House—and they served as the testing grounds for the first "organized" fund-raising strategies.

No doubt this is the reason why other historians date fund raising to the early 1900s when systematic solicitation of the general public really began to flourish. Changing social conditions and such life-altering events as World War I created an abundance of community needs and social service agencies that required expanded public support. New fund-raising methods were devised that would appeal to and attract large numbers of supporters. The times gave birth to the *job* of fund raising, to the *work* of the first paid fund raisers, and to two innovative fund-raising concepts—**the campaign method of fund raising** and **the federation (or combined) fund drive**. Together, these two fund-raising innovations broadened voluntary giving from the exclusive reserve of a handful of wealthy citizens to the involvement of mass citizenry.

The campaign method of fund raising was actually the YMCA's response to the excessive amount of time and money being spent on a form of fund raising that resembled *begging*. Charles Sumner Ward and Lyman Pierce, leaders in the YMCA movement, are credited with the idea of compressing "the drudgery of begging" into an intensive, highly organized and

> **The times gave birth to the job of fund raising, to the work of the first paid fund raisers, and to two innovative fund-raising concepts.**

publicized volunteer-led campaign: "to get the agony over quickly." Fund raising, in their view, wasn't necessarily an unworthy endeavor, but rather quite the opposite—for Ward and Pierce it was a conduit to something more meaningful. They were "driven by a missionary fervor, seeing their fund-raising roles as an expression of moral stewardship," Ward remarked. "I would leave this work immediately if I thought I were merely raising money. It is raising men that appeals to me" (Cutlip 1965, 43).

The YMCA's capital campaign of 1905 in the Washington, D.C. community stands "as a watershed in fund-raising history," for it integrated aspects of campaigning that are still present today in all capital campaigns and in some annual campaigns: specific campaign goals, a limited time frame, careful organization, selected volunteers, team competition, pyramid giving with large gifts first, detailed record keeping, report meetings, and lots of publicity (Harrah-Conforth and Borsos 1991, 22). The YMCA campaign methodology was not only successful financially, raising over $60 million in capital funds between 1905 and 1906, but these campaigns also served as a training ground for most first-generation fund raisers. The early YMCA fund raisers were grounded in a Christian philanthropic tradition, trained to be "engineers of movement in the service of other men" (Cutlip 1965, 43). Similarly, the Red Cross molded the character of pioneer fund raisers whose inseparable views of mission and morality led them on to become the first executive directors of the nation's fledgling social service organizations. This stewardship movement represented the first major ideological influence in the development of fund raising.

Not all of the pioneer-era fund raisers felt the same *calling*; some recognized the opportunity of fund raising as a money-making *career*. Frederick Courtney Barber is acknowledged to have been more interested in the commercial potential of fund raising, establishing what may have been the first consulting firm in 1913: Barber and Associates. To the then-popular campaign method Barber added another dimension—publicizing the activity with "fireworks and ballyhoo"—with remuneration based on a percentage of money raised. Unlike Ward and Pierce who typically remained out of the campaign limelight, Barber saw fund raising as a business venture with personal, financial rewards (Harrah-Conforth and Borsos 1991, 23). Today of course, percentage-based compensation is discouraged because of the possibility that the fund raiser may inappropriately pressure or influence the donor for potential self-gain.

In the early 20th century, the **federated or the combined fund drive** also began to take shape. Like the campaign method, it was driven by the need to improve the efficiency of fund raising by pooling resources and reaching out to more people. It was promoted by wealthy benefactors who wanted to cut down the increasing number of requests made to them by charities. The first recorded attempt to stage a federated fund drive was made by Matthew Carey in Philadelphia in 1829. Although unsuccessful, he was very creative in his approach, raising money for several needy institutions by selling subscriptions. Other mildly successful subscription drives were implemented to raise funds for the building of monuments to honor those who fought in the American Revolution. In 1877, the first "earnest" federated fund effort was waged in Denver to coordinate the financing of local community charities (Gurin and Van Til 1990, 14–15). Historic credit is given, however, to pioneer William J. Norton for leading and nurturing the successful federated fund drive movement (Harrah-Conforth and Borsos 1991, 20). Spurred by the success of the war drives, the "community chest movement" spread from 40 cities in 1919 to about 350 a decade later (Bremner 1988, 133). The federated fund drive concept proved effective in reducing competition, promoting the rational distribution of charitable dollars, expanding the number of givers beyond the wealthy, and increasing the amount of contributions to important social causes. Today we see the thriving, contemporary forms of the federated fund drive concept: the national and local United Way campaigns, regional United Arts fund drives, national United Negro College campaigns, the Combined Federal Campaign, community-based Combined Health Appeals, and more.

After World War I, a second major ideological influence emerged to further shape fund raising as a profession. In 1916, John Price Jones began working on a $10 million endowment campaign at Harvard, drawing on his background in journalism and advertising. Achieving success, he went on to form his own consulting firm after World War II, recruiting a professional staff with very different backgrounds from those who had come through the YMCA school of fund raising. In contrast to the YMCA "Christers," as Jones called them, the John Price Jones school of fund raising was based on businesslike, commercial, and secular principles (Cutlip 1965, 43).

At about the same time, Charles Ward and Lyman Pierce made their way into the consulting business as partners in the firm, Ward, Hill, Pierce & Wells. By the mid-1920s, the ideologies of the Jones and YMCA schools seemed to have merged: Fund raising was a philanthropic enterprise, a moral endeavor, that also made excellent business sense. The number of private consulting firms swelled, with over 20 firms in New York City alone. Their clients included leading colleges, churches, and community chest organizations (Bremner 1988, 133). The tension between *calling* and *career* was embedded in the center of the profession (Harrah-Conforth and Borsos 1991, 27).

During the 1920s higher education fund raising became more organized and competitive; fund raisers were hired to run campaigns for buildings, memorial football stadiums, and the first endowment funds (Broce 1986, 11). In the following decade, core fund-raising techniques were developed, designed to complement and enhance the original campaign methodology invented by the YMCA. These techniques were codified in the late 1920s by Harold Seymour in the two-volume *Standard Practices* guide for the John Price Jones company. Several decades later, Seymour published the first known book on fund raising, titled *Designs for Fund-Raising: Principles, Patterns, Techniques* (1966—first edition) (Harrah-Conforth and Borsos 1991, 26).

To summarize, the first-generation of pioneer fund raisers

- developed some of the first codified fund-raising techniques
- shaped and coalesced moral and business ideologies
- served as the initial training ground for future fund raisers
- established the first professional fund-raising firms
- produced the campaign and federated fund drive innovations

Generation Two—The Campaigners: 1930–1960

This second generation of fund raisers, most notably the group who became the first fund-raising consultants, now form the proverbial "old boys network" (Harrah-Conforth and Borsos 1991, 27). They established the first informal and then formal network of the American Association of Fund Raising Counsel (AAFRC), which served to cross-pollinate the field of fund raising with information about the philanthropic environment, the clients, and the donors. More importantly, AAFRC served as the first standard-bearer of integrity in the fund-raising field, with the charge of "to make our fund raising more dignified and worthy of respect" (26).

Many fund raisers worked as consultants, assigned to "resident" campaign work or "in the field," raising capital funds for higher education and health care institutions. This kind of campaign fund raising, short and intense, was highly successful. However, its very nature contributed to the public's negative attitude about fund raising. To the observer of the time, fund raisers appeared to be unstable and transient, given their lifestyle of travel and constantly changing short-term campaigns. Little defense could be offered, for there were no formalized professional requirements to enter the field of fund raising, nor was there formal training once there. It seemed anyone could be a fund raiser—no matter if you felt called or if you wanted a job. The

same criticism persists to the present time, as the entry to fund raising is still more often by *accident*, than by obvious plan.

The "Campaign of 1931," headed by Walter S. Gifford, director of the Organization for Unemployment Relief, helped strengthen the public's image of fund raising and their charitable response to it. This Depression-era effort used communication strategies to an extent never before imagined; it was purported to be the largest cooperative fund drive ever to appeal for public funds. The brainchild of then-President Hoover, the campaign enlisted the services of "one hundred leaders of business, industry, finance, and philanthropy." It used public advertising and promotion in the most auspicious and creative ways yet—movie theaters and college football teams gave benefit performances; radio broadcasts carried messages of inspiration; and billboards, newspapers, and magazines championed the campaign. According to Hoover's memoirs, this campaign was a success in "awakening" a sense of national responsibility for being "my brother's keepers" (Bremner 1988, 139–140).

World War II contributed greatly to the increase in public philanthropy; the fund-raising messages of national war campaigns were prominent, plentiful, and powerful. Although the war campaigns had forced the cancellation of many local fund-raising efforts, they established the momentum for larger, more successful post-war campaigns. With sizable monetary goals, the fund-raising campaigns that followed were artfully planned, with more style and communications than previously employed.

The American Cancer Society was the first to incorporate an element of public information *and* donor education into fund-raising materials. Their *communications* strategy had long lasting implications for the fund-raising profession. Fund raising evolved beyond the mere raising of money—it provided information, involved people in the mission, and called them to action. The emphasis on the mission over the money presented charitable organizations in a very different light; "most organizations dropped the word 'need' from the fund-raising vocabulary and replaced it with 'opportunity'" (Broce 1986, 13).

With the philosophical shift in thinking and communicating came the term *development*, offering a broader conceptual definition of fund raising. Seymour (1988, 115) explains, "The word development should not be taken merely as another word for raising money, but as a broad term for the planned promotion of understanding, participation, and support."

Not only was this era one of growing sophistication for fund-raising terminology and techniques but it was also an era of generous response from the donative public. In the early 1950s, public giving to religious, health, social welfare, and educational institutions exceeded $15 million annually for the first time. Private foundations were growing in number and impact, distributing significant numbers of grants. The concept of a **matching challenge grant** originated through the Ford Foundation's Special Program in Education served as an important incentive for other contributors; it is a tactic that remains successful today (Broce 1986).

By the 1960s, in-house development offices were opened—first in universities and teaching hospitals—and the use of resident/field managers declined. By the end of the decade, most major consulting firms had shifted from resident field assignments to campaign consultation with in-house staff and volunteers.

Capital campaigns reigned; they were prospering in almost every type of institution at a rate and amount never before anticipated. The late 1950s set the stage for the successful multi-million dollar campaigns of the early 1960s. The capital campaigns of Harvard, Duke, Stanford, and Chicago universities demonstrated that larger goals and shorter timelines were just as satisfying and successful as smaller, more drawn-out campaigns for volunteers, donors, and institutions alike. These multi-million dollar campaigns were the larger-than-life mirror images of the campaign methodology originated by the YMCA—a concept of which the fund-raising and donor community has never tired.

Meanwhile, in-house fund raisers had the freedom, in between conducting the big capital

> The annual fund and the legacy society were inventions of this generation— natural extensions of the traditional campaign methodology.

campaigns, to experiment with ways of raising funds to underwrite their institutions' operating budgets. The *annual fund* and the *legacy society* were the inventions of this generation—natural extensions of the traditional campaign methodology. Similar in design and technique, the annual fund and the capital campaign were both mechanically structured and bottom-line goal oriented. They were differentiated only by the *case* (for operating funds rather than capital expenses), and the size of the goal (for smaller, repeatable gifts).

To summarize, the second-generation of campaigners contributed greatly to the growth of the fund-raising profession in the following ways:

- Consultants were in high demand for resident campaigns and professional consultation.
- In-house fund-raising positions were created.
- Communications became an important component within fund raising, with the goal of educating and informing the public.
- Multi-million dollar campaigns flourished, growing in size and scope.
- The *annual fund* and *legacy society* were developed as methods to raise funds for the general operating budget.
- Challenge grants, initiated by foundations, served as incentives for matched contributions from others.

Generation Three—The Innovators: 1960–1980

The third generation of fund raisers were an eager and receptive audience for Harold "Si" Seymour's book on the principles of fund raising. Published first in 1966, reissued in 1988, and still widely read today, *Designs for Fund Raising* is considered the classic of the field and is "quoted more often in fund-raising circles than Benjamin Franklin is quoted in everyday life" (Seymour 1988, x). It provided a substantial review and rationale for the work that had been invented by the pioneer generation and enhanced by the campaigner generation.

During the third generation, fund raisers were growing in number and in competency. They were not only in high demand in educational institutions but were also being recruited for the arts, sciences, environmental causes, and the expanded number of combined fund appeal organizations. The establishment of professional associations, such as the NSFRE and the Council on the Advancement and Support of Education (CASE), contributed greatly to the skill-based training of fund raisers, the collegial networking, and the exchange of information about the latest fund-raising techniques.

Broce's 1974 edition of *Fund Raising: The Guide to Raising Money from Private Sources* describes *development* as three distinct but interdependent activities (planning, constituency relations, and fund raising) "that constituted the most sophisticated of all forms of *public relations*" (12).

By the mid-1970s, fund raising had become an innovative enterprise, with plentiful opportunities for entrepreneurs and volunteers. Fund raising was a high-profile activity with enormous public visibility fueled by the growing number of major benefit events, renewed interest in social issue fund raising, and high-visibility partnerships with major corporations. Innovative fund-raising tactics were plentiful and greatly reliant on communication tactics, thereby putting the real measure of success to the test: Was the money raised more important than the publicity generated or vice versa? The *commercialized* ideas seemed inexhaustible; there were nationally televised telethons, walk- and run-a-thons, raffles and auction events, pass-the-envelope neighborhood campaigns, major celebrity benefit events, and numerous cause-related marketing ventures. Charitable giving by individuals grew from 13.1 million in 1963 to 48.55 million in 1980; volunteerism was at an all-time high.

The experiential field of fund raising had become a *business* in its own right, looking a lot like its sister professions (public relations, advertising, and marketing) but delivering psycho-social benefits to donors in return for their gifts. Donors liked going to events with others "like them," volunteers enjoyed being in the limelight, the society-page editors relished in the social interactions. Social fund raising had become a cultural norm.

The 1980s saw the emergence of the fund-raising specialist whose acumen in specific areas of fund development was highly desirable given the size and scope of larger, year-round campaigns. People were hired for their expertise in special events, prospect research, direct mail, foundation grant writing, and major gifts solicitation. Specialists were beginning to replace the *generalists* who had gained their experience by "doing it all."

Two major developments of this period would challenge and change fund raising in fundamental ways—the large increase in the number of women entering the profession and the implementation of innovative technology.

The entry of a few women in the mid-1970s, followed by large numbers in the 1980s, altered the profile, image and culture of fund raising. Fund raising was a particularly attractive profession for women, many of whom had gained experience as volunteers. It was a field that focused on service and interpersonal skills, and it offered multiple and flexible opportunities. Current research on the motivation of women donors suggests that women, more than men, want to be involved in the implementation of organizations' fund-raising activities and events, suggesting a correlation in the historical expan-

> **Two major developments of this period were the increasing number of women entering the profession and the implementation of innovative technology.**

sion of both benefit events and the entry of women in the field.

The second development, advanced technology, made it possible for fund raisers to borrow business management principles and apply them in unique ways—in direct response marketing, telemarketing, computerized receipting, and donor file record keeping. The implementation of 20th-century technology further helped achieve the efficiencies that originally stimulated the invention of the campaign and the federated fund drive. Now an even higher level of sophistication could be attained; through high-tech systems and strategies, fund raisers could reach more prospects, solicit more donors, and move them up the pyramid of giving with carefully planned, economical communications. The *annual fund* was the most obvious and direct beneficiary.

Although these innovations made it possible to reach the masses, they also made fund raising more mechanical and much less personalized. Donors were at risk of being managed as computerized files, treated more like numbers than real people. Criticism began to surface from within the fund-raising field. Senior fund raisers expressed concerns that the profession had become too technology-driven, that philanthropy had been left out of fund raising. The tension between *calling* and *career*, money and mission resurfaced.

Signs of discontent came from both internal and external sources, questioning how much money was being spent to raise money in what were viewed as lavish, commercialized, and repetitive ways. Board members, volunteers, and donors wanted to know what the appropriate cost ratios and reasonable returns on investment were. The calls grew louder for sound business practices to augment the popular communications activities. Professional associations responded with advanced-practice standards, specific cost indicators and benchmarks for fund-raising activities, and principles for ethical professional behavior.

Also, this generation benefited from a variety of educational opportunities: a growing list of how-to books, local workshops taught by lead-

ing practitioners, and international conferences that offered cutting-edge techniques. Still, it was the fortunate fund raiser who worked in a full-service development department in a large institution and was mentored by an accomplished fund raiser of an earlier generation, for he or she had a laboratory for melding practice with theory.

Members of the innovator generation were experienced, knowledgeable, and skilled fund raisers who were rewarded with higher salary levels, making fund raising an even more desirable career.

To summarize, this third generation is noted for the following accomplishments and innovations:

- Fund raisers were widely recruited for many kinds of positions, in all types of nonprofit organizations.
- Professional societies established standards of practice, fund-raising benchmarks, and the first industry-approved code of ethical principles.
- Fund raising became a high-profile activity, stimulated by major public events and commercial activities.
- The most innovative fund-raising techniques in the history of fund raising were assembled, shaped, and fine tuned.
- Volunteer opportunities multiplied with the rise in fund-raising events.
- The implementation of advanced technology reinforced fund raising as a business strategy, gaining access to more donors.
- Women entered the profession in large numbers, altering the profession's profile and culture.
- Higher salaries reflected the growing level of professionalism.

Generation Four—The Professionals: 1980–2000

The fourth generation of fund raisers were the beneficiaries of career expansion, technology, and professionalism combined. So sophisticated was the terminology, the techniques, and development department organizational structures that fund raisers were no longer called fund raisers by title. By the mid-1980s they acquired new titles, such as *institutional advancement director, foundation president,* and *vice president of external relations,* to reflect the broad scope of responsibility and significance that development had come to encompass.

This generation had a very different mix of prospects and donors, complex and sophisticated techniques, and new management challenges. They also had a determination to turn fund raising into a profession—without apology or public criticism.

By now, the donor public was well informed and sophisticated in their view of the philanthropic sector and its activities and services. They were equally as intrigued and interested in the scandals as in the sector's achievements. Donors were ready to make their own giving choices and to have a deeper level of involvement in stewardship of their dollars. Although their discretionary time was more limited, their financial resources and interests were growing. The general public, and donors in particular, demanded more information, more accountability, and more contact with charities they chose to support. These requests led to an increase in the kind of information and activity level that fund raisers provided to donors to encourage their initial decision making and to keep them engaged and involved over time. High-level gift clubs, named funds, designated giving, tailored recognition, and "case management" were perfected during this era. *Prospect research* became somebody's job title, and almost every institution had its own *planned giving officer.* The **major gifts campaign** was promoted as the newest fund-raising trend; a reengineering of the original YMCA campaign model, stimulated by the anticipated $11 trillion "transfer of wealth" from one generation to the next.

Not only were individual donors more sophisticated but so too were businesses and corporations. Like individuals, businesses had come to expect something in return for their contributions. Although individuals expected an acknowledgment and recognition that their gifts

were needed and applied wisely, businesses used philanthropy to advance their self-interests. Quid pro quo partnerships flourished during this period, with businesses carefully selecting charities with constituencies that mirrored their purchase profiles and fit their marketing strategies. Cause-related marketing fueled criticism that commercialism was on the rise. This criticism was reinforced by the increase in the number of nonprofit organizations whose services were perilously close to their for-profit competitors— day care centers, health clubs, nursing homes, art gallery gifts shops, education-sponsored travel, and public radio product sales.

Professional fund raisers began to have a different look and a different agenda. Not only were women well represented in this fourth generation of fund raising but so were people of color and diverse ethnicity. Fund raising, or development as most called it, was a place where bright, committed, caring people could realize their aspirations and be remunerated. Parity and affirmative action were employment issues of this generation. In the 1980s throughout the mid-1990s there were jobs aplenty; one could make an entire career in fund raising by entering as a development assistant; moving up to special events manager, annual fund director, or development associate with management and major gift responsibilities; and finally to chief development officer.

In spite of all the opportunities and the sophistication, fund raising was still without specific entry requirements, save a college degree— it was available to anyone with passion for a mission, determination, interpersonal skills, and demonstrated fund-raising achievements.

For this generation, continuing education was not only readily available, it was a necessity as well. Local universities and colleges had added fund-raising courses and certificate-awarding programs. The Fund Raising School had found a permanent home at the Center on Philanthropy at Indianapolis University, and offered courses in more than a dozen states. Education was now classified as a continuum of experience mixed with theory and going from "cradle to grave"—for entry-level, mid-level, senior-level, and advanced executive-level fund raisers. Reflecting the life cycle of fund raising as a profession, continuing education was designed sequentially—first on what to do, second on how to do it, third on why we do it, and finally on how we might do it better. Continuing education was touted as the pathway to knowledge, knowledge to behavior, and behavior to credibility and professionalism.

A new and revised version of industry-approved ethical principles was distributed, and professional credentialing was promoted by professional associations as a way to safeguard the integrity of the profession. Two levels of credentialing had emerged within the Association of Health Care Philanthropy (AHP) and the NSFRE: baseline certification for the fund raiser with five years of experience, and advanced certification for the senior professional.

In the mid-1990s the emergence of academic philanthropic studies, research in the field, and the pursuit of a "higher order" of fund-raising practice greatly strengthened the field. Four generations of experience, combined with a little theory, gave fund raising its professional status, perhaps for the first time.

The definition of fund raising now reflected the complexity of its responsibilities. The following excerpt from The Fund Raising School's manual *Principles and Techniques* (1983) was far from the communications/public relations themes of the past and gave credence to the notion that fund raising is both art and science:

> Successful fund raising is based on successful **management of the highly complex development process.** Its complexity is derived from the extensive interrelationships required (board members and other volunteers, program and administrative staffs, vendors, prospects, and donors), as well as the scope of the development function itself (fund raising, public relations, records management).

The tension that existed earlier between calling or career now eased; realistically, it is not pos-

sible to be called without remuneration. Too, fund raisers' own opinion polls now suggested that those who selected fund raising as a career felt they were called to it in one way or another. The tensions of this generation seemed instead to be an extension of the earlier tension between technology and personal relations. As the profession became more technical (albeit professional), the focus tended to be more on the organization of things than on the relationship with the donor. And yet, it was this generation's research on donor motivations and motivating factors that emphasized the need for a more thoughtful and personalized approach—one in which the donor's interests were in balance with the organization's needs, though never to the exclusion of the recipient's needs. A later section addresses these present-day tensions.

To summarize, the accomplishments of this generation include

- efforts to make fund raising a profession
- multiple job opportunities, ranging from generalist to specialist in direct mail, special events, prospect research, major gifts, planned giving, and campaign management
- continuing education opportunities that promoted skill development and encouraged theory design
- increased emphasis on credentialing and the establishment of advanced certification levels within NSFRE and AHP
- a greater emphasis on the management of the integrated development program, reducing the kind and number of grassroots special events
- sophisticated donors demanded a more advanced level of communications, relationship building, and accountability

Fund Raising in the Year 2000

What does the future hold for those who choose fund raising as a career? Development will remain a worthy endeavor, one that is satisfying both to the soul and to the pocketbook.

People who enter the profession in the late 1990s and beyond will need to learn experiential methods alongside theoretical principles. They will need a solid educational underpinning on which to ground the necessary on-the-job learning. To be successful, they will need to be part psychologist, sociologist, anthropologist, economist, and historian.

The field will be more competitive—at the entry level and the top administrative level because of the increased interest of young people in the nonprofit sector and the staying power of those already accomplished in it. There will be at least four distinct career categories.

First, there will always be room for *consultants* who specialize in capital and endowment campaigns, development audits, board training, and recruitment/placement services. As the profession has evolved, consultants have come to play an essential role that cannot be filled by the employed professional.

Second, there will be more opportunities for *practitioners*—both generalists and specialists. The generalists will be needed for the small development offices, primarily in the social services, whereas the specialists will be in high demand in education, health care, the arts, and sciences.

Third, there will be enormous opportunities for fund development in other countries—Japan, Australia, Mexico, Canada, and the developing nations.

Fourth, because of the emergence of professional academic centers throughout the United States, there will be myriad opportunities for reflective development professionals to *train, teach, and write*. As the profession moves from an experiential to a theoretical body of knowledge, there is a great need for faculty who are grounded in philosophical, theoretical, and practical principles and their applications.

Certainly, fund raising has come a long way from its early days. Those who choose to be fund raisers in the 21st century will have the privilege of being *called to a career* that they can enhance and advance—for theirs, ours, and the public's good.

Changing Dynamics in Fund-Raising Practice: Finding a Balance Between Technology and Donor Relations

Today, there are two dynamic but conflicting trends—one practical and one philosophical—within fund-raising practice. The first is the increased practical application of know-how and technology and, with it, the growing commercialization of fund raising. The second is a shift from a purely organizational focus to a more donor-focused orientation, using exchange or marketing theory. Both have their critics and their advocates.

These and other changes are occurring in part because of changes in the charitable climate. Skepticism toward philanthropy is increasing; the base of giving—whether from individuals, foundations, or corporations—is undergoing fundamental change; new tax laws, mergers and acquisitions, and internationalization are affecting giving attitudes; concern for nonprofit corruption and inefficiency is rising; donors are overall better educated and more proactive contributors; and competition for the charitable dollar is greater than ever (Harvey and McCrohan 1990, 40–41).

Growth in Technical Skills and Business Approaches

The extent to which fund raising *know-how and technology* have achieved such dominance in the field fuels both pride and criticism among fund raisers. Driven by the need for more cost effectiveness and systems efficiency in an ever-increasing business environment, emphasis has been placed on the technical aspects of fund-raising principles. Where once there were positions called development directors, now there

> Driven by cost-effectiveness and systems efficiency, emphasis has been placed on the technical aspects of fund-raising principles.

are telemarketing managers, direct mail specialists, special event coordinators, volunteer coordinators, donor research specialists, planned giving officers, and, of course, annual fund directors.

Although the desired goal of specialization is laudable, the outcomes have been criticized as being too far removed from the original people orientation to fund raising. Harrah-Conforth and Borsos (1991, 33) write,

> There is room for concern and some validity to the fear that fund raising is becoming merely the business of raising money. . . . Technology has streamlined (to an extent) the methods and practices of fund raising, making it akin to a business more than ever before. Computer-related management has transformed people into numbers and "potential profiles" and helped increase the competitiveness of fund-raising firms and consultants. The goals of campaigns based on these methods may be seriously philanthropic; however, the process does not question the values of the person pushing the keys, the case, or the cause.

In a recent issue of the *Chronicle of Philanthropy*, an article entitled "High-Tech Fund Raising: Boon or Bane?" by Demko and Marchetti addresses the pros and cons of the increased use of technology, ranging from electronic pledge cards to automated telephone systems on the Internet. The article focuses on how technology is being used in annual employee fund-raising campaigns for the United Way and other federated funds. Companies like Ameritech, Federal Express, the Gap, and General Motors are using automated telephone systems that enable employees to indicate where they want to contribute and how much. At IBM, employees in 75 offices across the country can touch a computer screen and have access to information about their annual charity campaign. According to the authors, "Business executives and fund raisers agree the changes (automation) are necessary to streamline pledge drives" and electronic systems

"often turn ordinary campaigns into creative ventures" (1996, 21).

Yet, executives of nonprofits that benefit from annual employee campaigns are very concerned that technological innovations are eliminating the all-important face-to-face relationships with donors. For example, Mark O'Connel, executive director of the United Way of Metropolitan Atlanta, expresses his concern: "I want us to be more visible and present than we've ever been. . . . I don't think technology is the answer to that. I think wearing out your shoes is the answer" (23).

If computerized technology improves the efficiency of a campaign, does it also increase a campaign's effectiveness; in other words, does it enable more money to be raised? In certain cases, the answer is no; in other cases, yes. According to Demko and Marchetti (1996, 21), United Ways in Cincinnati, Indianapolis, and Milwaukee "reported drops in donations from companies that used technological innovations for the first time in their 1995–6 campaigns." On the other hand, companies like Microsoft Corporation have run electronic campaigns successfully for several years. In fact, at Microsoft in Redmond, Washington, a few automated donor-personalization features significantly increased the size of pledges this past year. Included in their campaign was an "electronic message to employees who had donated in the past thanking them for their previous gifts and asking if they wanted to increase their contribution" (23). As a result, 500 employees gave twice as much to the current campaign.

Critics of the technical growth in fund raising also suggest that it counteracts the movement of fund raising toward professionalism. "We believe that a professional is more than a technician. Fund-raising practitioners without a strong ethical sense and commitment tend to equate success with money raised—or more precisely, with their own income" (Payton et al. 1991, 279). Payton (1988), a highly respected scholar in the field of philanthropic studies, has gone so far as to challenge fund raisers whether we "are living *for* what we do" or "living *off* it" (88).

How did it happen that increased knowledge about fund-raising techniques would be viewed as less professional, rather than more professional? NSFRE President Patricia Lewis points out the dilemma by referring to recent research findings that indicate that the public is increasingly questioning fund-raising techniques and just plain doesn't like some of them. In her 1993 editorial in *Advancing Philanthropy*, Ms. Lewis comments on the problem: "In our quest for skill, systems, and techniques, we have overlooked the need to integrate the history and philosophy of philanthropy into our teaching and learning." In addition, although many solicitation techniques are "within the letter of the law, they are not within the spirit [and] mislead the easily led and easily confused. . . . Some fund-raising practices proliferate which stretch the bounds of trust. . . . [Are fund raisers] too timid about pronouncing them 'bad' out of respect for the freedom of individual initiative?" (Lewis 1993, 9).

But it is Payton who issues the strongest warning about the increased use of technology, pointing out how the technical and professional forces collide:

Increasing professionalism is in many ways positive, but there are associated risks. Professionals can tend to serve their self-interest and lose commitment to the service ethic—the very dimension that makes the professional worthy of admiration and deserving of trust—and in essence become technicians (Payton 1993, 13).

Regarding professionalism, he commented:

Technical rationality drives out emotion, and very often the emotional values are the ones that sustain philanthropy. Generosity, compassion, and benevolence are deeply personal, non-rational values. If our technical rationality displaces them, we will have lost the justification for the Third Sector. Philanthropy has to be somehow personal or it will die (14).

On commercialization, he added:

Success (is measured) in very narrow financial terms: who can raise the most money, who can conduct the biggest campaign. That's the same sort of reductionist thinking that has corrupted business in recent years. . . . Narrow business values have much too strong a presence, too powerful a voice, in fund raising today. Philanthropy has to address business problems, has to use business techniques, but it can't just live by business values (15).

There is no consensus among practitioners in this regard. Some support Payton's concern that fund raising is losing its compassionate voice, whereas others push for even more business-like accountability. In Frederick Walsh's article, "Big Lessons from Big Business," in the 1995 AHP *Journal*, he advises health care practitioners to become more business-like by examining what major corporations have done to restructure and strengthen themselves. He quotes *Fortune* magazine: "there will never be job security. You will be employed by us as long as you *add value* to the organization, and *you* are continuously responsible for finding ways to add value" (Walsh 1995, 32). He recommends that fund raisers "think of yourself as You, Inc. Focus on growth, accept responsibility, remember your customer, stretch your capacity and you will help ensure that there is a place for you and your institution in today's competitive marketplace" (33).

In the Spring 1994 issue of the AHP *Journal*, Michael F. Luck supports Payton's view in his article, "A Philanthropic Philosophy for the 21st Century":

We will fail as fund raisers if we ignore the unsightly elements of our profession. Too many of our fundraising activities are designed to create the illusion of productivity: bigger goals, larger gifts, and more prospects. Unfortunately, productivity by itself has little value, and our underlying and obsessive

> **There is greater emphasis on the business approach in annual giving campaigns than in any other aspect of fund raising.**

concern with it interferes with our pursuit of more humane activities....What will be the ultimate consequence of our continued reliance on the mechanical, formula-driven campaigns conducted by so many of today's organizations? (29).

Evidence of how the business orientation in fund raising has overshadowed the personal orientation in recent years can even be found in cartoons. In the January 25, 1996 issue of the *Chronicle of Philanthropy*, one fund raiser is pictured handing a computerized printout to a colleague saying: "The on-line search didn't turn up any new prospects, but I did find out that two of our current board members are deceased" (39).

By all accounts, there is greater emphasis on the business approach in the implementation of annual giving campaigns than in any other aspect of fund raising, except perhaps for the traditional capital campaign. It is in annual giving where technical expertise has flourished and perhaps where the personalization that Payton referred to is the least obvious.

Shift Toward Donor-Focused Exchange Approaches

The second dynamic change within the fund-raising environment runs almost counter to the first one. It is the movement from a purely institutional focus to a more donor-oriented one or, as some have referred to it, a shift away from *begging* (getting a gift) to *marketing* (giving and receiving a gift). This change seems small by comparison to the growth in technical skills, but is one that creates a lot of fervor. It is also one that professionals are advocating, rather than actually implementing to any great degree, particularly in the annual fund practice.

In her article, "Can We Throw Away the Tin Cup?" Kay Sprinkel Grace (1991) implies that

some organizations are moving toward a more donor-focused approach: "Increasingly, organizations are developing a sense of pride in their accomplishments and are emphasizing the community needs they are meeting. They are stressing the opportunities their programs provide for funders to help solve critical human and social needs" (184). This attitudinal change has enabled many organizations to "throw away the tin cup" and these new perceptions hold long-term promise for the nonprofit sector.

The literature from the 1960s through the 1980s contains many references to the importance of donors, but only an occasional reference can be found about the concept of *exchange* between donor and recipient (vis-a-vis the organization). This idea seems to be relatively new and is encouraged primarily by those who want to advance fund raising as a profession. In doing so, they highlight the importance of examining the attitudes and opinions of donors before determining what methods should be used to solicit them.

A few practitioners promote the notion that philanthropy is not just a gift from a donor, but rather a complex exchange of money, power, values, and expectations—between the giver and the recipient. In his 1990 book, *Critical Issues in American Philanthropy*, editor and author Van Til challenges fund raisers to "transcend the divisions of prevailing paradigms (how altruism can persist in an age of narcissism)" and see philanthropy "as essentially an exchange of values among people" (28). The exchange concept is based on the following three assumptions (28):

1. Individuals have a variety of needs, drives, and goals they seek to attain
2. some of these can best be achieved within the context of organization participation and
3. organizations need some mechanism to influence the behavior of their activists

The exchange concept described by Van Til highlights the dynamics of both internal donor motivations and external motivators; but it is Mixer (1993) who elaborates this dual dynamic best:

"The process of giving involves a circumstance in which individual prospects and donors have needs and desires that can be defined as internal motivations and that can be activated or channeled by external influences" (9).

The idea that two forces—internal donor motivations and external motivational factors—need to come together is not complicated, but it may be challenging for the fund raiser to apply at the annual giving level. Spending a significant investment of time trying to understand donors in return for a significant philanthropic investment, on the face of it, seems most justified at the major giving level. However, enough evidence from the field suggests that more donor research and segmentation of annual giving levels can produce larger gifts, more often, and more quickly than traditional one-time, one-case annual fund campaigns.

The Role of the Philanthropic Fund Raiser: Raising Money Isn't Enough

Ideally Positioned: Job, Role, and Responsibility

Reflective fund-raising professionals see their profession as one of the noblest, with its mission of facilitating the transfer of resources from people with interest to people with needs. It is also one of the most rewarding—fund raisers are the ones to see and feel the joy, the happiness, and the compassion in those who have both the ability and the desire to make a difference in the lives of others less fortunate. We see, first hand, the real changes in the lives of those who are helped, as they are transformed by hope, renewal, and opportunities. These are our rewards.

Even so, fund raising is the target of public criticism; some warranted, some not. Much of the criticism of late is related to the nonprofit sector's shift to be more corporate-like; in the last decade nonprofit cultures and systems, including fund-raising practices, have literally been *institutionalized*. Public skepticism is growing, as donors become annoyed by fund-raising techniques that are overtly *commercial*—life-insurance gimmicks, cause-related marketing, Sunday afternoon telemarketing, and charitable gambling. Public trust is threatened by the kind and number of reported abuses: fund-raising costs that are disproportionately high, executive salaries that appear exorbitant for charitable work, hospitals that report huge profit margins or *sell out* for a profit. Donor fatigue is growing with every direct mail letter, dinnertime phone solicitation, and mega-campaign upon campaign. With alleged abuses and doubt have come increased government regulation and intervention. Legislation to tax nonprofit income, property, purchases, and more is increasing. It is reasonable that one day soon commercial nonprofits (hospitals, nursing homes, health clubs, day care centers) will have a different IRS status, one that does *not* allow donors to claim charitable gifts to them as tax deductions.

Like it or not, it is our responsibility as fund raisers to defend the nonprofit sector and our role in it. We must accept responsibility for the shifts in values, behaviors, and the terminology that undermine the sector's integrity. As representatives of the philanthropic sector, we fund raisers deserve the severest criticism when we talk about our bottom lines instead of the people we serve, when we act like big business and still *beg* for money, when we use language like *hits* and *gets,* when we raise money for problems instead of solutions, when we put our institutional needs ahead of our donors' needs, or when we become technicians who know more about planning giving instruments than the complexities of philanthropic motivations.

Our own literature points out part of the problem: "The public feeling about professional fund raisers may be one of sympathy with the cause, yet irreverence toward the fund raiser" (Harrah-Conforth and Borsos 1991, 29). If irreverence isn't bad enough, put downs are: "Blessed are the money raisers—for in heaven, they shall stand on the right hand of the martyrs" (Murray 1993, 141).

For some reason, fund raisers are quick to criticize their own colleagues, to use derogatory rather than laudatory terms. It is embarrassing

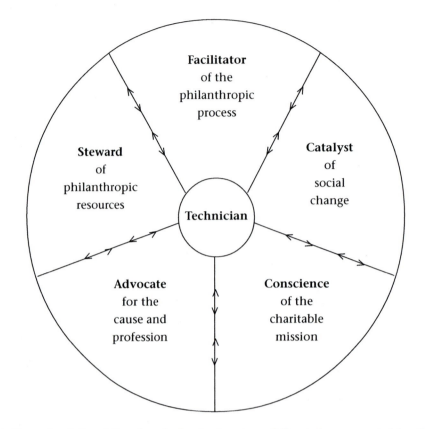

Figure 1–1 The role of the philanthropic fund raiser is multifaceted, represented by the wheel of responsibilities that permeate the internal organization, working outward to the external environment.

to admit that we are so willing to dishonor and discredit our own profession. A recent survey by Duronio and Temple of over 2,000 fund raisers revealed negative perceptions of fund raisers not only from CEOs and boards but especially from other fund raisers: "Many (fund raisers) differentiated themselves from unflattering stereotypes of fund raisers without refuting the stereotypes, suggesting that they felt they were exceptions to the rule—and part of the minority " (Duronio and Temple 1996, 12).

As philanthropic fund raisers, it our role to help clarify all these issues—to be good and to do good. We must defend all aspects of the philanthropic sector in order to strengthen it; we must espouse its virtues and remedy its shortcomings with energy, courage, intelligence, and passion.

We can start by considering how fund development *fits into* the organization we serve and discover how we can help institutionalize philanthropic fund raising beyond its technical aspects.

As Technical Experts

Knowing the craft and being able to apply the techniques skillfully is the first requirement of an effective fund raiser. Technical expertise is our core strength and a necessity of the first order. However, a typical job description reinforces the overemphasis on the technical aspects of project planning and goal setting; donor research, cultivation, solicitation, and recognition; organizing staff and volunteers; and office functions.

Exhibit 1–4 The Role of a Philanthropic Fund Raiser

Facilitator of the philanthropic process:
　Match people, ideas, resources
　Ensure all are heard
　Meet donor's interests and needs
　Teach and train others
　Accept that profession is indirect
　Encourage teamwork

Catalyst of social change:
　Articulate vision
　Serve as change agent
　Be courageous and tenacious
　Seek out entrepreneurs
　Inspire others to action
　Build mutuality
　Resist being self-serving

Conscience for the charitable mission:
　Present rationale for existence
　Link with community
　Balance competing demands
　Meet expectations
　Say things others will not
　Ask what's going on
　Be ethical about reproach

Advocate for the cause and profession:
　Voice without rhetoric
　Passionate and compassionate
　Cause above organization
　Involved and committed
　Understand and defend
　Act in collaboration, not competition
　Serve as role model

Steward of philanthropic resources:
　Take responsibility
　Moral action
　Openness and candor
　Ethical involvement
　Receive graciously
　Manage, invest, and expend wisely

Some clarification is offered by Burlingame and Hulse (1991):

All fund raisers should have the requisite technical knowledge, but the most effective are those working from a base of both knowledge and wisdom. They adjust to changing times and conditions because they have a sense of who they are as professionals, appreciate the role of fund raising in their organization, and understand what they do is important to the philanthropic sector and to society as a whole. Those who take fund raising seriously seek new perspectives on the profession to better understand the craft and enrich their professional lives. Only by addressing fundamental issues about fund raising and its role in a democratic society will the disparity between its negative public image and its importance to the third sector be reconciled (xxii–xxiii).

Fund raisers who look at their role broadly have the advantage of influencing the organization's culture to the greatest extent possible, and they benefit from the shared participation of others in the philanthropic process. Beyond technician, the fund developer's role delineations are as facilitator, conscience, advocate, catalyst, and steward (Figure 1–1 and Exhibit 1–4).

As Facilitators of Philanthropy—of People, Ideas, and Resources

As facilitators of philanthropy, fund raisers match people, ideas, and resources. It is our role to ensure that everyone is heard in the process and has a chance to *vote*. As was quoted earlier, "Apart from the ballot box, philanthropy represents the one opportunity the individual has to express his meaningful choice over the direction in which our society will progress" (Lord 1987). Fund raisers give donors this opportunity by recognizing that philanthropy begins with those donors, who may need to be educated about how to give in order to realize their own aspirations, and not be forced into contributing to something less meaningful. We must be sensitive to the motivations, desire for recognition, giving priorities, and need for involvement of our donors.

Fund development, fund raisers understand, is an *indirect* profession, ultimately practiced through others. We must recognize the importance of teaching others—executive directors, board members, volunteers, and professional staff—about the role of philanthropy in the institution and the place they hold as members of the fund-raising team. Teamwork, we know, is the basic tenet of a strong fund-raising program. We must coach and lead in order to bring out the best in those with whom we work.

Philanthropic fund raisers help organizations adopt philanthropic values and philosophies, build donor-responsive systems, and incorporate strategies necessary to attract and retain philanthropic support, now and in the future.

As Conscience of the Charitable Mission

Fund raisers stand at the critical intersection between the organizations and the communities we serve. This linkage requires the balancing of competing, sometimes conflicting demands and expectations of staff, colleagues, volunteers, trustees, and donors.

Fund raisers who assume the responsibility of acting as a conscience say things others won't when the charitable mission is at risk of being swallowed up by corporate strategies. We must be the ones to ask the tough questions that sometimes make people uncomfortable. We tug at people's elbows and ask, "What's going on here?"

Philanthropic fund raisers are passionate and compassionate. We are socially conscious, demanding that the patient, the client, or the student comes first, no matter what. We do everything in our power to ensure that our organization is effective in its reach and to its recipients.

In all that we do, we must be ethical above reproach. We must follow the strictest interpretation of the profession's code of ethics and take no action that would undermine the credibility of the organization or philanthropy itself.

As philanthropic fund raisers we practice philanthropy in our personal affairs. We believe in giving first, like Thomas Carlyle who said: "Let him who wants to move and convince others, be first moved to convince himself" (Murray 1993, 14). We encourage others to give and to volunteer their time to deserving causes—not just our own.

As Advocates for Our Cause and Profession

Philanthropic fund raisers are the voice for their cause in the community, all rhetoric aside. We must know the issues so intimately that we can speak about them without resorting to the annual reports, the brochures, or the telephone scripts. The cause might be children, life-threatening diseases, basic needs such as shelter and food, or education and cultural experiences. Whatever the issue, we must live and breathe it.

We must stand ready to help program staff articulate their dreams in ways that bring their case to life. Fund raisers must help develop the rationale for investing in programs and projects that benefit others. And fund raisers must continuously demonstrate that philanthropy is more about *receiving* money than *raising* it. As G. T. Smith said, "In fund raising, 95 percent is psychological or spiritual. Only 5 percent of it is financial. Actually, I don't ask for money. It's the other way around. People come to me and ask what they can do to help" (Murray 1993, 140).

As fund raisers, although we often enter the profession by chance early on in our careers, we must be deliberate in our decision to affiliate with an organization with a mission that mirrors our personal values. If we are fortunate to have such an opportunity, we make our "cause affinity" a lifetime commitment.

Philanthropic fund raisers are the voice for the profession too. We aspire to be the very best by understanding the craft and its subtleties. We must possess not only a technical knowledge of fund raising; we also must understand the philosophy and the theory—and defend them. We research, write, and teach. We give away everything we have learned, and we continue to learn.

We know that this profession is one without competition; it is a vocation of collaboration. We serve as role models and mentors. Through our enthusiasm and commitment, we encourage talented men and women to enter the profession, and we provide them support and guidance.

As Catalysts for Social Change

As philanthropic fund raisers we best articulate the vision of the institution and serve as change agents for society, being courageous and tenacious. We must seek out our organization's intrepreneurs (the term for entrepreneurs who work within organizational systems), helping them define their dreams, and work diligently to fund them—to serve people's dreams. Our energy must be endless, pursuing those dreams, inspiring others to action, and knowing when to lead and when to follow. As Jean Riboud said, "If you want to innovate, to change an enterprise or a society, it takes people willing to do what's **not** expected" (Murray 1993, 156).

Fund raisers build mutuality while pushing for the highest possible attainment, yet understand and resist the obvious risk of becoming self-serving.

As Stewards of Philanthropic Resources

As the front-line recipient of philanthropic funds, fund raisers must recognize the responsibility for stewardship. It is our responsibility not only to accept a gift in a meaningful way but also to regard these funds as our own precious earnings: managing them prudently, investing them wisely, and expending them judiciously. We must know precisely where they go and what good they do.

In our stewardship role, we know that accountability begins when we make a case for support that spells out realistic goals and objectives that make later accountability possible. Our practice must be open, candid, and ethical.

Professional Growth Cycle

Fund raisers tend to go through a growth cycle that is sequential and logical, and has three stages. Several authors have conceptualized this cycle and have given different titles to the stages—most notably Hank Rosso, who likely was the first to give it definitions. The notion of development stages are comparable to Maslow's hierarchy of needs in that each stage must precede the next, in order. The stages are (1) the collection of life experiences, (2) the fulfillment of needs, (3) the accumulation of knowledge, and (4) the achievement of one's potential. Understanding these different growth stages will help us manage staff and volunteers who are inevitably at different stages of experience, thinking, and skill.

Stage 1: Beginning Stage

When fund raisers first enter the profession, they are called *beginners* because of where they are in the experiential learning process, even if they bring senior level skills from another field, such as marketing, law, or estate planning. This stage is the time for learning the "how to's"— the everyday functions and tasks, ranging from putting solicitation letters *out* to receipting gifts *in*. Within a relatively short amount of time, beginning fund raisers can learn the mechanical techniques of direct mail, telemarketing, volunteer recruitment, and special event management. They learn by watching what others do, by asking a lot of questions, and by trial and error. They are *experts* in formula fund raising (direct mail can produce a 2 percent return; special events cost about 50 percent of the gross; the average first-time gift is about $25). Beginning fund raisers tend to mimic, rather than originate. Their fund-raising approach falls into the category of *begging* or *selling*, because their focus at this stage is on the needs of the organization—that is the subject area with which they are most comfortable.

Stage 2: Advancing Stage

In the middle stage, fund raisers progress beyond the "how to's" to the "what." They learn what works, theoretically speaking. They have come to the realization that fund-raising techniques are simply ways to *implement* the fund-raising process, not the reason for it. They begin to place more emphasis on the mission of the organization; that is, on what the organization accomplishes. In the *advancing stage,* fund raisers do research on prospects and donors, recruit and manage volunteers, and develop relationships with key donors and program staff. In terms of approach, they have moved from selling to *soliciting* contributions, a more advanced style of fund raising that may also involve training volunteers to solicit others.

Stage 3: Integrating Stage

The last of the three stages of fund development is called the *integrating* stage, in which the fund raiser learns the "whys" and the "ways" of philanthropic fund raising. At this level the fund raiser knows both the participants and beneficiaries of the philanthropic process. The focus is now on the total organization and on developing and maintaining interpersonal relationships with executive leadership, boards, volunteers, and donors. The fund-raising process is no longer begging, selling, or even soliciting—it is *facilitating a partnership* between the donor and the organization. At the *integrating* level, the fund raiser is actively involved in the organization's strategic planning and spends the majority of his or her time in the management of people, not things. Exhibit 1–5 illustrates this concept as developed by Hank Rosso.

Exhibit 1–5 Progress Growth Chart

	Development Stages		
	Beginning	Advancing	Integrating
Who	Inexperienced vendor	Experienced facilitator	Mature strategist
What	Product orientation	Mission orientation	Partnership orientation
Techniques	Sell products/raise money	Solicit contributions, develop relationships	Match resources/ needs, involve total organization
Results	Transfers	Involvement	Investment
Courtesy of Henry Rosso, San Rafael, California.			

References

Bremner, R.H. 1988. *American philanthropy*. 2d ed. Chicago: University of Chicago Press.

Broce, T.E. 1986. *Fund raising: The guide to raising money from private sources*. 2d ed. Norman, OK: University of Oklahoma Press.

Burlingame, D.F., and L.J. Hulse. 1991. *Taking fund raising seriously: Advancing the profession and practice of raising money*. San Francisco, CA: Jossey-Bass.

Cable, Carol. 1996. Cartoon. *The Chronicle of Philanthropy* (January 25): 39.

Cutlip, S.M. 1965. *Fund raising in the United States: Its role in the American philanthropy*. New Brunswick, NJ: Rutgers University Press.

Demko, P., and D. Marchetti. 1996. High tech fund raising: Boon or bane? *The Chronicle of Philanthropy* (January 25): 21–23.

Duronio, M.A. 1996. Fund raising: A portrait of the profession. *Advancing Philanthropy* (Spring): 11–22.

The Fund Raising School. 1993. *Principles and techniques of fund raising*. Indianapolis, IN: Indiana University Center on Philanthropy.

Gurin, M.G., and J. Van Til. 1990. Philanthropy in its historical context. In *Critical issues in American philanthropy: Strengthening theory and practice*, edited by J. Van Til. San Francisco, CA: Jossey-Bass.

Harrah-Conforth, J., and J. Borsos. 1991. The evolution of professional fund raising: 1890–1990. In *Taking fund raising seriously: Advancing the profession and practice of raising money*, edited by D.F. Burlingame and L.J. Hulse. San Francisco: Jossey-Bass.

Harvey, J.W., and K.F. McCrohan. 1990. Changing conditions for fund raising and philanthropy. In *Critical issues in American philanthropy: Strengthening theory and pracitce*, edited by J. Van Til. San Francisco, CA: Jossey-Bass.

Hodgkinson, V.A., M.S. Weitzman, J.A. Abrahams, E.A. Crutchfield, and D.R. Stevenson. 1996. *The Nonprofit Almanac 1996–1997: Dimensions of the independent sector*. San Francisco, CA: Jossey-Bass.

Hodgkinson, V.A., M.S. Weitzman, S.M. Noga, and H.A. Gorski. 1992. *Giving and volunteering in the United States: Findings from a national survey*. Washington, DC: Independent Sector.

Independent Sector. 1996. *Giving and volunteering in the United States*. Washington, DC: Independent Sector.

Lewis, P. 1993. Editorial. *Advancing Philanthropy* (Winter): 9.

Lord, J.G. 1987. *The raising of money*. Addendum. Cleveland, OH: Third Sector Press.

Luck, M.F. 1994. A philanthropic philosophy for the 21st century. *AHP Journal* (Spring).

Mixer, J.R. 1993. *Principles of professional fundraising: Useful foundation for successful practice*. San Francisco, CA: Jossey-Bass.

Murray, M. 1993. *Words of wisdom*. Silver Spring, MD: Philanthropic Service for Institutions, Seventh Day Adventist World Headquarters.

National Society of Fund Raising Executives (NSFRE). 1989. World Fundraising Council insert, *NSFRE Newsletter*. Alexandria, VA: National Society of Fund Raising Executives.

Ostrander, S.A., and P.G. Schervish. 1990. Giving and getting: Philanthropy as a social relation. In *Critical issues in American philanthropy: Strengthening theory and practice*, edited by J. Van Til. San Francisco, CA: Jossey-Bass.

Payton, R.L. 1988. *Philanthropy: Voluntary action for the public good*. New York: Macmillan.

Payton, R.L. 1993. Philanthropy's future: Insights from Robert Payton. *Advancing Philanthropy* (Winter): 12–17.

Payton, R.L., H.A. Rosso, and E.R. Temple. 1991. Take fund raising seriously: An agenda. In *Taking fund raising seriously: Advancing the profession and practice of raising money*, edited by D.F. Burlingame and L.J. Hulse. San Francisco: Jossey-Bass.

Seymour, H.J. 1988. *Designs for fund-raising: Principles, practices, and techniques*. Rockville, MD: The Taft Group.

Sprinkel Grace, K. 1991. Can we throw away the tin cup? In *Taking fund raising seriously: Advancing the profession and practice of raising money*, edited by D.F. Burlingame and L.J. Hulse. San Francisco: Jossey-Bass.

Van Til, J., and Associates. 1990. *Critical issues in American philanthropy: Strengthening theory and practice*. San Francisco, CA: Jossey-Bass.

Walsh, F. 1995. Big lessons from big business. *AHP Journal* (Spring): 29–33.

Chapter 2

The Annual Integrated Development Process:
A Multidimensional Activity with Eleven Steps

Fundamental Philosophies, Models, Principles, and Techniques

Fund Raising is Mission-Driven

Most practitioners agree that the development process exists and is justified because it facilitates the charitable *mission* of a nonprofit organization—it is the means, not the end. This clarification between means and ends is very important to achieving professional status, but recently challenged by the growing number of gimmicks, promotions, devices, and mass marketing programs that are so prevalent in our society today.

It is widely assumed by those in it that fund development is a noble and vital profession because it is more than promotion, more than communications, more than money raised. Its value is derived from the results achieved by the organization's use of the money. How well and how wisely the money is used are part of the moral imperative.

Peter F. Drucker (1990) helps clarify both the meaning of fund raising and its rationale:

The purpose of a strategy for raising money is precisely to enable the nonprofit institution to carry out its mission without subordinating that mission to fund raising. This is why nonprofit people have now changed the term they use from fund raising to fund development. Fund raising is going around with a begging bowl, asking for money because the need is so great. Fund development is creating a constituency which supports the organization because it deserves it.

Fund raising does not function in isolation; it is one of the central elements of a larger system of philanthropy and an integral force in the process. Fund development has an attendant role to the organization's mission and as such has ethical underpinnings. Given that philanthropy is values-driven, the same philosophical themes must also guide the fund development process. That process must function as if fund raising were the system's conscience, in addition to being its catalyst.

Because the fund development process is tied so intricately to the mission of the organizations that fund raisers represent, it is understandable that fund raisers are advised first to clarify their organization's mission before embarking on any fund-raising activities. It seems purposeless to raise funds for a cause that is not relevant, critical, and urgent. Nor is it ethical to stand aside if contributed funds are not used as directed or are spent unwisely.

This focus on the organization's mission does not, however, negate the importance of giving proper attention to the donor side of the philanthropic fund-raising process. There is general agreement within the development profession—from practitioners, scholars, and critics alike—that development is a multidimensional activity that matches the needs of the community (through the organization's mission) with the resources of the community (through philanthropic contributions). In that way it matches the donor's needs with organizational priorities. When an organization's mission merits the community's philanthropic support, fund raising becomes the process of facilitating transactions. Many authors refer to this function simply as "people helping people" and write eloquently about this philosophy (Greenfield 1991; Mixer 1993; Rosso 1991).

The obvious question is, Why are there so few concrete examples illustrating how to determine what donors want or how to go about meeting their needs? The fund raiser is hard pressed to find specific examples, particularly in the annual fund literature, illustrating how to research donors' attitudes, to develop communications with the donor in mind, or achieve a sophisticated match. Although the literature presents fund raising as a transaction, there is

an enormous gap in applying this concept. Without how-to examples, it is easy to see how annual fund strategies may end up being focused organizationally, technically, mechanically, or financially. The notion of a transaction between the organization and the donor, referred to as the exchange theory, is an important new concept within the fund-raising profession and in this book.

Core Principles and Techniques

Fund-raising principles and techniques are the products of tried-and-tested experiences accumulated over many generations. Some remain exactly the same as the day they were conceived. Others are slight iterations of their former self. Most of the fundamental principles and techniques emphasize the technical aspects of fund raising, focusing on how organizations should raise funds for their needs. Except for the more recent addition of promotional gimmicks, the current high level of technical skill, and the growing number of fund-raising specialists, such as direct mail managers or planned giving officers, the principles and techniques themselves have not changed much.

However, these techniques do vary. For instance, most trainer/practitioners recommend starting the fund-raising process at the bottom of the fund-raising pyramid (Rosso, 1991), whereas others promote turning the pyramid upside down to achieve more efficiencies after the pyramid is "filled" with donors (Flessner 1996). Although the *campaign* method of fund raising remains the dominant and most successful approach for capital and endowment campaigns, it is used less often in annual fund efforts. Many annual fund campaigns are now implemented *without* volunteers, and depend instead on mass marketing techniques, such as direct mail and telemarketing. Many fund raisers continue to use gift charts to determine the number of prospects and donors needed to achieve the stated goal; others use focus groups and surveys to determine the number of potential donors and set the goal accordingly. Some view the annual fund as a separate, almost self-

> **Fund raisers are advised first to clarify their organization's mission before embarking on any fund-raising activities.**

contained low-level fund-raising strategy, whereas others include major gifts and corporate grants in their annual campaign.

This chapter describes the overall management of the fund-raising process and the basic fund-raising models into which core principles and techniques are integrated. Other chapters elaborate on these aspects in relationship to the annual fund and provide practical applications and examples.

The Annual Integrated Development Process

As stated earlier, philanthropic fund raising is not merely money raising—it is the process by which a philanthropic exchange occurs that facilitates the accomplishment of the organization's mission, fulfilling a desired outcome. Some say that fund raising is the *engine* of philanthropy; others say it is the *fuel*. Regardless, fund raising is a dynamic human and organizational process that links people to values, values to mission, mission to outcomes, and so on. Actually, it is a sequence of carefully arranged steps, designed to **create an environment for philanthropy to flourish and to nurture and steward that environment for the long term.**

This process requires that core elements be constructed sequentially, although an arrangement of these elements in slightly different order will likely bring the desired successful outcome. An organization's culture and fund-raising readiness will have an impact on that sequence and on the width and depth of each element. Together, the following core elements create a synergistic relationship between people and organizations (Figure 2–1). The process includes the eleven steps in Exhibit 2–1.

The Pyramid of Giving

The **pyramid of giving** (or the pyramid of fund raising) is a time-honored principle in fund raising. The traditional way of explaining this basic principle is to divide the fund-raising activities into three integrated levels: first, annual giving; second, major giving; and third, estate/

planned giving. Fund raising thus becomes a *building* of activities that are designed to move prospects from the first level of giving (the acquisition stage), to repeat levels of giving (the renewal or retention stage), to the increased levels of giving (the upgrade stage), and over time, to major levels of giving (the special or capital gift stage), and ultimately to estate giving (the planned gift stage). The pyramid visually conveys several concepts (Figure 2–2): (1) the overall design of fund raising, (2) the sequential levels of giving with fund-raising strategies, (3) the proportion of donors at each level of giving, and (4) the increase of development activity, donor involvement, and donor giving.

The Campaign Model of Fund Raising

The **campaign** approach to fund raising has been the most dominant and colorful thread of the philanthropic fund-raising fabric. This **method** of fund raising has stood the test of time for almost 100 years, representing the essence of how fund raising was started, how it persisted, and how it is configured even today.

When the campaign methodology was invented between 1890 and 1900, it was done in response to the growing cost and time requirements of fund raising. The campaign model was a pioneer, innovative effort to facilitate fund raising in a more efficient and effective manner, thereby reducing not only the amount of time and effort spent by staff but also the amount of money expended on a long and, at times, arduous process. This campaign innovation came out of a belief that volunteers could be trained as facilitators of the philanthropic process; that volunteers would be energized by the high degree of organization, teamwork, and timelines; and that volunteers could be more successful than professional staff in raising more money from more people. The goal was to mechanize and publicize the campaign process to the greatest extent possible. The campaign method has endured for four generations and nearly ten decades.

Today, the campaign method or model is used in almost every capital, endowment, and

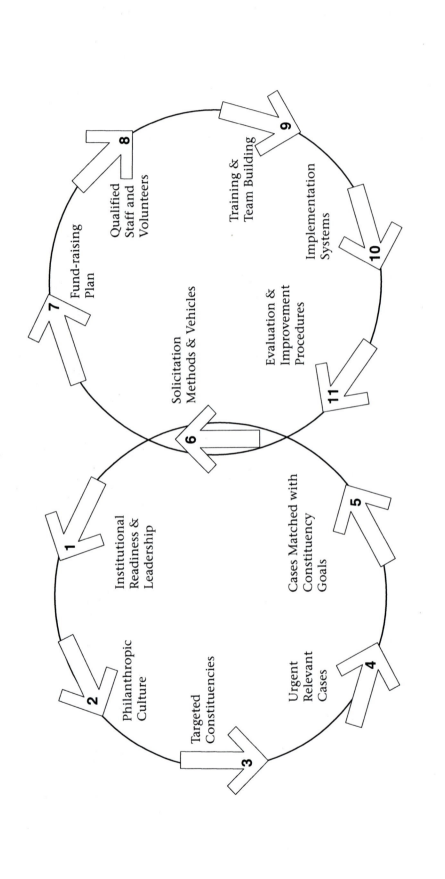

1. Institutional Readiness & Leadership
2. Philanthropic Culture
3. Targeted Constituencies
4. Urgent Relevant Cases
5. Cases Matched with Constituency Goals
6. Solicitation Methods & Vehicles
7. Fund-raising Plan
8. Qualified Staff and Volunteers
9. Training & Team Building
10. Implementation Systems
11. Evaluation & Improvement Procedures

This design represents the dynamic elements necessary for an annual integrated development program. Together they form a synergy that is essential to a successful philanthropic fund-raising endeavor.

Figure 2-1 Elements of the Annual Integrated Development Process

Exhibit 2–1 The Annual Integrated Development Process

Annual Integrated Development Process

Step 1. Determine the level of institutional readiness and external responsiveness.

Step 2. Develop strategies to create and nurture a philanthropic culture.

Step 3. Identify and qualify the constituencies; define market segments.

Step 4. Examine and validate the case(s); establish priorities for short-term, intermediate, and long-term goals.

Step 5. Match case(s) with constituencies, and set goal(s) for each segment and each case/campaign.

Step 6. Select appropriate solicitation methods and vehicles.

Step 7. Write a fund-raising plan with objectives and timelines.

Step 8. Establish roles and responsibilities for volunteers and staff.

Step 9. Recruit, train, and assign responsibilities to volunteers and staff.

Step 10. Implement fund-raising approaches and activities.

Step 11. Evaluate strategies and outcomes, and recommend improvements/changes.

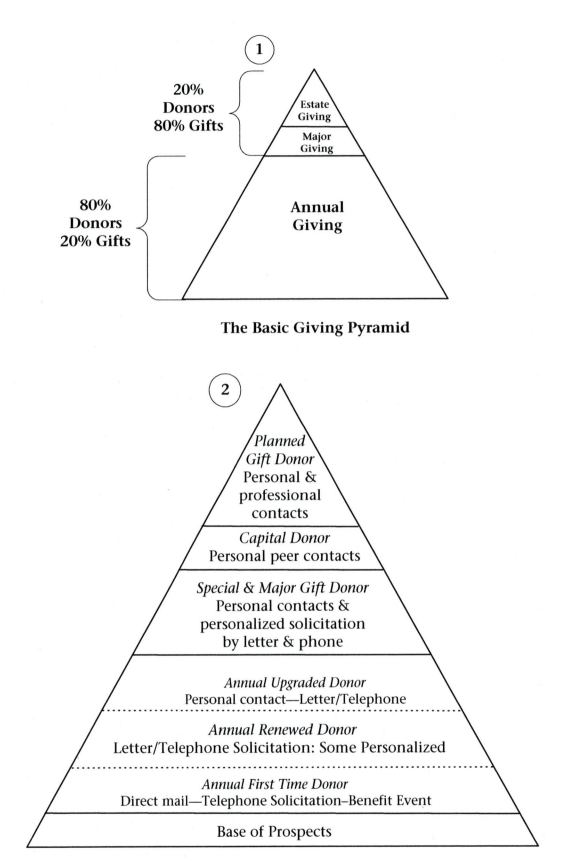

① The Basic Giving Pyramid

20%
Donors
80% Gifts

Estate
Giving

Major
Giving

Annual
Giving

80%
Donors
20% Gifts

The Basic Giving Pyramid

②

*Planned
Gift Donor*
Personal &
professional
contacts

Capital Donor
Personal peer contacts

Special & Major Gift Donor
Personal contacts &
personalized solicitation
by letter & phone

Annual Upgraded Donor
Personal contact—Letter/Telephone

Annual Renewed Donor
Letter/Telephone Solicitation: Some Personalized

Annual First Time Donor
Direct mail—Telephone Solicitation–Benefit Event

Base of Prospects

Donor Pyramid with Fund-Raising Strategies

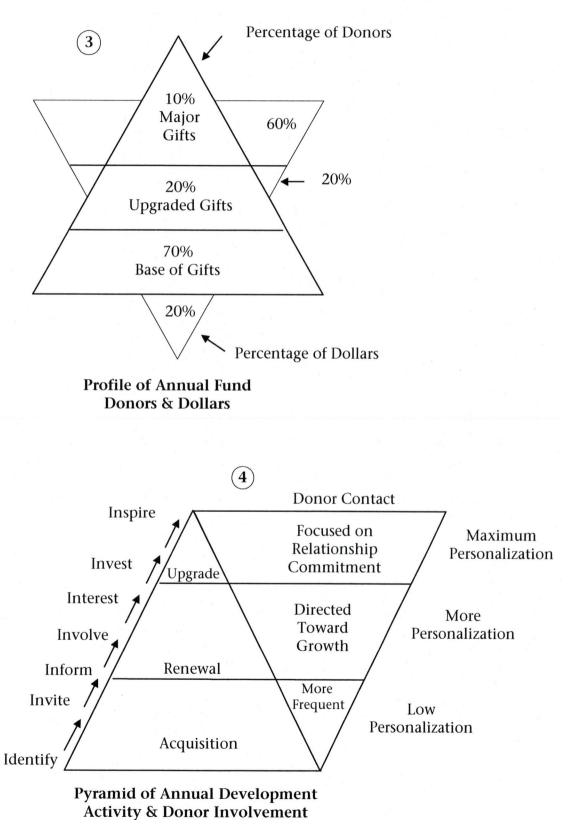

**Profile of Annual Fund
Donors & Dollars**

**Pyramid of Annual Development
Activity & Donor Involvement**

special-purpose campaign, including the newest trend—the major gifts campaign. It is the framework for most *annual* fund raising, including several subsets of the annual campaign—board campaigns, employee campaigns, special events, and the like. It is the approach used successfully in every United Way campaign across the county. It is also the approach used by most other federated fund drives. The campaign model is so much a part of the *culture* of some organizations that it is virtually synonymous with established social service organizations, churches, higher education institutions, and hospitals. As grassroots organizations emerge and as social service organizations reduce their dependence on United Way and government grants, they almost always put a structure into place that resembles the campaign model.

The campaign model (Exhibit 2–2) comprises specific elements that create an atmosphere and a structure that virtually guarantee success (to the extent the case merits support and the institution is worthy of it). In reality, there may be occasions when one or more of the elements listed are absent or weak; still, campaign success is dependent on the majority of them.

Annual Giving: The Building Blocks of Fund Raising

The overall success of fund raising is largely dependent on the successful implementation of *annual giving*, the base of the giving pyramid. Annual gifts are the building blocks of all other fund raising and the key component of an organization's development program because it builds and grows the base of loyal supporters. Annual giving is *central* to an organization's fund-raising program and philosophy. The way in which annual giving is practiced is a reflection of an organization's fund-raising culture, values, principles, and techniques. Is the organization's philosophy organization-driven? Is it donor-sensitive? Is it implemented by volunteers or staff? Is it organized as a single annual *fund* campaign ? Or does it include a series of seamless annual mini-campaigns, designed for specific donor segments?

Regardless of the strategy or style, generally all annual giving efforts include a variety of fund-raising methodologies, such as volunteer solicitation, direct mail, phone-a-thons, and special events. Orchestrated together, these activities are designed to "get the gift, to get it repeated, and

Exhibit 2–2 Campaign Model Elements

- A set, significant campaign goal

- A specific, fast-paced time frame

- A highly organized structure of people and tasks

- Research on prospects and detailed record keeping

- Trained volunteer solicitors with assigned prospects

- A tiered committee structure that stimulates competition

- A system of pyramid giving with large gifts first

- Regular committee meetings and status reports

- Lots of publicity, events, and donor recognition

to get it upgraded" (Rosso 1991, 52) while establishing habits and patterns of giving.

The terms *annual fund* and *annual giving* have quite different meanings (a little like charity and philanthropy). The term **annual fund** is historic, and is generally used to refer to the kind of fund raising or the name of the fund itself. Traditionally the annual fund was, and continues to be, a one-time volunteer-assisted campaign effort, undertaken at the same time each year to generate annual contributions that are used to underwrite the annual operating budget of an organization. Many universities and museums still refer to their campaign as "The Annual Fund"; others creatively call it "The Venture Fund"or "The Fund for Arts," and so on. According to Grasty and Sheinkopf (1982), Yale University was the first to initiate an annual fund drive in 1890, raising $11,000.

> The **Annual Fund** is an annual fundraising campaign that uses volunteer solicitors, as well as technical systems to raise unrestricted contributions from an organization's constituency.

Annual giving is a more contemporary term that better describes how many of the annual fund-raising efforts are designed today. Annual giving implies a broad range of activities that may be very different in size and scope, i.e., a personal solicitation campaign for board members or a special event to solicit parents of students. Many techniques are used within the broad definition of annual giving, including personal solicitations, direct mail, telephone solicitation, phonathons, benefit events, grant writing, and so on. These activities may be implemented throughout the year and raise funds for both general operating purposes and special needs.

> **Annual Giving** is a year-round effort to raise renewable funds from individuals and groups, for unrestricted and restricted purposes using a variety of solicitation methodologies and techniques.

The way fund raisers design an annual giving program is largely dependent on an organization's fund-raising history, culture, and level of experience; the type of organization; whether the organization has natural constituencies or needs to create them; the availability of voluntary and financial resources; and whether the organization has fund-raising affiliations such as with the United Way. The fund raiser has many choices, and none are mutually exclusive; all of the campaigns described in Exhibit 2–3 might have slight variations as well.

A description of the various models is given here, so you can be better prepared to use one or more facets, components, or strategies to fit your organization's culture, size, type, and stage. Model 4, the Annual Giving Strategies Development Program, is the newest and most comprehensive approach and the one used in the chapters that follow.

Model 1: The Annual Fund Campaign

The terms *annual fund* and *campaign* are almost synonymous. The annual fund campaign model is actually a mini-version of the original YMCA campaign model. It was added to most organizations in the early to mid-1900s as a way to raise funds to underwrite annual operating budgets, which were enlarged in part as a result of the successful capital, endowment, or *start-up* campaigns that formed the basis for most early fund raising. The term *annual fund* is used to describe both the way in which funds are raised and the purpose for which they are raised. It signifies one campaign, conducted once a year, for one program—in this case, the annual operating program(s). Annual fund campaigns differ from larger campaigns in that the *case* is more general and the dollar goals much smaller. The annual fund *theory* is to acquire, retain, and upgrade donors on an annual basis or to invite, inform, involve, and inspire donors over time. Annual fund gifts are relatively small, but repeatable on an annual basis and growing over time. Annual gifts come from a donor's discretionary funds, not accumulated assets, as in a capital or endowment campaign.

Exhibit 2–3 Annual Giving Models

❶ *Annual Fund* Campaign	**❷** *Annual Combined Fund* Campaign	**❸** *Annual Giving* Mini-Campaigns	**❹** *Annual Giving Strategies* Development Program
Run once a year for unrestricted operating funds; solicitations usually done by volunteers; direct mail and tele-phone solicitation done by staff or paid solicitors/ students	Run once a year for unrestricted operating funds; solicitations done by volunteers	Several small campaigns directed at different constituencies for unrestricted and restricted operating support; tend to utilize both volun-teers and staff	A year-long effort of multiple giving strategies, for restricted and unrestricted operating support; tend to utilize both volunteers and staff, and many solicitation methods

The Gift Range Chart

A basic time-honored element of the annual fund is the gift range chart (Exhibit 2–4) or "the arithmetic of fund raising." The gift range chart is a mechanism by which the fund-raising prac-titioner, together with volunteers, determine a realistic fund-raising goal. The process of as-sembling the chart requires that the fund raiser (1) estimate the size and the number of gifts re-quired to achieve the organization's "need" goal, (2) estimate the potential dollars to be raised, based on the size and number of previous do-nors at each giving level, or (3) use a combina-tion of both approaches.

The benefit of using a gift range chart is its ability to realistically display how many pros-pects and donors are needed to raise a specific amount of money, based on historical patterns of giving reported by practitioners over many decades. History with annual giving tells us that as few as 10 percent of the donors will give 60 percent of the dollars needed; while only 20 percent of the dollars will come from 70 per-cent of the donors. Taking volunteers through the process of designing a gift range chart not

only shows the arithmetic realities, it brings clar-ity to tasks at hand, and engages them in ulti-mate solicitation process. Volunteers will dis-cover that they need to identify a greater number of prospects than those who will become do-nors. They will discover that the largest portion of the money needed will come from a small number of contributors, and hopefully they will want to start there. And finally, the process will encourage the volunteers to recommend names of prospects/donors that they believe could make one of the larger gifts (and even volunteer to solicit them).

The annual range chart had its genesis in the 1900s as part of the pre-campaign strategy for raising capital funds. It remains as useful a tool today, as then, for each annual fund-raising effort, whether it is a small board cam-paign or a large special event.

After analyzing the gift potential in the do-nor base and creating a gift chart, the practitio-ner selects one or more fund-raising approaches: personal solicitation, telephone, or mail. Other important tasks include the recruiting, training, and supervising of volunteers who will help implement the annual fund campaign, as well

Exhibit 2–4 Annual Giving Gift Range Chart

$100,000 Goal

	Gift Range $	# of Gifts	# Prospects and Ratio	$ per Range	Cumulative $
10% donors 60% dollars	5,000	2	10 (5:1)	10,000	10,000
	2,500	6	30 (5:1)	15,000	25,000
	1,000	18	72 (4:1)	18,000	43,000
	500	34	136 (4:1)	17,000	60,000
20% donors 20% dollars	250	48	144 (3:1)	12,000	72,000
	100	80	240 (3:1)	8,000	80,000
70% donors 20% dollars	under 100	412	824 (2:1)	20,000	100,000

as establishing the time schedule and writing the annual plan.

The Volunteer Solicitation Pyramid

The second time-honored principle of the annual fund is the volunteer solicitation pyramid (Figure 2–3). As with major campaigns, today's annual fund requires a highly sophisticated volunteer corps. First, the annual fund volunteer *chair* is thoughtfully selected and strategically recruited for his or her leadership abilities. An organization cannot afford to have an unknown or inexperienced person lead its annual campaign, or to be turned down by the preferred candidate. The successful recruitment of the top position will set the pace for the entire campaign. Once recruited, the chair is responsible for assembling his or her campaign cabinet of approximately five to eight volunteers who will serve as *division captains.* The leader-

ship tier comprises the top third of the volunteer solicitation pyramid, and they have responsibility for rating and ranking prospects, as well as for adding additional tiers of volunteers so that no one has responsibility for more than 5 to 6 "assigned asks" or 8 to 10 volunteer committee members to oversee. The *division coordinators* form another tier which comprises the mid-third of the pyramid. The *division solicitators* form the last tier which makes up the final third of the pyramid, under which is a base of prospects to solicit. Over time, the prospects who become donors will eventually be recruited as volunteer solicitors, growing the pyramid larger each year.

Once the volunteer solicitation pyramid is assembled, the organization hosts solicitation training sessions to increase the volunteers' knowledge about the case for support, and to train them in the four-part solicitation process (described in Chapter 7). Once trained, the so-

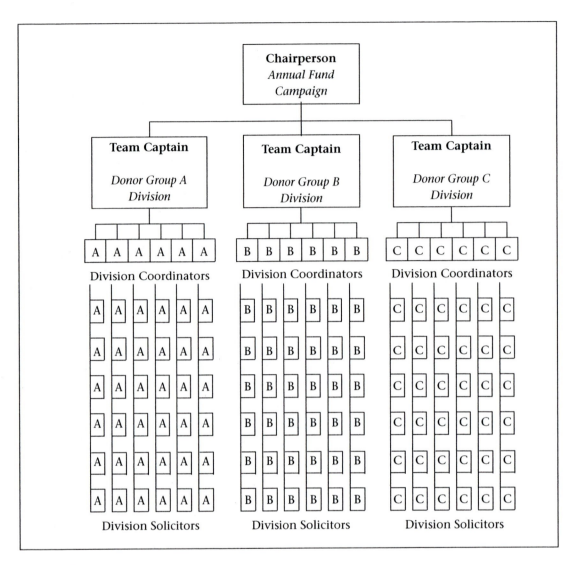

Figure 2–3 The Volunteer Solicitation Pyramid

licitors receive their assignments on computer-generated cards, containing information about the prospects' past giving history, their affiliation with the organization, other pertinent facts, and suggested gift amounts. Deadlines are set for the completion of the solicitation process; report meetings are scheduled; and follow-up assignments and suggestions are made (such as how to thank a donor, and what to do if the prospect says no). A campaign that utilizes the pyramid approach is not complete without a campaign celebration, with every volunteer captain, division coordinator, and division solicitor in attendance.

It is particularly interesting to note that the annual fund campaign model is still in use today at the YMCA, where it originated. Every year, all across the nation, YMCA branches roll out their annual campaign, led by community volunteers with pledge cards in hand, who call on their prospective donors and ask them for a larger-than-last-year gift for the *sustaining membership drive* (not a membership per se but an annual operating gift).

The reason the campaign approach continues to work year after year at the YMCA (though not everywhere else) is that volunteer-led campaigning is ingrained in the culture of the YMCA;

it is quite simply the way business is done. One telling feature of the YMCA fund-raising culture is the notation on employees' job descriptions that performance is measured by the extent to which the volunteers are successful and satisfied in their association with the YMCA.

Most higher education institutions use the campaign approach in their annual fund raising, strategically recruiting *class representatives* to provide volunteer leadership for each alumni class, and for reunion campaigns. Student volunteers (now paid in some way) perform the telephone calling services associated with most college or university annual fund drives.

The Annual Fund "Staffed" Model

Many organizations do not use volunteer resources to the large extent described earlier, relying instead on a staff-driven model that replaces personal solicitation by volunteers with paid telephone solicitors and direct mail appeals. Or there may be some combination of volunteer and staff fund raising, with staff providing the leadership. (To qualify as a *campaign* model, volunteers are integral to the fund-raising process; they are the leaders.)

The annual fund "staffed" model not only encourages technical and organizational expertise but it also mandates it. It uses the most sophisticated forms of mass communications, designed to acquire and to reinforce repeat giving among large numbers of lower-level donors. Although this model uses *impersonal systems*, it is decidedly more effective and efficient in large institutions with large numbers of prospects and donors who cannot practically be solicited in any other way. More information is provided in Chapter 7 about such techniques.

Model 2: The Annual Combined Fund Campaign Model

United Way campaigns are another contemporary example of the *campaign model*, used today to generate annual contributions for many affiliate organizations. The federated fund drives

of the 1920s, originating from the donors themselves who were being oversolicited by an increasing number of charities, were precursors to the United Way campaigns. One unique aspect of the United Way campaign is that the donors are primarily solicited in the *workplace*. In an effort to reach more donors, the United Way initiated the idea of recruiting business leaders as campaign solicitors, opening the door to hundreds and thousands of potential volunteers and supporters. Campaigns that are organized in the workplace offer many benefits, in addition to easy access to donors:

- Campaign leadership is recruited from the top of a corporation, setting the expectation of employee participation.
- Leadership sets an aggressive campaign goal, stimulated by competition with other companies and previous campaigns.
- There is a natural cadre of *askers* in the employees, who form pyramid-style solicitation teams.
- There is an ample supply of *friendly* prospects, who will be positively influenced by peer solicitation.
- Dollar goals are suggested for each earning level, making the expectations realistic and clear.
- Contributions can be *deducted automatically* from the employee's paycheck, making it possible to give more throughout the year than what one might give at one time.
- This activity is supported by campaign events, materials, posters, and on-site visits from representatives of the organizations who benefit from the campaign.

The United Way method of fund raising has changed very little since the initiation of the workplace campaigns, but in the past few years changes in the philanthropic environment have challenged it. First, the United Way national office scandal, which resulted in the departure of their CEO, William Aramony, threatened the public's confidence and trust in that organization and others. This scandal, coupled with increased donor fatigue, challenged the United Way to reexamine some of its fund-raising practices, and to seriously consider how to better meet donor needs and interests. For some time, contributors had been asking for more information about the effectiveness of nonprofit programs and services. They wanted to know precisely where their money was going and what it accomplished. Donors also were concerned about the cost of raising money and what top executives were paid. They were tiring of the pressure to give placed on them in peer solicitations and company-sponsored campaigns. And there was a growing interest in being able to designate contributions to *select* organizations represented by the campaign.

During the past few years, many of these issues have been acknowledged and addressed through strategically designed marketing tactics.

Note that not all these donor concerns can be fully resolved by the United Way, because the campaign model is dependent on a high level of organization, synergy, and control. Nevertheless, we can learn by example what might work or not work in an annual giving *campaign* in our respective organizations.

Model 3: The Annual Giving Mini-Campaigns Model

This model breaks the annual giving program into smaller, distinct components, driven by constituency segmentation needs/interests, campaign timing issues, and different case goals. Once an annual fund program is in place, the next step is to begin to discriminate activities that can stand alone, such as the board campaign or a major gifts drive. The mini-campaign concept allows the fund raiser to feature different cases, at different times of the year, to different groups or, if to the same groups, to appeal for a second contribution. This strategy gives more room for innovation, theme development, targeted communications, and the use of multiple techniques, such as individual solicitation for the board, personal telephone solicitation to major donors, direct mail for lower-level (in abil-

> The mini-campaign model allows the fund raiser to feature different cases, at different times of the year, to different groups.

ity and affiliation) donors, and a special event for qualified prospects and donors.

More and more fund raisers are adopting this model, because annual fund campaigns have become tired and flat. They can improve their communications, increase personalization and involvement techniques, and strengthen renewal efforts with relative ease with mini-campaigns.

Model 4: The Annual Giving Strategies Model

The concept of an integrated development program is not entirely new, but some of its component parts are. For many years, sophisticated fund raisers have attempted to integrate their fund-raising approaches in an effort to create a fund-raising program that closely resembles the pyramid of giving. To do so requires a series of strategically planned techniques that are linked to all others and are designed to build donor relations over time, ultimately producing the largest possible outcomes, financial and otherwise. The newest fund-raising efforts are designed to do the following:

- better understand donors, their motivations, and their interests through research
- segment donors into similar, discrete constituencies
- select and communicate specific *needs* to different donor segments, by way of an exchange
- select different fund-raising vehicles based on the donor segment
- provide a form of *case management* for each donor, allowing him or her to move more naturally into a relationship of giving and receiving

- provide a higher level of donor communications, recognition, and stewardship

The integrated annual development model is by and large the most donor-sensitive, complex, comprehensive, seamless, and effective fund-raising strategy for the long term. It raises money and makes friends 365 days a year. It is thus the preferred approach in the following chapters.

The integrated development model is the most donor-sensitive, complex, comprehensive, seamless, and effective strategy.

References

Flessner, B. 1995. Turning the fund-raising pyramid upside down: Starting with major gifts. Presented at the 1996 NSFRE International Conference (March 19).

Grasty, W.K., and K.G. Sheinkopf. 1982. *The annual fund: How to grow perennial rewards from an annual campaign.* Los Angeles: The Grantsmanship Center.

Greenfield, J.M. 1991. *Fund raising: Evaluating and managing the fund development process.* New York: John Wiley & Sons.

Greenfield, J.M. 1994. *Fund-raising fundamentals: A guide to annual giving for professionals and volunteers.* New York: John Wiley & Sons.

Mixer, J.R. 1993. *Principles of professional fundraising: Useful foundations for successful practice.* San Francisco, CA: Jossey-Bass.

Rosso, H.A. 1991. *Achieving excellence in fund raising.* San Francisco, CA: Jossey-Bass.

Chapter 3

Creating an Environment for Philanthropy to Flourish: Steps 1 and 2 in the Annual Integrated Development Process

Step 1 in the Annual Integrated Development Process: Determine the Level of Organizational Readiness and External Responsiveness

Characteristics of a Strong Organizational Environment

Fund raising is dependent on the character and strength of the organization it serves. If the organization is strong, philanthropy can flourish; if the organization has weaknesses, philanthropy can be stymied. Fund raising is most effective in organizations with a distinguished history, a worthy and relevant case, a respected image in the community, a strong culture of giving and receiving, and a commitment to grow by investing in the philanthropic process. The following characteristics are indicators of an organization whose culture is conducive to philanthropic giving and receiving:

- *The vision is entrepreneurial and achievable.*
- *There is confidence and trust in leadership.*
- *The organization values learning and teamwork.*

- *The staff and volunteers know how to transform ideas into action.*
- *The process of philanthropy is shared by all.*

Before fund raising can begin, it is essential that the fund raiser assess the extent to which the organization has achieved *internal readiness* and *external responsiveness*—basic conditions for effective fund raising.

Assessing Readiness and Responsiveness

Too often, fund raising is started in a hurry, without taking time to assess the organization's readiness and to *develop an environment for philanthropy to flourish.* The haste to raise money in the shortest possible time comes from a lack of understanding of the key management ingredients of success: analysis, planning, execution, control, evaluation, and professionalism. The fact is that fund raising takes time because it builds relationships that produce desired results for the long term, which requires a cultural readiness, organizational infrastructure, and institutionalized commitment.

Step 1 is a critical one, for it assesses four major areas: the organization's mission, leadership, structure, and culture—it measures the organization's *strengths, weaknesses, opportunities,* and *threats* (otherwise known as a *SWOT* analysis). The assessment and analysis form the basis on which fund-raising plans are developed, strategic decisions made, goals set, and projects implemented.

The process of assessing readiness and responsiveness for fund raising is similar to a campaign feasibility study, though not as complex and certainly not as expensive. This assessment should be done every few years, regardless of the size of the organization, the current level of financial and voluntary support, or the stage of the fund-raising program. This assessment will help renew, revitalize, and reengineer an annual giving program or build one from scratch if need be. A professional fund raiser can do this assessment with the help of other professionals in the

organization or, if needed, with an outside consultant.

1. Is the organization's **mission** relevant and its vision achievable?
2. Are there enough respected **leaders** and active **volunteers**?
3. Is the **organization** structurally sound and financially responsible?
4. Does the organization have a **philanthropic culture**?

The readiness and responsiveness assessment focuses on characteristics and conditions that must be present for fund raising to be successful. It is a systematic process for gathering information and testing assumptions through a specific sequence of activities:

- a series of **personal interviews** with key staff, board members, volunteers, and donors
- **focus group sessions** with key staff, volunteer leaders, and donors
- review of the **strategic plan** and supporting documents
- analysis of the **fund-raising program** from every aspect
- a comparative analysis of **similar organizations**
- assessment of the available **human and financial resources** for fund raising

These activities are designed to verify assumptions with quantified and qualified data about the organization's weaknesses and strengths. The findings are analyzed and recommendations are made and reported to the organization's leadership.

Question 1: Is the Organization's Mission Relevant and Its Vision Achievable?

This question can only be answered in the affirmative if the opinions of insiders match the opinions of outsiders. Often, after many years of existence, a nonprofit organization becomes fully institutionalized, a life-cycle stage at which things are taken for granted, rather than questioned. At this stage, an organization tends to behave in a way that prescribes what people need, rather then asking people what they need or want. Organizations who fail to validate their missions regularly find themselves in a survival life stage and are forced to go out of business because their missions have become obsolete.

Remaining relevant in the nonprofit sector takes work. It requires an inherent genuine interest in the external marketplace, a desire to be proactive and change-oriented, and the ability to be flexible. With change as an inevitable dynamic, an organization must engage in ongoing market research to find out if its mission is current and its vision realistic.

This assessment process serves as the organization's "reality check." It collects subjective and objective data from interviews and focus groups and compares responses of those who are on the inside with those on the outside. Some of the most accurate opinions of the organization's relevance come from its marketplace competitors. If the mission or vision has not been updated within the past five years, it probably no longer reflects the environment.

But being relevant isn't enough in today's marketplace—the mission must also be *critical* and *urgent* and built on a bright *future*. Fund raising is based on mission and vision; both are expressed through the *case for support*, the organization's rationale for philanthropy. If the mission is not current or the vision is not realistic, the case will be weak, and the ability to facilitate philanthropic exchanges will be diminished.

Questions to Ask
- When was the mission last updated?
- What is the status of social problems or issues addressed in the mission?
- What are emerging issues or conditions that could alter the mission?
- What is the effect of not achieving the mission?

- What impact does the organization have on the problem?
- What are the organization's distinct characteristics?
- What is its market share?
- Who are the organization's competitors? What are their strengths?
- What is the community's image of the organization?
- Does the community understand and support the mission? To what extent?
- What are the marketplace strengths, weaknesses, opportunities, and threats to the organization's need, place, timing, and cost?
- What are the organization's future plans, strategies, and objectives?

Documents to Analyze
- the strategic plan
- the long-range plan
- the annual report and financial audit
- program descriptions, often found in work plans or grant proposals
- communications materials, newsletters, brochures, and the like
- fund-raising materials, records, and reports

Insights
- Most nonprofit organizations are worthy of support not because they think so, but because others think so. Ask people on the inside why they are *personally involved* in the organization, and then ask people on the outside what would *cause them to be* involved in the organization?
- Some organizations focus on their strengths, rather than on the strength of the people who are served or the people who work there. Do the materials focus on the organization's mission (the means), or do they focus on personal accomplishments and successful outcomes (the ends)? The front page of the newsletter is a telling indicator of where an organization is in its *thinking*—is the lead article one that describes the problem or boasts

of the solution? Does it articulate the need for philanthropic support or report how funds were used? Do articles talk about the *way* the organization raises money (the Alumni Annual Fund) or *why* the organization raises money (for scholarships and library resources)?

- Can people outside the organization describe the organization's mission quickly or clearly, or do they seem confused by the complexity, or even the simplicity, of it? Take note of what people say when they talk about the organization. Do they say, "I know they do good work, but I'm not sure at all of what they do," or "I have seen first-hand the changes made in the lives of young people, and I believe no one else could do it better"? The first response seems apologetic, the second response prideful. What are the comments *saying* about your organization?
- Information is a powerful influence on people's attitudes. When people talk about their organization in terms of specifics—program examples, client statistics, real-life stories—they present verbal pictures of an organization that is *working*. In the absence of educated and inspirational examples, people send the opposite messages as if to say, "Nothing important is going on here."
- People prefer to contribute to what the future might hold, rather than paying for what has already happened, such as program deficits, declining numbers of clients, loss of employees, and so on.

Question 2: Are There a Sufficient Number of Respected Leaders and Active Volunteers?

As important as organizations are, they will never take precedence over the human systems that drive them. Few organizations survive and thrive without leadership—as differentiated from management. Leadership forges the path; management paves it. Leaders provide the vision, the inspiration, but charisma and an entrepreneur-

> **Leadership forges the path; management paves it.**

ial spirit are insufficient; today's *followers* require more. Participatory leadership is in; hierarchical management is out. Team building is in; orders and rules are out. Today's leaders must walk-the-talk and create an atmosphere where the first order of business is honesty and respect for each other. The extent to which people have confidence in and respect for the organization's leadership is a direct reflection of the organization's readiness and responsiveness. The assessment will discover if leaders are respected and valued and, if they are not, why not.

Leadership takes many forms in a nonprofit organization—*administrative* leadership, *board* leadership, *volunteer* leadership, and *staff* leadership. Leadership is not just positional, or at the top of the organization. Leadership can and should be exhibited at every level. On the other hand, a weakness in leadership at one level affects all other levels.

In today's nonprofit environment, administrative and development staff are assuming more and more responsibility for an organization's leadership. In many mature organizations, volunteers have roles that are perfunctory, rather than integral to strategic thinking and decision making. The recent shift from volunteer leadership to staff leadership does not bode well for the nonprofit sector. With the loss of volunteers comes the loss of community representation and community building. Staff can never replace the independent, objective role of the *socially conscious* or *conscientious* volunteer—not in policy matters, not in fund raising.

Questions to Ask
- Who are the designated leaders (administration, board, staff, and volunteers)?
- Whom do others regard as the leaders?
- What are their characteristics and distinctions?
- Do they have the influence and ability to take the organization where it needs to go?

- Do they demonstrate philanthropic leadership?
- Do they ask their friends to do likewise?
- Is there a waiting list for the board? Is there a healthy turnover on the board?
- Are many volunteers actively involved?
- What are their specific roles, responsibilities, and contributions?
- How are volunteers recognized? Do they feel special?
- Who are the organization's natural constituents?

Documents to Analyze
- board rosters and attendance lists
- administrative lists and charts
- contribution records, accounting procedures, and fiscal policies
- manual and computerized donor file profiles
- volunteer rosters, job descriptions, and recognition policies

Insights
- Invite important community leaders and key board member to review the organization's board list and ask them, "Who is **not** on this list who should be?" Keep a running list of names that people suggest, keeping track of the number of times they are mentioned.
- Inquire within the organization about the *brightest thinkers* and the people who get things done. These are usually the organization's intrepreneurs—those who have the ability to work within institutional systems without constraining their initiative and imaginative spirit. Often, these people are the source of the most innovative services and have the strongest following, be they social workers, physicians, faculty members, or neighborhood librarians—they are *popular*.
- It is common knowledge that people give to people, with causes. Identifying the organization's change agents and key influencers will enable the fund raiser to build the most effective and articulate fund-raising team, in partnership with

the development committee and department.
- If for some reason, the head of the organization is not seen as an effective leader, there is no substitute; a void exists. Confidence and trust in the organization's leadership are primary external motivators for philanthropy—its absence is problematic.

An organization that views its volunteers as partners, keeping them informed and enabled, will have the least amount of tension and the greatest amount of responsibility sharing. Tension between staff and volunteers is inevitable because of the shared roles and responsibilities. This is not to say that tension should be minimized—it should be *managed*. Pity the organization that does not have a maverick or two on the board to keep the executive director and board on their toes. Does your board rubber stamp recommendations and give lip service to its policies? If so, this board is unlikely to be interested in fund raising, because it will be insufficiently invested in achieving the mission.

Question 3: Is The Organization Structurally Sound and Financially Responsible?

All organizations have the responsibility to produce high-quality, needed services, based on the maximum utilization of all resources and the application of sound planning, management, financial, and personnel policies.

The internal workings of an organization or the management of it can make the difference between great ideas that go nowhere and those brought to successful fruition. Some organizations have systems that promote and facilitate new concepts or solutions; others have systems that perpetuate old programs. For instance, if an organization has a regularly scheduled, budgetary review process for the submission of new or enhanced programs, staff are encouraged to "think outside the box." This review process also puts pressure on existing programs to produce effective outcomes and remain competitive—

there's risk and reward. Everyone knows that the budget cannot handle unmanaged growth nor afford loss leaders.

Financial responsibility is a key characteristic of a healthy organization and one that will attract philanthropic support—donors prefer to support an organization when it is well managed, rather than in trouble.

The *effective management of human resources* is equally important. When an organization attracts and retains highly skilled and widely respected professionals, it not only remains competitive in the marketplace but it also becomes the leader. Parity compensation remains a major issue in the nonprofit sector. Attention must be given to reduce the compensation gaps between top executive positions and middle management and to compensate female and minority fund raisers fairly.

Well-designed organizational systems and structures make it possible for programs to be delivered to the public in effective and efficient ways. How wisely financial and human resources are allocated and used may be the most prevalent concern of today's donating public, governance bodies, and administrative personnel. *Program evaluation* has become as important a process as program origination was in the 1960s. Almost every organization has developed its effective benchmarks, continuous quality improvement systems, and devices to measure its levels of performance and customer satisfaction against similar organizations and competitors. Strategic positioning and market share are not only buzzwords of the 1990s but they also indicate the seriousness of program delivery and outcome effectiveness.

Questions to Ask
- Are organizational structures, systems, policies, and procedures in place and fully functioning?
- Is the organization accredited? What is its standing?
- Are program and funding priorities clear?
- How are program outcomes evaluated?
- What are the credentials of administrative and development staff?

- Are there any competency shortcomings?
- What is the budgetary process? Who participates in it and approves it?
- Are fund accounting practices fully utilized?
- Is the funding base diverse? What percentage comes from philanthropy?
- How are fund-raising goals established?
- What are the costs of fund raising, measured in return on investment by project?
- Are there stewardship and investment policies in place?

Documents to Analyze
- organizational charts
- personnel policies
- program descriptions, policies, and objectives
- program evaluation reports
- accreditation review reports
- financial reports
- fund-raising reports and cost analyses
- financial investment and stewardship policies

Insights
- Is the organization operating within its budgetary means and still able to provide cutting-edge services? Healthy organizations can do both. Because philanthropy is a litmus test of the community's needs, interests, and values, one has to consider the reality of receiving too little or too much support. When philanthropy does not seem to be forthcoming, one has to ask if the need is real; when philanthropy is in excess of the need, one must ask if the solution is large enough.
- The process by which fund-raising goals are determined is indicative of the organization's attitude about donors and the philanthropic process. All too often fund-raising goals are established by the finance office to balance the budget—this approach is based on need, rather than opportunity. With good fortune, the fund raiser might be successful, but the risk is high, given that the goal was set without any assessment of donor potential or spe-

cific program need. And the opportunity to facilitate meaningful gifts for valuable programs may be lost.

- How is success measured? There are many ways to determine success—people served, cases carried, number of "graduates," dollars earned, number of grants, net or gross figures, percentages of increase, comparisons with competitors, place in national standing and awards, and so on.

Organizations posture themselves by the way they choose to define success and failure. Some organizations focus on where they have been, others on where they are, still others on where they are going. How does your organization measure itself?

Question 4: Does the Organization Have a Philanthropic Culture?

An organization's culture is defined by the values and the actions of those who are affiliated with it—the people who work or volunteer there or who are touched by the organization's services. This culture is the environment, which is shaped by how people think and observed by how people act. Some organizational cultures are more conducive to the philanthropic process than others. That is to say, some organizations are more philanthropic in their attitudes, opinions, approaches, and actions; others are more charitable in their view.

These same principles apply to the staff and volunteers who work for an organization. How they think and feel about the organizations they are affiliated with will contribute to the organization's ability to survive and thrive. Too often, insiders think they are different from outsiders, resulting in attitudes, opinions, and ac-

> An organization's culture is defined by the values and actions of those who are affiliated with it.

tions that may undermine their communications and relationships with those on the outside.

For instance, staff may believe that the *charitable* services they provide should be supported by the philanthropy of others, not themselves. Instead they feel their programs are *entitled* to support from board members, wealthy donors, and others in the community—so they themselves won't make a contribution to the organization. Volunteers too may feel they are already contributing to the organization when they give of their time. Professional and program staff may feel that fund raising is the exclusive responsibility of the person who was hired as a fund raiser, yet they will be the first to accept the check when it is designated for their program. Board members may feel that they should not be asked to fund raise, because that is not the reason they were recruited.

This scenario is very real and very common. It points out that people from the inside can send very confusing, negative messages to the others on the inside and more importantly to people on the outside. These are the cultural and philosophical attitudes that undermine the potential for philanthropy. And most of them are derived from myths about money, about voluntary giving, and mostly about fund raising.

The philanthropic fund raiser is challenged in the assessment process to uncover both overt attitudes and opinions and subtle ones that undermine progress toward a philanthropic culture. Often the assessment will elicit sensitive information and as such will need to be presented honestly and respectfully. No one need be quoted directly; all comments must be recorded and all reported anonymously. Often, this process calls for an objective third party, perhaps a consultant, to help frame sensitive issues. The ultimate goal of the assessment is to propose solutions that people will embrace philosophically and hold in trust for the duration of their involvement.

Questions to Ask

- Why do we need to raise funds? What do we need to raise funds for?

- Who should support the organization? Why should they?
- What are the short- and long-range goals?
- Who will provide the leadership for developing a philanthropic culture?
- Who will comprise the fund development team?
- What is the role of volunteers? Of staff?
- What resources are needed to implement a fund development program?
- What strategies, models, and approaches will be used to fund raise?

Documents to Analyze
- board orientation manual
- nominating committee records
- fund development organization charts
- development and finance committee minutes
- development committee rosters
- development policies and procedures
- fund-raising plans and project descriptions
- volunteer and staff reports

Insights
- Two of the classic indicators of a philanthropic culture are the *place* the development report occupies on the monthly board agenda and who gives the report. If it is last on the agenda or not on it at all and is given by a staff member, this is pretty good evidence that fund raising is not a high priority. If it is not a high priority with the board, it cannot be fully successful.
- In the interviews with board members it is important to ask what *they think* their role is in fund raising. If you find they were recruited with the knowledge that they must contribute and be involved in fund raising in some way, you can be sure there is even greater potential for board giving. A good way to position board giving is to ask each person to make a gift that says "this is one of my favorite charities." Be sure to let board members know what is expected of them, where their funds are going, and why they are needed,

beyond balancing the budget. If your organization is *not* one of their favorite charities, they must be encouraged to let someone else sit in their spot. It is hoped that the line for board vacancies is getting longer.

- Gift *getting* is loaded with negatives and constraints, excuses, and apologies. But developing relationships with people who have a particular interest in your organization's work and share the same values is easy, rewarding, productive, and fun. The foundation of successful relationships is built on the *LIA* adage: *L*—linkage (an experience or a person that has *linked* another person to the organization and/or its mission), *I*—interest (a personal interest in and affinity for the organization's cause and/or its recipients), and *A*—ability (the ability to contribute resources—time, talent, or treasure). The LIA principle is promoted by Hank Rosso, founder of The Fund Raising School. A central theme in the Fund Raising School curriculum, the LIA principle is being used successfully all across the country by the School's alumni.

The Assessment Outcome

Having completed the assessment process, the fund raiser and team prepare a report for the executive and board chair (and for others as appropriate). This report identifies the key strengths, weaknesses, opportunities, and threats. It recommends strategies to create or nurture the philanthropic culture.

The assessment process should have enabled the organization to do the following (Boguch 1994):

- Focus its vision.
- Establish its priorities.
- Recognize opportunities.
- Measure progress toward long-term goals.
- Inventory organizational assets and debits.
- Connect aspirations and strategies.

- Predict changes within and outside the organization.
- Add a sense of fairness to even the most painful change.

Step 2 in the Annual Integrated Development Process: Develop Strategies to Create and Nurture a Philanthropic Culture

A Basic Understanding of Philanthropic Fund Raising

The most successful fund raisers—those who consistently facilitate the most extraordinary gifts—take their job very seriously and their role very broadly. Their fund development programs are more than narrow fund-raising efforts that focus on the money aspects; rather, they are driven by philanthropic values. They strive to build relationships that result in the formation of philanthropists, as opposed to getting donors. Their programs perpetuate the philanthropic tradition and nurture the spirit of giving and receiving. Successful fund raisers create organizational environments in which everyone is included and involved in the process in some way. Only then can philanthropy grow to its full potential.

The first step in building a successful development program is understanding and acknowledging the differences among philanthropy, development, and fund raising. *Philanthropy* is the giving and receiving *exchange* that fund raisers facilitate, *development* is the management of all the required relationships, and *fund raising* encompasses the methodologies and functions themselves. Understanding the relationships

among these activities forces fund raisers to reflect on why and how they do their work, rather than just on what they do. It is this distinction that leads to the "miracles" of philanthropy.

Successful fund raisers view *development* ultimately as a means of enabling donors to realize the fulfillment of their philanthropic dreams of helping create a society that reflects their most deeply held values. Development becomes the process of helping people move from prospects to philanthropists. It is the sum of our efforts to acquire, renew, cultivate, educate, and serve our donors. It is a long-term approach that helps people discover how the works of our organizations are congruent with their personal values and how they can be an "agent of good" to bring their value-based vision of the world to reality.

Development tells the story based on meeting human needs. It holds as a basic tenet that organizations don't have needs, but rather the people we serve have needs—and that an organization exists only to meet human needs. To the extent that we meet those needs in ways that are congruent with the values of our donors, we stand to help create philanthropists, not just givers.

Fund raising, in contrast with development, is more simply the carrying out of specific activities to raise a specific gift. It produces charitable gifts, but few philanthropists. Programs that are based on a narrow fund-raising approach tend to focus on organizational needs, rather than people's needs. Fund raising as a sole driving force frequently ignores donor interests and values and focuses on the agency's agenda; it commonly overlooks the key task of relationship building and puts the focus on obtaining the maximum annual gift even at the expense of possible future gifts.

The differences between a philanthropic development program and a narrow fund-raising program are much like the differences between charity and philanthropy.

Charity—or fund raising if you will—focuses more on the problem than on the solution. It is expressed in what the organization needs, rather than in what the community wants and needs. Charity is a limited concept that tends to be cri-

> **Philanthropy is the giving and receiving exchange that fund raisers facilitate; development is the management of all the required relationships; and fund raising encompasses the methodologies and functions themselves.**

sis oriented, indicating a weakness of some sort, for which there is almost always a sense of apology. This crisis orientation leads to a form of begging for support that results in alms giving; it is impulsive, based on emotion, and token in its gift amount. Charity is short term by nature, requiring minimal commitment *and* eliciting limited satisfaction on the part of the giver. The benefit is directed toward one person for one time, rather than to many people for all time.

Philanthropy, a much broader concept than charity, is aimed at systematically solving the problem—as is philanthropic fund raising (or development). It is based on carefully devised plans, built on previous successes that together garner a sense of pride. Philanthropy focuses on the community, rather than on the organization and, as such, benefits many people. It requires an investment on the part of the giver and produces a satisfying outcome for both giver and receiver—producing a transaction, rather than a transfer. Philanthropy is donor-focused, but always in balance with the interests and the concerns of the recipient.

Nowhere is the health of an organization's culture more critical than in the nonprofit sector. Culture is the force and the spirit that bring values, attitudes, and beliefs into sync—giving an organization the power and the ability to generate philanthropic support—which in turn gives an organization and its programs stability and sustainability. An organization with heart and soul is mission-centered, and vice versa.

In their article, "Selling the Institutional Soul: The Heart of Development," Terrence C. Deal and Casey Smith Baluss (1994, 95) address the role that development professionals play in helping strengthen an organization's culture:

> The further nonprofit organizations allow the cultural values to shift away from the responsibility to contribute ideas, services, and human capital to improve society, the more difficult fundraising becomes. Fundraising professionals should help nonprofit institutions renew their symbolic cores and

strengthen their links to donors and beneficiaries.

No one should singlehandedly be expected to or expect to create or change an organization's culture if it is seriously unhealthy, but a philanthropic fund raiser can have a significant impact because of the role he or she plays within the organization. It helps when there is already some evidence of a richness in values and character. Deal and Baluss challenge organizations to promote heroes and heroines; stories about myths and morals; rituals and ceremonies; networks of storytellers; and to employ a cultural mirror. For our purposes, we can borrow a few strategies, practices, and tools in Exhibit 3–1, which have been used successfully by our colleagues for many years. They are a good place to start if you want to *create an environment where philanthropy can flourish.*

Ethical Behavior

Ethics influences how an organization views the practice of fund raising, how it regards its donors, and how it behaves when conflict arises. Ethical behavior is built on an open, candid search for information that provides the framework for decision making. When you ask questions, search for answers, and consider options, the ultimate decisions are most likely to represent the ethical posture of your organization. Because philanthropy is based on ethical values, it is extremely useful to adopt an official code of ethical principles, which can be applied whenever the situation calls for it.

Members of NSFRE are required, as part of their application or renewal process, to sign the industry-approved Code of Ethical Principles. Member or not, all fund raisers are encouraged to subscribe to these principles and to ask everyone on their organization's fund-raising *team* to do likewise. The fund-raising team includes all development department staff, volunteers who in any way are involved in fund raising, and the executive, administrative, and program staff who participate in fund-raising functions

Exhibit 3–1 Nurturing a Philanthropic Culture

Cultural Evidence	Symbols to Borrow
● Ethical Behavior	● Code of Ethical Principles and Practices
● Donor Orientation	● Donor Rights Statement
● Expressed Values	● Philanthropic Values Statement
● Integrated Principles	● Development Maxims
● Mission Language	● A Mission that Sings
● Volunteer Partnered	● The Volunteer Credo
● Two-Way Communications	● The "I" Pyramid Strategies

on behalf of the organizations. The NSFRE code is self-explanatory and reprinted in Exhibit 3–2.

Donor Orientation

Donors are a key component of the philanthropic process, but can easily be taken for granted or viewed only as a source of money. If we see our relationships with donors as one sided (as in a transfer), we do them an injustice, a disservice. Donors are our partners, and the relationship is two-sided (as in a transaction). In the same way that fund raisers must give people the privilege of saying "no" to our appeals, we must give donors the rights they deserve when they say "yes." The Donors Rights Statement does that.

The Donor Rights Statement (Exhibit 3–3) was developed in 1994 as a collaborative effort by professional organizations to advance the field of development, to promote the values of philanthropy, and to ensure that donors are appreciated, respected, and entitled to certain rights. All organizations are encouraged to adopt this statement by having it approved by their boards as policy and giving the development department the authority to post it in public areas (lobby, waiting rooms, meeting spaces, etc.)

and to mail it to each and every donor on an annual basis.

Expressed Values

Many contemporary organizations have developed values or belief statements that articulate what they stand for, how they treat their employees, how their employees work with each other, what rights exist, and generally how people should behave. These statements mirror each organization's existing or desired culture. The same kind of reflection and agreement should go into the drafting of a statement about the role that philanthropy plays in the organization's culture.

For example, the Statement of Philanthropic Values presented in Exhibit 3–4 is one I drafted several years ago in an effort to attain a common understanding among volunteers and staff of how and why development efforts should be designed and implemented. Its genesis was the mutual agreement by both volunteers and staff that the existing fund-raising program needed to be more donor-focused and market-driven. The actual writing of the statement took about 30 minutes, but the concept had emerged over a period of 12 months or longer. It was officially

NSFRE Code of Ethical Principles and Standards of Professional Practice

Statements of Ethical Principles

Adopted November 1991

The National Society of Fund Raising Executives exists to foster the development and growth of fund-raising professionals and the profession, to preserve and enhance philanthropy and volunteerism, and to promote high ethical standards in the fund-raising profession.

To these ends, this code declares the ethical values and standards of professional practice which NSFRE members embrace and which they strive to uphold in their responsibilities for generating philanthropic support.

Members of the National Society of Fund Raising Executives are motivated by an inner drive to improve the quality of life through the causes they serve. They seek to inspire others through their own sense of dedication and high purpose. They are committed to the improvement of their professional knowledge and skills in order that their performance will better serve others. They recognize their stewardship responsibility to ensure that needed resources are vigorously and ethically sought and that the intent of the donor is honestly fulfilled. Such individuals practice their profession with integrity, honesty, truthfulness and adherence to the absolute obligation to safeguard the public trust.

Furthermore, NSFRE members

- serve the ideal of philanthropy, are committed to the preservation and enhancement of volunteerism, and hold stewardship of these concepts as the overriding principle of professional life;
- put charitable mission above personal gain, accepting compensation by salary or set fee only;
- foster cultural diversity and pluralistic values and treat all people with dignity and respect;
- affirm, through personal giving, a commitment to philanthropy and its role in society;
- adhere to the spirit as well as the letter of all applicable laws and regulations;
- bring credit to the fund-raising profession by their public demeanor;
- recognize their individual boundaries of competence and are forthcoming about their professional qualifications and credentials;
- value the privacy, freedom of choice, and interests of all those affected by their actions;
- disclose all relationships which might constitute, or appear to constitute, conflicts of interest;
- actively encourage all their colleagues to embrace and practice these ethical principles;
- adhere to the following standards of professional practice in their responsibilities for generating philanthropic support.

Standards of Professional Practice

Adopted and incorporated into the NSFRE Code of Ethical Principles
November 1992

1. Members shall act according to the highest standards and visions of their institution, profession, and conscience.

2. Members shall avoid even the appearance of any criminal offense or professional misconduct.

3. Members shall be responsible for advocating, within their own organizations, adherence to all applicable laws and regulations.

4. Members shall work for a salary or fee, not percentage-based compensation or a commission.

5. Members may accept performance-based compensation such as bonuses provided that such bonuses are in accord with prevailing practices within the members' own organizations and are not based on a percentage of philanthropic funds raised.

6. Members shall neither seek nor accept finder's fees and shall, to the best of their ability, discourage their organizations from paying such fees.

7. Members shall effectively disclose all conflicts of interest; such disclosure does not preclude or imply ethical impropriety.

8. Members shall accurately state their professional experience, qualifications, and expertise.

9. Members shall adhere to the principle that all donor and prospect information created by, or on behalf of, an institution is the property of that institution and shall not be transferred or utilized except on behalf of that institution.

10. Members shall, on a scheduled basis, give donors the opportunity to have their names removed from lists which are sold to, rented to, or exchanged with other organizations.

11. Members shall not disclose privileged information to unauthorized parties.

12. Members shall keep constituent information confidential.

13. Members shall take care to ensure that all solicitation materials are accurate and correctly reflect the organization's mission and use of solicited funds.

14. Members shall, to the best of their ability, ensure that contributions are used in accordance with donors' intentions.

15. Members shall ensure, to the best of their ability, proper stewardship of charitable contributions, including timely reporting on the use and management of funds and explicit consent by the donor before altering the conditions of a gift.

16. Members shall ensure, to the best of their ability, that donors receive informed and ethical advice about the value and tax implications of potential gifts.

17. Member's actions shall reflect concern for the interests and well-being of individuals affected by those actions. Members shall not exploit any relationship with a donor, prospect, volunteer, or employee to the benefit of the member or the member's organization.

18. In stating fund-raising results, members shall use accurate and consistent accounting methods that conform to the appropriate guidelines adopted by the American Institute of Certified Public Accountants (AICPA)* for the type of institution involved. (* In countries outside of the United States, comparable authority should be utilized.)

19. All of the above notwithstanding, members shall comply with all applicable local, state, provincial, and federal civil and criminal law.

Amended: March, 1993; October, 1994

Courtesy of National Society of Fund Raising Executives, 1994, Alexandria, Virginia.

Exhibit 3–3 A Donor Bill of Rights

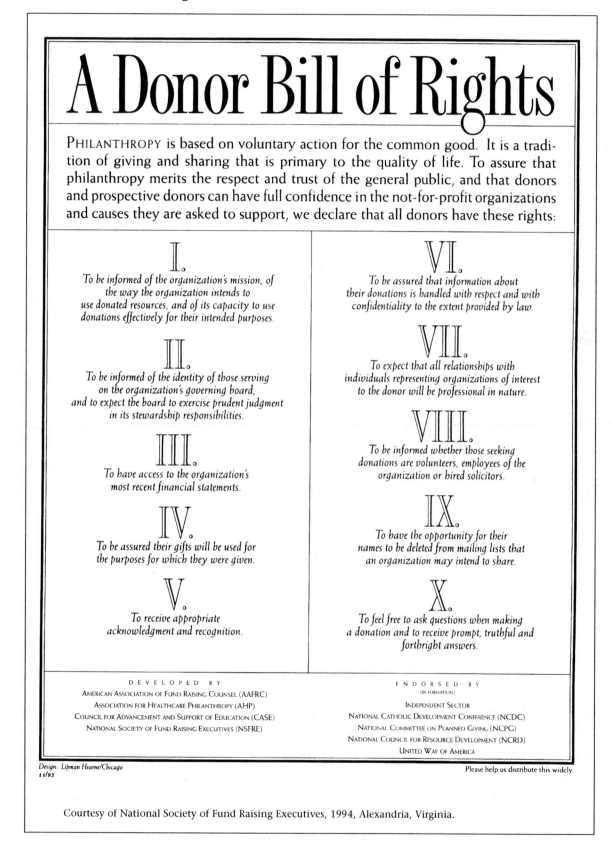

A Donor Bill of Rights

PHILANTHROPY is based on voluntary action for the common good. It is a tradition of giving and sharing that is primary to the quality of life. To assure that philanthropy merits the respect and trust of the general public, and that donors and prospective donors can have full confidence in the not-for-profit organizations and causes they are asked to support, we declare that all donors have these rights:

I.
To be informed of the organization's mission, of the way the organization intends to use donated resources, and of its capacity to use donations effectively for their intended purposes.

II.
To be informed of the identity of those serving on the organization's governing board, and to expect the board to exercise prudent judgment in its stewardship responsibilities.

III.
To have access to the organization's most recent financial statements.

IV.
To be assured their gifts will be used for the purposes for which they were given.

V.
To receive appropriate acknowledgment and recognition.

VI.
To be assured that information about their donations is handled with respect and with confidentiality to the extent provided by law.

VII.
To expect that all relationships with individuals representing organizations of interest to the donor will be professional in nature.

VIII.
To be informed whether those seeking donations are volunteers, employees of the organization or hired solicitors.

IX.
To have the opportunity for their names to be deleted from mailing lists that an organization may intend to share.

X.
To feel free to ask questions when making a donation and to receive prompt, truthful and forthright answers.

DEVELOPED BY
AMERICAN ASSOCIATION OF FUND RAISING COUNSEL (AAFRC)
ASSOCIATION FOR HEALTHCARE PHILANTHROPY (AHP)
COUNCIL FOR ADVANCEMENT AND SUPPORT OF EDUCATION (CASE)
NATIONAL SOCIETY OF FUND RAISING EXECUTIVES (NSFRE)

ENDORSED BY
(IN FORMATION)

INDEPENDENT SECTOR
NATIONAL CATHOLIC DEVELOPMENT CONFERENCE (NCDC)
NATIONAL COMMITTEE ON PLANNED GIVING (NCPG)
NATIONAL COUNCIL FOR RESOURCE DEVELOPMENT (NCRD)
UNITED WAY OF AMERICA

Design: Lipman Hearne/Chicago
11/93

Please help us distribute this widely.

Courtesy of National Society of Fund Raising Executives, 1994, Alexandria, Virginia.

Exhibit 3–4 Statement of Philanthropic Values

Statement of Philanthropic Values

- We believe that philanthropy is the initiative that occurs when people see a need and the response they give to effect change. Philanthropy is the fundamental human impulse to say how life should be, or could be.

- At this institution, philanthropy is not merely about money-raising or money-giving. It is a dignified process based on marketing principles and an exchange of values. We express our mission in ways that invite funders to participate in programs that mirror their values, preserve their interests, and meet their need for recognition, belonging, and a feeling of making a difference. The institution's needs become opportunities for donors to invest in. For this reason, we seek and encourage donor-designated giving to the greatest extent possible.

- Philanthropy at this institution is directed toward community initiatives and new programs for medical education, research and development, the purchase of high-tech equipment, and capital expansion. Gifts and grants are applied toward projects that cannot be funded through general operating revenue, demonstrating to donors and the community that their discretionary philanthropy dollars are vital in an extraordinary way.

- At this institution, philanthropy is never taken for granted. We recognize that when we receive a gift, be it large or small, our responsibility is to steward the funds in the most prudent way possible and exactly as the donor intended. We will respond to our donors with respect, giving due recognition and timely reports.

- The role of staff and volunteers in the philanthropic process is as:

  - facilitator   (of people, ideas, and funds)
  - conscience   (of our charitable mission)
  - advocate   (for human rights and dignity)
  - catalyst   (for program initiatives and advances)
  - steward   (wise use of funds)

- It is our responsibility to serve both the interests of donor and the institution, while working as part of a professional and volunteer team. We practice *case management*, which assures that donor relationships are properly built and nurtured and which offers staff members the opportunity for individual growth and leadership. Together, development staff facilitate a fund-accounting process that involves both donors and the institution in the distribution of assets.

- Our communications focus on how philanthropy addresses real problems, enables people and programs to flourish, and serves as an expression of community volunteerism. Our communications emphasize the human dimension, focusing on donor motivations and the patient outcomes, not fund-raising methodologies or balance sheets.

endorsed by the organization's board of directors, the supporting organization's board of directors, and the development committee and staff. Not only did it serve to advance the practice of philanthropic fund raising, but it was also a poignant reminder of what was important when opportunities arose that were not philanthropically rooted, i.e., cause-related marketing activities.

Since 1990, this statement has been circulated widely, and adapted to meet varying organizations' distinct characteristics, cultures, and views. It can be found today in hospital foundations, social service organizations, and universities.

Integrated Principles

Over the years, many professional fund raisers have built their own list of "do's and don'ts" based on their experiential learning. Such lists of *maxims* have been printed and distributed, edited, and expanded by other fund raisers, becoming the foundation for a body of knowledge in fund development and philanthropy. They comprise a core set of values, practices, assumptions, and expectations that affect every significant philanthropic exchange. The maxims included in Exhibit 3–5 are those of a fellow reflective practitioner, consultant, and scholar: Tim Burchill, CFRE, President, the Metanoia Group, St. Mary's University of Minnesota.

Mission Language

An organization's mission is the basis for its fund raising. Too often a mission statement is written *by committee* and, as a result, is not very energetic or inspirational in its presentation. It becomes hard to quote verbatim because it seems so rhetorical. This being the case, we can observe people describing their organization's mission in their own way, using personal examples of what the mission means to them in *real life*.

It may be useful to have several versions of the mission statement: one for the institution's internal use and one for external use. When used in fund raising, a mission statement should get people's attention, inspire them, and motivate them to action.

The two mission statements in Exhibit 3–6 are provided by colleagues; they offer good examples of exciting, inspiring, compelling mission/case language.

Volunteer Partnering

Few organizations view volunteers as their partners as thoroughly as does the YMCA, which has mastered the art of balancing the needs of the volunteer with the needs of the organization in fund raising. To their credit, they were one of the first institutions to involve volunteers in fund raising, and they continue to maintain the belief that volunteers are fundamental to their success, despite a national decline in volunteerism in recent years. Undoubtedly the YMCA will be among the last organizations to continue to use volunteers in spite of the professional growth of paid fund raisers. The YMCA's credo addresses how much they value volunteers (Exhibit 3–7).

Two-Way Communications

When someone is asked to describe his or her favorite charity, the answer usually falls into two response groupings: (1) The donor will rationally describe how the organization fulfills its mission in ways that are meritorious and distinct, or (2) the donor will emotionally describe his or her relationship and involvement with the organization. These reactions point out the importance of relationships between donors and the organization's representatives or recipients. When donors are involved, informed, invested, and inspired in the work of a charitable institution, their interest, commitment, pride, and willingness to do more, grow—they become afficionados for the cause. Even times of trouble can't keep a philanthropic afficionado from standing up and supporting an organization.

The pyramid of giving has long been used to illustrate the increased level of involvement necessary to the building of relationships with donors as the fund-raising process moves donors

Exhibit 3–5 Philanthropic Fund-Raising Maxims

Philanthropic Fund-Raising Maxims

- Institutions have no needs.
- Requests for support must focus on the impact the support will have on the beneficiaries, not the recipient.
- For both donors and volunteers, the single greatest motivation is the perceived opportunity to make a difference.
- People support what they help to create.
- Hope is not a strategy.
- Neither the focus nor the objective of philanthropy is money.
- Seek investments not donations.
- Empower volunteers.
- Invite people to stakeholder status.
- The most common (and least forgivable) reason for not securing a gift is the failure to ask for the gift.
- Ask for enough.
- Passion is more powerful than facts.
- The threshold for a major gift is in the donor's heart.
- First, work smart. Second, work hard.
- Insiders must give first.
- We aren't asking for ourselves.
- Two on one is the best scenario.
- The most important skill in communications is listening.
- It's easier to get the gift than it is to get the appointment.
- Capital campaigns in the future will be briefer and involve fewer donors and raise more money.
- One of the best ways to create and sustain momentum in a capital campaign is to secure one or more challenge grants.
- Every development officer should at all times have on the desk or in the drawer a list of the top prospects for whom he or she is responsible and an action plan for dealing with each of those prospects.
- Neither tax laws nor the ill-advised initiatives of legislators constitute the single most critical threat to the future of philanthropic support for the nonprofit sector; indeed, philanthropy's most dangerous enemy comes from within: the unethical, misleading, self-aggrandizing, amoral, dishonest actions of some in our profession whose actions desecrate the concept of stewardship.
- The most successful nonprofit organizations are those with credible, moral, visionary leaders who have the power to move people toward realization of common goals.
- Philanthropy is the voluntary giving and receiving of time and resources, frequently within an organizational context, directed toward charitable purposes and/or betterment of the quality of life.
- Development, within philanthropy, is the creative process of building and facilitating relationships with an ever-expanding pool of stakeholders who are encouraged and invited to invest themselves in the mission and vision of charitable organizations.

Courtesy of St. Mary's University, Winona, Minnesota.

Exhibit 3–6 Sample Mission Statements

MISSION OF A FAMOUS BALLET COMPANY

We dance before we speak. Transcending race, national origin, geography, ethnicity, gender, economic station . . . even species, dance is the universal language of the soul. We dance to express our deepest emotions from ultimate joy to abject despair, from total devotion to absolute abandon. Dance is a transcendent prerequisite to the fullest expression of life. This ballet company brings voice through dance to the soul of the City.

MISSION OF A LOCAL GIRL SCOUT TROOP

Sunlight filters through the mountainside forest, creating patterns of light and shadow on the front porch. One girl carefully handcrafts a dulcimer. A small group of girls hold their final rehearsal for an original play. Two girls head hand-in-hand down the trail, discovering nature's bounty. Everywhere there is laughter—learning, living, growing up. It's just another day at Camp.

Courtesy of Jim Reid and The Fund Raising School No. 101 participants, Indianapolis, Indiana; and Hornets' Nest Girl Scout Council, Charlotte, North Carolina.

---

up the pyramid. It is unclear precisely where the multiple pyramid adaptations came from, but the most interesting one uses "*I*" words—*i*nvite, *i*nform, *i*nterest, *i*nvolve, *i*nvest, and *i*nspire. The two-way communications build strategically with each step.

- **Invite** is the process of attracting a prospect's/donor's attention by encouraging participation in the organization's mission.
- **Inform** is the process of educating prospects/donors about the organization's mission, its programs, and need for funding through a newsletter, an annual report, or an invitation to an activity.
- **Interest** is the process of exploring the donor's needs and interests while increasing his or her awareness and desire to participate. At this point the donor and organization are considering their options.
- **Involve** is an action that reaches out to

donors and involves them in meaningful ways, seeking their input and advice as a committee member, on a site visit, or to attend an event.

- **Invest** conveys the high level of involvement and investment (time and money) that both the organization and the donor are giving to the process. This involves the highest possible level of communications and interaction.
- **Inspire** is an activity that causes the donor to have a more profound experience or connection to the organization's mission. It might be a visit by the board chair or executive to discuss the organization's vision or meeting one of the students who benefited from a scholarship in the donor's name.

Figure 3–1 illustrates how the "I" words become a process that builds in quantity and quality.

Exhibit 3–7 Acting on Principle: Goals and Guidelines for Volunteer Development in the YMCA Movement

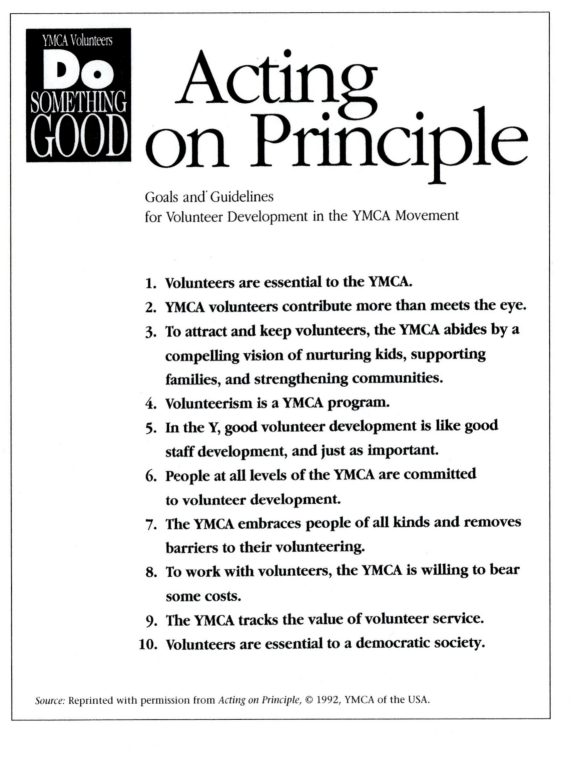

Acting on Principle

Goals and Guidelines
for Volunteer Development in the YMCA Movement

1. **Volunteers are essential to the YMCA.**
2. **YMCA volunteers contribute more than meets the eye.**
3. **To attract and keep volunteers, the YMCA abides by a compelling vision of nurturing kids, supporting families, and strengthening communities.**
4. **Volunteerism is a YMCA program.**
5. **In the Y, good volunteer development is like good staff development, and just as important.**
6. **People at all levels of the YMCA are committed to volunteer development.**
7. **The YMCA embraces people of all kinds and removes barriers to their volunteering.**
8. **To work with volunteers, the YMCA is willing to bear some costs.**
9. **The YMCA tracks the value of volunteer service.**
10. **Volunteers are essential to a democratic society.**

Source: Reprinted with permission from *Acting on Principle,* © 1992, YMCA of the USA.

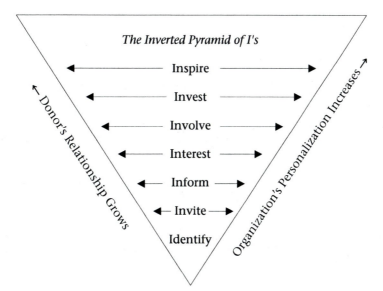

The Inverted Pyramid of I's

Inspire
Invest
Involve
Interest
Inform
Invite
Identify

Donor's Relationship Grows

Organization's Personalization Increases

Figure 3–1 The Inverted Pryamid of I's. The inverted pyramid illustrates how the donor's relationship with an organization grows with time and involvement, and how the organization's personalized communications increase quantitatively and qualitatively.

References

Boguch, J. 1994. Organizations readiness for successful fund development: A systematic and holistic approach. *New Directions for Philanthropic Fundraising* (Fall).

Deal, T.C., and C.S. Baluss. 1994. The power of who we are: Organization culture in the nonprofit setting. *New Directions for Philanthropic Fundraising* (Fall): 5–16.

Chapter 4

Building a Constituent Base by Focusing on Donors' Wants, Needs, and Interests: Step 3 in the Annual Integrated Development Process

Applying Marketing Principles to Annual Giving: A Different Way of Thinking That Is Donor-Directed

Marketing has changed the way Americans think and behave. As we moved from a product-oriented society to a consumer-driven one, people turned to the principles of marketing to guide the way. Since marketing concepts were first introduced in the mid-1970s, the for-profit sector has literally reengineered its business strategies from selling the customer what is produced to producing what the customer wants. The business sector views marketing as the way to gain a competitive edge, to direct proactively the growth of business.

The nonprofit sector, on the other hand, has been less than enthusiastic about adopting a marketing philosophy, resisting the idea that theirs is a *business*, and people their *products*. The terminology used in marketing, such as the word "customer," represents a foreign concept to many nonprofits—the mere idea of looking outside the organization for direction conflicts with the belief that "experts" are on the inside. These attitudes have become institutionalized and are difficult to overcome. Too, the nonprofit sector's reluctance to incorporate marketing principles was and still is deeply rooted in a misperception that marketing is selling and therefore manipulative. Or worse, there are those who think of marketing only as effective public relations, not as a consumer-centered philosophy. Marketing is not promotion or selling; it is a perspective that identifies people's needs, and in turn designs programs/products to meet them.

Understandably, it is a challenge to apply for-profit fundamentals in a nonprofit setting, because corporate monetary cultures are very

> **Marketing is not promotion or selling; it is a perspective that identifies people's needs, and in turn designs programs or products to meet them.**

different from nonprofit mission cultures. A close look at the nation's business schools uncovers ongoing debate about whether nonprofit administration (or nonprofit marketing) is an original theory or merely a "borrowing" of business theory. If borrowed, is it as applicable? Faculty and students alike struggle to explain exactly how marketing fits the nonprofit "consumer"—the client in need of counseling, the hospital patient, the college student, the museum or theatergoer, or the nature center visitor. For some, the interpretation is as difficult as translating one foreign language into another—something seems to get lost in the process. Until recently, the practitioners who were interested in applying marketing techniques to their nonprofit organization found very few resources to help them. Now, workshops, books, and journal articles enthusiastically promote the use of marketing in response to the ever-increasing competitive environment. In recent years, the use of marketing principles has become a widely accepted way of determining which programs or services to initiate, to promote, and to eliminate.

Given the nonprofit sector's slowness in incorporating a marketing perspective, it should be little surprise that, within the sector, the development profession was one of the last to look at how marketing might fit—mere reference in the literature is given to the use of marketing in fund raising. It is even more challenging to view the donor as the organization's "customer," given the ambiguity about what the donor is "buying," from a social and psychological perspective. The irony is that marketing theory may be the *most natural* approach for fund raising because it places the donor in a prominent position—in partnership with the organization. Because marketing requires that an exchange occur between giver and receiver, the fund-raising

marketing objective becomes one that matches a donor's needs and interests with the organization's needs and interests.

A marketing perspective in fund raising acknowledges that donors want to get something in return for their charitable and philanthropic contributions—albeit intangibles, like appropriate recognition, timely reports, invitations to *insider* events, and to be "heard." This is supported by experience which shows that prospects and donors are more likely to contribute if (1) the donor and the organization have shared values, and (2) the donor and the organization achieve their mutual goals.

Shared Values:

- Donors recognize that the institution mirrors their own deepest desires, values, and aspirations.

Mutual Goals:

- The institution demonstrates a capacity to solve the problems and address the opportunities that the prospects themselves consider most pressing. (Lord 1981).

For development professionals, the theory of marketing provides a fresh new focus that is more about receiving, than getting; more of a transaction, than a transfer; more of a relationship with the giver, than with his or her money. A marketing perspective changes our orientation from a begging/selling mode to one that is donor-oriented. And finally, and most importantly, marketing is a sound business approach that is based on information, rather than intuition. According to Kotler and Andreason (1987, 36), marketing is a discipline:

> To survive and succeed, organizations must know their markets; attract sufficient resources; convert these resources into appropriate products, services, and ideas; and effectively distribute them to various consuming publics. These tasks are carried on in a framework of voluntary action by all the parties. The organization does not employ force to attract resources, convert them,

or distribute them. Nor does it beg for resources or distribute them wantonly. The modern organization relies mainly on offering and exchanging values with different parties to elicit their cooperation.

Marketing is distinguished from promoting and selling by three key elements:

1. **Research**—to find out what people want, think, or need
2. **Segmentation**—to place people into groups based on similarities
3. **Targeting**—to tailor communication messages to high-potential groups

Marketing Life-Cycle Stages: How It Works with Annual Giving

Philip Kotler and Alan R. Andreason, authors of *Strategic Marketing for Non-Profit Organizations* (1987, 36–65), may be the first to describe for the nonprofit sector what is known as the "market exchange theory." They advocate two-way interactions with customers (donors), rather than one-sided transfers of money. They embrace the concept that fund raising has a marketing life-cycle with three stages: the (1) product orientation, (2) sales orientation, and (3) strategic marketing orientation. See Exhibit 4–1.

Using the three-phase marketing model, fund raisers can pinpoint their current annual giving status and where they would like it to be.

These three approaches to annual giving are not necessarily discrete; fund raising can be very effective with a combination of all three, or two out of three. The key is to use the marketing approach in the annual giving program to the greatest extent possible, recognizing that resources are needed to achieve the highest level of market positioning and personalization.

Stage 1: Product Orientation

During the *product orientation stage*, fund raising takes the form of *begging*. This stage focuses on the organization's needs. The commu-

> **The key is to use the marketing approach in the annual giving program to the greatest extent possible.**

nications are about the organization's deficits, its shortcomings, its limitations, and problems. (Remember, institutions have no needs; only their clients-students-patients have needs, and donors have the opportunity to provide solutions that match their own goals and aspirations.) At this first stage, there is a belief that the more talk there is about the organization's needs, the stronger the case will be and the more money will be raised. This of course is not very effective because donors by and large prefer to support success, rather than the status quo and certainly not failure. During the product orientation stage, fund raising seeks sympathetic patrons who are inclined to make charitable handouts. When these are not forthcoming, fund raisers blame the organization's lack of success on recalcitrant donors.

With Annual Giving. At this stage, the annual giving program asks donors to contribute once a year to the general operating budget because the institution deserves it. The emphasis is on a donor's **ability** to give—if he or she has money, the organization should ask for it. Not only is the case the same but also the solicitation techniques are the same, the communication messages are the same, and the time of year is the same for every donor. Very little or no research is done on prospects or donors to qualify them, no segmentation is made, and no targeting is done. Volunteers may be involved, but their assignments are to get a repeat gift, not necessarily an increased gift. This kind of annual giving program is probably flat in terms of growth, and no doubt, most of the donors are at the bottom level of the pyramid, making small annual gifts.

Stage 2: Sales Orientation

During the *sales orientation stage,* the focus is on the "ask." Fund raising is *selling*, with fund

Exhibit 4–1 Marketing Life-Cycle Stages Applied to Fund Raising

Three Stages of Marketing and Development

Stage 1	Stage 2	Stage 3
Organization focused	Seller focused	Donor focused
"It is up to you to keep us going, and if we have to close down you'll be responsible." *	*"There are a lot of people out there who might give money, and we must go out and find them and convince them to give."* *	*"We're here to help you realize your aspirations, and provide opportunities to deliver benefits. With your support, we can do even more."* *

Product Behavior	*Sales Behavior*	*Marketing Behavior*
Acting entitled to charity Talking about the problem Having an internal focus	Convincing people to give Using guilt or pressure Emphasizing the bottom line	Analyzing the marketplace Targeting those with linkage Presenting cases of interest

Product Language	*Sales Language*	*Marketing Language*
Financial deficit Program needs Overworked/limited staff Inadequate facility Insufficient donor base	The annual campaign/ goal Direct mail and telemarketing Membership drive Special event Incentives and deadlines	Donor needs and interests Natural constituencies Segmented, target markets Research/positioning strategies Distinguishing characteristics

Product Activities	*Sales Activities*	*Marketing Activities*
Tired campaigns Lack of innovation Appeals that beg for support Charitable expectations One campaign a year *"Give to the institution"* *	Campaign "theme" overload Staff driven Messages that convince Mass marketing Computerized letters/calls Emphasis on techniques *"Give to the annual campaign"* *	A series of campaigns, for specific programs Messages that invite investment Volunteer solicitors Personalized solicitations *"Give to make services available to people like you"* *

*Lord, J.G. 1981. *Philanthropy and Marketing*, Cleveland, Ohio: Third Sector Press.

raisers resembling salespeople in the business sector, with business tactics, such as quotas, incentives, tickler files, and call-backs. At this stage, fund raisers work to achieve *quid pro quo* exchanges, replete with financial investment vehicles (as in insurance policies and annuities) and incentive rewards (ranging from mugs and T-shirts to name-a-building opportunities). The emphasis seems to be to "go out and get the order," with proficiency being paramount; hence, the overemphasis at this stage on mass direct mail appeals, mass telemarketing, and mass-produced communications. The transaction itself, such as the campaign's theme or financial goal, is the most significant element—rather than who gives or who receives and what is achieved as a result of the gifts.

With Annual Giving. This stage of annual giving is a little more sophisticated; there may be one or several mini-annual campaigns, each with specific goals and perhaps even one or more cases. At this stage, the emphasis is on the theme of the campaign, i.e., "Give to the Annual Fund." There might be a little research on a donor's **linkage and ability**, but not much about what the donor might be interested in, other than the organization per se. With the emphasis on money, the tactics at this stage may appear aggressive. They tend to be one-way "selling" messages, repeated many times throughout the year. Some segmentation is occurring at this stage, but it is probably limited to giving levels, such as first-time givers, repeat givers, upgrade givers, and major givers. Gift clubs and recognition events/ activities are very popular at this stage, as are incentive items, challenge grants, and heavily promoted campaign deadlines.

Stage 3: Strategic Marketing Orientation

The third, and most advanced stage, is the *strategic marketing stage,* in which development professionals acknowledge that the relationship between the donor and the organization is an inherent quality of philanthropy. In this stage fund raisers incorporate marketing principles

into their practice, redirecting their approach from a *need* mentality (internally focused) to a donor-directed philosophy (externally focused). Fund raisers work to *involve* donors in the accomplishment of change by funding solutions, rather than perpetuating problems. Research is first done on donors, after which they are segmented into like-groups. With knowledge about the donor's wants, interests, and needs, the fund raiser develops the case, the message, and the solicitation method—all designed to facilitate a match between the donor and the institution.

With Annual Giving. The third stage of annual giving is identified by a series of strategic giving opportunities (many mini-campaigns) run 365 days a year, designed for segmented audiences, and targeted for the highest returns. At this stage, annual giving programs are designed to fit the various levels of donor **linkage, interest, and ability**. Extensive research is done in advance of designing strategies for the annual plan. This research will uncover data that give the fund raiser the ability to segment donors by similarity, such as all "donors who are giving over $100, are personal friends of board members, and have expressed interests in preventing teen pregnancy" or "all donors whose accumulated giving exceeds $500, whose children or grandchildren were hospitalized in the past few years, and who attended the last charity ball." Only people who are known to have some linkage and interest and ability are targeted for a solicitation. Each segment of meaningful size is approached to support a particular program within the annual operating budget. The method of solicitation is determined by their potential—the larger the potential, the more likely a personal solicitation strategy by volunteer, by staff, in person, or by phone will be used. The smaller the potential, the more likely the solicitation will be a mail appeal, albeit personalized to the maximum extent.

Exhibit 4–1 was influenced by the work of Kotler and Andreason (1987) and of James Gregory Lord (1981), whose reflective study of the adaptation of marketing principles to fund-raising practices I greatly admire.

How the Marketing Exchange Works with Fund Raising

When fund raisers apply marketing principles, fund raising become a systematic, *managed* process of matching donor interests with an organization's needs, it is strategically targeted at selected high-potential markets, rather than the general public. This exchange concept, or marketing view, can best be graphically illustrated as a scale (Figure 4–1), with the prospects/donors on one side of the scale and the program providers/recipients on the other side. The center pole represents the organization, strongly positioned to hold the weight of both entities. The cross-bar represents the two-way communications and linkages that are formed as a result of relationships.

Not only does a marketing perspective encourage the design of more effective strategies but it also forces us to **reexamine** existing programs—assessing the benefits of mass market appeals, impersonal "personalized" computer letters, excessive telemarketing, and laborious special events. Have these broad-based efforts contributed to the short- or long-term growth of support? Marketing encourages greater emphasis on the personal relationship built through informal telephone conversations, personal visits, hand-written notes, and social occasions that bond donors as members of the organization's family. Marketing enables us to put the emphasis where it belongs: on the people who give, not on the goods we sell.

Because marketing is a business methodology, it has an orderly process that fund raisers can follow (Exhibit 4–2). The first three elements are presented in this chapter and the rest in subsequent chapters.

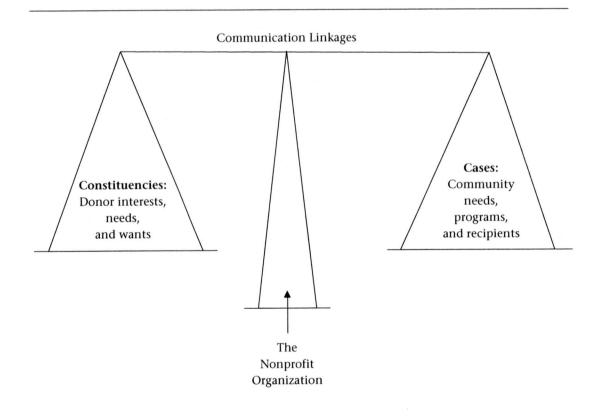

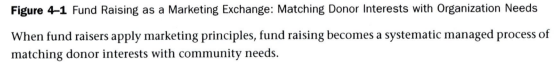

Figure 4–1 Fund Raising as a Marketing Exchange: Matching Donor Interests with Organization Needs

When fund raisers apply marketing principles, fund raising becomes a systematic managed process of matching donor interests with community needs.

Exhibit 4–2 Distinct Marketing Elements

- Marketplace analysis and psychographic research

- Market and audience segmentation

- Targeting those with highest potential

- Organizational positioning with distinguishing characteristics

- An integrated marketing, communications, and development plan

- Targeted and matched case messages and methods

- Demonstrated benefits to the donor

Philanthropic Motivations Are Complex and Varied: Why Do People Give and Why Not?

Philanthropy plays a significant role in American life, contributing two percent of the gross national product in 1995, according to *Giving USA* (1996). The great majority, over 80 percent, of the $143 billion contributed to charity in 1995 came from individuals. Observers of this philanthropic phenomenon, and fund raising professionals in particular, have always been interested in *who* gives, *when,* and *how* much they give. Over the years, market research studies, most specifically by the Independent Sector, have focused on the *demographic* characteristics of givers (location, age, income, gender) and *patterns of giving* (time of year, gift amounts, types of charities).

Although demographic factors play an important role in indicating who is likely to give (zip codes with high-income residents tend to give more than low-income zip codes), how much they will give (older people tend to give more than younger people), and when they will give (November and December are the highest giving months), in recent years professionals have become more interested in answering the question: Why do people give and what do they expect in exchange? The following questions deserve answers:

- Why do donors give to certain charities and not others?
- What causes them to make a first gift as compared to making repeat gifts?
- Why will a donor suddenly stop giving, after having supported an organization for many years?
- What influences a donor to select a *favorite* charity?
- What factors elicit a significant gift as though "out of the blue" while seemingly attentive efforts to solicit gifts over many years produce no response?
- Why do some give to a few selected charities, and others give to many?
- Why don't people give? (28 percent do not.)
- What do donors expect in return for their gift—anonymity or public recognition, an invitation to join the board, or regular project reports?

The time-honored "rule of rights" maintains that **a person will give when the right person, asks the right prospect, for the right amount, at the right time, in the right way, for the right reason.** In reality, philanthropic fund raising is not so simple. The motivations, behaviors, and motivational factors behind philanthropic giving are very complex. Most gifts, at least the significant ones, are thoughtfully decided on, they reflect a donor's personal values, are influenced by a relationship, and are in response to an effective external motivator. As stated earlier, a donor looks for shared values and the achievement of mutual goals. Other benefits to donors include respect, acknowledgment, appreciation, truthfulness, information, involvement, and results. Exhibit 4–3 shows donors' primary expectations. The more fund raisers know about what motivates donors to give, to give again, to give more, or not to give, the more the process of philanthropic exchanges will be improved, donor fatigue will be tempered, and resources will not be wasted.

The need to understand donor motivations better and to create more sophisticated fund-raising practices is especially pressing given today's environment of intense competition, an uncertain economy, and reduced governmental support. It is ineffective to spend time and money on mass marketing efforts to those who are unlikely responders. And, systematic analyses of donor motivations make it possible for fund raisers to carry out their tasks more effectively and efficiently.

Understanding donor motivations is not altogether a new idea. One of the first people to advocate for a better understanding of donors was John D. Rockefeller, Jr. His classic statement, printed and reprinted over the years, is a poignant reminder of the importance of understanding motivation:

> It is a great help to know something about the person whom you are approaching. You cannot deal successfully with all the people in the same way. Therefore, it is desirable to find out something about the person you are going to—what are his interests, whether he gave last year, if so, how much he gave, what he might be able to give this year, etc. Information such as that puts you more closely in touch with him to make the approach easier (Rosso 1991, 218).

How do fund raisers learn about donor motivations, behaviors, and motivational factors? One way is to be cognizant of the growing number of research projects on donor attitudes and to read the latest fund-raising journals and books (see the bibliography at the end of this book). Another way is to study human behavior; an education in psychology provides an excellent foundation for relationship building. According to Kay Sprinkel Grace, "Although intuition may serve most people well during challenging or sensitive transactions, a background in psychological principles can improve interactions with various constituencies (Sprinkel Grace 1991, 218). Yet another way is to begin collecting and analyzing information, beyond demographics, about your own donors. It is equally important, and perhaps more so, to gather data on a donor's initial affiliation, personal values, expressed program interests, linkages with others, and responsiveness to external motivators, such as the type of solicitation or time of year.

And it is useful to understand why people *don't* give, as those reasons are often mirror images of why they give. The reasons in Exhib-

Exhibit 4–3 Market or Social Exchange Benefits to Donors

- To be thanked in a timely, appropriate way

- To be recognized and treated as an investor in the organization's mission

- To achieve a meaningful impact/outcome on a social problem or cause

- To be given assurance that the gift was stewarded properly

- To be able to realize their own aspirations through giving

it 4–4 were elicited as part of a discussion by Fund Raising School participants and give testimony to the importance of understanding the annual donor from a marketing perspective.

Donor Research from the Field: Donor Motivations, Patterns of Giving, and Demographic Characteristics

There has been enormous growth in the number of field research projects relating to donor motivations. Fund raisers can learn from demographic research; research on giving patterns; behavior and "social exchange" research; research on relationships between religion and philanthropy; research on the motivations of the wealthy, women, and ethnic groups; research on people who volunteer; and research on people of different age groups, such as the elderly and the Baby Boomers. In addition to the reported research, a vast amount of information is collected by practitioners on their organization's donors, but these data have not been put to a comparative analysis test or published.

The following research projects are examples of how complex the subject of donor motivations can be; they point out how important it is to do your homework and "get into your donor's shoes" before embarking on a fund-raising program.

Research on Donor Giving Patterns

The Independent Sector is best known for its research on national patterns of giving by profile groups. Its annual publication, *Giving and Volunteering in the United States*, reports correlations between socioeconomic, life-cycle, ethnic, and religious attributes of donors and their giving levels and targeting of donations. The 1994 report shows the percent of respondents *who give*, their average contribution, and the percentage of household income represented by their contributions. It indicates, for example, that males contribute a higher share of their income than females, whites more than minorities, the elderly more than the young, the poor and the rich more than the middle class, Protestants and

Exhibit 4–4 Why People Don't Give

Why People Don't Give

- Not asked

- Didn't get around to it

- Prospect's needs, interests, and readiness not understood

- Absence of future plans

- Inadequate communication and cultivation

- Wrong solicitors

- Not asking for a specific amount relative to need and ability

- Not involving people who could influence or participate in gift

Courtesy of The Fund Raising School, Indianapolis, Indiana.

One way to distinguish people's attitudes is to look at their generational similarities or differences.

others more than Catholics, married people more than singles, and so on.

In addition to researching the demographic correlations of donors, the Independent Sector uses data collected by the Gallup Organization to learn more about *why people give*. These data have substantiated the widespread view that multiple reasons underlie charitable behavior, ranging from functional altruism to highly pragmatic benefits. See Chapter 1 for a list of 11 motives for giving funds and volunteering time to nonprofit causes. This information has helped improve fund raisers' understanding of why people are responsive to their appeals or not.

Demographic and Psychographic Research

Judith Nichols, a fund-raising practitioner/ consultant, is well known as a specialist in the area of demographics and psychographics. At last count, she had published five books on the subject. Nichols asserts that five major societal trends are significantly affecting fund raising: (1) overall aging and increasing longevity, (2) the unique demographics and psychographics of mid-life Baby Boomers, (3) new life patterns caused by the presence of women in the work force, (4) the diversification of the population, and (5) the different perspective of the young. She points out the need for fund raisers to understand that people have *different points of reference* and *different childhood experiences* that shape their views (1995, 2). One way to distinguish people's attitudes is to look at their generational similarities or differences. As a predictive tool, she groups people into four generational personalities—civic, adaptive, idealistic, and reactive (16–20).

1. *The Civics (1900-1924): "We fought for it . . . save, save, save":*

The civic personalities are those aged 70 and older. Coming out of the Depression and several world wars, they share two key characteristics: frugality and patriotism. "They are the 20th-century's confident, rational problem-solvers, the ones who have always known how to get big things done." With boundless civic optimism and a sense of public entitlement, they are good volunteers and good givers. Nichols suggests that the civics should be approached with "rational and constructive messages, with an undertone of optimism."

2. *The Adaptives (1925-1945): "We earned it . . . save, then spend":* The adaptive or silent generation members were born around the Depression and World War II, learning how to be seen but not heard. "They are consensus builders rather than leaders; they make the best of things." Members of the silent generation tend to be good givers, believing more in a fair process than final results. Like the civics, they are organization-loyal and value-oriented. Nichols suggests they be approached with "sensitive and personal messages, with an appeal to technical detail."

3. *The Idealists (1946-1964): "We deserve it . . . spend, then save":* Born after the war, the Baby Boomers are the largest and most idealistic group. Members of this group were told they could do anything; thus they believe in changing the world, not changing to fit it. "They display a bent toward inner absorption, perfectionism, and individual self-esteem." Nichols recommends approaching the Baby Boomers with "meditative and principled messages, with an undertone of pessimism."

4. *The Reactives (1965-1977): "We won't get it . . . it's hopeless":* Children of Baby Boomers, the reactive personalities or the Baby Busts, were touched by divorce and poverty and grew up as the first generation not believing that life would be bet-

ter for them than their parents. They "weren't trusted or appreciated as youth and carry the scars into adulthood. They are the most conservative-leaning youths of the 20th century." Nichols recommends approaching them with "convincing proof that your organization is reliable" and to use a "blunt and kinetic message, with an appeal to brash survivalism."

Research on Relationships between Religion and Philanthropy

Studies on American's beliefs and practices have substantiated strong ties between religious affiliation and giving; nowhere else in the world is religious commitment and religious diversity so prevalent. Somewhere between 65 and 71 percent of the adult public belong to a church or synagogue. Wuthnow and Hodgkinson, in their book *Faith and Philanthropy in America* (1990, 6), report that "church attendance, belief in God, confidence in organized religion, and sales of Bibles all show much higher levels of religiosity in the United States" than elsewhere. Total giving to religious causes is in excess of 50 percent of all monies contributed annually, and a higher proportion than given to any other type of charity.

What stimulates religious giving? The literature points out that religion teaches that believers have responsibilities to their fellow human beings; the messages are said to be codified in the Golden Rule, the Beatitudes, and the parable of the Good Samaritan. According to Wuthnow and Hodgkinson, "some experimental research suggests that guilt (also) may enhance the likelihood of someone engaging in altruistic behavior," (1990, 9) while other research suggests that believers view God as a wrathful deity instead, motivating people to do good deeds to appease God. Other theories argue that religious giving is stimulated as a result of people having a strong sense of self-esteem, suggesting they may be concerned with the social status that results from giving. Still others suggest that religious giving is situational, triggered by what someone else does, by how busy one is, or where the opportunity for giving arises. Wuthnow and Hodgkinson assert that religion is more than a simple set of moral and ethical dictums, and that donors are influenced instead by the way traditions are transmitted by sermons, stories, and other oral communications—the "narrative discourse that concretizes, objectizes and above all personifies what it means to be charitable" (11). According to Mixer, most believe that religion may actually motivate philanthropy by reinforcing a sense of obligation, putting moral and ethical pressure on individuals to contribute and providing some material incentives (1993, 8–11).

Research on Motivations of the Wealthy

It is not surprising that there is more research interest and activity on motivations of the wealthy than on any other group because of their potential giving power. Experience and some research have suggested, however, that wealth, in and of itself, is not a predictor or motivator of philanthropy. Rather, it is their belief that private contributions and nongovernmental charitable organizations are integral to the American way of life that serves as the foundation of their philanthropy (Odendahl 1990).

Researcher, author, and Harvard University sociologist Francie Ostrower agrees: "Donors are giving to things they choose to support, not what politicians say they should support." In an article describing a research project of 100 donors undertaken in the late 1980s, she reports that many wealthy donors value philanthropy precisely because it nurtures organizations and activities that the government is unlikely to support, such as universities, museums, hospitals, churches, and parks (Ostrower 1996).

In one of the largest and most recent research field studies on wealthy giving, Prince and File (1994) developed a framework of donor behavior from interviews with 800 donors. Their research, published in *The Seven Faces of Philanthropy* (1994), places each affluent donor into one of seven distinct segments based on needs, motivations, and benefits. Each segment (personality) represents a characteristic and distinctive (1) approach to philanthropy, (2) set of typical attitudes and beliefs, (3) range of considerations, (4) process of evaluation, and (5) style of involvement with a nonprofit organization (13–16).

- The *Communitarians*—Doing Good Makes Sense (26.3 percent)—tend to be local business owners, who credit their success to their community and want to give back.
- The second largest group, the *Devouts*—Doing Good is God's Will (20.9 percent)—gives mostly to religious causes, and sees giving as a moral imperative
- The *Investors*—Doing Good is Good Business (15.3 percent)—have one eye on the cause and one eye on personal benefits. They give because they are financially able to do so.
- The *Socialites*—Doing Good is Fun (10.8 percent)—are women who prefer to raise funds in social settings through social networks. They give because they are charitable at heart, and because they have the resources.
- The *Altruists*—Doing Good Feels Right (9 percent)—are selfless donors, who associate giving with spiritual self-fulfillment and self-development.
- The *Repayers*—Doing Good in Return (10.2 percent)—give because of the good results that follow. They are the only philanthropic personalities who make a distinction between the responsibility that those who are affluent have to help those in need.
- The *Dynasts*—Doing Good is a Family Tradition (8.3 percent)—are philanthropic because they grew up in an environment where giving was a way of life, believing that philanthropy is everyone's responsibility.

The framework provided in *The Seven Faces of Philanthropy* is a model for understanding the motivations of affluent individual donors. With this knowledge, fund raisers may be able to craft a vision that will meaningfully link the mission of a nonprofit to the benefits sought by donors with specific philanthropic personalities. Then, the fund raiser can select appropriate charitable giving strategies to transform the wealthy prospects into donors and repeat donors.

Schervish (1996) points out the need for more research on giving patterns by income and wealth as a means of "settling the debate about the relative generosity of the rich and poor" (27). His analysis of the *Survey of Consumer Finances*, which provides information about 400 individuals at the upper income and wealth level, concludes that "virtually all the rich are contributors, that they donate very large amounts to charity, and that they give higher proportions of their income to charity than do the poor or affluent. . . . In every category of income and wealth there is a small proportion of extraordinary givers . . . [and] some evidence that among the highest income and wealth groups there may in fact be a greater proportion of such extraordinary givers" (Schervish 1996, 27–28).

Research on Women as Philanthropists

In the past several years, fund raisers have become more interested in how they might approach female donors, who appear to have more influence in philanthropic decision making than was earlier thought. The National Council for Research on Women (1994) reports that, according to the Internal Revenue Service, most of the wealth in the United States (60 percent) is owned by women; in addition, wealthy women are more likely than wealthy men to make charitable bequests (48 percent compared to 35 percent), and younger women especially are giving money to support social action causes (Ostrander and Fisher 1995, 67).

A research project using interviews, focus groups, and discussions with 150 development professionals and women philanthropists was completed in 1994 by Shaw and Taylor and published in 1995 as *Reinventing Fundraising*. Their research points out a rich history of American women in philanthropy that is vastly divergent from that of men. Several themes emerge:

Women care deeply about making the world a better place for themselves and others; they want to pass on the responsibility of philanthropy to their children; their philanthropy involves a high measure of fellowship obligation and ability to make a difference; and they are rewarded by feeling a part of a larger community. Shaw and Taylor grouped women's motivations into six categories of desire: "to change, to create, to connect, to commit, to collaborate, and to celebrate their philanthropic accomplishments" (88).

The importance of research on women's attitudes lies in the applications that can be made to advance philanthropy. In their book, Shaw and Taylor demonstrate how fund raisers can involve women in nonprofit institutions by showing how, as donors, they can change the course of society by supporting a particular cause. Through philanthropy, women can be entrepreneurs and create a program or an opportunity for someone who would otherwise lack that opportunity. By collaborating as volunteer fund raisers, women can connect with an organization and with other women who share their visions. Women's commitment to volunteer efforts can be well directed when they work to help other women express themselves through giving. And finally, Shaw and Taylor suggest that through philanthropy, woman can celebrate their achievements with well-deserved fun. They advise fund raisers to become more gender sensitive, to improve communications with women, and to recognize and overcome the barriers to woman's philanthropic giving.

Ostrander and Fisher (1995, 73) go so far as to say that being sensitive to women's priorities while addressing social causes and building common connections "has the potential to create a different and better kind of fund raising—one that is perhaps more ethical and socially responsible than the approaches most frequently used."

Research on African-American Philanthropy

African-American philanthropy may be distinguished from other forms of philanthropy in that it is based on the concept of giving back, rather than reciprocity. African-American giving tends to be more spontaneous and unplanned and not influenced by tax advantages. If the need is present, the response is made—no matter that the gift is to a tax-registered charity or directly to an individual. Writer Jean Fairfax explains, "Black philanthropy has been shaped by the realities of life on this continent; that is, often the harsh reality of oppression" (Fairfax 1995, 10). As an expression of solidarity for the oppressed, African-American philanthropy has been a "mechanism for survival, mutual assistance, and self-help, for social protest, for the struggle for justice, for the enhancement of the educational and economic status of blacks, and for the establishment of institutions" (10).

Although Independent Sector research suggests that African-Americans, along with other minorities, give much less proportionately than whites, another study shows that they are very generous givers. In a paper prepared for the Center for the Study of Philanthropy, Emmett Carson (1990) asserted that in 1989, 60 percent of African-Americans in households with incomes under $20,000 were givers and 30 percent were both givers and volunteers. In households with incomes over $40,000, 88 percent were givers, and 62 percent were both givers and volunteers (13). Over two-thirds of their contributions were directed to black churches, which is no surprise because "giving to the black church represents an outpouring of thanks for its critical role in establishing other kinds of institutions in areas where public authorities failed to assume their responsibilities" (Fairfax 1995, 14).

To increase African-American giving beyond its traditional "crisis" approach, Fairfax urges fund raisers to do more asking and more educating. She advises against a one-shot drive for the big gift, but instead encourages a long-range coordinated effort within communities to educate African-Americans about philanthropy as a lifetime commitment, with the mission of "taking the concept of stewardship to another level." One way to involve them in the process is to invite more African-Americans to become board members of nonprofit organizations.

Research on the Correlation of Volunteering with Philanthropic Giving

Volunteering plays a vital role in an individual's propensity to give. In a 1992 Independent Sector study (Hodgkinson et al. 1992), households that both gave money and volunteered gave an average of $1,155 in 1991, almost two and one-half times the $477 average contribution from households that did not volunteer. The study estimated the total number of adult volunteers to be 94.2 million, a significant group with fund-raising potential.

Research on Social Exchange Relationships

In recent times, reflective professionals such as Joseph Mixer have explored the exchange concept in an attempt to build more responsive fund-raising methods. Mixer's book, *Principles of Professional Fundraising,* is one of the first comprehensive fund-raising texts to bring together the latest concepts and theories from psychology, organizational behavior, development, and management with the goal of providing a framework that enhances the effectiveness of professional fund raising. He describes tools that can help fund-raising professionals discern the attitudes, influences, and values of potential donors. Except when referring to the techniques of fund raising, he does not reduce fund raising to an economic or mechanical system; he presents a strategic view, rather than a task/functional one.

Mixer's social exchange model is based on the assumption that people's giving decisions are influenced by internal motivations (something desired, satisfying needs, relieving tension, or feeling good) that are stimulated by external influences (persons, events, or conditions): "Donors' internal motivations must be appealed to, stimulated, or triggered by external events" (Mixer 1993, 13). The framework for determining why people give includes both internal motivations and external influences.

According to Mixer, *internal motivations, needs, or drives* have three dimensions—personal (I factor), social (We factor), and negative (They

> People's giving decisions are influenced by internal motivations stimulated by external influences.

factor)—and are most strongly evident in the individual's concepts of self. Therefore, fund-raising efforts involve self-esteem, achievement, cognitive interest, growth, guilt reduction or avoidance, the meaning or purpose of life, personal gain or personal benefit, spirituality, immortality, and survival. Donors' internal motivations are also linked to feelings about others. The social factors of motivation include status, affiliation, group endeavor, interdependence, altruism, family and progeny, and power. Because individuals' motivations are not always positive, it is equally important to recognize the negative motivations. These include frustration, unknown situations, insecurity, fear and anxiety, and perceived complexity.

According to Mixer, *external influences* affect the individual's state of being and may condition or cause a response. He cautions against preciseness here, but believes three categories of influences show promise as external influences: rewards, stimulations, and situations. The *rewards* fall into three overlapping types—recognition (most tangible and visible to others), personal (coming from one or more people, less visible to others), and social rewards (less tangible of all). *Stimulations* are actions that directly prove human needs, make requests, present a vision, promote initiative, stress efficiency and effectiveness, and offer a tax deduction. *Situations* can arise from an individual's own actions or are created by others. They include personal involvement, planning and decision making, peer pressure, family involvement, tradition, networks, culture, role identity, and disposable income.

Mixer promotes the social exchange model of the charitable transaction as a "rationale that elevates the practice of fund raising, and gives impetus to both parties, the donors and the recipients, to perform well" (1993, 36).

Behavioral Research: Mobilizing and Motivating Factors

Paul G. Schervish offers the most extensive research on motivating factors for charitable giving in a new paper, *Inclination, Obligation, and Association: What We Know and What We Need to Learn about Donor Motivations* (1996). He sets the stage for the topic as follows (3):

> The current literature on the motivating factors for charitable giving is extensive; however, it is uneven in its level of theoretical sophistication and empirical complexity. For a number of reasons, including the fact that volunteering is tied to charitable giving, the literature on motivations for volunteering is always indirectly, if not directly, relevant to the discussion of charitable giving. Also, the fund-raising and prospect research literature is invariably related to the mobilizing factors for giving insofar as this literature addresses the organizational techniques and personal strategies fund raisers employ to induce donors to contribute. . . . In the absence of more complex research, we know little about the relative importance of these factors. . . . Also, this literature is both repetitive and partial. . . . We have not yet reached a point at which the theories, conceptual frameworks, measurement techniques, statistical analyses, and findings of one research effort build explicitly on previous research and become the bases for subsequent research designed to confirm, disprove, or amend previous findings.

Schervish proposes eight factors that are sufficient to induce at least a minimal level of philanthropic response. These variables grew out of his analysis of intensive interviews with millionaires in a 1988 study with Herman (5–6):

1. **Communities of participation:** groups and organizations in which one participates

2. **Frameworks of consciousness:** beliefs, goals, and orientations that shape the values and priorities that determine people's activities

3. **Direct requests:** invitations by persons or organizations to directly participate in philanthropy

4. **Discretionary resources:** the quantitative and psychological wherewithal of time and money that can be mobilized for philanthropic purposes

5. **Models and experiences from one's youth:** the people or experiences from one's youth that serve as positive exemplars for one's adult engagements

6. **Urgency and effectiveness:** a sense of how necessary and/or useful charitable assistance will be in the face of the onset of an unanticipated or previously unrecognized family, community, national, or international crisis

7. **Demographic characteristics:** the geographic, organizational, and individual circumstances of one's self, family, and community that affect one's philanthropic commitment

8. **Intrinsic and extrinsic rewards:** the array of positive experiences and outcomes of one's current engagement that draw one deeper into a philanthropic identity

Schervish's research findings indicate that the first factor, communities of participation, has the strongest and most consistent relationship to giving behavior and that "charitable giving is largely a consequence of forging a connection between the existing inclinations and involvement of individuals and the needs of recipients" (Schervish 1996, 21).

In Conclusion

The literature providing clues to donor motivation is growing, and it is offering the fund raiser a better view of the complexities and variations of philanthropic behavior. What little research has been done on the application of the donor motivation data does indicate, as does years of experience, that systematic analysis of such information will influence the fund raiser's own donor research, the selection of prospects, the identification of appropriate cases (needs), and the design of solicitation vehicles. This kind of donor and organization-specific information makes it possible to employ donor segmentation techniques—the selection of small groups based on similarities and potential (demographic and psychographic). Communications can be tailored to influence internal philanthropic motivations. External activities can be designed to influence and facilitate relationship building, and resources can be applied more effectively. Evaluations and analysis of outcomes can become more scientific and used to achieve future efficiencies.

A Disclaimer

All this knowledge, and the ability to use it cannot be driven merely by a need to improve fund-raising techniques and financial outcomes. The needs and the interests of donors must take precedence over the needs of the fund raiser and the nonprofit institution, but should never take precedence over the needs of the recipients. Should the balancing scale tip, the philanthropic process will not retain its integrity as a mutual exchange.

Step 3 in the Annual Integrated Development Process: Identify and Qualify the Constituencies; Define Market Segments

Once organizational readiness has been assessed (Step 1) and strategies are in place to ensure a philanthropic culture (Step 2), the development team is ready for Step 3 in the annual integrated development process—identifying and qualifying constituents. This step is a critical one, because it focuses on the *people* who will support your organization's mission—To approach fund raising with a marketing/donor perspective, requires that the development team first examine the potential base of support, be-

fore developing the case(s), before determining the solicitation methods, before designing the communication strategies, before "fund raising." This is especially important in annual giving, because annual gifts are the base of all support for the organization. If this step is not done well, the potential for major or planned gifts is diminished greatly.

The annual integrated development program is based on a *managed* process to acquire, renew, and upgrade a *base* of donors for an organization (Exhibit 4–5). In this process, fund raisers are able to invite, inform, involve, and increase the investment of donors for the cause.

Annual giving programs are designed to "fill up" the bottom and middle levels of the giving pyramid. The basic giving pyramid, illustrated in Chapter 2, depicts the typical fund-raising program, which has more donors at the lower-level giving tiers than the higher-level giving tiers. It shows that, on average, annual givers may represent as much as 80 percent of the total constituency base while generating only 20 percent of the funds because their gifts are the smallest.

The art of creating and nurturing *relationships* with groups of people who have an affin-

---

Exhibit 4–5 Purposes of Annual Giving Strategies

To build constituencies and to

- acquire donors

- renew donor support annually

- cultivate donors to increased giving levels

- build donor loyalty

- identify and involve leaders

- identify and solicit major annual prospects

ity or linkage with your organization is called "constituency building." *Every* organization has constituent groups who are *naturally* linked to it and thus naturally inclined to support it. *No* organization that provides worthy services is absent a constituency base. However, *some* organizations have constituencies that are smaller and less affluent than those of large, established institutions and thus have to create responsive constituencies by building linkages. For example, a university by its nature will be able to raise more money from its alumni than a social service agency will be able to raise from its client bases. Still, the social service agency has the ability to build significant linkages with people who have experience with or knowledge of its programs—these people become that organization's "nearly natural" constituency. The key to building constituencies, cultivating them, and retaining them is the process of linking people to people. The old adage of "people don't (just) give to causes, people don't (just) give to people, but people give to people, with causes" remains as true today as it was when organized fund raising began nearly 100 years ago.

There are two main constituent groups—**prospects** (those who have never given) and **donors** (those who have given at least once). Throughout this book, the terms "prospects" and "donors" are used interchangeably. This is not to suggest that prospects should be approached the same as donors—quite the contrary. Examples are given to show the differences between the two groups when appropriate.

How Are Annual Constituencies Segmented and Targeted?

According to a recent article in *Business Week,* marketing has moved past mass marketing in which a selected "mass" of people received identical messages, to market segmentation, in which smaller groups of people received the same information, to smaller niche marketing. The ultimate goal given computer technology is to reach the smallest consumer segment of all—the individual. *Technology* alone has made it possible to market, to segment, and to target in ways never before imagined.

The extent to which organizations are able to segment their constituency base is determined by how many resources they have: staff, computerized systems, research expertise, and time. Not all organizations are able to do a lot of segmentation, but those doing so are increasing their base of support not only in number of donors but also in increased gift amounts. When donors are segmented into groups that are defined demographically or configured psychographically, communications can be tailored to the interests of that group, and thus, the external motivators are more efficient and more effective.

Each organization will have different and various options for segmentation based on who their prospects/donors are, how they behave, and what their needs and interests are. The most frequently used determinant of segmentation is level of giving, followed by frequency of giving. For instance, it is relatively easy to segment donors into giving levels; for example, under $25, between $25 and $100, over $100, over $500, over $1,000, and so on. It is equally as easy, given computerized record keeping, to segment by frequency of giving: first-time donor, renewed donor by years, upgraded donor by years, and so on. Both level and frequency can be combined into segments and the time of year added; for example, $25 first-year donors who made a gift last year in November or former donors who gave $100 or more at any point in time.

For-profit market specialists point out the very real advantages of marketing by age group. Research has proven that older generations make purchasing decisions differently—they pay by cash and checks, are charitable but skeptical of computerized gift giving—while Baby Boomers love credit and computers and are charitable, but not necessarily in the workplace.

Other creative and effective segmentation characteristics are affiliation or interest groupings. For instance, a hospital has obvious and closely linked constituencies: physicians, nursing staff, employees, patients, board members, or volunteers. Within the patient segment, one could further segment those who were seen in the emergency room, had surgery, or recovered from a life-threatening illness or are self-insured, un-insured, or double-insured. For a social service agency, the obvious segmentation is board members, volunteers, employees, clients, and families of clients. As a subgroup, the board could be segmented further into those who have the most financial ability, are past board members, who served in a leadership capacity, or have special interests because of their experiences as a client. Additional segmentation breakdowns are offered in subsequent chapters.

Informal Research Techniques

The process of identifying and qualifying a constituent has components: research, segmentation, and targeting (Exhibit 4–6).

Research is the systematic acquisition and recording of important data on current and prospective donors. The goal is to identify the shared values between the organization and donors/prospects in order to build and maintain the exchange relationship (matching). The concept of matching was graphically presented earlier as a scale—with constituencies on one side and cases on the other. The constituency side is filled with information about prospects' interests and needs, and it is then balanced with information about what the organization does through cases that are based on similar interests and needs.

All three components—research, segmentation, and targeting—are interrelated and sequential; once the research is completed, the segmentation can be accomplished, followed by the targeting of specific groups with the highest potential. The objective is to determine through

Exhibit 4–6 Constituency-Building Components

RESEARCH AND ANALYSIS OF ALL PROSPECTS AND DONORS

- Who are they (demographics)?

- What do they think, need, and want (psychographics)?

- What external motivators elicit a response (influences)?

SEGMENTATION OF ALL PROSPECTS AND DONORS

- How can they be segmented into smaller similar groups?

- How are they alike and different?

TARGETING OF HIGH-POTENTIAL PROSPECTS AND DONORS

- Which groups have the greatest potential for short-term response?

- For the long-term investment?

---

the collection and analysis of information which donor groups have the greatest potential for giving and to design solicitation approaches that will motivate these groups to respond. Those who are not high-probable responders may not be solicited or will be the last to be solicited. Informal and formal research segmentation, and targeting strategies are shown in Exhibit 4–7.

The Annual Giving Donor Profile

One of the best ways to start looking at who might give to your organization is to look at who is already giving. Your existing annual giving profile can be used as a tool to map out where your current donors fit onto the pyramid of giving. Simply draw a pyramid, leaving enough room to put detailed information on it; you might use a flip-chart sheet to start. You will be surprised at how much data you already have.

Exhibit 4–7 Techniques to Research, Segment, and Target Prospects and Donors

---

INFORMAL

- the annual giving profile

- the constituency circle model

- the board and friends techniques

- linkage, interest, and ability ranking model

- the prospect evaluation grid

- technique with volunteers

FORMAL

- prospect donor management system

- record review

- personal interviews

- donor surveys

- focus groups

- professional prospect research

To be sure your organization's current donor base is profiled accurately on the donor pyramid, it is necessary to examine all giving records by source, date, amount of gift, and whether each is a first, second, third, (and so on) gift.

- How many are new donors?
- How many are renewing at the same level?
- How many are renewing at higher levels over time?
- How many donors are making more than one gift a year?
- What is different about each donor; what is the same? Are too many stuck at a low giving level?
- Is retention of donors within industry standards?
- Are the solicitation strategies different or the same for each group? Each level?

This profile should graphically present both weaknesses and opportunities in the base of support. Does your donor profile look more like an hourglass—wider at the bottom and at the top—than a pyramid? Is it bulging in the middle and out of sync with the desired pyramid shape? A sample donor profile is found in Exhib-it 4–8.

Going through the exercise of examining the different types and levels of donors often produces a picture that is vastly different than what may be expected. For instance, those 3,000 donors whom everyone talks about are not logged on the donor profile because only 500 of them are currently contributing—the other 2,500 are lapsed givers. Or of the 3,000 donors, over 2,500 are repeat givers at the lowest giving level (under $100) and have not shown any significant increase in the past five years.

The *greatest resource* an organization has is its existing constituency/donor base. Within fund-raising practice, there tends to be too much emphasis placed on *acquiring* donors to the detriment of *retaining and upgrading* existing donors. Perhaps the acquisition strategies and techniques are more mechanical, and therefore, fund raisers resort to them out of ease. Retaining and upgrading donors, on the other hand, take a more sophisticated, tailored, and time-consum-

Exhibit 4–8 Annual Giving Donor Profile

The Annual Giving Donor Profile

Number of Donors	Total	Types, Sources, Levels, Designations
Category 1: Number of donors who consistently give large gifts.	_____	_____ _____ _____
Category 2: Number of donors who have given a cumulative or single gift of $10,000 or more in the past 5 years.	_____	_____ _____ _____
Category 3: Number of donors who have made a cumulative or single gift of $1,000 or more in the past 3 years.	_____	_____ _____ _____
Category 4: Number of donors who give multi-year gifts.	_____	_____ _____ _____
Category 5: Number of renewed donors who have increasased their giving over time.	_____	_____ _____ _____
Category 6: Number of second and third time renewed donors.	_____	_____ _____ _____
Category 7: Number of new first time donors.	_____	_____ _____ _____
Category 8: Number of prospects.	_____	_____

Divide donors and prospects into eight categories. Indicate the total number for each category, dividing into sub-categories as appropriate, such as the constituency type, the solicitation method or source, the giving level and frequency, and by gifts that are designated for specific programs. For every five donors in a discreet group, fill in a square on the blank GRID, using different colors and codes as appropriate. The final GRID is a profile of your donor base, and hopefully it is shaped like a pyramid (though not a perfect one). This exercise will point out where donors are "stuck," and where strategies are needed.

continues

Exhibit 4–8 continued

Donor Profile Grid

Donors in Category 1.

Donors in Category 2.

Donors in Category 3.

Donors in Category 4.

Donors in Category 5.

Donors in Category 6.

Prospects in Category 7.

Category 8.

ing approach; it is difficult to use mass marketing techniques further up the donor pyramid. Mid-level donors are often an organization's most overlooked and underrated philanthropic resource, and a good first place to look to generate additional funds. The concept of targeting high-profile markets values quality over quantity. Why pursue new donors where costs are the highest, when existing donors will likely increase their giving, if properly approached, at far less cost? Furthermore, the sooner the donor starts moving up the pyramid of giving—after the first gift—the less likely he or she will form habits of giving at the lowest levels. If the donor is not encouraged to move up in giving and is left in the same place for several years, the donor will get the impression that any larger gift is not needed or expected.

The Constituency Circle Model

Another efficient way to identify and qualify prospect and donor constituents is to *scan* the constituency marketplace and see who might be out there by using the constituency circle model, a time-honored tool originated by the Fund Raising School at the Center on Philanthropy in Indianapolis. The constituency circle is a planning device that is best used with the entire development team, encouraging input that is "value-added."

The concept of constituency circles is based on the premise that people are essential to the philanthropic process; organizations are merely conduits for *people* to receive services, provide services, administer services, contribute to the services, and be connected to any of these people. The constituency model is made up of a series of interlocking circles around a core that is "home" to the people who are closest to the organization's mission: the board of directors, clients/patients/alumni, the organization's administration, and current major donors. This core represents the organization's strongest energy, like the big splash of a rock thrown into a pond. In Figure 4–2, an example of a university's constituency model, the second circle signifies those who are the first "ripple" in the pond: the

parents of alumni, relatives of clients, colleagues of administrators, friends of board members, or peers of donors. The third circle and on contain those people who have more distant relationships because of personal experience or timing—for instance, an alumnus who attended the university but did not graduate may belong in the constituent circle, but because of his limited experience will be further from the center than an alumnus who graduated. Thus, as more ripples occur, they are progressively a little more obscure, a little less connected.

The constituency circle model can be used (1) to identify *prospect* groups and (2) to group *donors* into smaller, similar segments (donors of $10,000 or more are placed in the center, whereas donors of $100 or less are placed in an outer circle). The ultimate goal is to identify those with the greatest linkage, interest, and ability (LIA). The LIA indicators are proven to be strong determinants of philanthropic motivations and behavior.

The constituency circle model together with the annual giving donor profile will begin to give the development team a good idea of the unrealized potential for fund raising. Of course, these tools require a good understanding of the organization's prospect/donor base—how many prospects/donors, how many general groupings, how many discrete groupings, what is their current giving behavior, and what is their potential giving behavior. Answers to these questions cannot be made solely by intuition; they ultimately must be researched to be predictive. Unless a fund raiser has evidence of donor behavior and understands the dynamics affecting that behavior, he or she cannot predict with any certainty what the organization's constituency will do. Budgeting then becomes a need, rather than an opportunity.

The Board and Friends Technique

The question of which groups to target is answered by "those who have the greatest short- and long-term capability and impact on the organization's mission." Therefore, the organization's board of directors is the first and most

CONSTITUENCY MODEL

The Organization's Universe

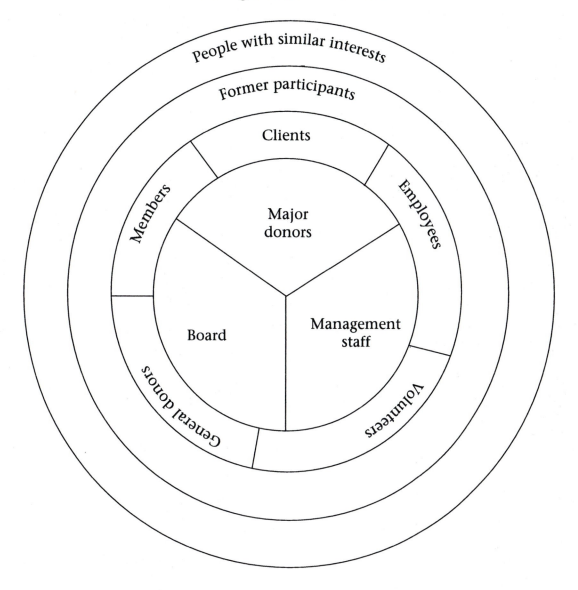

People with similar interests

Former participants

Clients

Members

Employees

Major donors

Board

Management staff

General donors

Volunteers

Figure 4–2 The Constituency Model. Courtesy of The Fund Raising School, Indianapolis, Indiana.

important group to involve in the philanthropic process.

As trustees of the philanthropic community and stewards of the organization's mission, board members are central to any fund-raising effort. When they are enthusiastically involved and committed to the role of fund raising, they send messages to others that the organization is worthy of support. If they do not view their organization as one of their *favorite* charities or make an annual gift at a level that does not reflect such a commitment, board members send the opposite message. Interestingly enough, others seem to know which organizations have boards who are generous supporters and those who do not. The board's level of giving greatly influences others' decisions to give; this is especially true with foundations, corporations, and individual major givers. When you can say that your **board** is the organization's largest collective donor (and it should be), it is evident to all other prospects that something good goes on there.

Sometimes board members are recruited who do not have much board experience or without being informed of their responsibility for the financial (fund-raising) welfare of the organization. Therefore, they may need to be educated about their responsibilities in order for them to understand how important their personal involvement is to achieving the organization's mission. This is particularly important for organizations that do not have large natural constituencies to draw on and must instead build a constituency of linkages with people—through their board members.

A popular and successful technique to build linkages with people where none naturally exists is to ask board members and key donors to **invite their friends** to make a contribution to the organization. The old adage, "people give to people, with causes," reminds us how important a person's testimony is to building linkages with other people and establishing a sense of credibility because of who the "invitee" is.

Once a year or more, those who are in the constituency circle core should be asked to provide lists of friends or colleagues who they think might be interested in the organization's mission. It is quite a simple process to prepare solicitation letters for their friend, and to follow up with a phone call/personal request. The successful solicitations will eventually grow into annual donors, who in turn will invite their friends to support one of their favorite organizations, and so on.

The Linkage, Interest, and Ability Ranking Model

One of the more obvious questions when looking at the organization's constituencies is how does one *qualify* them—how does one determine high response potential? A relatively easy way, which is more effective when augmented by research, is to determine the linkage, interest, and ability (LIA) of prospects/donors. Although people have individual, complex, and varied motivations for their philanthropic behavior, the LIA formula focuses on the three primary, experiential indicators observed by fund raisers over the years—linkage, interest, and ability.

1. **Linkage** is the notion that people must have some connection to the organization, its mission, or its people in order to give. That connection is on a continuum, ranging from a profound experience such as a life-saving event in the hospital's trauma center to merely hearing about a neighbor who was treated successfully for cancer at a local hospital. Linkages are both direct and personal or indirect through others.

2. **Interest** is the notion that people must have a particular interest or concern for the organization's mission, programs, and clients. The stronger the interest, the more often and more money a person is likely to give. For instance, some donors have a specific interest in children who are abused, whereas others will support a host of organizations whose mission is the general health and welfare of children.

3. **Ability** is the notion that people must have resources, be they time, talent, or treasure, to be able to give—though ability is a far less important determinant of giving than linkage and interest. Many examples can be given to demonstrate that people wanting to ameliorate a problem or advance a cause will "find" the resources to contribute when they believe their help is critical to the cause. To rank and rate LIA factors on paper, a matrix can be designed, similar to the one illustrated in Exhibit 4–9.

Exhibit 4–9 Identifying Targeted Constituencies with LIA

Identifying Targeted Constituencies with LIA

DIRECTIONS

- Fill in the total number in each audience group below (donors and prospects).
- Add audience groups as necessary; break out donors and prospects, if distinctive.
- Add as many subgroups as you feel appropriate.
- Rank and rate each audience group by *Linkage, Interest,* and *Ability* on a scale of 1–5.
- Total your ratings, and rank your top three groups as follows:

Audience Group	Total Number	Linkage*	Interest	Ability	Total Score
		(Rate using Scale of 1–5; low >high)			
Board members	____	____	____	____	____
Staff/employees	____	____	____	____	____
Affiliates (professors, physicians, artists)	____	____	____	____	____
Alumni (graduates, patients, etc.)	____	____	____	____	____
Volunteers	____	____	____	____	____
Neighbors	____	____	____	____	____
Friends	____	____	____	____	____
Cause-interested	____	____	____	____	____
Organization-loyal	____	____	____	____	____

Others:

_____	____	____	____	____	____
_____	____	____	____	____	____
_____	____	____	____	____	____

#1. Highest Potential Audience _____
     Those with strongest ties, have given on a regular basis, and have the greatest potential to give.

#2. Second Highest Audience _____
     Those who have some linkage and who are thought to have the ability and interest in giving.

#3. Third Highest Audience** _____
     Those who will, over time, move to #1 or #2.

*Linkage refers to the linkage to your organization.

**Continue process with the next highest audience, continuing down until no longer practical.

The Prospect Evaluation Grid

The prospect evaluation grid (Figure 4–3) should be used to help identify the prospects and donors who are capable of giving the largest annual gifts. The grid is especially effective in a group setting, with board members who are knowledgeable about your donor list.

Ask each person to review a list of the top contributors (you can code them to make it easier to put them on the grid) and to rank them by two indicators: (1) their interest and involvement and (2) their financial capability. Financial capability is defined as "what a prospect is capable of giving today taking into consideration his or her present business or financial situation." It is not based on what they have given in the past. Each prospect can be rated on a scale of 1–9 for both indicators.

Those who receive the highest evaluations are assigned to a board member for cultivation and solicitation. Those given lower scores are assigned to volunteers or staff for more extensive cultivation and involvement. Eventually, with planned attention, the prospects will begin to raise their interest levels and be better prepared to give at their financial capacity.

Rating and Ranking Technique with Volunteers

Often, there is not enough time or resources to undertake a sophisticated research effort to identify the top prospects/donors. One way to identify them quickly is to use a prospect evaluation grid; another way is to use a gift range chart. The latter technique, which is still used in the campaign model, involves gathering a group of board members or donors and circulating among them a list of "known" people who seem to have the potential to give large or larger gifts. This process is always a confidential one, in which attendees are asked to estimate, based on what they know about a particular person, each person's interest and ability. Often people know more about other people than scientific research will ever uncover.

The rating and ranking process uses a gift chart (Exhibit 4–10), with identified levels of gift support needed, to rate and rank prospects/donors at a particular level.

Formal Research Techniques

Formal donor research can be as complex a subject as donor motivations; fund raisers do research in numerous and pragmatic ways, and there are equally as many, if not more, methods that the researchers themselves prescribe. The fact remains that although prospect research is widely accepted as a way of doing business at the major gifts level, it is woefully weak at the annual giving level. This is understandable because the allocation of the time and resources required to conduct sophisticated research is not viewed as cost effective at the lower gift levels. In the future, however, prospect research, segmentation, and target marketing will become an accepted way of improving and expanding all annual giving programs. There are at least four formal research applications appropriate for annual giving programs: (1) record review, (2) personal interviews, (3) donor surveys, and (4) focus groups. Professional prospect research is not covered here because of its limited use in annual giving programs; admittedly it could be used more.

Before deciding which one or more of the research methodologies are useful to your fund-raising program, it is a good idea to make a list of the information you *think* you need to know. Then list the information you already have. Chances are that you have an abundance of data in your computer—most of it on gift transactions and little on donor linkages, interests, and abilities. One of the greatest challenges that fund raisers face is to collect only the kind of data they need and then to use it. My thesis survey of annual giving directors revealed that they spent only 7 percent of their time on prospect/donor research; yet they collected enormous amounts of data, most of which were irrelevant to donor research, and they used only a fraction of what they had.

Prospect Evaluation Grid

Interest & Involvement

1	2	3	4	5	6	7	8	9	
									8
									7
									6
									5
									4
									3
									2
									1

Financial Capability

Rank each contributor on a scale of 1–9 on their interest and involvement (across) and then by their financial capability (up/down). Financial capability is defined as what a prospect is capable of giving today, and not based on what they have given in the past. Those receiving the highest scores will be prioritized for personal peer-to-peer solicitation; those with lower scores are assigned for more extensive cultivation and involvement.

Top Ten Contributors   Score   Contact

A. _____   _____   _____

B. _____   _____   _____

C. _____   _____   _____

D. _____   _____   _____

E. _____   _____   _____

F. _____   _____   _____

G. _____   _____   _____

H. _____   _____   _____

I. _____   _____   _____

J. _____   _____   _____

Figure 4–3 Prospect Evaluation Grid.

Exhibit 4–10 Gift Ranking Chart

Rating and Ranking Prospects and Donors

Determine the number of prospects needed, based on a detailed Gift Rage Chart. Score each prospect using the Prospect Criteria Form. Fill in the number of total points for each prospect; note the gift solicitation level, and best contact person.

Prospect's Name	Number of Points	Gift Level	Best Contact
Prospect's Name	Number of Points	Gift Level	Best Contact
Prospect's Name	Number of Points	Gift Level	Best Contact
Prospect's Name	Number of Points	Gift Level	Best Contact
Prospect's Name	Number of Points	Gift Level	Best Contact
Prospect's Name	Number of Points	Gift Level	Best Contact
Prospect's Name	Number of Points	Gift Level	Best Contact
Prospect's Name	Number of Points	Gift Level	Best Contact
Prospect's Name	Number of Points	Gift Level	Best Contact
Prospect's Name	Number of Points	Gift Level	Best Contact
Prospect's Name	Number of Points	Gift Level	Best Contact
Prospect's Name	Number of Points	Gift Level	Best Contact
Prospect's Name	Number of Points	Gift Level	Best Contact
Prospect's Name	Number of Points	Gift Level	Best Contact
Prospect's Name	Number of Points	Gift Level	Best Contact
Prospect's Name	Number of Points	Gift Level	Best Contact
Prospect's Name	Number of Points	Gift Level	Best Contact
Prospect's Name	Number of Points	Gift Level	Best Contact
Prospect's Name	Number of Points	Gift Level	Best Contact

continues

Exhibit 4–10 continued

Prospect Criteria Form

Description	Points	Score
Prospect has contributed regularly and frequently to the organization.	10	_____
Prospect has known linkage to organization, as a client, a board member, or another obvious connection.	9	_____
Prospect has demonstrated an interest by being involved, as a volunteer or donor in our or like causes.	8	_____
Prospect is personally known to a volunteer solicitor, and has discussed the organization's mission in some way.	7	_____
Prospect is approachable and accessible, has financial ability.	6	_____
Prospect is active in the community, is religious, educated, and married.	5	_____
TOTAL SCORE (possible 45 points)		_____

A Prospect/Donor Management System

Managing a successful integrated development program requires that you have the information needed to make decisions about how to use your time effectively, and to determine the best solicitation strategies and matches. Given the amount of data that are needed about prospects/donors, it almost goes without saying that an information management system is essential. Most often an information management system is computerized, and in this high-technology era there are many computer software systems to purchase or design to fit the particular needs of each fund-raising program.

However, the lack of a sophisticated computer program should not get in the way of collecting and analyzing donor data—it is possible to maintain manual files of information through color coding, comprehensive donor profile sheets, and tracking forms. The primary goal of a prospect management system is to establish long-term gift relationships with as large a percentage of the organization's constituency as possible. Prospect/donor information management includes the steps listed in Exhibit 4–11.

Record Review: What to Ask

The review of development and fund raising records includes a review of individual donor files (manual and computerized) with donor data, that contain transaction and financial data. The following list contains the basic type of information to look for. Chapter 9 also discusses using this information as part of Step 11 in the Annual Integrated Development Process, the evaluation step.

> **The primary goal of a prospect management system is to establish long-term gift relationships.**

Exhibit 4–11 Prospect/Donor Management System

- Identify and research prospects.

- Collect and catalog the data.

- Store and retrieve the data in a user-friendly way.

- Evaluate, rate, and rank the prospects.

- Design a solicitation plan for each prospect.

- Update the prospect/donor files each time an activity occurs, including call reports and donor history.

---

1. **Demographics**
   - Age (different age groups behave differently)
   - Gender (women make giving decisions differently than men)
   - Income (an indicator of capability)
   - Geography (place may have a correlation with giving attitudes)
   - Family composition (with or without children)
2. **Psychographics**
   - Values (helping others may be family tradition)
   - Attitudes (some people want to change things; others are content with the status quo)
   - Interests (childhood experiences can be carried into adulthood as interests)
   - Lifestyles (is work, family, or community a priority)
3. **Linkages**
   - How and when did they first learn about your organization?
   - Are they linked directly, i.e., a patient, an alumnus, a client?
   - Are they linked indirectly? Through whom?
   - Have they been involved as a board member, volunteer, or event attender?
   - Are they donors? How often, how much, for what area?
4. **External Motivators**
   - What is their preferred giving mechanism?
   - What program do they prefer to support?
   - What is unique about their giving patterns or methods?

Personal Interviews: What to Ask

A personal interview is an excellent technique to find out what is important to someone, because they surely will tell you. People are generally very responsive to a request for an interview, provided you have adequately justified it as something more than a pre-solicitation step. There must be a good reason to schedule time with an important board member or donor beyond collecting information for your donor file. An interview is an occasion to learn about what they think matters, and they will be flattered and willing to offer their counsel. You will want to follow up on any recommendations or concerns, of course.

These questions can be asked in an interview:

- How did you happen to get involved with (name of organization)?
- What caused you to make your first gift?
- What do you see as the strengths of the organization?
- Is there a particular program you are interested in?
- How did you come to be interested in (the program issue)?
- What do you think the organization might be able to do to resolve those issues?
- What would it take to get you more involved?

Donor Surveys: What to Ask

There is a science to preparing a written or a telephone donor survey so as not to influence

Exhibit 4–12 Sample Donor Survey

Donor Survey

We value your opinion. You can help us focus our efforts in coming years. Your response is confidential and, if you would like, anonymous. Thank you for your help!

1. **We currently fund or are considering funding care in the areas listed below.**
   Please indicate how important each of these areas are to you as a donor.

	Very Important	Somewhat Important	Not Important
Family Health Center	☐	☐	☐
Cancer	☐	☐	☐
Heart Disease	☐	☐	☐
The Birth Center	☐	☐	☐
Visitor and Family Services	☐	☐	☐
Hospital Quality Initiatives	☐	☐	☐
Other _____	☐	☐	☐

2. **How do you want your contributions to be used?**

   ☐ Capital Needs   ☐ Program Needs   ☐ Endowment
   ☐ I have no preference   ☐ Other *(please specify)* _____

3. **How would you like to be approached by the Foundation for a gift?**

   ☐ Telephone   ☐ Mail   ☐ Special Events
   ☐ A personal visit   ☐ Other *(please specify)* _____

4. **What fund-raising special events do you enjoy?**

   _____
   _____
   _____

5. **How much did you give to the United Hospital Foundation last year?**

   ☐ Under $99   ☐ $500-$999   ☐ Over $5,000
   ☐ $100-$499   ☐ $1,000-$5,000
   ☐ I do not contribute because _____
   _____

6. **What other organizations do you support?**

   _____
   _____

Courtesy of United Hospital Foundation, St. Paul, Minnesota.

Exhibit 4–13 Sample Board Campaign Survey

LEADERS FOR LEARNING
1996 BOARD CAMPAIGN SURVEY

This year the board campaign focused on school success. We would like your opinion of the campaign focus, format, and information. And, we would like to gain a better understanding of you, as a donor. Your views about the campaign are very important to our evaluation of this effort.

Please take five minutes to fill out this survey and return it in the stamped, self-addressed envelope by **February 10**, so that results may be shared at the February 19 Board Meeting.

CAMPAIGN FOCUS

1. Please indicate your *level of interest* in the FACT program and/or school success, as a donor.

   ☐ Very Interested   ☐ Somewhat Interested   ☐ Not Interested

2. What other issues are *important* to you as a donor?

	Very	Somewhat	Not
Prevent violence	☐	☐	☐
Family counseling	☐	☐	☐
Child abuse prevention	☐	☐	☐
Building community leadership	☐	☐	☐

   Other: _____

CAMPAIGN FORMAT

1. Indicate your *level of satisfaction* with the following aspects of the board campaign.

	Very Good	Somewhat	Not Good
Time of year (November/December)	☐	☐	☐
Time given to make giving decision	☐	☐	☐
Contact by fellow board member*	☐	☐	☐
Suggested gift amount	☐	☐	☐

   I was not contacted by a fellow board member.   ☐

continues

Exhibit 4–13 continued

CAMPAIGN INFORMATION

---

1. Indicate which information aspects of the campaign were *most helpful* to you.

	Very Helpful	Somewhat	Not Helpful
Printed materials about FACT	☐	☐	☐
Financial information about FACT	☐	☐	☐
Giving pyramid showing campaign goal	☐	☐	☐
Philanthropy Committee leadership	☐	☐	☐
Client presentation*	☐	☐	☐
Program staff presentation*	☐	☐	☐
Information given during board meetings	☐	☐	☐
Discussion with a fellow board member	☐	☐	☐

*I did not attend a presentation. ☐

2. Are there any other suggestions or comments you would like to offer?

_____

_____

_____

DONOR PROFILE

Please give us information about yourself.

1. Rank the *level of importance* of being able to designate your gift to a particular program.

☐ Very Important   ☐ Somewhat   ☐ Not

2. Identify the top three charitable organizations that you support, in order of priority.

1. _____
2. _____
3. _____

3. What are the *most influential* factors when you make a contribution decision?

☐ Understanding of program need
☐ Knowledge of program outcomes
☐ Awareness that others are supporting it also
☐ Responsibility of my position in the organization
☐ Personal request by a peer

THANK YOU FOR YOUR TIME AND IDEAS.

Courtesy of Family & Children's Service, Minneapolis, Minnesota.

the answers. It is equally necessary to have a statistically significant response, and the data must be assessed carefully and thoughtfully. Donor surveys can be used to collect information about the donors themselves, which will help you identify your typical donor profile. Or you can seek feedback about donor satisfaction with the fund-raising program. The idea is not to focus on the organization; that is the responsibility of the marketing department.

The survey may pose questions about specific subjects, ranging from solicitation methods to recognition opportunities, or be focused on one campaign or the entire fund raising endeavor. The questions may be open ended, or you may use a scale of 1–5 (very satisfied to dissatisfied), or a combination of both. To obtain the highest-quality information it is a good idea to make the survey confidential; to ensure a high written response, give a deadline and a stamped return envelope; to be taken seriously, report the findings within a reasonable amount of time and resurvey next year.

Two real-life examples of donor surveys are offered here: a survey (Exhibit 4–12) sent every year to the entire donor list of a hospital foundation and a survey (Exhibit 4–13) to evaluate the first board campaign at a social service agency.

Focus Groups: What to Ask

The purpose of a focus group is to involve people who are influential to the organization, to gain both objective and subjective insights, to elicit concerns and provide an opportunity for suggestions, and to determine the key characteristics of others who could be involved. It is an exploratory process, unstructured except for a few pre-determined questions. As such, it is one of the best ways to elicit perceptions, attitudes, and opinions and to clarify mis-perceptions.

Ideally, a focus group is facilitated by someone who is not employed by the organization and is trained as a facilitator. Participants are selected not on their familiarity with the organization, but on their expertise in professional matters and their involvement in other community organizations and activities. Participants will range in number from 10 to 15 and will spend up to two hours exploring a few questions. The entire process is taped, the discussion comments are compiled, and the collective data are reported to the sponsoring agent. The key is to keep the discussion focused on *what*, as opposed to the why, how, who, and when. Use questions such as these to start the discussion:

- What organizations do you think of when you hear (type of mission, such as youth)?
- What comes to mind when you hear (name of organization)?
- Read the mission statement; which aspects are important?
- Describe who (the kind of people) you think should be involved in (name of organization).

References

American Association of Fund Raising Counsel (AAFRC) Trust for Philanthropy. 1996. *Giving USA*. New York: AAFRC Trust for Philanthropy.

Fairfax, J.E. 1995. Black philanthropy: Its heritage and future. In *New Directions for Philanthropic Fundraising*, edited by C.H. Hamilton and W.F. Ilchman. San Francisco, CA: Jossey-Bass.

Hodgkinson, V.A., M.S. Weitzman, S.M. Noga, and H.A. Gorski. 1992. *Giving and volunteering in the United States: Findings from a national survey*. Washington, DC: Independent Sector.

Independent Sector. 1994. *Giving and volunteering in the United States*. Washington, DC: Independent Sector.

Kotler, P., and A.R. Andreasen. 1987. *Strategic marketing for nonprofit organizations*. 3d ed. Englewood Cliffs, NJ: Prentice-Hall.

Lord, J.G. 1981. *Philanthropy and marketing*. Cleveland, Ohio: Third Sector Press.

Mixer, J.R. 1993. *Principles of professional fundraising: Useful foundations for successful practice*. San Francisco, CA: Jossey-Bass.

Nichols, J.E. 1995. *Global demographics: Fund raising for a new world*. Chicago: Bonus Books.

Odendahl, T. 1990. *Charity begins at home: Generosity and self-interest among the philanthropic elite*. New York: Basic Books.

Ostrander, S.A., and J.M. Fisher. 1995. Women giving money, women raising money: What difference for philanthropy? In *New Directions for Philanthropic Fundraising,* edited by C.H. Hamilton and W.F. Ilchman. San Francisco, CA: Jossey-Bass.

Ostrower, F. 1996. Rich people: No safety net. *The Chronicle of Philanthropy* (January 25): 12.

Price, R.A., and K.M. File. 1994. *The seven faces of philanthropy.* San Francisco, CA: Jossey-Bass.

Rosso, H.A. 1991. *Achieving excellence in fund raising.* San Francisco, CA: Jossey-Bass.

Schervish, P.G. 1996. *Inclination, obligation, and association: What we know and what we need to learn about donor motivations.* Paper distributed to the alumni of the Executive Leadership Institute. Indianapolis, IN: Center on Philanthropy.

Shaw, S.C., and M.A. Taylor. 1995. *Reinventing fundraising: Realizing the potential of women's philanthropy.* San Francisco, CA: Jossey-Bass.

Sprinkel Grace, K. 1991. Resources for strenghening fund raising skills. In *Achieving excellence in fund raising,* edited by H.A. Rosso. San Francisco, CA: Jossey-Bass.

Wuthnow, R., and V.A. Hodgkinson. 1990. *Faith and philanthropy in America.* San Francisco, CA: Jossey-Bass.

Chapter 5

Identifying and Building the Case for Annual Support: Step 4 in the Annual Integrated Development Process

Key Ingredients in the Case for Support

Experience and research provide strong evidence that donors make giving decisions based on a multitude of internal motivations stimulated by external motivating factors. The most obvious external motivators for a "yes response" are the strength of the case, the credibility of and linkage to people involved, the evidence of organizational leadership and a high success factor, and the potential impact of the requested gift. The successful solicitation process attempts to incorporate all these aspects, but one stands out as the primary motivating factor in philanthropic giving—the organization's *case for support*: why funds are needed and what will occur as a result.

The case for support motivates gifts based on *philanthropic intent*, an influence far more effective than peer pressure, guilt, social recognition, or tax benefits. A gift with philanthropic intent comes from a sincere desire to improve the *human* condition. As such it is intentional, long lasting, likely to repeat itself, and likely to increase over time. Perhaps this is why the time-worn phrase, "you make a difference," has no substitute.

A strong case has the power to pull people, rather than push them—causing them to give *seemingly* without asking. When the case is matched effectively to the donor's interests, it seems to sell itself. As Peter Drucker, a leading management theorist, said, "The aim of marketing is to make selling superfluous" by understanding the customer so well that the product or service fits him and sells itself (Kotler and

> The case for support motivates gifts based on philanthropic intent, an influence far more effective than peer pressure, guilt, social recognition, or tax benefits.

Andreasen 1987, 36). Among practitioners, stories are shared about donors who make large, unsolicited (sometimes anonymous) gifts, with no apparent previous history of support or linkage. For these donors, the organization's case is so compelling that it elicits a gift without an official ask. Such unsolicited gifts are undoubtedly the result of an accumulation of information and experiences over time, which spark a response when the time is right. External motivators influence a donor's attitudes, opinions, and ultimately behavior as well. Consistent and meaningful communications have a building effect, resulting in significant gifts that are not made haphazardly but are almost always "planned." Although it's inadvisable for fund raisers to count on unsolicited donor-directed gifts to the annual fund, such real-life occurrences remind us of what a difference the case makes in the philanthropic fund-raising process and of how important it is to send regular informational mailings (not just promotional ones).

Key ingredients to building a successful case(s) are the following:

- knowledge of the organization's programs and its recipients
- ability to identify, build, and validate the organization's case(s) for support
- awareness of, and adeptness with, numerous communication principles and channels
- creative skill in positioning the organization through its distinguishing characteristics
- ability to match the case(s) with targeted constituencies and design effective case messages
- skill in the selection and implementation of relationship-building steps, or the management of "moves"

Chapters 3 and 4 focus on the organization and constituency ingredients. This chapter presents the case and communication ingredients, and Chapter 6 focuses on the strategic *matching* of donors to cases.

What Is the Case for Support?

The *case for support* provides the stimulus for philanthropic giving, regardless of whether it is a small first-time gift, a repeat annual gift, or an occasional special gift. As such, the development of the organization's case must be taken very seriously. That is, it should never be assumed, taken for granted, unsubstantiated, understated, or presented merely as a way to balance the annual operating budget. The case for support is the fund raiser's *rationale for fund raising*—the right to seek philanthropic support from others. It is the *cause* for which funds are sought and the *criteria* for which funds are given.

Nowhere is this concept more important (and perhaps more neglected) than in annual fund/annual giving strategies. The lack of attention to the case in annual giving is endemic. The annual fund was initiated as an effort to raise unrestricted funds for the general operating budget. The assumption was made, and continues to be made, that the mission of the organization is worthy enough to merit support—it doesn't need to be explained or "positioned." It has become obvious, and very frustrating, to many administrators that the annual giving program of the future must be run differently, and articulating a compelling case is key. Justin Fink says it well: "The savvy agency executive director today realizes that it is neither an indignant expression of entitlement nor strident ideological rhetoric but rather a demonstrable need for services and an incessant scanning of the grants economy that enable an agency to survive and grow" (Fink 1990, 145).

The case for support (whether written or spoken) is the who, why, what, when, how—and the *"so what?"*—behind the solicitation process. It is the organization's justification to seek funds, whether for a specific type of program, a particular fund, a new initiative, an expansion project, or all or part of the general operating budget. The *case* is the accumulation of all the reasons behind an organization's decision to provide services to a particular recipient group (its mission), the decision around how and when to deliver those services (its strategic goals), the decision as to who will provide them, and how much they will cost (its operational objectives).

The case also includes outcome objectives—what will happen to the recipients as a result of the services or if they are not provided (its evaluation of impact). The case also states how the donor and the community will benefit (its future plans). An annual fund-raising effort will not be successful without a strong case, as the effort is only the means—why and how the funds are to be used are the end result. The case answers the donor's question: "What difference does it make?"

Because the word *case* is an accepted fund-raising term (sometimes confused with case

management in the social work field) and because it has so many components and applications, it is useful to define it. Exhibit 5–1 lists the most common uses and definitions of the word *case*.

Step 4 in the Annual Integrated Development Process: Examine and Validate the Case; Establish Priorities for Short-Term, Intermediate, and Long-Term Goals

As stated earlier, the ability to match a donor's interests with an institution's needs is conditional on a fund raiser's *knowledge* of the

---

Exhibit 5–1 Case Terminology

Case for Support:	All the reasons why someone should contribute to the cause; the rationale for fund raising
Case Components:	The information needed to develop and validate the case for support: the organization's mission and history, problems/causes to be addressed, strategic solutions, target markets, goals and outcomes, structure and systems, financial and resource needs, and future plans
Case Statement: (*Internal Case*)	A written document that contains all the information needed to communicate the case for support, in any and all forms; it is concise and cogent, demonstrates success, is targeted to a specific audience, describes how philanthropy will solve the problem, is compelling/urgent/relevant/realistic, and is built on the future
Case Communications: (*External Case*)	Written and verbal communications that tie internal and external information together to position the organization for development; shows how philanthropy addresses social issues and solves problems that concern the donor community
Case Messages:	Messages to a particular audience, designed to establish an organization's needs and merits and articulate the benefits to the prospects, which in turn will stimulate a response

organization's programs and its recipients. This knowledge comes from understanding the organization's work from every aspect. Not only must fund raisers be well versed in their quests for philanthropic support but they also must be able to defend their organization's right to exist. The very process of identifying and building the case from the inside out forms that body of knowledge.

Case Components

The information that *makes up* the case can be divided into seven main groupings of data (Exhibit 5–2). Fund raisers are advised to collect, study, analyze, clarify, challenge, and assimilate the "internal" data to build the organization's *case for support*. Some of this information may have already been collected in Step 1 in the Annual Integrated Development Process, determining institutional readiness, and will be applicable here. Step 4, however, has a different focus; institutional readiness is about the entire organization, whereas case development is about fund raising and, in this instance, about annual giving. The case components should answer these questions:

- What will annual gifts be used for?
- How will annual gifts finance program objectives?
- Who will benefit from annual contributions?
- For each program/project within the annual operating budget, how much is needed from philanthropic sources and why?
- Which programs have the highest organizational and/or community priority?

According to Payton et al., "The organization justifies itself in terms of the merits of its case, its ability to translate the social values and beliefs of its mission into an action program—goals and objectives that can be used in the measurement of results" (1991, 6).

The Case Establishes Priorities and Goals

Too often, fund raisers are hired to raise money for a *case* that they had little or any part in shaping. It is not uncommon, especially in annual giving, for others (an organization's administration and board) to make decisions about how much money should be raised and for what. Annual giving frequently is relegated to meeting the gap between other revenue sources and expenses, to balancing the bottom line. Or annual gifts are used to meet an unexpected crisis during the year, for an expense not covered by other revenue, or to cover the year-end shortfall.

Annual gifts have traditionally been viewed as discretionary funds, solicited for general operating purposes. It is thus not unusual for organizations to set their annual giving budget based on their financial *need* (the operating budget shortfall) or on an *incremental* increase over the previous year (on the number/size of gifts received), rather than on marketplace *opportunity* (the anticipated response based on donor research). When the budget is based on need or history, the fund-raising team misses out on critical parts of the development process—the building of the *annual case for support* and the setting of an achievable goal for the annual giving program. When the budget is established on need or history, even if the underlying case is worthy and the goal realistic, the absence of Step 4 in the Annual Integrated Development Process, building the case, puts the fund raiser and the development team at a disadvantage.

With full knowledge and understanding of the case development/ budgeting process, the fund-raising team will have the level of com-

> **With full knowledge and understanding of the case development process, the fund-raising team can promote, articulate, or defend the annual case.**

Exhibit 5-2 Case Components

1. **The Organization's Mission**
   - Why does it exist?
   - What does it intend to accomplish?
   - What sets it apart from other organizations?
   - Who are its targeted customers/clients/recipients?

2. **Problems/Causes**
   - What are the social problems/causes that exist?
   - What is the nature of these problems/causes, and how do they compare to others?
   - What is the organization's history of addressing these problems/causes?

3. **Strategic Solutions**
   - What makes this organization best able to understand and address the issues?
   - What programs, projects, and services will the organization provide that solve the problems or advance the causes?
   - How was the need assessed? How much of the need will be met?
   - What are the unique, relevant, or important features of the programs/services?
   - Who else is providing them?
   - Why should these services be provided, as compared with others?

4. **Customer Markets**
   - Who are the primary recipients of the services?
   - How are they identified and reached?
   - What are the recipient needs and characteristics?

5. **Programs/Services Objectives and Outcomes**
   - How were the programs and services determined?
   - What are the specific programs, projects, or services?
   - How will they be delivered?
   - What are the program objectives? For the short term and long term?
   - What are the anticipated outcomes? Based on what information?

6. **Organizational Structure and Systems**
   - How will the programs be managed? By whom?
   - Who has ultimate responsibility for the program delivery and outcomes?
   - What resources are in place or need to be put into place?

7. **Financial and Resource Needs**
   - What is the budget for each program and service?
   - How was the budget determined—by need or opportunity? By whom?
   - How much of the annual budget is dependent on philanthropic sources?

mitment necessary to promote, articulate, or defend the annual case(s) as needed. They will be able to creatively segment a general operating case into easier-to-understand program/case components or to tailor case messages effectively to particular groups of donors. Opportunities will not be missed. The fund-raising emphasis will be placed on building exchange relationships by meeting the needs of both donors and recipients, rather than on the technical aspects of raising money (the means). And as a result, fund raising falls back into begging or selling modes—orientations that are the most unsophisticated, perhaps the most unprofessional, and the most unethical.

The Case Involves and Enables People

In addition to collecting printed material about their organization, what is the best way for fund raisers to learn about their organization's mission and programs? To experience them. The most productive time a new fund raiser can spend is in the field, learning how to build a campfire, watching the zookeeper feed the dolphins, reading to a hospitalized child, volunteering in the local soup kitchen or at a crisis nursery, repairing a torn theater costume, bringing library books to a senior citizen, becoming a mentor to a disadvantaged teenager, or hearing a graduating student express appreciation for a college scholarship.

How else? The fund raiser can initiate meetings with each program director and learn first hand how programs are managed. The development team (including volunteers) might invite program managers to present their "case" at a monthly meeting (including a client testimonial). The development team can schedule an annual all-day orientation to programs as part of the strategic fund development planning process. Program managers could add the development team to their mailing list so they can receive regular updates, current articles, and other materials. And the development team could be invited to programs and events as a way of observing them in action. The idea is to make the process of case data collection an integral part of the organization's culture and the accepted role of the development team. Just as an organization is dynamic in its functioning, so is the building of the annual case. It should be an ongoing, thorough review and update, officially undertaken once a year but continuing year-round.

Over time, with this level of cooperative activity, the program and fund-raising staff will become partners in the management and exchange of information. The result will be *true teamwork* in the following activities:

- shared building and prioritizing of the organization's case(s)
- early identification of new or expanding programs/areas
- meaningful involvement of key volunteers
- shared responsibility taken by all for fund raising
- increased knowledge of and access to the case recipients

Through these organizational dynamics, a stronger, more sustainable philanthropic program is built and the most important outcome is achieved: The organization's donors are ultimately *drawn closer,* via the case, to the organization's recipients, and a social exchange relationship is formed.

Formulating, Validating, and Testing the Annual Case

The obvious question at this point in the case-building process is, What does one do with all the case component information? The next step is to synthesize it, prioritize it, write the case statement, and put it to the test. The information behind the annual case is generally abundant in detail and scope. For example, most organizations have many different programs and deliver a multitude of services that comprise their work. Some of these programs are more visible than others, some are more cutting edge than others, some are at the end of their life cycle, others need to be expanded, and *some are more dependent on philanthropic support than others.*

The goal is to examine all the case material and its component parts and then determine which programs and services have the *greatest priority for fund raising.*

Programs that *need* philanthropic support and have the *ability* to generate philanthropic support become the priority of the annual giving program.

An organization with many different programs may elect to build their case on all of them; another organization may choose two or three programs for its case. Yet another organization may decide to focus on a couple of programs/services for the next few years and change the program case mix in subsequent years.

The decision about which programs/services will constitute the annual giving case requires careful consideration and agreement by many participants, because the case becomes the organization's public philanthropic platform. How this decision is made and who is involved are all part of the case development process. The notion that one person (the CEO) decides how much money is needed or that one person (the fund raiser) writes the case statement is at times the reality, but certainly is neither ideal nor advised. The fund raiser may facilitate the process of collecting, refining, validating, and composing the case materials, but the more people who are involved at each step, the more successful the fund-raising efforts are apt to be. Once the case is accepted by internal constituencies, it will be relatively easy to integrate all organizational communications. In annual giving, especially, the organization's marketing, public relations, and development case messages must all be synchronized in order to achieve the highest possible fund-raising impact and donor response.

Formulating the Case: Writing It

There is no substitute for formulating the case except to write it. All the collected data must now be put on paper. That is the only way that others can fully grasp the meaning of the case,

analyze it from their point of view, give feedback and suggestions, add value to its substance, and, ever important, buy in.

At this point in the process, the case becomes the *case statement.* It is a written document that describes, on several pages, the reason why annual gifts are needed and what they will accomplish. It does not include all the information that was gathered, but rather synthesizes it in a clear, concise way, similar to an executive summary of a major grant request. More than likely, there will be a need to write one overall or umbrella case statement for the annual integrated development program, with individualized case statements for each annual giving component; for instance, if the board campaign raises funds for one program while the alumni campaign raises funds for another, a separate case statement will be written for each constituency/campaign. Ideally, each case statement is written from a marketing perspective, taking into account the information that was gathered in the analysis of each prospect group (see Chapter 4 on constituency building). Remember, the overall or "umbrella" case statement serves primarily as an internal document that substantiates the need for philanthropic gifts per se and gives fund raising its impetus. Although it may never be used externally in this format, it serves as the foundation for all subsequent external communications, be they printed or verbal.

Validating the Case: Internally

The preparation of the case statement serves as a device to involve key people in the organization: program staff, volunteers, administration, board members, donors, and development staff. The goal is to engage the total organization, bottom up not top down. By starting with *key program staff,* the case will be validated as an organizational priority, even when there are competing interests and limited resources. The next step is to involve the *board of directors,* who will look at the case statement from a dual perspective: internally from a governance standpoint and externally from a community need standpoint. Their involvement brings an objective/subjective balance to the validation process and elicits important investment by board members who will ultimately serve as chief advocates and constituent "links." Next, the case statement should be validated by *key volunteers* who provide a different kind of filter, one that is more objective and representative of the donor marketplace and a little further removed from the inner circle. The volunteers will give a good indication of the effectiveness of the case—does it make sense, is it compelling, will it move people to action? And finally, it is wise to test the case with *major annual donors* as a way to recruit them into leadership positions, motivate them for future gifts, and keep them involved.

Testing the Case: Externally

The way to ensure that the organization's case is viewed by its donor market as relevant, urgent, and compelling is to test it with identified constituent groups. This external process focuses more on the testing of the individualized case statements, which form the basis of individualized annual strategies and mini-campaigns, than on the testing of the umbrella case statement.

Testing individualized cases may involve simply talking them through with key donors at a luncheon scheduled for this purpose, hosting a formal focus group of potential donors by segment (alumni by graduate area, clients by service received, patients by diagnosis type), or writing a telephone script or direct mail letter and testing its response with a statistically significant number of prospects. The case should be tested for clarity, relevance, urgency, and its "call to action." The bottom line is whether people will respond to this appeal and to what extent.

Kotler and Andreasen (1987) have developed a framework of testing communications copy. The first method is *comprehension testing* with

an instrument that assesses what readers understand. This kind of testing is usually done by market testing firms. The second is *direct mail testing*, in which several direct mail samples are sent to a group of potential donors who are asked to rank the solicitations for copy, style, graphics, and the like. It is important that the test be statistically significant. The third method is a *portfolio recall test*, which asks a group of people to list all the information they can recall from reading the materials and to describe their meaning. This survey method helps weed out information that is not relevant or useful. The fourth method is *focus group interviews*. This process yields information quickly and creates a synergy that produces value-added input. According to Kaye Ferguson-Patton, case/copy testing helps the development professional find answers to the following questions (1995, 97–98):

- How much do these constituents know about the organization, its mission, and its need for funding?
- What else do they want to know about the organization, its mission, and its need for funding?
- How do they want to hear it said? What language do they best relate to when it comes to hearing about the organization, its mission, and its need for funding? What language do they readily understand and would move them to respond with financial support if they were asked?
- How do they feel about what the organization has said to them through these messages? What emotions are they feeling? Are they positive or negative? Do those emotions support your communications plan? Are they what you were after at its creative inception?

Establishing Priorities

Given the growing need that organizations have for philanthropic support, it is important that fund raising be given top administrative priority in both focus and resources. It is also imperative that individualized cases within the

> **The case should be tested for clarity, relevance, urgency, and its "call to action."**

overall case be prioritized so that the appropriate amount of commitment and energy is devoted to their successful actualization. It is equally important for staff and volunteers to look at changing times, fluctuating conditions, and the possibility of over- or undersubscribed cases/campaigns, and to make priority adjustments along the way. An annual integrated development program must have annual goals for the current, upcoming, and subsequent years and advisably even a priority plan for five years hence.

Communicating the Case: Principles, Techniques, and Messages

The *case for support* and the written *case statement* are built from information that resides *within* the organization, whereas *case communications* are built with information that resides *outside* the organization, for external purposes. The basic purpose of communications, within fund raising, is to build relationships that are sustainable, adaptable, and resilient and that grow over time. Communications are internal/external two-way exchanges. Communicating the case effectively requires an understanding of communication principles, techniques, and messages.

Basic Communication Principles

Whether you are communicating with only one person, with a small group, or with many people, the same basic process occurs, and the same misunderstandings can arise. The basic elements of the communication process are: sender (person A) to receiver (person B), stimulus and motivation, encoding and decoding, and frame of reference.

Sender to Receiver. This element simply indicates that two interchanges will be occurring. In annual fund raising it is most often one sender (albeit representing the organization and the recipients it serves) communicating to many receivers (all the more important for the fund raiser to know the audience so that case messages can be tailored to improve their reception).

Stimulus and Motivation. Two things must happen. First the sender must stimulate the receiver (either internal or external). In other words, something in the communication has to get the receiver's attention. Stimulus, however, is insufficient to trigger communication. The second requirement is to send a message that will be sufficiently motivating. In fund raising, we must acknowledge that most donors are not simply waiting to hear from us; thus, our messages must first be heard and only then listened to. According to Kotler and Andreasen, "The sender has an intended message, but whether or not the received message is in most respects identical to it is determined by the extent to which the communications process is relatively noise-free and the sender and receiver share the same cultural codes" (1987, 506).

Encoding and Decoding. The message that the sender has formulated (which could be the case) is in an encoded form. Because senders encode messages before communicating them, the sender is often referred to as the encoder. When the encoder's message is picked up, the receiver tries to make sense out of it; that is, to decode it.

Frame of Reference. Encoding and decoding may seem simple, but they are not because of the complexity of each person's frame of reference. These factors come into play: the choice of words (the tone of a letter), ineffective communication channels (the person hates direct mail), faulty feedback mechanisms (the receiver has questions, but the letter didn't address them), an unconducive environment (the wrong time to call), and too much noise (three other appeals arrived on the same day).

Four Conditions of Effective Communications

Of course, the goal of all communications, especially in fund raising, is to elicit a response—an action-oriented response. As in marketing, fund-raising communications are designed to influence attitudes and opinions, which then influence decision making. Educating prospects/

donors or expanding public awareness of the organization itself is not marketing. Marketing requires a transactional outcome: a favorable exchange relationship between the donor and the organization. Kotler and Andreasen (1987) offer a view of communications—as a process creating an exchange that elicits an action response. An exchange assumes that four conditions exist:

1. **There are at least two parties to the exchange.** In fund raising, the two parties are the donor and the organization's representative. Although others (the donor's family, friends, or representatives; the organization's volunteers, staff, or recipients) may be involved, the exchange generally starts and concludes with two people.

2. **Each party can offer something that the other perceives to be a benefit or benefits.** An exchange requires a perceived benefit for each party. The benefit to the organization is obvious: financial contributions, volunteer time and expertise, leadership on behalf of the organization, advocacy and influence with others in the community, and the like. The benefit to the donor is multifaceted, with both tangible and intangible benefits: a satisfaction in helping others, recognition, involvement in the organization, affirmation that the gift was needed and spent wisely, and so on.

3. **Each party is capable of communication and delivery.** For an exchange to take place, the two parties must be capable of communicating with each other. All fund-raising methods are designed to send and receive messages, some more effectively than others. For instance, direct mail is used heavily in annual giv-

ing, and although it promotes an exchange via the mail, it is an impersonal fund-raising strategy—it gives the appearance of being one-way. More effective communication and solicitation strategies are those based on two-way "open" systems, such as via the telephone or in person. When two people have a conversation, the desired exchange is more immediate; there is an opportunity to explore, dialogue, negotiate, clarify, and construct a mutually beneficial exchange.

4. **Each party is free to accept or reject the offer.** The essence of an exchange is its voluntary nature. It is each person's right and privilege to say "yes" or "no" or even "maybe." Both the giver and the receiver may elect to accept or reject the process. A prospect may not see the benefit of making a charitable contribution at this particular point in time to the organization that is soliciting his or her support. On the other hand, an organization may not accept a gift from a donor for a purpose outside its mission and strategic priorities or if the donor expects benefits that cannot be delivered.

Six Decision-Making Steps

Understanding *how people make decisions* is an important aspect of communications and marketing theory. Yet, one could take a semester class on customer behavior and still not be able to anticipate or predict how people will respond to communications/solicitations. But experience in the field *can* help fund raisers develop a more sophisticated understanding of consumer behavior, which can be augmented by formal and informal research that provides the facts. Over time, it is possible to understand these relationships and patterns better and to predict behavioral responses more reliably.

Several decision-making models can be applied to fund raising. Exhibit 5–3 describes a one-time exchange, with a minimum of three steps, that is applicable to the donor acquisition process.

Exhibit 5–3 Donor Acquisition Communications

> 1. The prospect must need or want to make an exchange.
>
> 2. The prospect must understand that the organization's offering will meet those needs and wants.
>
> 3. The prospect must behave as desired.

Exhibit 5–4 describes a continuing exchange with multiple steps that is applicable to the donor renewal and upgrade process.

Although decision making is more complex than these illustrations reveal, it is easy to see why fund-raising strategies must approach those prospects whom we want to inform and cultivate differently from first-time donors whom we want to stimulate and from repeat donors whom we want to evaluate their previous decisions and reaffirm them, and from upgrade donors whose commitment we want to increase.

How do we translate these decision-making steps into fund-raising communications?

Exhibit 5–4 Donor Renewal and Upgrade Communications

> 1. The prospect must need or want to make an exchange.
>
> 2. The prospect must understand that the organization's offering will meet those needs and wants.
>
> 3. The prospect must behave as desired.
>
> 4. The project assesses the previous exchange outcomes for satisfaction level.
>
> 5. The prospect repeats behavior, with renewed expectations for desired benefits.

First, fund-raising communications must be structured to *attract peoples' attention*. Given the noisy marketplace, this challenge can be met by making sure the communications are written and designed for the target market, not a mass market. Copy tone and graphic design play a significant role here.

Second, communications must be written to focus on the prospects' interests sufficiently enough to *be considered*. A personalized approach, as if directed only to the receiver and from someone familiar to him or her, improves the likelihood that the communications will be read or heard. If the appeal "gets into the bill box," it stands a good chance of being considered seriously.

Third, communications must sustain a *test of evaluation* against other options. At this point, the evaluation/decision may be influenced by the strength of the case, the preciseness and value of the match, or the influence of others who are involved in the cause.

Fourth, the communications must *be situationally correct*. Timing is everything, and everything must be right—the amount, case, and organization. If a personal situation prohibits response at this point, it negates previous steps, and communications need to start over.

Fifth, communications must include a "call to action" and *make it easy for the prospect to respond*. The message must be compelling and urgent enough to eliminate the option of decision delay. When the response vehicle, card, or envelope offers all the needed information, the donor has only to write a check.

Sixth, after the donor decides to respond affirmatively, follow-up communications must provide *a positive reinforcement* for the decision, validating the reasons behind the exchange. These communications must set the stage for future, repeat gift decisions.

As decisions become more complex, the exchange process becomes more complex—with more information, more involvement, more investment, and more benefits. The rule is to move communications from impersonal to personal, from simple to complex, from occasional to ongoing as donors move up the giving pyramid.

> **As decisions become more complex, the exchange process becomes more complex—with more information, more involvement, more investment, and more benefits.**

Communication Models

In describing the relationship between fund raising and marketing, Kotler and Andreasen (1987) offered a staged approach to marketing (see Chapter 4); they also divide fund raising into four stages based on a marketing perspective: *begging*—"people should give because we have needs"; *collecting*—"people will give if we just ask them"; *campaigning*—"people will give if we convince them"; and *development*—"people will give if we develop relationships with them." These sequential stages portray how an organization thinks, acts, talks, and communicates and where it is in an evolutionary process that starts with an internal organizational focus, moves to a systems focus, then to an external focus, and finally to a balanced donor market focus.

Another communication model is derived not from a marketing perspective but from a public relations model. Kathleen Kelly (1994) presents four communications models that represent the values, goals, and behaviors held or used by organizations when they practice fund raising: press agentry, public information, two-way asymmetrical, and two-way symmetrical. She asserts that fund raisers use all four models to some extent, but usually practice one predominantly—the press agentry model.

The *press agentry model*, which emerged in the early 1900s within the YMCA, is known to fund raisers as the campaign style of fund raising. According to Kelly, this model's practice rests on a foundation of pressure, competition, emotion, and even coercion. Yesterday as today, this model is predominantly used in campaigns that are time-based, implemented by volunteer teams, and have aggressive goals. This type of fund raising can be seen in most federated fund drives, annual fund campaigns, and capital cam-

paigns. Educational institutions, religious groups, and United Ways are the frequent users of this model. The communication is predominantly one-way from organization to donor, with an emphasis on emotions, embellishments, and deadlines. This model uses very little research. It is best described by a quote from the study research instrument: "The more people who know about our cause, the more dollars we will raise" (Kelly 1994, 16).

The *public information model* was introduced in 1916 by Bishop William Lawrence and Ivy Ledbetter Lee. The underlying theme of this approach is that people will give, not because of emotional appeals or a high-pressure campaign, but because they have all the facts and figures needed to reach a decision. This model is used predominantly by health and human services organizations, with a heavy reliance on publicity and direct mail. Communications are designed to influence and convince: "We disseminate factual information, which prospective donors then use to make a rational decision to give" (Kelly 1994, 16). Again, the communication is one-way, with little research, but with an emphasis on truth.

The *two-way asymmetrical model* emerged in 1919 under John Price Jones. Devoted to research and planning, the purpose of this model is to use research to stimulate giving: "Before starting, we look at attitude surveys to make sure we describe the organization in ways our prospects will be most likely to support" (Kelly 1994, 16). Communication is two-way, but is unbalanced in that it depends on the extent to which donors are open to influence. More common in major gift programs than annual giving, it uses formative research to shape persuasive communications.

The *two-way symmetrical model* of fund raising emerged in 1980, some 80 years after the other models. It is based on the notion that fund raising is dependent on agreement between donors and charitable organizations—on a partnership or an exchange. Kelly (1994) writes, "In contrast to the reliance of press agentry on donor emotions, of public information on enlightenment, and of two-way asymmetrical practices on accessibility, the two-way symmetrical model is dependent on donor agreement with the organization's mission and the means by which it carries out that mission" (3). This model uses formative research not only to match donor interest and shape communications but also to influence an organization's philanthropic culture—how it thinks about its donors. Kelly's study's finding that the press agentry is the predominant fund-raising model practiced today "bodes poorly for the success and even survival of the nonprofit sector" (30), while the use of the two-way symmetrical model by some reflective practitioners "will help practitioners and their organizations be more effective in an ethically and socially responsible manner" (32).

Although these models do not include all the available types of communications, they do cause one to pause and consider how important the philosophical dimensions are in a fund-raising program (see Chapter 2).

Communication Techniques and Key Messages

Fund-raising communications are designed to inform, educate, and influence behavior, so donors "become involved with the cause as advocates, contributors, volunteers, and informed constituents" (Rosso 1991, 47). Fortunately, there are a number of tried-and-true communication techniques handed down from generation to generation that we can use. The test of effectiveness is and has always been the bottom line—how many people responded and how many dollars were raised. Though not tested empirically, the following four *themes* are prominent in a successfully stated case:

1. The case reflects what the community needs and wants.
2. The case has clarity and focus.
3. The case has both emotional and rational components.
4. The case evokes a response.

Case communications take the form of both written materials and verbal expressions. The *case statement* is the basis for a personal solicita-tion, a letter, direct mail or telephone solicitation, a campaign brochure, a grant request, a presentation or testimonial, and the like.

Whatever the form, effective case communications incorporate most of the following 12 messages:

Message 1: **Invite people to give to others with needs.** The demonstration of human needs is a powerful catalyst to giving and a crucial element of the case message. P.M. Blau, author of *Social Exchange*, asserts that "most gratifications of human beings have their source in the actions of other human beings" (Mixer 1993, 10). The key is to portray that need in a way to which others can relate, using words, phrases, and other stimuli that will help them recall their own situations and will elicit feelings of compassion and a belief that their gift will help somebody.

Message 2: **Tell people what the result will be, and who benefits.** The concept of making a gift to charity is more complicated than it used to be. Growing skepticism and donor fatigue have created a need for more information— enough to show that programs can respond to problems properly and seize opportunities. People want evidence from outside sources that an organization meets charitable standards. In addition, today's donors have a results orientation, fueled by performance expectations in their own workplace. The United Way movement to encourage their agencies to define their outcome measures better comes at a time when people expect more from nonprofits for less. People need to be reassured that their gift is needed and will benefit the recipient, the family, the neighborhood, and the community. They want to know precisely what will happen as a result. These are reasons why donor-designated giving is on the rise.

Message 3: **Explain how much is needed and what is required.** More and more, donors want to be advised of the big picture, as well as the details. This is especially true when it comes to financial aspects of the organization. They want information about the budget, the revenue, and the expenses. If asked for a specific amount, they will consider the relative impact of that gift against the total need—how much difference will their gift make or not make. Donors want to know who else is contributing and at what level; they want to "do the right thing, with the right people." When an organization is able to communicate the case/program in sound bites, such as "$146 will feed one child for one year," the prospect is better able to understand his or her role and responsibility.

Message 4: **Give an example; tell a story.** An age-old method of communicating—going back to biblical times—is to use real-life examples to illustrate the case. Telling stories is an effective way to create visual images, supported by audio messages. When people can imagine a situation, in technicolor and stereo, they are better able to assimilate the information, process it, and react to it. Visual and audio messages are especially useful when the case/problem

is outside someone's personal experience. For instance, most people have *never* been homeless, gone to bed hungry, or been abused as a child—they can feel empathy, but cannot relate to those problems. A story told about such a situation can illustrate the case emotionally, because the donor's experience may not.

Message 5: **Provide a balance of emotional and rational information.** Most people are able to make decisions when they are given a sufficient amount of data, but those data need to be both emotional and rational in its delivery. Psychology tells us that when people make decisions that come from their heart *and* their head, they have less post-decision dissonance. Carefully crafted case communications can offer emotional information through examples, quotes, choice of words, and visual enhancements. Rational information is provided through statistics, facts, reference points, and clear succinct language.

Message 6: **Convey a sense of urgency.** Many donors seem to follow the same practice: They put solicitation appeals in the proverbial bill box, where they surface each month until a final decision is made. At bill-paying time, the decision is often made to delay, and that may mean until the end of the year. To reduce the possibility of delay, communicate a sense of urgency, given there is one. Urgency is tied to the case/condition being so critical that to delay a response would impose a hardship on those who may not be served. A campaign deadline does not convey a legitimate sense of urgency—deadlines seldom stimulate the right kind of gift. On the other hand, challenge gifts are legitimate stimuli when available for a limited amount of time and when they will be lost if not met.

Message 7: **Treat people as individuals; be personal.** With technological advances in fund raising, it seems that every appeal is computer "personalized" in one way or another. The problem is that everybody recognizes this so the effect is lost. Therefore, fund raisers must use other methods of personalizing their appeals. Using first-person language, hand-written salutations, signatures and notes, tailored case solicitations, and phone calls all help let people know they are more than a computer record. Tell people how *they* will benefit too—research says that giving satisfies a donor's fundamental needs and desires. Use language that gives the donor a feeling of pride, achievement, status, and belonging. "The more personal the involvement in the cause, the stronger the relationship" (Mixer 1993, 12).

Message 8: **Articulate how efficient and effective the effort is.** The very essence of the nonprofit sector is derived from the public's belief that the people can address social issues more effectively than government. Not only does the public pridefully promote nonprofit ventures as an expression of American philosophy but it also fully expects that nonprofits will operate in a less

costly and more productive fashion than government. Donors want to be reassured that their giving decisions are good ones, that their gifts were used in the best possible way, and that they "went as far as possible."

Harvey and McCrohan (1990) report that the two major concerns of prospective donors are the purpose served by the funds raised and the temporal efficiency by which the funds are raised: "Having a clear purpose gives prospective donors easily understood information about the use of their contributions, and has a considerable positive effect on donor behavior. . . . The proportion of funds raised . . . also appears to be of considerable importance to donors" (55). A significant increase in giving occurred when perceived efficiency (the ratio of income to expense or the amount directed at program delivery) rose 60 percent (57).

Message 9: **Demonstrate past success and future potential.** People give to ameliorate problems and advance causes—to serve a purpose much larger than themselves. Show donors how they can fund solutions and demonstrate that your organization has capable management, visionary leadership, and past successes. Donors will be inspired by knowing where the organization is going rather than where it is today. When donors are asked to invest in the future, they do so in ways similar to how they do their own financial planning—thoughtfully with an expectation of a greater return on their investment. Any attempt to raise money for a financial *problem*, rather than a program *solution*, forces the organization to resort to begging and apology.

Message 10: **Articulate vision and leadership.** Repeatedly we hear that there is no substitute for leadership, in contrast to other areas of organizational dynamics that can be weak and still function. The presence of leadership is a powerful force; it results in an environment that is both value-centered and value-added. Messages that convey vision and leadership are inspiring and influential. According to Mixer, "Expectations that arise from looking to the future create fundamental psychological drives that involve many of the personal and social motives such as self-esteem, achievement, status, and group endeavor" (1993, 24). Donors are strongly influenced and challenged by the thought of what can be done, what the organization should be or do, and the part they might play in the grand plan.

Message 11: **Use creative and energetic ideas and language: get their attention.** Social behavior research points out that people's attitudes differ if they were born at different times, raised with different values, and have different experiences. Thus, they must be communicated with through different styles, moods, and methods. For instance, younger, career-oriented women respond to crisper copy and bolder graphics, whereas traditional older women seem to re-

spond better to subdued colors, graphics, and copy. Baby Boomers respond to straightforward language because of their somewhat pessimistic outlook on life, whereas older generations look at the world with more optimism and respond best to language that describes "the way the world can be" (Nichols 1995). Although everyone will react differently to a fund-raising appeal, nearly everyone will respond positively to a case that is presented with excitement, is creative, is action-oriented, and has vitality. Anything less is likely to elicit a yawn.

Message 12: **Ask people to respond and show them why and how.** So many fund-raising appeals approach people timidly and with apology. Doing so will evoke little more than a timid response. There is no need for apology when the case is worthy of support and no way to invite people's participation except to ask, straightforwardly and with pride. "The case is the way the fund raiser spells out goals and objectives that make later accountability possible" (Payton et al. 1991, 9). We can't tell people too many times why they should make a contribution—positive reinforcement is an essential component of the decision-making process. The appeal should provide a balance between the reasons to give and the benefits of giving for the exchange concept to be clear. And finally, fund raisers can offer a multitude of ways for people to give, making it possible for them to consider the largest possible gift. For instance, some donors are influenced by the prospect of charging their contribution on a charge card that awards frequent flyer miles. Other donors will give more if they can spread their gift out quarterly or over 12 months. The United Way success with payroll deduction has resulted in larger gifts made monthly in affordable increments. Creatively, clarity, and flexibility are key.

Missed Signals

For as many reasons as people give, there are equally as many why they do not give. Many of the latter reasons are tied to ineffective communications. There are the simple explanations—the case did not give the right information or the right amount of it, or the tone and style were incongruous with the prospect (too gaudy, too slick, too trite). There are the more complex ones—the manner of asking is wrong, or the case is not matched properly to the audience. Mixer groups the reasons for why people do not give into four categories: communication problems, organizational image problems, reactions to solicitations, and personal characteristics and situational problems.

Communication Problems. Mixer writes,

The leading error [in communications] is a failure to make up for prospects' *lack of information*. Prospects may know little or nothing about the agency. The purpose or mission is obscure and no record of service is apparent. The results and benefits from gifts seem remote. The case for supporting the organization is not transmitted to the prospects. In this case, prospects simply have insufficient information on which to base their giving (1993, 32).

Citing Harvey and McCrohan (1990), Mixer asserts that *ineffective communication* leaves many

prospects cold. When publications appear too slick and expensive in relation to campaign goals and the sponsoring organization's needs, the apparent unwise use of promotional funds deters support. This diminishes the effect of urgency and severity of the need. Mixer (1993, 33) concludes that "negative publicity results more often from the manner in which problems are reported than from the event itself."

Organizational Image Problems. These key image/outreach concerns consistently emerge as factors that contribute to a prospect's lack of interest and response (Exhibit 5–5).

Reactions to Solicitations. A reason why people do not give is very personal and tied to the manner of being asked. Does the prospect feel he or she is being over-asked and pushed or, on the other hand, under-asked and ignored? The first stage in Kelly's model of communications/fund raising, the press agentry model, is an aggressive and manipulative way of fund raising that is pervasive in the industry and yet effective in raising money. Some of the poor image of fund raising seems to be related directly to this style of fund raising, and it may be the reason behind why people do not give again, having once given reluctantly.

Personal Characteristics and Situations. There is also the issue of timing—the fact remains that most everyone will allow financial wherewithal to dictate the philanthropic spirit. But nothing is as wasted as the invitation to give to someone without any previous linkage, interest, or involvement. As James G. Lord writes, "If the prospect is not already interested in what you have to offer, you aren't very likely to change his or her mind" (1981, 58).

Positioning Your Organization's Case: Examples of Annual Giving Cases

The marketing term "positioning" refers to the organization's image (real or desired) in the marketplace. Is the organization the community's charity of choice, a traditional charity among many, an emerging up-and-coming char-

Exhibit 5–5 What Went Wrong?

What Went Wrong?

- The organization's messages are not clear, consistent, and specific.

- The organization is viewed as a "fair share" charity, not as a priority for many donors.

- The organization is perceived as "a player," not as a leader, by the general public and especially by major potential donors.

- Many confuse the organization with other similar mission-focused charities.

- The organization's mission has no urgency, sizzle, or prestige.

- The organization's purpose is unclear to the community.

- The organization is seen as impersonal and institutionalized.

Source: Data from J.E. Nichols, *Global Demographics: Fund Raising for a New World*, p 42, © 1995, Bonus Books.

ity, or a unknown quantity? An effective case positions the organization, making it more visible and distinct from others, particularly from those in the same market grouping, such as social services, health care, or arts and culture. When an organization is well-positioned, it stands out; people know about it, talk about it, and are involved in it. It has a competitive edge against like charities. Often, in response to environmental and organizational changes, an organization will need to adopt a re-positioning strategy; one that regains a lost position or attains another desired position. Positioning is so important today because of the growing number of new nonprofits, increased sophistication in fund raising, increased competition among donors for annual contributions, and the abundant number of capital campaigns.

What does positioning have to do with fund raising? The success of a fund-raising program is dependent to a large extent on the image of the organization—is it well known, how is it regarded, and how does it compare to the competition? Though the organization's positioning strategies are the primary responsibility of its marketing department, fund raising relies on

them. Fund raising also relies on a case that is positioned in much the same way. How is the case distinguished from others? Is it competitive? Is it clear, or will it be confused with like cases?

Fortunately, there will always be donors who have confidence in the organizations they support, and trust that organizations can identify the best uses of funds. But there is growing discontent among well-informed donors; they want to make decisions for themselves and this requires that we allow them more choices about how their gifts are applied. In the future, even the most successful annual fund programs will need a stronger, more compelling, definitive case if they are to prosper.

What should the annual giving program raise money for? Tradition has it that the annual giving program raises money for the general operating programs of an organization. The thesis promoted in this book is that an annual giving program is most effective when it incorporates a variety of fund-raising strategies that communicate specific case components, tailored to specific donor/prospect groups, using a variety of solicitation methods on a year-round ba-

> An annual giving program is most effective when it incorporates a variety of fund-raising strategies.

sis. That is not to suggest that funds are raised for something other than the general operating budget, but instead it promotes drawing out or elaborating on a few programs/services within the operating budget that need and merit philanthropic support. And at times, annual giving strategies may include raising funds to start up a new initiative, expand an existing successful program, or make small capital improvements that will enhance current program delivery. The obvious point is that annual contributions are raised for budgeted programs and services. The examples that follow are successful cases from a social service organization, a hospital, a zoological society, and a college.

Example 1—A Social Service Organization: Positioning with Three Cases

It is customary for social service organizations to have many, and sometimes diverse, program services including counseling for families, shelters, and treatment centers, youth intervention and mentoring services, adoption and foster care placement, and innovative programs that address teen violence, pregnancy, and drug use. Because of their distinctions within the organization's mission, social service programs usually have their own individualized names, budgets, goals, objectives and identity, at least with certain client groups. Some programs have wide public visibility, such as a battered women's shelter; others have a more obscure image, such as a family counseling program.

Given this scenario, social service agencies must consider the best way to communicate with the donating public. Should the agency promote the identity of individual programs, or promote name recognition and visibility for the agency itself? Is it possible to communicate the comprehensive nature of an organization's mission

and services, or is it better to feature a few programs with the goal of bringing value-added visibility to all of them? What is the best approach for fund raising?

A century-old Minneapolis-based social service organization faces just such a challenge. The organization has a well-established history, an excellent reputation, a moderately influential board, a competent and highly respected executive director, and a small professional development staff. It has a solid track record of United Way support, and an excellent relationship with corporate and private foundations, but very little history of individual giving. It has 21 different programs, all of which need some level of philanthropic support.

This social service organization made a decision to strategically position its communications and fund raising using a two-pronged communications approach: (1) to focus on a few problems and issues of greatest concern to the community, and (2) to feature a few programs (solutions) in which the organization has significant history and success. The development committee researched, reviewed, and selected three different cases as the focus of their two-year fund-raising and communications plan. They decided to feature three social issues rather than promote individual programs by name, although many of the agency's 21 programs do fall within the following initiatives:

- School Success
- Violence Prevention
- Community Leadership Building

The volunteer committee identified three constituency groupings with high levels of affinity and interest in the organization.

- board of directors, friends, and current donors
- neighborhood residents, churches, clubs, and businesses
- major prospects and donors who have demonstrated interest in the agency, and have supported other projects designed to ensure the community's quality of life

Fund-raising strategies were designed with the goal of raising money for the smallest, neediest issues first from constituents who were the most involved and informed. The fund-raising methodologies included the following:

- a personalized board, friends, and donors campaign, and a corporate-sponsored public-participation campaign
- a targeted neighborhood campaign
- a major donor initiative

The sequential approach of three campaigns over a two-year period would create a synergy of building constituency linkages, moving from the board of directors toward the outer rings of the organization's constituency circle. The second campaign component within the *School Success* initiative, the Book Reading Sponsorship Program is critical to the agency's image building. This campaign is designed to increase visibility for the agency's work with youth, and to encourage more broad-based public support.

Compared to raising money for the organization itself (all 21 programs), the communication plan promotes one initiative at a time, to more effectively crystalize the agency's image, making it more distinguishable and memorable. This approach greatly enhances the community's understanding of what the organization does, where the money is needed, and what it will do.

Case 1: School Success

The social service agency's first organized fund-raising effort/campaign is based on a case to underwrite a program which identifies "baby truants" and intervenes in a family's way of life by giving them the necessary skills to ensure a child's success in school. The case materials point to the success of the model program ("over 95 percent of the children/families demonstrate improved behavioral outcomes") and the extent to which the program is dependent on philanthropy ("every $2,000 will sponsor one child/family for an entire school year, without which the family will not be served"). The case for support points to specific outcomes: "a high per-

centage of parents also returned to school as a result of seeing their own child experience success." And, the case articulates there is a benefit to donors "when they help one child at a critical time of life, they improve an entire community because that child ultimately gives back."

The *School Success* campaign has two components, designed for two different audiences: (1) *internal constituencies* (board members, employees, donors, friends of the board, and designated United Way donors), and (2) *external constituencies* (corporate partners and qualified individual prospects). The internal campaign is titled "Leaders for Learning;" the theme is "Unleashing the Potential of our Littlest Ones." The first board and friends campaign raised $110,000, a 500 percent increase over the board's giving for the previous year.

The case materials for the external constituency are designed to appeal to a broader audience. This campaign component, the Book Reading Sponsorship Program, includes both a fund-raising effort as well as a volunteer recruitment effort. People are invited to give $25 to sponsor books for each child, as a symbolic gesture of ensuring that child's school success. In turn, the donor receives a thank you from the child who receives the books. Volunteers are invited to become reading tutors for one year, and are assigned to the four participating schools. Corporate sponsors underwrite the actual program costs by sponsoring a school.

Case 2: Violence Prevention

The second organized fund-raising effort/campaign is based on a case "to prevent the kind of violence that puts neighborhoods at risk." The case for support points out that violence is "the #1 health risk facing children and youth, and the #1 threat to a community's health." The written materials describe how violence affects people in multiple ways, and emphasizes the need for a continuum of solutions ranging from public policy initiatives to youth diversion projects.

The *Violence Prevention* fund-raising campaign is targeted at organizations, businesses, and churches who are located geographically near the agency's four neighborhood centers. The communications show prospects how they "are stakeholders in the community's well-being and safety," and asks them to contribute in order to make *their* neighborhoods violence-free. The campaign, in addition to seeking philanthropic support, promotes public education about "how to avoid potentially violent situations," demonstrating ways in which the agency's partnership programs (in the homes and schools, with police and community groups) have a direct benefit to the donor/community. The case theme is "zero tolerance for violence."

This geographically-oriented campaign utilizes a personal contact strategy; volunteers who represent each of the neighborhood centers solicit other neighborhood residents, as well as churches, clubs, and local businesses. Volunteers serve on development sub-committees, where they are also involved in designing promotional strategies that are unique to each neighborhood *Violence Prevention* campaign, and to each center's type of services and philanthropic goals.

Case 3: Community Leadership Building

The third organized fund-raising effort, the *Community Leadership Building* campaign, is dependent on the success of the two other campaigns because it is designed to appeal to donors who are capable of becoming major givers, and to raise significantly more funds. When implemented, this campaign will have had two years in the planning stage, and a goal to raise between $500,000 and $1 million from donors who understand and are interested in funding social policy and systemic social change in their community. The prospects for this campaign are board members, current and lapsed donors, donors to the agency's 1985 capital campaign, and other prospects qualified through research as having a high level of linkage, interest, and ability. All prospects are known to have a sophisticated understanding of the community's infrastructure, and an appreciation of the agency's credibility in building community.

Case communications focus on the high quality of the agency's services, and point out what tactics are necessary to achieve the desired changes or outcomes. The case communications feature several of the agency's programs that are designed "to work through community-based organizations with the goal of identifying low-income individuals who are committed to helping their communities develop effective solutions to problems such as housing, drugs, violence, unemployment, and poverty." The *Community Leadership Building* case for support demonstrates that success is measurable, by showing that a model demonstration project implemented last year produced "four leadership trainees who involved 86 community members in projects that now benefit some 340 children and their family members."

This campaign is scheduled after the successful completion of the other two campaigns, because together they serve as the platform for informing and involving this campaign's key prospects. Cultivation strategies include informational luncheons, site visits, personal solicitations, and tailored grant requests to major donors and funders.

Timelines for all three campaigns can be found in Exhibit 5–6.

Example 2—A Children's Hospital: Creating and Matching Cases for Specific Target Markets

In today's rapidly changing health care arena, hospital fund raisers must be more in touch with their organization's donors than in any other time in the organization's history. As health care has moved from an independent, physician-driven delivery modality to a complex, multifaceted managed care system, hospitals have assumed a commercial, big-business persona. Annual operating budgets for a medium-sized health care entity are in the multi-million dollar brackets, while philanthropy represents a small, declining portion—as little as 1 to 10 percent of the hospital or health care system budget. This creates an awkward dilemma; with the commercialization of health

School Success

Constituency/Type of Campaign		Solicitation Method	Timeline
Internal Constituency Campaign: To raise $138,000 for the School Success			
Donors:	Board Members	Small Group Presentation and Personal Follow-up	Oct 96
	Employees	Personal Mail Solicitation	Nov 96
	Past Donors	Personal Mail/Telephone	Nov/Dec 96
Prospects:	Friends of the Board	Personal Mail Solicitation	Nov 96
	Designated Donors	Direct Mail	Nov 96
External Constituency Campaign: To raise $200,000 for Book Reading Program			
Donors:	Corporate Partners	Personal Solicitation Grant Request	Jan 97
Prospects:	Individuals on Qualified Lists	Direct Mail Media Coverage	April/May 97
	School Children in select ZIP Codes	Personal Presentation Posters/Stickers/Mail	April/May 97

Violence Prevention

Constituency/Type of Campaign		Solicitation Method	Timeline
Neighborhood Based Campaign: To raise $200,000, or $50,000 per site			
Prospects:	Local Businesses	Grant Request Personal Solicitation	Mar 97
	Local Foundations	Grant Request Site Tour	Mar 97
	Civic Clubs	Personal Solicitation Site Tour	April/Oct 97
	Churches	Personal Mail	April/Oct 97
	Community Leaders	Personal Mail/Telephone	April/Oct 97

Community Leadership Building

Constituency/Type of Campaign		Solicitation Method	Timeline
Major Donors/Social Change Endowment Fund: To raise $500,000–$1,000,000			
Donors:	Major Individuals	Personal Solic/Grant	Jan 98
	Private Foundations	Personal Solic/Grant	Jan 98
	Community Foundations	Personal Solic/Grant	Jan 98
	Corporation Foundations	Personal Solic/Grant	Jan 98
	Board Members	Personal Solicitation	June 98
Prospects:	Major Individuals	Personal Solicitation	Aug 98

Courtesy of Family and Children's Service, Minneapolis, Minnesota.

care, hospital donors who have been "institutional loyal" for decades are now questioning the rationale for funding costly medical services—"Why do those big hospitals need my support?" Hospital administrators are beginning to question the cost benefits of philanthropic efforts—"Why bother with fund raising when it represents such a small proportion of the operating budget?" The rationale, of course, is that as long as hospitals maintain their nonprofit status, there will be a need for *charitable* services which may only be provided if philanthropy is available. And grateful hospital patients will continue to want to demonstrate their appreciation for the services they received by making a philanthropic gift, as well as wanting to have a voice in the kind of services that "their" hospital provides the community. If ever there was a time to invite health care donors to voice their interests by making *designated* gifts to their programs of choice, and to restrict those gifts for services that would not exist without philanthropy, it is now.

Given this scenario, a hospital fund-raising effort must focus on specific, critically needed services which constituent groups indicate a high level of interest in. Research on prospect and donor attitudes and opinions is fundamental to this strategy. It is also important to have a comprehensive understanding of the unique dimension of "consumptive" philanthropy—a term used to describe the relationship between a donor's contribution, and the benefit that donor, family, and friends may derive as a result. For example, most hospital donors are former patients, physicians, employees, or others who have been affected in some way by a medical condition or disease. As such, they have a natural desire to "give to get"; they may want to say thank you for the services they or their family members received; they may want to find a cure for their disease; they may want to advance a particular area of research or program (as in the case of hospice or a cancer center); or they may simply have institutional loyalty to "their hospital." Special interest is a fundamental force behind philanthropic giving to a health care organization, regardless of whether it provides services to adults, youth, or children. But a hospital dedicated to the care of children elicits an even higher level of attachment and a more powerful form of philanthropic response.

In this scenario, a well-established children's hospital in St. Paul, Minnesota faced a particularly unique challenge to build a development program in the face of a proposed merger with another hospital. This children's hospital had a loyal following of donors, excellent visibility within the community, a prestigious board of directors, and a well-established development program. It faced the challenge of professionalizing the fund-raising efforts from a traditional, annual fund approach to a more creative, tailored, targeted effort. Not only would this strategy prove to reassure donors and prospects that their support was "really" needed, but it would reinforce the partnership between donors and the organization by inviting donors to support what they wanted to.

Few other nonprofit organizations can develop a philanthropy program that is as donor-driven as can a children's hospital. In the true marketing sense, patient families are the ones who ask for counseling services when they are not provided; parents are the ones who ask for sleeping accommodations when there are none; the grown-up cancer survivors are the ones who demand more research into the disease; and the Child Life staff are the ones who advocate for a children's library, a playroom, or a plant therapy garden.

In the following examples, there were occasions when the case "need" preceded the interest of donors; there were as many times when the "grateful" donors wanted to fund a project or a service that they thought important. These examples point out the delicate balance where the fund raiser may find him- or herself managing the potential conflict between need or want, nice or necessity. The following four "matches" are representative of what was a much larger annual giving program, which over a period of four years boosted annual giving to the 160-bed hospital from $800,000 to $3 million dollars; from 3,800 donors to 10,000 donors.

Constituency I: The Board of Directors—
Case I: The Southeast Asian Initiative

A review of the hospital board's giving records showed poor support; there was not 100 percent participation, nor were the giving levels anywhere near the financial capability. Personal interviews revealed that most of the board members did not know what was expected of them; most were unclear about where their support was needed, and few were familiar with what others were contributing. In other words, they were not involved or engaged in the philanthropic process, nor fully aware of the hospital's charitable needs. With research results in hand, the development committee began to query the board members about their particular areas of interest; they found that board members felt a responsibility for the provision of services that fulfilled unmet community needs, for projects that had high accountability and that were directed at special-need populations. It was clear that board members had not, and were not going to be, responsive to a campaign that appealed for contributions to underwrite the general operating budget.

In an effort to select a specific case that the board members would respond to, members of the development committee held an all-day orientation and review of the hospital's community-based programs. Following the review, the committee selected the Southeast Asian Program for its board campaign case. This initiative proposed hiring interpreters from the Southeast Asian community to help bridge the cultural gaps, the different medical practices, and the language barriers that existed between the hospital and the growing population of Asian immigrants in the area. The project's goal was "to increase the comfort level of parents whose child was ill so that the child would receive medical treatment *before* the condition became an emergency."

The newly designed board campaign differed from all previous ones: board members personally solicited each other; case materials were written in Q & A style to address the issues raised earlier about the board's role, participation, and identification of where funds were needed; regular updates were sent weekly during the campaign, and status reports were made at every board function, until the campaign was concluded.

Board giving increased from 70 percent to 100 percent, and level of giving increased 130 percent. The success is attributed to the board's sense of ownership in the case selection, the personal level of involvement by volunteer solicitors, and the unique and distinct nature of the project.

Constituency II: Hospital Employees—
Case II: Patient Emergencies

Although the hospital had held an employee campaign every year for the previous four years, the participation level was sporadic and unimpressive given the perceived level of commitment to the mission by its employees. In an effort to discover what was wrong, the development department held personal interviews with key staff, and distributed a written survey to gather opinions and attitudes about philanthropy. The research uncovered a high level of interest by employees in giving to the patients themselves, as opposed to funding the cost of delivering a program. The employees said they wanted to do something for the children that the hospital could not, such as providing vouchers for cab fare and for cafeteria food, purchasing child safety seats, providing clothing, and purchasing special take-home medical equipment. Research also uncovered an especially high interest by employees to designate their gifts and to see evidence of beneficial outcomes. It also revealed that employees were influenced in their giving by what their peers gave.

A committee of volunteer employees was convened for the purpose of selecting the case for support and for redesigning the annual employee campaign. The committee created a new project called the "*We Believe Fund*" that acted as a checking account to fund emergency grants to families in need or distress. As part of the campaign, employees were informed that a request for a grant could be made by any employee, for any family, so long as they fit the established criteria. *We Believe* grant requests could be made 24 hours a day, 365 days per year.

Employee giving nearly doubled, and the number of donors increased from 251 to 387, with gifts averaging $75. Payroll deduction became the predominant method of payment. The campaign was so successful, it was repeated the following year, and the *We Believe Fund* grew large enough to act as an endowment, producing enough investment earning to fund almost every request made each subsequent year. Reports of the use of the *We Believe Fund* were mailed quarterly to employee donors, and published annually in newsletters that were mailed to all donors. A sample brochure for the *We Believe Fund* is found in Appendix 5–A at the end of this chapter.

Constituency III: Hospital Physicians— *Case III:* Medical Research

Physicians have long been thought of as poor prospects for philanthropy, and yet when motivated have the potential of being a hospital's most influential and generous supporters. This certainly proved to be the case at the Children's Hospital. Development staff started their research with a review of articles about fund raising, with particular emphasis on physician giving. This research, coupled with personal interviews with key physicians, identified two influencing factors in their giving: there was an interest by physicians in giving to projects that benefited their patients or their particular area of practice, and there was a high level of influence by peer giving with physicians. It was felt that a campaign with personalized solicitations, public recognition, and personal benefits would be the best approach for physicians.

Key members of the medical staff volunteered to head up the next physician campaign. They made a decision to redesign their campaign, and selected a case that had wide appeal

with the medical staff. The campaign would raise funds to establish the first endowed fellowship fund, to honor a physician peer who had recently been diagnosed with cancer. The endowed fund would create a position in neonatal research, the specialty area of the physician whose work was being memorialized. The hospital's chief of staff, together with a colleague who was personally interested in the case, made weekly presentations at medical staff meetings about the new fund and the campaign until the campaign was concluded. Physicians received individualized solicitation letters, with personal follow-up; no solicitation requested a gift of less than $1,000. A list of donors, posted in the medical staff lounge, was updated every week, with special notation of every gift over $1,000. Physician giving rose 400 percent, and participation increased from 56 to 206. Within two years and two campaigns, the fellowship fund was fully endowed at the $500,000 level, with contributions from family and friends of the physician for whom the fund was named.

Constituency IV: Hospital Patients and Parents—*Case IV:* Overnight Accommodations

A children's hospital has the distinct advantage of having a particularly large natural constituency, given the number of patients and parents who come into contact with it. This constituency is composed mostly of young families, often with limited discretionary funds. However, because an experience with a children's hospital tends to involve a life-altering event, parents will support a hospital for years after, and sometimes for life. Their small gifts accumulate into large contributions over time. Grandparents also have the potential to contribute even more generously, given their lifetime of accumulated resources.

The development department researched the motivations of patient families by examining the hospital's patient satisfaction surveys. A correlation was found between the levels of patient satisfaction with certain services (such as cardiology) and giving by the families who benefited from those services (it has long been felt there is a correlation between patient family satisfaction and philanthropic motivation in health care settings). Research of donor records focused on the type of hospital use and compared it to giving levels. Analysis of the data revealed some interesting behaviors: parents whose children had a surgical procedure had higher levels of giving than those whose children were seen in the clinic. Parents who were self-insured, or double-insured were the highest givers. Parents whose children had a life-threatening disease were generous supporters, both as volunteers and donors. But patient families who had contact with certain "favorite" physicians, in this case the oncologists, contributed the most regardless of their financial ability.

A volunteer task force was formed to discuss existing patient family needs which were not currently being met; they uncovered a critical and growing need for parents to stay overnight when their child was critically ill and for families who lived a long distance from the hospital. The task force proposed building *The Family Center*, a facility with eight rooms to provide overnight accommodations for families. *The Family Center* would be constructed on the roof of an existing building, adjacent to the pediatric intensive care unit.

A telephone solicitation program was initiated, as a year-round effort to call the annual 10,000 plus patient families. Printed case materials provided a visual description of the proposed facility, with testimonials from parents who would benefit from it. Patient family giving increased from $30,000 to $135,000, with an average gift amount of $36. The telephone response rate was 25 percent, and the fulfillment rate 80 percent. Combined with gifts from individuals at the higher levels, a total of $500,000 was raised within 18 months to fully fund *The Family Center*. A sample brochure is found in Appendix 5–A.

Timelines for all four cases are shown in Exhibit 5–7.

Example 3—A Zoological Garden: Coordinating One Case, Three Constituencies, and Three Methodologies

Public institutions whose facilities are conducive to membership programs, like zoological gardens, performing arts theaters, and museums, have the unusual challenge of designing an annual giving program which is not overshadowed by membership. By their very nature, membership programs are effective relationship-building devices, more so than annual giving programs are designed to be. Membership programs are highly visible, economically attractive, replete with tangible benefits, and they include psychosocial events that reinforce belonging.

For annual giving to compete with a quid pro quo membership effort, it will need to target: (1) prospects who do not use the facility on a regular basis, (2) prospects who have the inclination and resources to make a gift over and above the somewhat nominal membership fee, or (3) prospects who have a high degree of interest in accomplishing something significant—in the case of the zoological garden, "to fund a breeding program for an endangered species."

In this scenario, the zoological garden is a state-owned facility with not just two fund-generating programs, but *three: membership, animal sponsorship, and annual giving.* Imagine the confusion that three marketing programs bring, not only to internal administration but to the external community of supporters.

First, the chances of people learning about the membership program are far greater than the annual giving or animal sponsorship programs because membership is more visible, more popular, and financially more beneficial. Interestingly, membership programs do not produce huge profit margins; they sometimes lose money because of the "gate overuse."

Second, a member who does not regularly use the zoo will not support the annual giving program, feeling "I only used my membership card once last year—isn't that money donated to the zoo?"

Exhibit 5–7 Hospital Positioning with Cases Matched to Constituencies

The Board of Directors & *The Southeast Asian Initiative*

Constituency Research	Strategies	Solicitation Methods	Timeline
Unsure about need	Board ownership	Committee initiated	March
Not certain about roles	Clear expectations	Personalized letters	June
Wanted accountability	Designated project	Peer phone calls or visits	June
Interested in community	Increase responsibility	Regular status reports	June–July
	Specific dollar request	Stewardship reports	Aug–Jan

Hospital Employees & *Patient Emergencies:* The We Believe Fund

Constituency Research	Strategies	Approaches	Timeline
Not interested in programs	Employee ownership	Employee initiated	March
Unclear about need	Focus on patients	Group presentations	June
Wanted specific outcomes	Crisis oriented	Materials hand-delivered	June
Influenced by peers	Designated project	Personal follow-up	July
	Increase involvement	Ongoing status reports	July–Jan

Hospital Physicians & *Medical Research*—The Stephen Boros Fellowship Fund

Constituency Research	Strategies	Approaches	Timeline
Select constituency	Physician ownership	Medical staff initiated	May
Poor record of giving	Focus on med research	Group presentations	July
Influenced by peers	High expectations	Personalized letters	July
Interested in benefits	Challenges from peers	Weekly updates	July–Aug

Patient Families & *The Family Center*

Constituency Research	Strategies	Approaches	Timeline
Large constituency	Compelling project	Creative print materials	Jan
Mostly young with children	Easy to understand	Telephone solicitations	Mar–Oct
Many special interests	Visually appealing	Follow-up mailings	April–Nov
Hospital satisfaction key	Testimonials/Parents	Status reports	June–July
Wanted to "give back" and "help others"		Stewardship reports	May–Dec

Courtesy of Children's Health Care. Children's Hospital of St. Paul merged with Minneapolis Children's Medical Center in June 1994 to form Children's Health Care.

Third, when asked to support the zoo, people may choose the animal sponsorship program or annual giving because they get more in return; they get a tax deduction plus a certificate, a stuffed animal, recognition at the zoo, and if they like they can give the animal sponsorship in someone else's name as a gift.

Clarity, distinctiveness, and constituency development are fundamental to an organization with only one case (the animals and the zoo habitat) with three different, but similar methodologies. Is it essential that research uncover which ones are most effective. Do they attract different supporters, and if so, what are the unique characteristics? Which program should receive the greatest amount of resources, in terms of priorities? How do supporters distinguish between the three programs?

To determine each program's effectiveness and potential, it is necessary to research the motivations and characteristics of various constituencies; individually by membership, animal sponsorship, and annual giving, and collectively for overlap (some members are also annual giving donors, some donors are also animal sponsors). If the three methodologies attract three different or similar constituencies, then each of the programs can be expanded by targeting high-potential prospects, rather than relying on the constituencies to self-select. In the case of members who never use the facility because of distance or other obvious reasons, it may be possible to "move them, and move them up" after they have become regular supporters, and are well informed. They are less likely to resist the managed "move" when they are part of the zoo family. Research can uncover what is unique about the person who chooses to be a member, a donor, and a sponsor. Once the research is completed, the greatest challenge is to design a communications program that will eliminate the confusion between the three programs, so that supporters will select the best one for them from the beginning.

This zoological garden utilized volunteers to do their constituency research, using telephone interviews over a period of several weeks. The findings confirmed early assumptions about supporting behaviors.

Research identified the profiles:

Members are primarily motivated by the economics of multiple zoo admissions—those closest in proximity to the zoo visit more frequently than those outside the metropolitan area. The 23,000 members are predominantly young to middle-aged, families with children. Non-using members view their membership fee as a contribution, because they support the zoo by "saving the zoo money." Their renewal rate is 75 percent after one year.

Animal sponsors are drawn to the zoo in a novel way—the sponsorship of a favorite animal, frequently as a gift for someone else on a special occasion: birthdays, anniversaries, Mother's or Father's days. But Valentine's Day is the biggest draw of all. Animal sponsors tend to make their "purchase" decisions emotionally and spontaneously. They believe they are making a contribution, but not as altruistically as annual donors because they receive much in return: recognition, certificates, stuffed animals, decals, and the like. The 1,300 animal sponsors are young, independent, and want something tangible for their support—some are also members. Their renewal rate is 60 percent.

Annual giving donors are more philanthropically inclined, overall. They give to other charities, and they support the zoo for its conservation, research, and educational contributions to society. Demographically, they are older, middle-class, professionals and business owners, and single-income households. Psychographically, they are interested in quality-of-life issues, the environment, and being a part of a community that supports its institutions.

Profiles shaped the communication strategies and goals:

Because all three programs are important to the zoo's vitality, the challenge lies in creating a strong and distinct communications image for membership, animal sponsorship, and annual giving. The goal is to target only those constituents that match the profile of each program and to develop a sophisticated effort that moves supporters from program to program as their interest and life-stage permit.

First, it is important to minimize confusion among the programs—each must have its own case theme, color, mood, copy, and clarity of purpose. Second, it is essential to target, and not to over-solicit people for annual giving just because they are members, or sponsors. The key is to target prospects that most resemble the current profile of each program. Third, it is necessary to improve customer satisfaction by providing the benefits people most want, but not too many; to personalize messages so there is consistency in tone and look; and to begin to build relationships that allow sequencing to occur. Members are invited to be animal sponsors, animal sponsors are invited to be annual donors—as if the three programs comprised the giving pyramid. At the appropriate time, each program works to upgrade the supporter within the program (individual membership to family membership; otter sponsor to Siberian tiger sponsor; Curator Club donor to Zoo Director Club donor).

The fund-raising strategy is planned and managed, based on research and results. The higher the level of giving, the more frequent the giving, the longer the tenure of giving, the more time and energy is expended on the exchange relationship—more invitations, more information, more involvement, and more investment opportunities.

Communicating the case differently:

The *membership materials* are designed to be fun, interactive, family oriented, and to "sell" the economics of joining. A colorful brochure is mailed each spring to members and prospective members, with heavy emphasis on prospects who live near the zoo. The direct mail packages help to keep renewals high. They also encourage members to upgrade to a higher level of membership, with guest privileges. These economics can be more clearly articulated in print than in a verbal exchange. Nevertheless, on-site promotion at the zoo entrance and ticket booths is key; when the visitor can see that a membership may actually be less than the day's admission for a family of four, zoo memberships sell themselves.

The *sponsorship materials* are designed to evoke emotion, and a quick response; people are asked to "give." The color red is used throughout, close-cropped photos feature favorite animals, copy is limited, and emphasis is placed on the "chart" of benefits. Special-occasion giving is emphasized—birthdays, holidays, Mother's Day, etc. Sponsorship is promoted through the mail, on-site, and as seasonal "inserts" in corporate partner publications. Mail solicitation is the most appropriate communication vehicle, given the complexity of the offer—each animal category is priced differently, with different corresponding premiums.

The *annual giving materials* are designed to communicate a "conservation" message, with earthy colors, and sketches rather than photos. People are invited to become part of the Conservation Circle, a status more important to the zoo's mission than membership or sponsorship. The brochures are available on-site, but donors are telephoned for renewal, and upgrading, becoming more personalized as the gifts grow in size and frequency.

A mini-campaign strategy was instituted to invite donors to make a second annual gift when the zoo had an unexpected opportunity to purchase a herd of Saiga antelope from Russia. A personalized appeal was mailed to high-potential prospects, articulating a compelling and urgent case for a rare opportunity. The appeal was targeted to current annual donors, members of six years or more, and repeat animal sponsors. This first-time designated appeal generated an extra $25,000 from individuals, foundations and businesses who had not previously supported the zoo.

The timeline for all three cases is found in Exhibit 5–8.

Exhibit 5-8 Case Communications Matched with Zoo Constituencies

The Conservation Circle: Annual Giving	
Donor Profile	**Case Communications**
Philanthropic	Conservation messages
Middle-aged, middle-class	Earthy, environmental design
Interested in conservation	Personalized appeals
Community minded	Designated cases

Animal Sponsorship	
Donor Profile	**Case Communications**
Young families, professionals	Evokes emotion
Interested in tangible benefits	Photos of animals
Looking for a gift to give	Focus on premiums
Love animals	Emphasis on occasion giving

Zoo Membership	
Donor Profile	**Case Communications**
Young families	Creative packaging
Live near the zoo	Emphasis on fees and dollars saved
Interested in the economics	Mass market delivery systems
Are joiners	Easy response device

Courtesy of Minnesota Zoo, Apple Valley, Minnesota.

References

Ferguson-Patton, K. 1995. Saying what donors want to hear. *New Directions for Philanthropic Fundraising* 10: 89–98.

Fink, J. 1990. Philanthropy and the community. In *Critical issues in American philanthropy: Strengthening theory and practice,* edited by J. Van Til and Associates. San Francisco, CA: Jossey-Bass.

Harvey, J.W., and K.F. McCrohan. 1990. Changing conditions for fund raising and philanthropy. In *Critical issues in American philanthropy: Strengthening theory and practice,* edited by J. Van Til and Associates. San Francisco, CA: Jossey-Bass.

Kelly, K.S. 1994. Building fund-raising theory: An empirical test of four models of practice. *Essays on Philanthropy* 12.

Kotler, P., and A.R. Andreasen. 1987. *Strategic marketing for nonprofit organizations.* 3d ed. Englewood Cliffs, NJ: Prentice-Hall.

Lord, J.G. 1981. *Philanthropy and Marketing.* Cleveland, Ohio: Third Sector Press.

Mixer, J.R. 1993. *Principles of professional fundraising: Useful foundations for successful practice.* San Francisco, CA: Jossey-Bass.

Nichols, J.E. 1995. *Global demographics: Fund raising for a new world.* Chicago: Bonus Books.

Payton, R.L., H.A. Rosso, and E.R. Temple. 1991. Toward a philosophy of fund raising. In *Taking fund raising seriously: Advancing the profession and practice of raising money,* edited by D.F. Burlingame and L.J. Hulse. San Francisco, CA: Jossey-Bass.

Rosso, H.A. 1991. *Achieving excellence in fund raising.* San Francisco, CA: Jossey-Bass.

Appendix 5-A

Sample Case Communications

A Social Service Agency

Brochure

Family & Children's Service
The School Success Program

Family & Children's Service

*Unleashing the potential
of our littlest ones . . .*

*"For equality of opportunity to become real,
education must enable and encourage children
to become more than they thought they could
be . . .to choose, in fact, an 'improbable
destiny.'"*
　　　　　–Patricia Graham
　　　　　Harvard School of Education

*"We're either going to see these kids in the
schools—or on the streets. With this school
success program, there's a better chance that
school will win out."*
　　　　　–Patti Frisch, board member,
　　　　　Family & Children's Service

*"Education is not the filling of a pail, but the
lighting of a fire."*
　　　　　–William Butler Yeats

*"All who have meditated on the art of
governing mankind have been convinced that
the fate of empires depends on the education of
youth."*
　　　　　–Aristotle

(Brochure Front & Back)

Family & Children's Service's Approach to
School Success

Our *school success program* began just three
years ago, as an effort to help children who
were failing in school—or simply weren't
showing up. Our goal today is to link families with teachers and schools, and in the
process build stronger communities. With
100 years of history in the human services,
Family & Children's Service recognizes that
responsibility-taking is necessary if our
communities are going to survive, and
thrive.

This idea of providing families with the
tools and resources to help themselves is
not a new concept, but it is especially hard
work. It means that our progress is slow,
like growing up . . .a baby step at a time. It
also means that our successes are life-
changing . . . breaking the cycle of dysfunc-
tion, one child and one family at a time.

How do we measure the importance and
the impact of this work? First, in the outcomes—our results show measurable improvement, and behavior changes. Our
families are taking responsibility for their
children and themselves, and they are suc-
ceeding on their own. Second, in dollars
saved. For every child who might otherwise
end up in foster care at the cost of $12,000
a year, our cost of $2,000 seems like a bar-
gain. Can we measure the cost of lost potential?

We wish we could do more. The number of
children we serve is entirely dependent on
the amount of philanthropic support we receive from the community. That's the true
bottom line.

Terrence J. Steeno
President and Chief Executive Officer

Courtesy of Family & Children's Service, Minneapolis, Minnesota.

One Child's Story

Seven-year-old Lisa got up that morning after falling asleep sometime after midnight. She stepped over her mom and some other people sprawled on her living room floor. She made her way to the refrigerator, only to find it empty. She put on yesterday's dirty clothes and headed for the bus stop. On the way, she heard taunts from the neighborhood drug dealers and prostitutes. Some days, she didn't go to school at all.

That was the day before Family & Children's Service heard about Lisa from her teacher. Ten months have gone by. Lisa's home life is more nurturing and, consequently, her school performance is stronger.

At Family & Children's Service, Lisa's mom has learned how important she is to Lisa both at home and at school. She's there now to get her up in the morning, and she knows Lisa has to get to bed at a reasonable hour at night. She helps with homework, monitors her TV, talks to her teachers at school. As a family, Lisa and her mom come to family events at Family & Children's Service and have made new friends.

Lisa and her mom have learned a new way of life.

(Brochure Inside)

Courtesy of Family & Children's Service, Minneapolis, Minnesota.

Brochure

The Family Center
A place for parents to stay by their critically ill child.

Each year more than 600 children from Minnesota and surrounding states are treated in the Pediatric Intensive Care Unit (PICU) at Children's Hospital of St. Paul. These children have medical crises caused by accidents or sudden illnesses and require sophisticated care to save their lives.

At times like these a parent needs to be close by. There is, however, no place within the PICU for them to stay.

To address this problem a task force was formed of parents, physicians, nurses and child specialists. They researched how other hospitals resolved the need for overnight accommodations. When interviewing parents here, it was discovered that parents were creating make-shift beds by pushing two chairs together or sleeping in staff offices on the floor. Because most of these parents are facing large financial obligations related to their child's illness, they can't afford to leave the hospital—emotionally or financially.

After reviewing research which confirms that children recover faster when surrounded by love ones, the task force recommended we build THE FAMILY CENTER.

THE FAMILY CENTER will be built this year and will be located on a roof-top, just steps away from the PICU.

–Five fully-equipped bedrooms will be built for family members to stay overnight, change clothes, make phone calls and have private time away from others. There will be private bathrooms, including separate showers, complete with accommodations for people with disabilities.

–A large waiting space, divided into three distinct gathering areas, will provide a calming atmosphere for families to quietly wait out their child's medical crisis.

–A dining room will allow families to have meals together without leaving the PICU area, so they can be reached by the medical staff.

Families will not be expected to pay for the use of THE FAMILY CENTER, but their stay will be limited to the time their child's life is in immediate danger.

Your help is essential. Contributions are our only source of funding.

Children's Hospital development committee and volunteers are committed to raising $454,000 to begin construction this fall. Nearly half of this project is already funded, but there is still $229,000 to raise during the next few months to make this dream a reality. Won't you help us provide a place to stay for parents whose children are critically ill?

Send your contribution today, or call 220-6059 for more information.

Courtesy of Children's Health Care. Children's Hospital of St. Paul merged with Minneapolis Children's Medical Center in June 1994 to form Children's Health Care.

THE FAMILY CENTER Budget

Family Lounge $9,141
  Furniture
    2 Love Seats, 3 Chairs, 3 End Tables, 2 Lamps, 10 Side Chairs
    2 Tables, 1 Coffee Table, 4 Conference Chairs
  Construction
    Ceiling, Floor, Glass, Molding, Cabinetry, Mechanical/Electrical   84,249
Dining Area
  Furniture
    Table, 4 side Chairs, Microwave, Refrigerator, Television, Coffee Pots   2,511
  Construction
    Ceiling, Floor, Glass, Molding, Cabinetry, Mechanical/Electrical   37,635
Five Bedrooms
  Furniture (each room)
    2 Beds, 1 Desk, 1 Side Chair, 1 Lamp   ($1,780/5)   8,900
  Construction (each room)   ($45,281/5)   226,405
Contingency   25,000
Architectural Fees   60,000

TOTAL EXPENSES   453,841
Grants/Gifts Received as of 6/1/93   224,375

BALANCE NEEDED FROM PHILANTHROPY $229,466

Courtesy of Children's Health Care. Children's Hospital of St. Paul merged with Minneapolis Children's Medical Center in June 1994 to form Children's Health Care.

Brochure

We Believe Fund
1993 Employee Campaign

We believe employees care deeply about the children we serve.

We believe the family is critical to a child's recovery and that the best way to help a sick child is to help their family cope.

We believe employees can be of great help to families through simple acts of kindness.

Employees like yourself have been very generous donors to Children's Hospital. Past campaigns have supported programs to protect abused children, provide charitable care in our clinic, and to build the Launching Pad. Because of your support, Children's Hospital continues to provide the very best and most innovative health care to the children of our community.

This year employee campaign volunteers have elected to raise $35,000 to create the *We Believe Fund*. This fund will provide immediate, emergency grants to needy families in distress. When a family is coping with a child's serious injury or illness, it is often the simple things that can make a dramatic difference. For instance:

– Buying safety cabinet locks for a Southeast Asian mother whose 2-year-old was poisoned with cleaning supplies.

– Provide a manual suction pump for a boy with a tracheostomy whose home is without electric power.

– Buying a helmet for a boy who has seizures so he'll be safe both in the hospital and at home.

– Provide an answering machine for a single mother of four who needs to receive frequent, timely lab results and instructions for her sons's chemotherapy.

– Pay the phone hookup charges so a family can ask for frequent and immediate guidance on he care of their premature infant now that she's home.

continues

continued

Suggestions for family assistance grants can come from *any* employee and be acted upon quickly. Simple guidelines will be set up and reviewed by a rotating committee of employee campaign volunteers. Requests would be phoned to child and Family Services for an immediate decision and allocation of cash. Each grant would come with a card acknowledging that it comes from employees.

In the first year we expect to award between $7,000 and $8,000 in grants. With future grants from employees we hope to finish endowing the *We Believe Fund* so that invested principal will generate enough income to fully fund future grants.

Participation in our annual employee campaign is voluntary. Your gift should be given freely and will be accepted as your willingness to be listed as an annual supporter of Children's Hospital. If you would like your annual gift to be used in some other manner than the *We Believe Fund* please note this on your card. Your wishes will be honored.

Payroll deduction is an easy way to make your gift. Your pledge will be spread out over 26 pay periods, with a portion taken out of each check. Your gift is tax deductible.

Children's Hospital of St. Paul
345 North Smith Avenue
St. Paul, MN 55102

Courtesy of Children's Health Care. Children's Hospital of St. Paul merged with Minneapolis Children's Medical Center in June 1994 to form Children's Health Care.

Brochure

Minnesota Zoo Animals Depend On People Too

A Couple of Good Reasons to ADOPT

When you ADOPT an animal at the Minnesota Zoo, you help defray the cost of feeding and caring for more than 2,800 wild, wonderful creatures who live here. That's really important, because our grocery bill alone amounts to more than $250,000 each year. Of course you get to choose the animal you most want to help. The larger your sponsorship, the more food you buy.

When you ADOPT an animal as a GIFT for someone else, you are doing something doubly important. You are making someone else feel special, plus you are helping your favorite animal at the Zoo. There are lots of good reasons to give an ADOPT GIFT: Father's or Mother's Day, Valentines Day, birthdays, graduation, retirements, and so on.

And, your ADOPT sponsorship lasts for an entire year.

A Bunch of Wild Reasons to ADOPT

When you ADOPT an animal in your name or as a gift, you get a bunch of stuff that shows how important you are. With each level of ADOPT sponsorship, from $25 to $1,000, the recognition items grow in number. Think how much fund you will have receiving all this stuff, or giving it to someone else sas an ADOPT GIFT.

There's everything from a personalized ADOPT certificate, a refrigerator magnet, a color photo of your animal, a subscription to the Zoo's newsletter, name recognition on our animal's exhibit and your level of sponsorship. Now that's pretty wild.

It's Easy to ADOPT

All you have to do is:

1) Choose your favorite animal.
2) Select your ADOPT sponsorship level.
3) Fill out the application—and we'll do the rest.

We'll send out the ADOPT recognition items right away; and/or we'll personalize your ADOPT GIFT package for the person and the occasion you choose. We'll put your contribution to good use, and we'll make sure your animal never goes hungry.

Or, you can call our ADOPT program manager at (612) 431-9216 or 1-800-366-7811. It's just that easy.

Courtesy of Minnesota Zoo, Apple Valley, Minnesota.

ADOPT Sponsor's Benefits	$25	$50	$100	$250	$500	$1000
	Your Contribution					
A personalized certificate	✔	✔	✔	✔	✔	✔
Animal fact sheet	✔	✔	✔	✔	✔	✔
Refrigerator magnet	✔	✔	✔	✔	✔	✔
Invitation to the ADOPT annual family reunion	✔	✔	✔	✔	✔	✔
Recognition on the Zoo's ADOPT sponsor board	✔	✔	✔	✔	✔	✔
Framed 3 × 5 color photograph of your animal		✔	✔	✔	✔	✔
A hand-painted animal figurine		✔	✔	✔	✔	✔
10% discount coupon at the Minnesota Zoo store			✔	✔	✔	✔
Subscription to *Minnesota Zoo* newsletter			✔	✔	✔	✔
Plaque with photo of your sponsored animal				✔	✔	✔
Recognition on Zoo Donor Wall					✔	✔
Name recognition on your animal's exhibit						✔

Courtesy of Minnesota Zoo, Apple Valley, Minnesota.

June 26, 1996

Linda Johnson
Box 22
8656 Ivywood
Cottage Grove, MN 55016-0022

Dear Ms. Johnson:

Recently we made a critical decision that, if all goes well, will have long-lasting consequences for generations to come. Because you are an active supporter of the Minnesota Zoo, we want you to be among the first to know, and if possible, to help.

This spring, we had the rare opportunity to acquire eight Saiga antelope from Russia. While this purchase was not part of our 1996 acquisition plan, it is one that is crucial to the Saiga's survival.

Threatened in its Homeland
The Saiga antelope is seriously threatened in its native territory of Russia and Mongolia. The populations are declining at an alarming rate for several reasons. The Saiga are illegally over-hunted for their horn, which is thought to be an aphrodisiac. Their habitat is overgrazed by domestic livestock. What was once grassland is becoming desert—20 percent has been reduced to blowing sand.

Fewer than 500 of one subspecies can be found in Mongolia, while the number of the Russian subspecies is a mere 15 percent of its peak population. Forty years ago, populations of this species ranged in the several millions.

The Chance of a Lifetime:
The opportunity acquire Saiga antelope was not planned. But—we knew the precarious nature of the species—and we knew that our professional contact with Russia is planning to retire soon.

The facts are clear. There are no viable herds of Saiga in the zoo world. There are only a few female Saiga in another zoo in the United States, the San Diego Zoo. Without this acquisition, long-term genetic diversity to ensure their future will be lost.

Faced with a now or never situation, we responded quickly when the time came. We made arrangements with our Russian contact to secure five females and three males. Our short-term goal is to open a new exhibit area for the Saiga this fall. Our long-term goal is to provide Saiga to other zoos interested in managing this special species.

continues

continued

An Unforeseen Opportunity and Expense:
Seizing an opportunity like this one seems most reasonable given the unusual circumstances. But, it does present a challenge as well. The purchase of eight Saiga antelope for the Minnesota Zoo is $68,000. Since this cost is not part of our current budget, it will likely impact other budgeted projects—unless we can cover the costs through extra contributions.

Our hope is that we will be able to raise all, or a portion of the unforeseen costs through special gifts from friends of the Zoo. We count you as part of this group. We have created a new, restricted account for this purpose, and we are embarking on a special campaign effort. The **Save the Saiga Fund** will help underwrite the acquisition costs, as well as future operating costs.

Your previous contribution demonstrated that you have an active interest in the Minnesota Zoo. Because of that interest, we are inviting you to be one of the first supporters of the **Save the Saiga Fund.** We hope that you will, very simply, help to establish a viable Saiga herd that will be here for future generations to enjoy.

Another Success in Conservation:
There is a two-fold benefit here—in animal conservation and public education. We will save a threatened population of Saiga antelope, and at the same time, be able to educate people about the threats to animals throughout the world.

The Minnesota Zoo is immensely proud of its position as a world-wide conservation leader.

- The Zoo is the international conservation headquarters for the world's population of tigers.

- The Zoo adopted a park in Sumatra to preserve one of the last homelands for the Sumatran tiger. Much-needed equipment is being purchased to help park rangers fight the war against poaching.

- The Zoo has worked with the Minnesota Department of Natural Resources and Hennepin County Parks to reintroduce more than 240 trumpeter swans to their native habitat in Minnesota.

Your interest in the Minnesota Zoo is very important. A tax-deductible gift will not only be greatly appreciated—it will demonstrate that the Zoo should seize opportunities of this magnitude. After all, it's really for generations to come.

Sincerely,

Kathryn R. Roberts, Ph.D.
Executive Director
Minnesota

Nicolas Reindl
Northern Trail Curator
Minnesota

Courtesy of Minnesota Zoo, Apple Valley, Minnesota.

Chapter 6

Strategies for Success: Annual Giving Objectives

Objectives for Annual Giving: An Organization's Lifeline and Lifeblood

Annual giving programs are an organization's *lifeline* to the community. By making

annual gifts, people show their interest and confidence in an organization. In the process, donors become advocates for *their* organization and afficionados for the cause. When an organization's value is affirmed by a significant number of annual donors, it sends an encouraging and influential message to others—community leaders, granting organizations, public entities, and the like.

Annual giving programs are also the *lifeblood* of an organization's charitable mission. Because annual gifts come predominantly from *individuals*, they are a source of financial and psychosocial support for which there is no substitute. Annual gifts underwrite unrestricted operating expenses, restricted programs and services, new service initiatives, capital improvements, and the purchase of specialized equipment. They are a predictable resource; annual donors keep on giving year after year out of institutional loyalty, as if by habit. Annual donors are the ones who care most about an organization for personal reasons, make decisions voluntarily and independently of others, and are willing to be invested and involved in ways that other funders cannot or will not. Once established, an annual giving program can produce all the individual donors and dollars needed for larger and ambitious endeavors: a major capital campaign, an endowment drive, and a planned giving program.

As *giving opportunities,* annual fund-raising projects are exciting, satisfying, challenging, and rewarding. Exciting, because they use a vast array of solicitation techniques in enterprising combinations. Satisfying, because they involve a diverse group of people—board members, volunteers, program staff, donors, grantors, and vendors. Challenging, because they entail the management of multiple strategies, techniques, systems, policies, and procedures. Rewarding, because they result in long-lasting relationships that produce an ongoing stream of financial support for worthy programs and services to people in need. An annual integrated development program draws on both management abilities and leadership skills.

Annual campaigns generate both small gifts (under $25) and large gifts (over $10,000) from a few donors (under 100) to many (over 25,000). These gifts constitute between 10 and 80 percent of an organization's annual operating budget, depending on the type of organization and the emphasis given to the annual giving pro-

gram. The potential is enormous—there are no limitations to the kind or number of fund-raising efforts (campaigns) run on an annual basis nor are there time constraints. Gifts can be solicited and received 365 days a year.

However, programs that are run every year, year in and year out, demand a high level of energy, enthusiasm, and attentiveness. This continuing dependence on energy and expertise *can* wear people down. When an annual giving program has reached its desired goals, the natural response is to let up and take things for granted. Annual giving programs left to implementation by technology or relegated to the youngest and least experienced fund raisers will plateau and deteriorate without warning. The magnitude of the task of systems management easily camouflages the real problem: the need to improve the quality of *relationships*, rather than the *mechanics*.

Staff and volunteers need to be flexible, creative, and persistent from start-up to wind-down and then start all over again. *Continuous quality improvement* is a must; without it a program will succumb to the status quo and become weary and ineffectual. Experience tells us that all annual giving programs need to be nurtured and rejuvenated occasionally. Now and then, they benefit from a complete overhaul.

The real challenge for today's practitioners is to create an annual giving program with a unique *personality*, one that mirrors their organization's culture, life stage, and resources. Each organization's distinctiveness necessitates that its annual giving program have its own style, look, feel, and tone—one that is easily recognizable and consistent, year to year. Although there are a number of tried and true annual giving models to copy (see Chapter 2), even these models must be adapted and realigned if they are to function at their best. What works for one organization does not routinely work for another. There are no quick formulas for success in annual giving, save hard work, strategic focus, and ample resources. Marketing savvy will set one apart from another—fortunate is the organization with an entrepreneur who will take the annual giving program apart and put it back together again, breathing life into it in imaginative ways. Annual giving is unmistakenly both art and science.

The Annual Giving Models— A Continuum

The various annual giving models are presented as a continuum in Exhibit 6–1. They range from a once-a-year campaign to support the general operating budget to a series of mini-campaigns for designated cases targeted at segmented constituencies. As pointed out in Chapter 4, the fund-raising approach can vary depending on the organization's life stage, from one that is organization-focused (begging), to campaign-focused (selling), to donor-focused (marketing).

Not only will the philosophies and strategies of these annual campaigns differ, but so will the implementation tactics. The annual effort may be organized and run by a team of volunteers who solicit others or be implemented by staff who use personal and telephone solicitations, direct mail, and special events, or there may be any combination of the above.

A first-time annual giving program will likely begin in a simple way, with limited strategies and methodologies. It will develop over time to a more comprehensive effort that garners an increased number of prospects/donors. It takes between four and five years before donor giving patterns are set and reliable, predictive relationships are built. Although one seasoned annual giving program may use every conceivable approach and technique, another may rely on only a few basic approaches with proven effectiveness. The objective is to achieve an *integrated development program* that does the following:

- understands donors, their motivations, and their interests—through research

- segments donors into similar, discrete constituencies
- selects and communicates specific needs to different donor segments, by way of an exchange
- selects different fund-raising vehicles based on the donor segment
- provides a form of *case management* for each donor, allowing each to move more naturally into a relationship of giving and receiving
- provides a high level of donor communications, recognition, and stewardship

How do you determine the best strategies for your organization? You ask a lot of questions, elicit a lot of answers, and then proceed. This process is similar to buying a pair of gloves in advance of winter. As a consumer, you need to consider the appropriate color, size, style, source, design, durability, and price for you. If you make the right decisions, you will weather the storm in style. If the gloves don't fit right, you will have wasted precious resources, and worse, your hands will get cold.

We are reminded once again that **fund raising is a dynamic, strategic, problem-solving process—one that requires shopping around (analysis), considering options (planning), making decisions (execution), living the consequences (control), and reviewing results (evaluation).**

Annual giving programs have three main objectives: **donor acquisition, donor renewal, and donor upgrading** (Exhibit 6–2). These objectives encompass a functional series of steps that form relationships, from the initial stage to the actualization stage. The notion is simple— people move from prospects to *first-time donors;* first-time donors move to *repeat donors;* repeat donors move to *established donors;* established donors move to *loyal, frequent donors;* loyal, fre-

Exhibit 6–1 Annual Giving Continuum

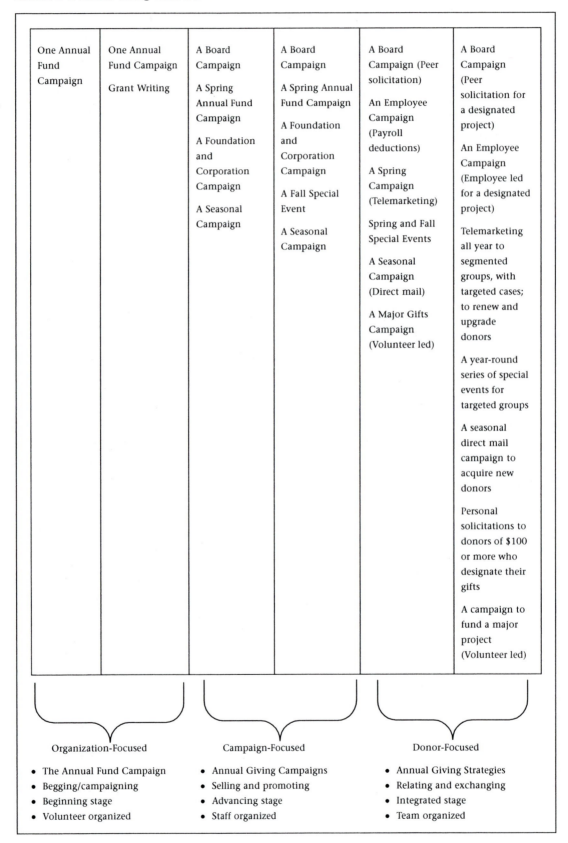

One Annual Fund Campaign	One Annual Fund Campaign Grant Writing	A Board Campaign A Spring Annual Fund Campaign A Foundation and Corporation Campaign A Seasonal Campaign	A Board Campaign A Spring Annual Fund Campaign A Foundation and Corporation Campaign A Fall Special Event A Seasonal Campaign	A Board Campaign (Peer solicitation) An Employee Campaign (Payroll deductions) A Spring Campaign (Telemarketing) Spring and Fall Special Events A Seasonal Campaign (Direct mail) A Major Gifts Campaign (Volunteer led)	A Board Campaign (Peer solicitation for a designated project) An Employee Campaign (Employee led for a designated project) Telemarketing all year to segmented groups, with targeted cases; to renew and upgrade donors A year-round series of special events for targeted groups A seasonal direct mail campaign to acquire new donors Personal solicitations to donors of $100 or more who designate their gifts A campaign to fund a major project (Volunteer led)

Organization-Focused

- The Annual Fund Campaign
- Begging/campaigning
- Beginning stage
- Volunteer organized

Campaign-Focused

- Annual Giving Campaigns
- Selling and promoting
- Advancing stage
- Staff organized

Donor-Focused

- Annual Giving Strategies
- Relating and exchanging
- Integrated stage
- Team organized

Exhibit 6–2 Annual Giving Programs and Objectives: Building and Managing Exchange Relationships

---

DONOR ACQUISITION

Build the base of support (identify and invite).

- Identify and acquire donors.
- Initiate an exchange relationship.
- Raise unrestricted and restricted funds.
- Identify and involve volunteers.

DONOR RENEWAL

Strengthen the base of support (inform, involve, and interest).

- Renew donor support annually.
- Communicate with and inform donors.
- Give donors choices.
- Build donor loyalty.
- Recognize and reward donors.

DONOR UPGRADE

Increase the base of support (invest and inspire).

- Cultivate donors to increase giving.
- Form lasting relationships.
- Expand giving options.
- Involve volunteer leaders.
- Identify major annual gift donors.

Exhibit 6–3 Donor Levels of Giving

FIRST-TIME DONOR:
  One year
REPEAT DONOR:
  Two to three years
ESTABLISHED DONOR:
  More than three years*
LOYAL DONOR:
  Larger gift every year and/or gives frequently*
COMMITTED MAJOR DONOR:
  Gives every year in a major way*
ACTUALIZED DONOR:
  Achieves aspirations through philanthropy*
LAPSED DONOR:
  Has not given during the past three or more years

*Core group.

---

quent donors move to fully committed *major donors*; and finally major donors move to *donor actualization*. Exhibit 6–3 describes the donor levels of giving. This sequence is not an absolute one, but it is one that works most of the time (see relationship section in this chapter). And it does not imply that later steps are less important than earlier ones: The first objective, donor acquisition, does not take precedence over subsequent objectives of renewal or upgrading, but rather quite the opposite.

There are two ways to visually present an annual giving program: by using the pyramid (Figure 6–1) or the circle (Figure 6–2). Both articulate the sequential nature of relationship development; depending on your conceptualization style (as translated to your teaching style), you may prefer one way over another.

Donor Acquisition: Building the Base of Support

A donor acquisition program may be the fund raiser's most rewarding and most risky solicitation strategy. The potential for success is great, but the results are unpredictable. First, acquisition requires that more prospects be approached than will become donors. As such, acquisition is dominated by mass marketing techniques that use expensive commodities, such as staff, technology, and printed materials. Even so, an acquisition program is necessary and, over time, well worth its cost, time, and energy.

In many ways, donor acquisition works like a child's sand toy. Sand is poured into a sifter, allowing small particles to pass through and capturing the larger ones, along with a few pebbles and sea shells. For both novice and seasoned professionals, it takes a lot of patience and effort to locate a few perfectly sized "treasures." The difference is in the experience; the seasoned professional is a little more discriminating about where to do the sifting.

In practice, successful donor acquisition is more than a process to gain donors; it is a process that selectively acquires *high-potential donors*. A sophisticated, *selective* acquisition program targets the most qualified prospects—those who have the potential to become fully engaged and invested in the organization over time. The goal of donor acquisition is to increase the organization's base of support, not to generate an immediate profit. Initially, the cost of acquiring new donors may be as high as $1.50 for every $1.00 received, but that expense becomes an investment when it is recovered many times over through renewals. Each subsequent renewal is less costly to implement, generating greater net returns with each repeat gift.

A donor acquisition program has four steps, which are repeated in the renewal and the upgrade process with donors who are then *prospects* for repeat and larger gifts:

1. *identification* of prospects
2. *cultivation* of prospects
3. *solicitation* of prospects (when the organization asks) and the actual *acquisition* of donors (when the donor responds)
4. *appreciation* given to donors

Prospect Identification: Seeing Who Is Interested

Prospect research, focus groups, and volunteer rating and ranking sessions help uncover prospects with the highest potential (see Chapter 4). Although most prospect identification is done by the development team, some of the

> A sophisticated, selective acquisition program targets those prospects who have the potential to become fully engaged and invested.

most successful leads come from people in the field: donors, staff, and volunteers. As representatives of the organization, volunteers and staff are the first to hear from others, "Oh, you are involved in that organization—I think they are doing a wonderful job," or "I had such a great experience there." These comments are really *signals* of special interest—the person has identified *him- or herself* as a prospect. When these prospect names and circumstances are reported to the development office, they can be incorporated effectively into the acquisition process. This personal kind of prospecting occurs without plan per se, depending instead on a philanthropic culture of well-informed, conscientious ambassadors and listeners who value their role in the philanthropic process.

Prospect Cultivation: Creating Awareness

The really successful acquisition program involves everyone in the organization, every day of the year—not just in prospect identification, but in prospect/donor *cultivation*. And the efforts are always focused on prospects with the strongest connections, the greatest interest, and the best ability.

Cultivation is a method of making prospects aware of the need for an organization's services and for their support. Awareness actually begins when the prospect is first introduced to the organization and cause, either through someone who is already involved, attendance at an event or organization activity, or communications from the organization. Awareness is *built (cultivation is occurring)* with high-quality, frequent, informal, and formal communications between the organization and the prospects.

The obvious goal of planful cultivation is to improve the chances of an acquisition by preparing the prospect for a solicitation. During cultivation, information is exchanged that will help the prospect better understand the organization's mission and case and simultaneously give the organization a better understanding of the prospect's interests. According to Mixer, "the prospect's cognitive interest in an agency's clients or service ranks as a fundamental prerequisite in the process of building awareness" (1993, 39).

Once prospects are adequately qualified (their needs and desires are known), these attributes become the focus of the cultivation process, which may be an interest in helping youth, reducing violence in the community, meeting other people, or improving self-esteem.

Cultivation *activities* are a key ingredient to bringing people together, and they can dramatically increase the probability of raising funds. Such activities are as diverse as the organization and may range from newsletters, invitational tours, luncheons hosted by board members, presentations made by program staff, to videotapes showing the programs in action. Events have a compounding effect, providing prospects with the opportunity to meet the organization's representatives, socialize with other donors, and learn first-hand about the organization's needs.

Remember that the more people know about an organization that is in their area of interest, the more likely they are to support it. The more relevant the information, the more compelling the case. The more urgent the need, the more responsive the prospect (or donor).

Prospect Solicitation and Donor Acquisition: Inviting Them to Join

For the sake of clarification, prospect *solicitation* is the process of inviting someone to consider making a philanthropic gift, and donor *acquisition* is the organization's way of saying the solicitation was successful. In reality, the organization controls only the solicitation process, whereas the donor determines whether he or she will be "acquired." Stories are told about donors who say, "I don't want to be asked—I just want to give." What they are probably saying is "there are certain ways that I don't like to asked, and I will give when the asking feels good." The balance between the asking (solicitation) and the giving (acquisition) is a delicate one. If the transaction is unbalanced—the asking is stronger than the giving—then the donor experiences a post-

giving dissonance, an "uncomfortableness," which negatively affects subsequent giving decisions. If the giving is stronger than the asking, the donor may have equal discomfort, wondering whether the organization really needed the gift because it was not asked for. Most donors fail to give a second gift (becoming lapsed donors) because they were not treated respectfully in the acquisition process or in post-acquisition stages (acknowledgement or appreciation). Either their satisfaction level was not met, or their interest level declined and they moved elsewhere. Only occasionally is a donor's decision not to give again related to financial ability, though often that is given as an excuse.

Prospects are new to your organization and thus need more information, a more compelling case, a solicitation that "breaks through," assurance that the organization is worthy and successful, and a communication tactic that elicits a response. In contrast, **donors** need information about how their last gift was used, recognition for that gift, a personal appeal to continue support, and assurance that they are part of a growing, successful concern.

A prospect solicitation/donor acquisition program is very complex—the chances of success in donor acquisition programming differ with the approach and the variables around timing, person, and place.

Not all prospects become donors the first time they are solicited. And some never become donors. The key is to solicit all prospects at least three times. Every qualified prospect should have the privilege of saying yes or no. It is a disservice not to solicit those who appear to be capable and interested in giving and a detriment to the building of a strong philanthropic community.

The success or failure of donor acquisition rests to a large extent on the quality of fund raisers homework, and follow-up work. Are prospects sufficiently *qualified?* Are the acquisition efforts designed properly to ensure a substantial "yes" response? How effective and efficient are the time allocated, money spent, and methodologies used? How satisfied are the donors with the philanthropic match and the relationship "services" (ultimately measured by renewal rates)? In other words, the success of a donor acquisition program is correlated directly to these factors:

- quality of the prospect (your research on motivational indicators)
- quality of the case (your case development and communications)
- influence of the solicitor or the vehicle (your choice of the external influences)
- image, mission, and vision of the organization (your institutional readiness)

A successful donor acquisition program is measured by the following:

- response rate
- number and level of the gifts received
- total amount of money raised
- effectiveness of each strategy and each vehicle
- amount of time spent, proportionately, on each activity
- total cost and net proceeds
- donor's satisfaction with the experience

Each campaign has individualized acquisition goals. For example, a college's annual campaign may include one strategy to "acquire 300 alumni as new donors at the $100 level from the graduating class of 1996" and another strategy to "acquire 50 new donors at the $500 level, who are parents of current alumni." Or a social service agency may embark on a special-purpose campaign to "acquire 250 new donors who have an interest in children, at the $25 level." *A donor acquisition effort requires very different strategies from a renewal or upgrade effort.*

Historically, fund raisers have spent a major portion of their time and effort on donor acquisition, seeking a few likely responders from a large pool of prospects. Because acquisition is hard and costly work, fund raisers traditionally tried to approach as many people as possible— "as long as we are going to make the effort, let's add more names." What followed was the need to use solicitation techniques that worked best with large numbers, such as mass appeals via direct mail or telemarketing. It seems incongru-ous that fund raisers traditionally use the least effective techniques for such important work as the acquisition of new donors. One wonders what the outcome might be if a donor acquisition program approached only as many prospects as *volunteers* could personally approach. For example, 300 *qualified* prospects personally solicited might produce a response rate of 33 percent or 100 donors versus a *staff*-driven direct mail campaign to 5,000 prospects, which might only yield a 2 percent response rate or 100 donors. The numerical outcome might be the same, but the effectiveness is dramatically different. What are the costs, benefits, and returns measured by quality versus quantity? In this example, is there a perceptible difference between the two sets of donors? Are the donors who were solicited personally better informed and more involved? Do they have a higher satisfaction level, and if so, will it improve their renewal rate? Or are the donors who were responsive to the direct mail effort equally as satisfied and committed? What then is the *measurable impact* of the post-acquisition steps of acknowledgment, recognition, information, and involvement?

Remember, a successful donor acquisition program does not waste resources soliciting non-responders, low responders, or people who have little in common with the organization or little evidence of interest in its mission. Experience has proven that nothing is gained by frequent acquisition of small or one-time donors who make token gifts without intentional investment. The idea is to solicit *qualified* prospects, to acquire *high-potential* donors, and to encourage the rest to support their favorite charities, whatever they may be.

> **A successful donor acquisition program does not waste resources soliciting non-responders, low responders, or people who have little in common with the organization.**

Donor Appreciation: Expressing Thanks

From the organization's point of view, the donor acquisition effort is *finished* when the donor is acquired. This is understandable, considering how much work has already occurred—prospect research, cultivation and communication activities, and the actual solicitation itself. However, from a donor's point of view, the relationship exchange progress is *just starting* with the gift. Having made their gift, donors are looking forward to the part of the exchange that benefits them—acknowledgment, recognition, information, education, and gift stewardship. This is not the time for the organization to sit back and celebrate; the money may have arrived, but the returns are still out. The acquisition process is but one day in the *life* of a philanthropic relationship. Every activity and interaction that follow contribute to the building of the desired relationship and complete the exchange.

How to Structure a Donor Acquisition Program

The following questions will stimulate your thinking about how to structure a donor acquisition program that is the most effective and efficient one for your organization.

Question 1: What Should Be the Size of Your Prospect Base?

The first consideration is the size of the prospect universe. Does your organization have a universe of 1,000 or a universe of 10,000? It goes without saying that there are many more people who will support your organization than presently do, but there is *not* an *unlimited* pool of donors.

How many prospects will it take to generate the desired number of donors per year—the prospect-to-donor ratio? How many donors are needed this year, next year, and in following years? How long will it take with the best techniques to sift the universe? How can you focus on the best possible prospects from the beginning?

Many ask, "How long do we keep a prospect on our mailing list, and how many times do we solicit them before taking them off?" The answer depends on the quality of the prospect. When organizations have a natural constituency, such as alumni, patients, clients, or members, they need to solicit each prospect on a regular basis, keeping each on the mailing list for all time. When organizations have to create a constituency, they should solicit these prospects several times and then assess the benefits of keeping them on the mailing list every few years. When a prospect becomes a donor, even a one-time donor, that individual should never be removed from the mailing list, unless he or she personally requests it. The stories of one-time $25 donors leaving a bequest to an organization support the value of keeping donors informed, even after they lapse in their giving. Their decision not to give may be due to financial insecurity, not disinterest. A "no" response to a solicitation means "not now"; it does not mean "no never." The key is to build a prospect list *only* of qualified, high-potential names.

Question 2: What is Your Organization's History of Donor Acquisition?

How many new donors has your organization acquired per year for each of the past few years? Is this number growing or flat? What is the average gift? Is it increasing in size or flat? What are the desired numbers/sizes given the organization's growth and recipients' needs? Chances are, the historical averages will be close to your current growth going forward, the trend line already exists unless monumental changes occur in the program.

Are you acquiring enough donors to replace those who are lost every year? How else will your donor base grow? Consider the benefits of improving retention rates, along with increasing your acquisition rates—for now.

Question 3: What Is the Profile of New Donors?

What are your donor characteristics (their profiles)? Are there commonalities among the donors, demographically and psychographically? Are they young, middle-aged, or older? Are they representative of the community as a whole, or do they come from a particular segment of the community? Do they have linkages with the organization or linkages with people who are close to the organization? Do they have the capacity, the giving potential needed in the future?

Once your organization has researched its existing donor profile, it is advisable to design and target acquisition programs that mirror previous successes—generating like donors. If your *desired* profile is different than the existing one, then acquisition efforts should be vastly different.

Question 4: Who Is Giving or Not Giving?

Is everybody in the family giving? Donor acquisition always starts with the organization's family, beginning with those closest to the center of the constituency circle and moving incrementally outward as appropriate. Reaching out to family first is a continuous process, not a one-time event. Every year there are *new people to solicit* within the organization's constituency circle—new board members, new employees, new clients, alumni, patients, new neighbors, new friends, and so on. Each requires a specialized approach, tailored to specific needs and interests; the same solicitation letter will no longer do.

In this area, *key problems* with a fund-raising program are: (1) members of the family who do not financially support the organization at a level that indicates it is a priority in their lives, (2) members of the family who do not speak out on behalf of the organization outside the organization, and (3) members of the family who are not willing to ask others for support.

Question 5: What Are the Acquisition Response Rates?

Assuming you are using selective acquisition methods, what are your response rates? Personal solicitation efforts to *qualified* prospects should be generating a 30 to 50 percent response rate, direct mail should be pulling a 10 to 15 percent response rate, and telephone marketing should be yielding a 15 to 25 percent response rate. If not, check the determinants listed earlier, especially the first one on the quality of the prospect list. Maybe your prospect research is inadequate. Maybe you have a lot of information—almost too much—but it has too little relevance (this is a big problem in the field). The answers to all these questions will clarify what works and does not work. For even one-way communications have a positive effect if someone is receiving them. Benchmarks are given in Exhibit 6–4.

Question 6: What Are the Acquisition Gift Levels?

What is the gift level of first-time donors? Is your program acquiring most of the donors in the lower levels ($25 or $50)? Although every size gift should be appreciated, and received graciously, are you sending a message that your organization needs "charitable" gifts or "philanthropic" gifts? A meaningful gift—one that probably took some thought and investment—is $100 or higher today. The idea is to acquire high-potential donors, or the cost of acquiring them will not be justified economically, even if there are other benefits. Should more time be spent acquiring donors at the top of the pyramid or the bottom?

Question 7: What Are Gifts for?

What are your annual gifts supporting? How many giving choices and pay options do you offer? Are more donors designating their gifts? Are certain programs more appealing than others? Donor acquisition includes every type of gift and every gift size. A first-time contribution may be in response to a personal, telephone, or mail

Exhibit 6–4 Benchmarks for Fund Development

Benchmarks for Fund Development

Fund Raising Activity	Reasonable Cost per Dollar Raised
New Donor Acquisition	
• Direct Mail	Up to $1.50
• Telephone	.50 to .65
• Personal Solicitation	.10 to .15
Donor Renewal	
• Direct Mail	Up to .75
• Telephone	Up to .50
• Personal Solicitation	10 to .15
Major Gifts	Up to .15
Planned Gifts (after 4–7 yrs)	Up to .15
Corporations & Foundations	Up to .20
Overall Fund Raising Program	.18 to .20
	(not to exceed .30)

Acquisition and Renewal Strategies	Response Rates:	
	Moderately Qualified	Highly Qualified
New Donor Acquisition		
• Direct Mail	.01 to .02%	10 to 15%
• Telephone	.05%	15 to 25%
• Personal Solicitation		30 to 50%
Donor Renewal		
• After 1 year	20%	50 to 60%
• After 3 years	40%	60 to 70%
• After 5 years	60%	80 to 90%
Donor Upgrade	15%	15 to 20%
Overall Fund Raising Program/Renewal		80 to 85%

solicitation or attendance at a benefit event. It may be paid in cash or pledged with monthly payments. It may be charged now or put in a bill box until the end of the year. The gift may be for unrestricted purposes, designated for a favorite program, or for a special purpose, such as a program initiative, replacement or new equipment, capital enhancements, or even endowment. It may be a gift to honor someone else.

A donor's first gift may be small, or it might be major. A good number of first-time gifts fall into the major gifts category; well-established organizations will regularly attract direct mail gifts of $1,000 or more. And there are numerous stories about a first gift in the $10,000 plus range, reinforcing the fact that the first gift is stimulated by the critical, urgent, and relevant nature of the case.

Question 8: What Is the Cost of Acquisition Efforts?

Now, consider how much money is spent on acquisition and how much is raised as a result. Has the acquisition effort been a break-even venture or a loss leader? If your acquisition program has a profit margin of any sort, it is probably worth the effort, and the cost. Finally, how much staff time is expended on donor acquisition? Given small returns, high costs, and limited staff and volunteer resources, is it not wise to expend more than 20 to 30 percent of staff time on donor acquisition? The greater portion of time, 70 to 80 percent, is spent more effectively on donor cultivation, renewal, and upgrading to major gift levels.

Question 9: Which Techniques Are Successful?

Which solicitation techniques do you use—the most effective ones or the easiest ones? What is the cost of each technique and the return on investment? Although certain techniques are not as cost effective as others, they are a necessary part of an integrated development program. However, total fund-raising costs should not exceed 30 percent of the amount raised.

For many organizations *direct mail* is the technique of choice for donor acquisition, despite the confirmed successful performance of more personal techniques. Perhaps fund raisers are quick to take the biggest, easiest way to acquire donors and the one "furthest from having to ask." Whatever the reason, let us remember that donor acquisition is our organization's invitation to potential donors to join an effort that is worthy of their support. Would we invite a new friend to our home with a computerized letter, a third-class stamp, and expect them to show? Or would we shop for the perfect invitation, write a note on it, hand-address it, and mail it first class? The fact is, we would probably call.

For many large national organizations, the most logical approach will be *direct mail*, given the size of the prospect base, the geographic limitations, and the lack of a volunteer base. Interestingly, such large organizations as the American Cancer Society use both direct mail (nationally) and personal solicitation (regionally), resulting in one of the most successful acquisition programs in the country. For a small social service agency just starting a development program, *personal or telephone solicitation* would seem to be the best mechanism to acquire new donors. For a college or university with a long-standing annual fund program, telephone solicitation by students has proven to be the most effective acquisition approach. Too, *telephone solicitation* is the preferred acquisition technique for hospitals and health care organizations and for others with natural constituencies. Although there are many solicitation options, there is no disagreement—*personal solicitation remains the most effective approach.*

The Practice of Thanking: The Acknowledgment Process

The relationship between the donor and the organization really begins in earnest when the gift is received. Prospect identification, cultivation, and the solicitation itself are important preliminary steps that set the stage for a social exchange relationship. However, there is no replacement for the exchange part of the relationship—when the donor begins to benefit—this is the thanking or *acknowledgment process*. The thanking process has two aspects: (1) acknowledging the gift in a timely way and (2) showing the appropriate kind and level of appreciation for the gift. *Donor recognition* comes later, by way of giving proper attention officially and publicly to the philanthropic act.

> **The thanking process involves acknowledging the gift in a timely way and showing the appropriate kind and level of appreciation.**

Having received a first-time gift, what are the important next steps? Who should do the thanking, and how should it be done? What do donors want and expect? **Donors want an acknowledgment that is personal, sincere, timely, and appropriate.**

As a rule, the practice of thanking should be *equivalent* to the practice of asking—if the gift was $100, the thank you should be "worth" $100. The prevailing practice is to thank a donor within 36 to 48 hours. A telephone call to say, "Your generous contribution just arrived—I wanted to let you know, right away, how much it is appreciated," will long be remembered. A call to a long-time donor to say, "Your loyal and generous support means a lot to us; I called to personally thank you," will reinforce the donor's interest and indicate the value of his or her part in the relationship. Conversely, do not thank a donor for a generous gift when it is not generous. We send mixed messages when we are too gracious just for the sake of it. It is important that the acknowledgment of appreciation be appropriate to the gift.

It only seems natural that the person who did the asking should also do the thanking. An official letter from the chief administrator is most appropriate, a personal note or a phone call from a board member or volunteer is always appreciated, and a follow-up report from the program director is a respectful gesture, one that will reinforce the gift's meaning. If the gift size is at a "club" level, the thank you should also include a certificate, a recognition item, or whatever else is appropriate. If the gift giver has more potential, the thank you might include a copy of the annual report, the last issue of the newsletter, an invitation to an upcoming event, a brochure on a program of interest, or business cards of those with whom contact is important. And if a gift comes unsolicited, the thank you should express surprise and appreciation that is *special*; this situation merits extra attention, as does a large first-time gift.

One thank you is expected. Two thank yous are impressive. Three thank yous are not too many over a period of several months if the gift size or the donor is significant to the organization.

Many organizations invite their volunteers to help thank donors. This is a way to help volunteers overcome their fear of soliciting and to impress on the donors that their gift is deeply appreciated, and needed. Volunteers may gather once a month or every quarter for a "thank-a-thon." Or staff may prepare thank-you letters for volunteers to sign on a weekly basis. If asked, volunteers may be willing to send their own personal notes to people they know. Every gift of $100 merits a quick thank-you phone call the same day it is received—how many might there be on any given day? What better way is there to let donors know they are special, find out what motivated them to give, and encourage them to give again. A donor survey is another method of eliciting information; this is best sent out immediately when interest is highest. Such a survey has two benefits: gathering information and sending a message at the same time that the donor is special and his or her opinions matter.

On the subject of personalization, a computer-generated "boiler-plate" thank-you letter is not a personal communication. Technology has streamlined much communication, but it has also undermined the human elements, and donors know the difference between a personal thank you and a computerized one. Fund raisers must allocate sufficient time and resources to the acknowledgment process if they want to retain a high percentage of donors in the renewal stage. It is the thanking and reporting that reinforce the donor's gift decision while setting the stage for a second gift. The marketing perspective is about exchange; receiving an acknowledgment (and recognition) is central to the transaction.

The final step in the donor acquisition process is to catalog as much information as possible about the donor and to set about the process of finding out a little more. A donor file should include these three elements:

1. *demographics:* name, address, phone number, and age
2. *giving history:* date and gift level, type, source, and designation
3. *psychographics:* relationships with organization or others, community involvement, and lifestyle, expressed values, and the like

This information belongs in a computer if the capability is present or in a manual file of sorts. Gather as much information as you are able for the purpose of establishing a closer relationship in the future. Record the date and signature of the thank you(s). If a telephone call is made to thank the donor, make notes in the file with any relevant information. If a survey was returned, record the significant data.

Donor Renewal: Strengthening the Base

A donor renewal program is more cost effective, efficient, and meaningful to an organization than a donor acquisition program, and, frankly, more important to the donor. The irony is that in the first few donor renewal cycles, donors may be more interested in us than we are in them. A fund-raising program built for the long term is one that focuses on donor retention, rather than short-term gains seemingly obtained through donor acquisition. This perspective, however, is not obvious in practice. Jim Greenfield (1994, 44) says, "The greatest sin of omission in fund raising is not paying attention to the people who already love us and, instead, chasing after those who we hope will begin to love us." A well-known fund-raising axiom says: "Your donors are your best prospects." Bottom line, it is better and easier to keep a donor than to acquire a new one.

Why is it that fund raisers allocate a greater portion of their resources to donor acquisition

to the detriment of donor renewal? A widespread problem, this becomes more harmful with time. Once a donor is lost for one or more years, the likelihood of renewal drops to 22 to 25 percent, which is not much higher than the probability of acquiring a new qualified prospect. The loss of one donor who gives $100 per year, say for 25 years, will be $2,500 or more (without annual increases and special gifts).

One reason why fund raisers spend more time on acquisition than renewal is the pressure that board members and administrators put to get more donors. Many are mistakenly under the impression that more is better, influenced by their own experience with the corporate sector's pursuit for market share. In the philanthropic sector, however, success is measured by the *value* of long-time donors who have relationships with their charities of choice, not by the numbers or the dollars. Practically speaking, current donors have the potential to give many more years than anyone anticipated, perhaps as many as 30 more years if they are in their fifties. At the same time, younger generations seem to be giving less as a group; on average, they are giving fewer but *larger* gifts to their favorite charities. Thus, keeping existing donors involved and engaged must be a key strategy.

Another reason behind the board's insistence to acquire new donors is the need for immediate dollars. A quick fix or crisis orientation to fund raising puts undue pressure on volunteers and fund-raising staff to go out and get the money, rather than to acquire friends and funds for the long term. One very startling fact: a philanthropic program will not grow if a donor is lost—to find a new donor may be five times as difficult as retaining a current donor (Nichols 1995).

Therefore, reassess the amount of time allocated to your renewal processes, and consider the relevance of the results, quantitatively (in dollars) and qualitatively (in relationships). The *middle* of an organization's giving pyramid has far more potential than the bottom, and it is the best place to focus if the goal is raising more money, rather than raising more donors. The primary objective in fund raising must be to form lasting relationships with donors whose willingness to solve problems grows more generous with every year and each gift.

Although the acquisition effort can be compared to sifting for treasures, the renewal effort can be compared to planting seeds. The gardener spends a little money to purchase perennial seeds, cultivates the soil before planting, arranges the seeds carefully in the flower bed, and fertilizes and waters them. Having made the original investment, the gardener needs only to take care of the flowers until they bloom. The following spring, the perennials reappear, ready to bloom again.

A renewal program is designed very differently and managed separately from the acquisition efforts. Renewal too is an objective, not a program in and of itself, with subgoals for each renewal aspect of each annual campaign. For instance, a campaign run every year at the same time would use

- a *different appeal* for acquiring donors
- a *slightly different appeal* for first-year renewing donors
- a *significantly different appeal* for third-year renewing donors
- a *highly personalized appeal* for mid-level and major donors

For different groups, it is *inappropriate* to send the same generic appeal. Not taking the time to write a personal letter or make a personal phone call to an established, loyal, or major donor is taking the donor and philanthropy for granted in the worst possible way—it is telling the donor that he or she is not special nor really needed.

Renewal and acquisition *do* have some similarities. Both articulate the case in rational and emotional ways. Both use the same techniques—personal, phone, and mail solicitations. Both are targeted for a particular group of people. Yet, renewals differ in four ways: (1) the level of segmentation, (2) the degree to which the solicitations are personalized, (3) the kind of

information given, and (4) the sequence of the solicitation with other communications.

The Level of Segmentation

Once a prospect becomes a donor, the marketing strategy changes. Because it is difficult to research prospect needs and interests, mass marketing acquisition techniques—direct mail or telephone marketing—are used. Not so with renewals. Research is much easier with donors, but more critical. Donors are accessible and willing to give information about themselves and others. With information about donors' particular interests, we are better able to make the appropriate distinctions and segment renewing donors into smaller constituent groups. Once segmented, the most appropriate solicitation strategies and techniques can be determined, which can vary from group to group.

- **Segmentation by Giving Levels and Cumulative Amounts:** Renewal is the place to differentiate donors whose gift is under $100, over $100, over $250, over $500, over $1,000, and so on. If a donor has been giving $100 per year for the past ten years, their loyalty is something that ought to be acknowledged in a special way. The higher the level, the higher the contact, the higher the personalization. Gift level designation is often linked to donor clubs, which function simultaneously as recognition and incentive mechanisms.
- **Segmentation by Number of Years (Longevity) and Gift Frequency:** Donors tend to fall into several giving categories, and each requires a different approach. The established, loyal, and committed donors constitute an organization's *core group* (noted by the asterisk in Exhibit 6–3), whom staff and volunteers treat as family, making regular contact, involving them in a variety of ways, and giving them special treatment and insider information. A sophisticated development program will

> A sophisticated development program will have an individual strategy for each donor in the core group.

have an individual strategy for each donor in the core group, as if each were a mini-campaign in themselves.

- **Segmentation by Giving Patterns and Original Source:** There is a need to differentiate donors by giving patterns, such as those who give monthly or those who give only at the end of the year. Another way to segment donors for renewal is by source—the way they originally became a donor; for example, a special event or a tribute gift.
- **Segmentation by Giving Designations and Interests:** Differentiating donors by their area of designation and interest is essential. For instance, don't invite a donor to make a contribution for emergency room services, when he or she originally made a contribution for the pediatric cancer program. Separate donors into as many interest groups as appropriate.
- **Segmentation by Linkage and Relationships:** Donors fall into many linkage or relationship groupings, which necessitate different types of appeals and different solicitation techniques. For example, there are board members, employees, physicians, clients, alumni, students, grandparents, neighbors, and vendors. Your organization has linkages unique to each, and relationships with different levels of potential.
- **Segmentation by Ability:** Donor renewals also need to be divided by ability. If your research indicates a particular donor has the ability to make a $1,000 gift, after having made a $100 gift the previous year, you would not want to send this donor the same appeal letter you send to the other $100 donors. This is the time to ask a peer volunteer to solicit this donor for a larger amount or a special project.

The Kind of Personalization

Renewal is not the time to "batch" donors; it is the time to treat each donor as an individual who is special to the organization. As compared to prospects, it is much easier to personalize communications to donors. First of all, when donors made their initial gift, they gave you an enormous amount of information about themselves—their preferred name(s), who sent the gift (who signed the check), what they are interested in (if they designated a particular service or responded to a particular appeal), the type of solicitation they are responsive to (personal, mail, or phone), and their level of interest (size of first gift).

With subsequent communications and especially at renewal time, there are many ways to personalize the messages. It may be the right time to use first names of both solicitor and donor. The renewal appeal should be personalized to make note of the donor's previous gift (size and designation) and its use (what happened as a result). Other personalized information can be added, such as reference to a previous phone call, a visit or tour, survey comments, or attendance at a special event.

> As donors move up the giving pyramid, so do the techniques. If the acquisition occurred by direct mail, renew with a personal letter; if acquired by personal letter, renew with a letter and a telephone call; if acquired by personal letter and telephone call, renew with a personal visit; and if acquired by personal visit, renew with a personal tour/lunch/meeting.

If a renewing donor gave as a result of a telephone solicitation, the renewal should be done by phone, with a mail follow-up. If the gift was solicited by a volunteer or staff person, the same person should seek the renewal.

Personalized In-Person Tips

- Greet the person as a friend; make no mistake about his or her name.

- Thank the donor again and again for being a friend of (name of organization).
- Be sure to thank the right person(s), who may or may not be the spouse of the donor.
- Never refer to gift amounts in a public setting.
- Take every opportunity to give recognition in front of others, as appropriate.

Personalized Telephone Tips

- Call to say thank you for a gift on the same day it is received.
- Leave a short message on the answering machine, without stating the amount of the gift.
- Call to personally invite the donor to a special event, after a printed invitation is mailed.
- As a courtesy, call as a reminder of an upcoming meeting.
- Never call at home during the dinner hour.
- Be sure to thank the right person(s).

Personalized Mail Tips

- Hand-write the donor's name, right over a "Dear Friend" salutation.
- Hand-address the outside envelope.
- Enclose a photo of a recipient with a notation on the back.
- Enclose a hand-written note thanking for the last gift by amount.
- Hand-sign the letter, and add a P.S.
- Enclose a donor report, with a list of names, and his or her name highlighted.

The Kind of Information

The actual renewal may be done in one visit, one call, or one letter—but the activities leading up to and following the renewal set the stage for other *yes responses*. The renewal process is designed to achieve a series of communication goals: interest, inform, involve, invest, and inspire.

To achieve those goals, several decisions must be made—how much information should be given, when, and what kind. The *how much* is determined by the level of the gift, the frequency of the giving, and the interest indicated by the donor. The *when* is determined by *how much*, after which a schedule is developed to coordinate all communications to ensure there is not too much and to eliminate duplication. Nothing offends a donor more than receiving duplicate mailings. Few donors, on the other hand, complain about receiving too much information, although their interest and its readability factor are determined by *what kind* of information. The general rule is that the longer, the larger, and the more invested a donor, the more important the quality of the information and its frequency.

What kind of information do donors want?

- whether the organization is doing what it said it would
- changes in the organization or its leadership
- new programs and ventures
- news of philanthropic activities
- the results of the program they supported
- the exact use of their gift
- who are the beneficiaries, with case/client examples
- what is needed in the future
- who else is giving and is involved

The Sequence of Other Communications

Once a prospect becomes a donor, it is as if he or she said, "I am interested in your mission; now show me what there is to be interested about." And once a donor goes on the organization's regular mailing list, it seems as if *everyone* in the organization now wants to communicate with him or her—the marketing department, the public relations department, the alumni association, the medical staff office, the program department that received the gift, the president's office, and the like. Now is the time to determine the appropriate type and amount of communications, as well as the timing and the sequencing for the following:

- project reports
- newsletters
- event invitations
- annual reports
- updates, fact sheets, and press releases
- other solicitations
- invitations to volunteer

Policies are needed so that communications from all departments are coordinated and approved by the development department. For instance, it may **not** be a good idea to mail a four-color magazine to donors under $100, though doing so may be quite appropriate for others on the mailing list, including some who are not donors. It would **not** be a good idea for every donor to receive a 30-page annual report; for lower-level donors, it is better to send an annual summary inside a newsletter. An inexpensive quarterly newsletter should be sent to all donors, as well as to qualified prospects. As a rule, it is **not** wise to mail two items within a few days or even weeks of each other—the subtle message is that the organization does not "have its act together" or "has money to burn," especially if the two could have been combined into one mailing.

As for solicitations, it is advisable to solicit every donor several times during the year, especially for different projects—a seasonal campaign, a tribute program, or a benefit event. The donor will decide which projects to support, but not to inform them of those projects is to exclude them from the opportunity of giving and from "being in the know."

> It is advisable to solicit every donor several times during the year, especially for different projects.

Thinking Like a Donor

More and more, as fund raising incorporates a marketing perspective, fund raisers are encouraged to take off their shoes and "put on their donors' shoes." This is not as easy as it seems, because people naturally look at the world from their point of view.

What Do Donors Feel?

Donors give in order to get. They do not want to feel like they are giving their money away—they want to *feel like they are investing it* and getting something in return that is bigger than their dollars. This is why the emphasis cannot be on the dollars per se or on the money the organization needs. The emphasis must be on the investment itself. As an investor, you want to know how your stock is doing. Is it competitive with other stocks (is the organization the community's charity of choice)? Who is investing the money, and are there gains? Is there a good return, and is it being spent wisely (was the stated purpose achieved)? As an investor, you want to know when the stock splits or if it is sold. Was the investment a wise one (did it make a difference), and is it time to reinvest? And donors want to know the costs associated with the management of their investment; how much is spent on overhead (what is the temporal efficiency)?

Donors naturally *feel attached* to their gift, they *feel entitled* to information about its use, and they *feel good* when there is a return on their investment—when they get something for it. Like all good investors, donors *feel a sense of ownership* for the institution and its work.

What Do Donors Think?

Having made a thoughtful gift, donors *think that everyone in the organization knows* who they are and what they did. Obviously this is not all that it seems—it would not be possible or practical for everyone to know the donor. Nor does it mean that donors expect to be placed on a pedestal for what they did; most donors prefer anonymity of a sort. But it is imperative that the *right* people know, remember, and act on the information they have about their organization's donors. The people who represent the organization—the administration, the program staff, the board of directors, and the volunteers—should receive regular reports of gifts received so that they are prepared to acknowledge and thank donors when they come into contact with them.

Like other consumer purchases, donors reflect on the wisdom of having made a decision to contribute to charity. They need reassurance, as with any purchase, that it was a good decision. Given that their decision had impact, they need to *be encouraged to think about making another gift* (and the sooner the better).

What Do Donors Want?

When fund raisers are philanthropists first, it is easy for us to understand what donors want, which is the same kind of things we want—thanks, thoughtfulness, respect, reminders, information, appreciation, and insider news. When unsure about what they want, we just have to ask donors, and they will tell us. According to Christine Graham,

> You owe your prospects respect, kindness, and appreciation. You should be frank and straightforward about the organization's needs when you solicit them, and grateful when they help. You should remember that it is the cause they are supporting, not your personal needs. Anytime you wonder how to deal with a prospect, put yourself in his or her place. How would you want to be treated? You and your prospects and donors are partners, working toward a shared goal. One of the most remarkable aspects of the nonprofit world is the focus on others. Learn to spear that generosity of spirit, which you certainly have for the beneficiary of your work, to your donors and prospects as well (Graham 1992, 44).

Donors want what we want—an enhanced degree of self-esteem, a feeling of achievement, a sense of belonging.

What Will Donors Do?

People have an inherent need and ability to be change agents. When motivated by the right reasons, donors will not only give money (over and over again) but will become the organization's best spokespersons too. As they become further invested, they give more, they become more adamant, dedicated, and outspoken and eager to be involved as volunteers. They will do what ever they can to help, but they need to be asked.

Donors can be asked to do the following activities:

- participate in a focus group
- fill out a survey
- work at an event
- join a committee
- sign up as a program volunteer
- bring a friend to an event
- make or secure an in-kind gift
- offer expert advice and counsel
- identify people needing service
- introduce prospects to a board/staff member
- host an information event at home or work
- solicit others

Renewal Benchmarks

The best way to measure the success of your renewal programs is to analyze each renewal activity. Once the development program is established, benchmarks are needed to assess progress and make improvements (Exhibit 6–4).

- **What is your retention rate (what percentage of donors renewed)?** A one-year retention rate should be between 50 and 60 percent. A second-year retention rate should be slightly higher, with increases each year. A five-year retention rate should be about 90 percent. Overall, the entire renewal program should have an 80 to 85 percent retention rate.

- **What is the average gift size for each renewed group?** The average gift size should be greater with each renewed group: first year, repeat, established, loyal, and major. Overall, the gift sizes may fit the traditional giving pyramid, with the lowest level representing 80 percent of the number of donors and 20 percent of the total dollars. Efforts are needed to increase the giving at the middle of the pyramid, where the potential is greater and the costs less. The ideal giving pyramid is taller than wider.

- **What is the total amount of dollars received as measured against cost?** The dollars raised overall should grow each year. It is customary to budget an increase in renewal contributions of 10 to 25 percent annually. The cost of fund raising should not exceed 30 percent of the overall amount raised, while established programs will average about 18 to 20 percent of the amount raised. Special events are the most costly at 50 percent; direct mail at up to 150 percent for acquisitions and up to 75 percent for renewal; telemarketing at 50 to 65 percent for acquisitions and 50 percent for renewal; personal solicitation at 10 to 15 percent.

Donor Upgrading: Increasing the Base

The third sequential objective in annual giving is to **invite donors to become more involved in the organization by making larger and more frequent contributions.** This objective, like renewal, would be accomplished better with a little more effort, making it a higher priority in the integrated development plan than is currently practiced.

Upgrading donor giving moves donors further up the giving pyramid, allowing them to become more involved with the organization, providing them with more opportunities to give

and more options to give to, and sharing with them the organization's accomplishments and its future directions. The rewards that come from being *a donor of significance*—an established donor, a loyal donor, a committed major donor—are felt very personally because of the voluntary nature of philanthropy. When donors recognize how much they can do to ameliorate a problem or advance a cause, they are eager to give as much as they are able. They do, however, need to be listened to and then asked.

As a strategy, donors are invited to upgrade a gift in the early stages of renewal, when they are first becoming involved and are enthused about what they can do. Upgrading is not as successful once a donor's gift level is firmly established. Not to invite a donor to upgrade his or her gift is saying "we don't really need more money," and "your gift is nice, not critical." Not inviting donors to make larger gifts is not only a disservice but it is also an insult to their capacity and the organization's worthiness.

If donors have satisfactory experiences from the first gift on, they are ready to give more when the case merits it and the solicitation articulates it. It is not a good idea to wait for a capital campaign to ask donors to make a significant leap in their giving; upgrading is intended to be a gradual increase over time.

A donor upgrade program is best designed as an individual strategy for each donor, implemented *immediately* after the first gift. The thank-you letter should include an *indirect courtesy invitation* to participate in another way, such as a tribute envelope that can be used at any point in the future. Within two months, the donor should be invited to give again—this time more directly—for a different project or program or a benefit event. If there is an annual holiday campaign, the donor should receive another solicitation. During the year, the donor should receive

> A donor upgrade program is best designed as an individual strategy for each donor, implemented immediately after the first gift.

newsletters that carry appeal envelopes, another form of indirect solicitation. In all, new donors should receive as many as four to six solicitations to give and five to seven invitations to participate during the year.

As donors respond to these appeals, a pattern of giving—the number of times and number of cases—is established. By plan, future requests should increase incrementally and should always include a stated dollar amount, as donors want to know what is needed and expected. For instance, if a donor is giving $25 in the spring and $50 through a special event in the fall, the spring solicitation should ask the donor to consider a gift of $100, a level that moves him or her to the *Century Club* along with other special donors. The invitation to the special event should also include a request to consider a higher category of participation. Finally, this donor should receive an invitation to attend the annual *Century Club* dinner in appreciation for being "one of the family."

Meanwhile, other $100 donors should be invited to consider giving $500 and $1,000, which would be designated for programs of interest to them. They too should be invited to attend a benefit event and a recognition event and be solicited for at least two other campaigns during the year (the holiday appeal, the tribute program, and perhaps a special project campaign). The goal is to upgrade with larger-sized gifts and more frequent gifts and to acknowledge this increased level of giving with more tailored communications and involvement opportunities.

As is obvious, upgrading is not a mass marketing technique—it is an individualized strategy, with many complexities. But it is worth the effort: At least 15 percent of your donors will upgrade every time they are asked.

What Motivates Donors to Give More?

Donors who are firmly committed to an organization and are treated properly can be motivated to give more through the use of gift clubs, challenge grants, giving choices, payment options, and tangible recognition items. Even the time of year will influence a donor's decision to give more. Some donors give more as a result of the psychosocial benefits they receive—when they gather with others who have similar interests their involvement is reinforced and stimulated further. Special events and donor clubs make this reinforcement possible. It is interesting to note that donors who have made a major capital campaign gift or a bequest provision often then increase their annual giving. Most annual donors who make major gifts are motivated by the strength and relevance of the case and the feeling of being needed.

What Motivates Donors to Give More Frequently?

Donors who are highly satisfied are inclined to give more frequently if they are properly motivated by a combination of influences—the case, the message, the solicitor, and the ease of giving. It is not uncommon to see established donors (those who make a large annual gift) giving to several campaigns during the year—as many as three or four. When donors give frequently, it is tempting to treat their gifts individually, as if each was completely separate from the other gifts. This is a mistake. The key to frequent giving is to openly acknowledge each gift as part of a "package," giving donors credit for their cumulative giving.

About Core Donors

An organization's *core donors* are those who give regularly and generously and have indicated a keen interest in the organization. They are the organization's best friends. Usually affluent and influential, they are the ones with the greatest potential. Typically, the core group of donors give 80 percent of the contributions made annually and comprise 20 to 30 percent of the total number of donors. These are the donors who will contribute most of the gifts to a capital campaign and the ones who seriously consider making a planned gift, including a bequest.

Every day of the year, core donors must be the development team's top priority. They should receive the most staff attention, be contacted by influential people in the organization, receive invitations to exclusive events, be invited to join a special committee, and be considered for the board. The organization's leaders and key volunteers should maintain a list of the core donors; most should be assigned to a staff member or a volunteer to ensure that regular communication is occurring. Comments, questions, feedback, recommendations, ideas, and dreams should be recorded in each donor's file.

Phone calls from core donors should always be taken or returned immediately. Suggestions or ideas from a core donor should go right to the top. Contributions from core donors must be acknowledged the same day. They should be the first to know about organizational changes or crises, just as they are the first to be solicited for a volunteer committee and for a major campaign. They are special enough to merit a birthday card, a get-well call, an article about something they are interested in, and invitations to tour behind the scenes and meet the people who benefit from their gifts.

Core donors must never be taken for granted; their gifts should never be expected. Instead, they should be recognized as if they were a new donor every time they make a gift, and given the same level of gratitude, enthusiasm, and stewardship they received the first time, the second time, and so on.

About Major Donors

A major donor is someone whose gift is a major decision given his or her financial circumstances and which in turn has a major impact on the organization's mission. The two go hand in hand.

There are several ways to measure the meaning of "major." There are benchmarks, but no absolute criteria for determining what is a major gift. For some organizations a major gift is any contribution over $1,000; for others a major gift is over $10,000. In addition, does the donor consider your organization one of his or her top three charities? That's major. Would the

organization find it difficult to replace such a donor? That's major.

Major donors may give once, regularly, or cumulatively over time. Any donor who makes an annual gift of $1,000 would probably fit the category, given his or her obvious potential. There is a well-founded notion that a donor's potential is ten times the size of his or her annual gift. If donors are linked closely to the organization and are keenly interested in its mission, this potential can be realized. Although it is important to discover the financial capability of donors, it is even more important to find out what they are interested in and what their needs are if their potential is to be realized.

People with financial capability seldom "wear it," so it is not obvious who among your mid-level donors have the financial ability to become major donors. We do know that people over the age of 50 control much of the nation's wealth. Research and experience tell us that older adults are also among the most philanthropic. And they are going to live longer, making it possible for them to be major donors longer. So, although it is not always possible to determine people's wealth factor, we can determine their philanthropic factor. Today's best donors are mature individuals with a philanthropic attitude—they will find the resources if they see the need and believe they can make a difference.

About Lapsed Donors

In many ways, donors whose annual giving has lapsed are like prospects, albeit *no longer qualified* ones. Of importance is the fact that they no longer give; the fact that they once gave is less relevant. Something has happened to cause them to decide to "un-give," and that "something" is going to be a barrier to their renewal. Perhaps something happened to offend them or to draw their interest elsewhere, or perhaps their financial situation prohibits them from making continuing contributions. More likely, they did not feel a sense of appreciation as a result of their previous gift(s), did not sense an urgent need for support (as compared to another charity), or did not connect with someone in the organization and, as a result, no linkage developed beyond the initial motivational influence.

Lapsed donors therefore are not great prospects, though one might think so given how many times organizations try to get them to renew their giving, as though they had never stopped giving. In part, the organization's lack of appreciation for what caused them to lapse is part of the problem. Organizations need to treat lapsed donors as new prospects; their previous contribution(s) is not proof that the relationship should continue—entitlement is not a stimulus for philanthropy.

Recognition, Incentives, and Rewards: Thanking and Motivating Donors at the Same Time

The movement from first-time donor to repeat donor and so on often requires external influences that will stimulate or trigger internal motivators; recognition, incentives, and rewards can be effective tools (Exhibit 6–5). According to Mixer (1993, 22), "When donors are shown that their gifts make a difference in meeting a human need, their reward comes from a sense of both achievement and power."

Special Needs Lists

It is fundamentally important for an organization to have an updated "needs list" of items for which philanthropic support is sought. Many organizations have come to understand the tremendous impact that a one-page wish list has with donors. Its effectiveness lies in its simplicity, its clarity, and the fact that a wish list gives donors a choice. The opportunity to select one need over another is easy, exciting, engaging, and empowering for donors. Wish lists can be assembled quickly, changed as often as necessary, and printed inexpensively. The list can include a wide variety of needs in a wide range of prices. A special needs list can be used as a hand-out or a "leave-behind," referred to in a phone call, included with a letter, be the focus

Exhibit 6–5 Annual Giving Recognition, Incentives, and Rewards

Special Needs Lists

Gift Clubs and Gift Levels

Recognition Items and Privileges

Donor Listings

Philanthropy Awards and Events

Tours and Program Presentations

Volunteer-Hosted Events

Newsletters and Mailings

Financial and Program Updates

Invitations to Events

Volunteer Opportunities

of a mailing, or published in the organization's newsletter. Variations of needs lists can be produced for different donor segments as needed. Exhibit 6–6 is an example of a needs list, and Exhibit 6–7 is an example of a wish list.

Gift Clubs and Gift Levels

For the organization, gift or donor clubs are very effective mechanisms of accomplishing several aims: recognizing donors, cultivating and upgrading donors, and gathering donors with similar interests. For the donor, gift clubs offer tangible benefits and privileges. Organized in gift level tiers (starting at $100 or $1,000), the benefits grow in number and value as the gift increases.

First and foremost, a gift club allows the organization to express honest gratitude in a distinguished way. Second, a gift club is an incentive to donors to "belong" to a giving club where their peers are. Third, gift clubs are inexpensive

Exhibit 6–6 Special Needs List

Real Options for City Kids (R.O.C.K.)

1997–1998 Special Needs List

$25,000   **ROCK'S High Sierra Residential Sports Camp**
- Send inner city children and youth, ages 9–17, to camp in Sept. 1997.
- Children will experience sailing, archery, ropes course, climbing, and mountain biking. (Serving 75–100)

$18,000   **ROCK Van**
- Purchase a van that will enable staff and volunteers to provide transportation for children who, without assistance from ROCK, would not have the resources to get to the activity sites or the events.

$15,000   **ROCK Scholar**
- Sponsor a ROCK youth while they are in junior or senior high school, with hope and financial resources to look beyond the walls that surround them to a future of college and opportunities for success.

$ 7,500   **Sports Development Clinic**
- Underwrites an 8 week sport clinic featuring basketball, soccer or volleyball, for 120 children ages 9–12 who have never had the opportunity to play organized sports and benefit from the lifetime lessons learned outside the classroom.

$ 5,000   **ROCK Sport Team**
- Provides a team of 12–15 girls with the equipment, uniforms, trained coaches and facilities necessary to successfully participate in soccer or basketball.

$ 5,000   **ROCK-n-Read Children's Library**
- Underwrites a comprehensive library filled with age-appropriate and engaging historical literature for children grades 1–6.

$ 2,500   **ROCK Book Angel Project**
- Provides 150 children from low-income families with a book of their own during the holiday season.

Courtesy of Real Options for City Kids, San Francisco, California.

---

ways to bring donors together for the purpose of involving, informing, and inspiring them.

A gift club can be designed in a variety of ways to fit the organization's culture. For instance, a hospital may name its club in honor of its founder. Members of the club may be any donor with an annual gift of $1,000 or more or a planned gift of $25,000 or more. The criteria for entrance into the club can be as broad or as focused as determined appropriate; there seem

Exhibit 6–7 Wish List

Wish List

Volunteers to donate
4 hours of office assistance one day a month

Computer professionals to provide
technology expertise and training
1 day a week, 2 hours per day

Business to donate
meeting space for monthly volunteer training

Frequent Flyer Miles to fulfill a child's wish

35 mm cameras

Laser Copy Paper

Small, safe toys to fill hospital toy chests.

Photo albums to hold 4×6 prints

Courtesy of Make-a-Wish Foundation, Sacramento, California.

to be benefits to inclusion and exclusion in this regard, depending on your objectives. Gift clubs typically have at least one annual event for their members, during which special donors are recognized publicly, and program staff and administrators have an opportunity to reinforce the benefits of philanthropic support. Exhibit 6–8 is an example.

Recognition Items and Privileges

The merit and expectation of giving donors tangible *items* in recognition of *their* gifts are hotly debated, and opinions are a direct reflection of an organization's culture. It is a popular practice for public radio and television stations to give away membership premiums, such as mugs and T-shirts. Higher education institutions give away football blankets and baseball caps.

Museums give art posters, calendars, and books. Zoos give stuffed animals, hospitals give first-aid kits, and environmental groups give bumper stickers. Advocates for the practice remind us that the overcrowded and competitive marketplace demands that we give donors something tangible, as they have come to expect it. Critics of the practice argue that commercialization has already undermined the noble nature of philanthropy, turning it into a business enterprise with marketplace products.

Aside from the true membership programs, such as with institutions that charge admission, donors do not seem to want recognition items unless they are inexpensive, are utilitarian, or have status associated with them (in the case of a major gift). Donors frequently say, "Please don't waste my money on that stuff—just say thank you." Of course, experience tells us that some donors do appreciate a token of apprecia-

Exhibit 6–8 Gift Clubs

Your Gift Matters
The University Annual Fund 1996–97

	Annual	Quarterly	Semi-Annual
Centennial Society:	$5,000	$1,250+	$2500+
Presidents Club:	$1,000–4,999	$250+	$500+
Cornerstone Club:	$500–999	$125+	$250+
Friends of the University:	$100–$499	$25+	$50+
Viking Club:			

Centennial Society:
The Centennial Society is essential to the overall student experience. Members are invited to meet with the president and trustees to share their counsel and to hear from campus leaders about critical issues and opportunities at the University. Thirty-six members now comprise the committed group. Gifts are renewable annually.

Presidents Club:
The Presidents Club is a long-standing organization whose support provides a strong foundation for the Annual Fund. These annually renewable gifts have provided more than $100,000 each year for the University. Members receive a quarterly memorandum from the president and are invited to events to meet campus leaders.

Cornerstone Club:
Newly formed in 1996, the Cornerstone Club already has a number of members on board who pledge to give between $500 and $999 annually.

Friends of the University:
Among the University's most faithful supporters. Friends of the University has been an important backbone of the Annual Fund for more than 30 years.

Viking Club:
The Viking Club recognizes gifts from alumni, parents, and friends to athletics at the University.

continues

Exhibit 6–8 continued

	Annual	Quarterly	Semi-Annual
Nyvall Society: The Nyvall Society is a critical new organization that recognizes gifts for institutional scholarships to help support Seminary students.	$1,000+	$230+	$500+
Friends of the Seminary: Friends of the Seminary is a long-standing organization whose annual support offsets funds, including scholarships for the Seminary	$100–$999		
Heritage Circle: The Heritage Circle recognized donors who provide for the future of the University and its students through a deferred gift or through mentioning the University in their estate plan. A colleague from the Trust Company can assist with these arrangements.			

Courtesy of North Park College.

tion when it is appropriate and inexpensive. The measure of appropriateness might be a proportionate amount of the donor's gift (say one percent) or the extent to which the item will have ancillary promotional benefits (a framed certificate or a paperweight that visibly promotes the organization and elicits an inquiry). There are numerous sources for such items and encouragement by salespeople to purchase them, because others have. You do not have to settle for stock items, as vendors are happy to design an item to fit your organization's personality. The primary question should be, Is a gift necessary, useful, expected, and a statement about the organization's mission? If not, a better substitute may be a personal phone call, an invitation to tour behind the scenes, or a hand-written thank you from a recipient.

However, there is increasing evidence that donors do want recognition *privileges*, for lack of a better term. Privileges are indications that a donor has reached a level that merits special attention, just as you would extend to a member of the family. Many organizations have found creative ways of recognizing their donors without spending money, which makes these efforts even more attractive to our conscientious, conservative donors. Free parking, special access, library privileges, and toll-free lines are some of the generic privileges that every organization can offer. Museums invite donors to "be a curator for a day," symphonies allow donors to "practice in a rehearsal," zoological gardens let donors "feed the dolphins," hospitals invite donors to "experiment with a laser device," and social service agencies invite donors "to read to a child." The benefit of giving privileges instead of tangible items is profound, as doing so brings people together to gain insight into the issues that concern them.

Remember, just as in the acknowledgment process, the form and the degree of appreciation and recognition should be appropriate to the size and the nature of the gift. If not appropriate, the credibility of the recognition deteriorates; "efficient administration of gifts reinforces donors' decisions to donate" (Mixer 1993, 43).

Donor Listings

The listing of donor's names, whether in the annual report or on the lobby donor wall, is a form of recognition and promotion. It is common practice to annually publish donor names somewhere, although there are differing opinions about the appropriateness of listing names without obtaining permission or listing names in identified gift categories. Social service agencies are the most reluctant to list donors by amount, whereas hospitals are quick to do so. Donor lists do have tremendous promotional impact. They send powerful messages that people are supporting the institution, and they encourage others to follow their lead. The investment of dollars in a donor recognition wall is more likely to occur at institutions that are established and have high-traffic areas, such as hospitals and museums.

Philanthropy Awards and Events

One of the newest methods of recognizing donors, promoting philanthropy, and providing a psychosocial experience is an annual Philanthropy Day awards program. Stimulated by the popular national and regional NSFRE Philanthropy Day celebrations, nonprofits are creating their own version to give awards to *their* loyal volunteers, key donors, corporate sponsors, major foundation funders, youth groups, and the like. The event is typically a luncheon or dinner, which provides excellent photo opportunities, good newsletter copy, and in-demand public relations releases.

Tours and Program Presentations

There is no better way to inform and involve donors than to invite them to meet the program staff and service recipients, be they Nobel Prize-winning faculty or promising medical students. Only those providing the services and receiving them can speak as sincerely about the need for philanthropic support.

A donor's greatest reward (and philanthropy's self-actualization) is to see first hand where one's gift is applied and to become involved directly in the problem's *solution*. The philanthropic spirit is fueled by meeting someone whose life situation can be altered or by meeting someone whose interests and concerns are the same as yours. To be considered special enough to merit a private behind the scenes tour, to be invited with a small number of other donors to meet a highly regarded faculty member or a prominent zoologist is a rare treat for a donor, not soon to be forgotten. When donors can see their interests and concerns reflected in the lives of others, contributions flow.

There is another benefit that comes when donors have an opportunity to meet the philanthropic recipients. The recipients themselves benefit, gaining confidence and power from articulating their needs and respectfully collaborating in the solution. Ostrander and Schervish's (1990) research on interactions between donors and recipients suggests these mutual gains: "Engagement between donors and recipients has the potential for transforming the practice of philanthropy in a more profound way. The projects funded may be more in line with what people need and less with what they can get funded" (95).

Volunteer-Hosted Events

For staff, too often the celebration of philanthropy is limited to a hallway "hurrah" when a significant, unsolicited check arrives in the mail. For board members and volunteers, too often the celebration of their involvement is relegated to a once-a-year event at which volunteers are given pins for their years of service.

Just as a thank-a-thon is a rewarding way for volunteers to be involved in development work, donors are rewarded and celebrated when they are invited to someone's home or workplace to learn more about the charity's programs. And board members, volunteers, and donors are flattered to be asked to host one of the organization's annual "informational, inspirational" events. The personal relationships that are developed during this kind of activity are long lasting and powerful. The information presented is similar to that given during agency tours and program presentations, but the volunteers are more visible than staff, serving as personal testimony of donor and/or recipient. This mood is one of celebration and ongoing emphasis on the money received, rather than on the money needed. Together, staff, volunteers, and donors celebrate, and benefit from the interaction.

Newsletters and Mailings

Most people neither have the time nor inclination to become very involved in a charity—their life stage does not enable it, nor does their lifestyle facilitate it. Nevertheless, they do read their mail and often with interest. Organizational newsletters provide a wonderful opportunity to promote philanthropy, recognize donors, and feature clients and services. The rule of thumb is to eliminate anything that is institutionally based in favor of articles about people. The more successful newsletters are filled with photos, success stories, achievements, and aspirations, rather than campaign or financial reports. The newsletter may be the best place to tell stories—in the words of those served and those supporting them.

Financial and Program Updates

Donors are entitled to a report about how their gift(s) were applied and what happened as a result—in human terms. Practically speaking, it may not be possible to prepare a separate report for each and every donor that details their gift's use, the program, the recipients, or the outcomes of their contribution. Therefore, much of the generic information can be reported in a newsletter, the annual reports, and in presentations. However, any donor making a gift of $1,000 or more might expect to receive a report specific to his or her gift before being asked to renew or upgrade the next annual gift. A report can be as simple as a one- to two-page summary of the program or of the designated fund activity, with a notation of any changes going forward. Once prepared, the annual "donor report" can become a boiler-plate for other reports, until eventually it is possible to produce them with little effort. When program staff are involved in the preparation of the *fund request*, they are more enthused about participating in the preparation of the *fund status or donor report*. Then the development staff may only have to edit, print, and mail the reports once they become a regular part of the stewardship process.

Invitations to Events

As a donor becomes more interested in a particular charitable organization, he or she tends to want to be involved—the two go hand in hand. The easiest way to test someone's involvement interest is through invitations to special or benefit events. When people are unable to attend but call to decline the invitation (which was mailed to them personally with a note from you), it is a pretty good indication that their interest is increasing. Donors who are fully engaged will become regular attenders at events (open houses, lectures, and the like) as they begin to feel more like insiders and thus want to be a part of these special occasions. It is not particularly useful to mail invitations to donors for every agency event—be particular, be personal, and be a good host when the person responds affirmatively.

Volunteer Opportunities

Despite the decline in volunteerism in recent years, there remains a solid base of volunteer support to draw on, albeit for more important work than such tasks as envelope stuffing. There are two ways that organizations and volunteers get together. First, the organization seeks volunteers for functions that have already been defined. Second, the volunteer seeks out an organization, offers his or her help, and the organization in turn creates a volunteer position to fit the interest of the volunteer while meeting the needs of the organization. It is very important to have a good number of volunteer positions (those that exist or could be created) to offer to donors as they become more interested in the organization. There should always be an opening on the development committee, the special event committee, or the planned giving committee. Every organization benefits from the vigor, vitality, and values that come with a new committed volunteer/donor—with or without plan.

Relationship Management: Cultivating Friendships and Nurturing Partnerships

Establishing strong relationships with donors does not happen by itself; as in all relationships, there must be an environment of mutual goodwill based on an appreciation of each other's similarities and differences, needs and interests. Strong relationships develop when there is openness, respect, honesty, patience, commitment, and give-and-take from both parties. Relationships are, in reality, partnerships developed through effective, balanced interpersonal communications, which over time increase in frequency, complexity, and intensity. Dominance by one party diminishes the essence of the partnership, and exchange does not occur. The challenge for donors and fund raisers alike is to maintain balance in their relationships, even under pressures of self-interest. Relationships are undermined when organizations "convince" their donors to support something outside their area of interest under pressure that the organization's needs are paramount. Conversely, relationships are tested when donors insist on contributing to programs that are not a priority of the organization's mission. The role of the development professional is to manage the relationship between the donor and the organiza-

tion in a way that creates an ethical, moral, and synergistic partnership for the long term. J.D. Ragsdale discusses the relational nature that is fundamental to fund raising:

> People do not give money either to strangers or to unknown causes. . . . They give most fully and happily to someone who has taken the time and exhibited the concern to develop something akin to friendship with them, someone whom they like, trust, and feel comfortable with, someone whom they know will still be in a relationship with them even after they have made a gift (1995, 18–19).

The Relationship Pyramid

Two models describe the movement that occurs in the building of donative relationships: the relationship pyramid and the cultivation and commitment circle. The relationship pyramid (Figure 6–1) is commonly used to describe the way donors move up the giving pyramid as their interests, needs, and desires grow incrementally—in direct proportion, fund raisers are informing and involving donors in the organization's mission and programs, building interest and desire for future support. As donors move from annual giving decisions to major giving decisions, they require more influences and inputs and rationale justification. At the top of the giving pyramid, as in Maslow's theory, the philanthropic partnership is realized fully—donors have achieved their aspirations, and the organization's mission is fulfilled (implied).

The Cultivation and Commitment Circle

Another model used to describe the management of donor relationships, the cultivation and commitment circle (Figure 6–2), is a more dynamic, synergistic model that works in circular fashion. Its conceptual framework is a ball of energy that attracts donors to the outer surface and moves them incrementally toward the cen-

The Relationship Pyramid

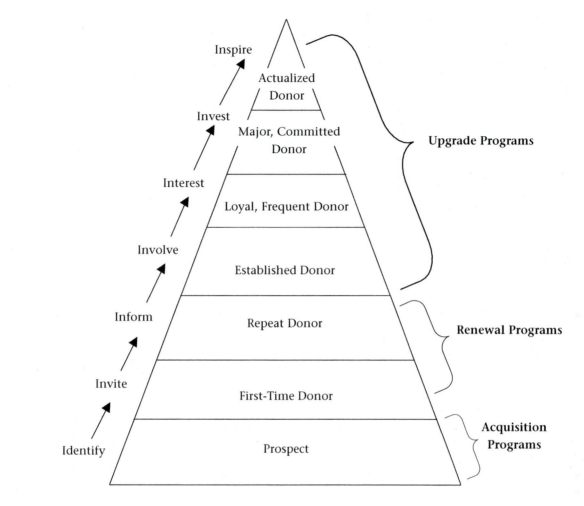

Figure 6–1 Annual Giving Objectives. As donors move up the giving pyramid, their interests, needs, and desires grow incrementally. In direct proportion, fund raisers are informing and involving donors in the organization's mission and programs. As the donors' commitment grows, so does the organization's attention to the relationship, and vice versa.

ter. The cultivation and commitment circle describes how donors pass through a series of cultivation steps designed to increase their commitment to the mission over time or, in the absence of satisfaction, are spun off. As the donor is cultivated and grows more committed, the connections grow stronger, the exchanges multiply, the interactions build in quantity and quality, and the satisfaction multiplies. A synergy develops that brings the donor and the mission into sync. In the absence of synergy, some donors decide to leave—their experience did not meet their expectations, their interests changed, their needs were not met, and others come into the circle to replace them. The goal is to add more donors to the circle over time, to build a larger, stronger donor constituency that is propelled forward by the infusion of energy gained.

Finally, Exhibit 6–9 shows the various donative relationship stages—the sequence of moves that donors make in the relationship and the corresponding moves that the organization makes to facilitate the philanthropic partnerships. This Donor Relationship Management

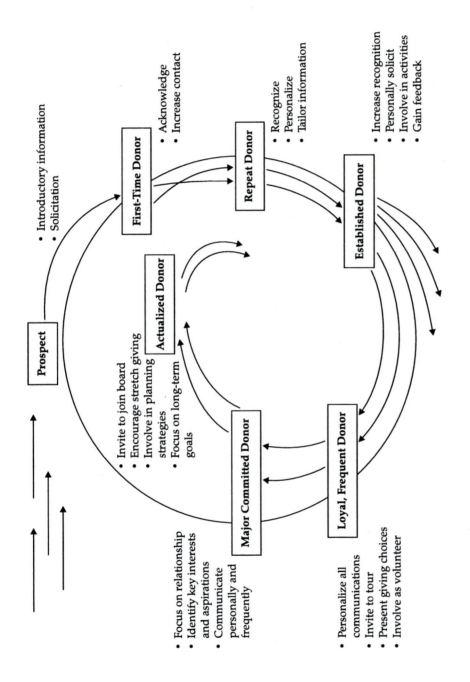

Figure 6–2 Constituency and Commitment Circle

Exhibit 6–9 Donor Relationship Management Chart

PROSPECT: INTRODUCTION STAGE (Organization and Prospect Are Introduced)

Information has been collected about the prospect that indicates that a relationship might be developed. The organization introduces the prospect to its charitable mission, using the appropriate communication method—in person, by phone, by mail. The introduction stage *may* include three steps: presentation of the organization's mission (a newsletter), a cultivation activity (invitation to a benefit event), and a direct solicitation (an annual appeal). Or this stage may start with a direct solicitation for an appropriate case.

FIRST-TIME DONOR: INTEREST STAGE (Organization and Donor Become Interested)

Having made a first gift, the donor has indicated some level of interest in the organization. The organization now collects additional information about the donor and begins to explore areas of mutual interest, shared values, and future support. The organization's interest is expressed by the way the donor is thanked, recognized, and re-solicited. The communications shift from why support is needed to what a difference the donor's gift made.

REPEAT DONOR: INITIATION STAGE (Organization and Donor Initiate Contacts)

Interest is growing as the donor decides to make repeat gifts. There is a desire on both parties to learn a little more about each other, to make contact. The organization makes contact by mail or telephone to thank the donor in a more personalized way. The donor is initiating contact in other ways by attending a special event, supporting a particular program, or having a discussion with a volunteer or a board member. Observation takes place, information is processed, questions are asked, and opinions about the relationship are formed. The communications begin from what "I" can do to what "we" can do.

ESTABLISHED DONOR: INFORMATION STAGE (Organization and Donor Share Information)

Having initiated contact, communications turn to sharing more detailed and personal information about the donor's interests and the organization's specific or special project needs. Personalized invitations are made to the donor that call for a response—an offer to tour the facility, attend a luncheon, join a giving club, participate on a volunteer committee. By now, the donor has revealed interest in a particular area and will continue to participate in dialogue, asking more questions and looking for a stronger rationale as the gift decisions grow in size. The donor's expectations and needs are being met—the organization determines there is benefit to the investment of more time and effort in the relationship. Agreement about the relationship is established, and contacts are increasing.

continues

Exhibit 6–9 continued

LOYAL, FREQUENT DONOR: INVOLVEMENT STAGE (Organization and Donor Are Involved)

At this stage both parties are actively involved in the relationship exchange. Common interest is apparent; pride of association is made public. Interpersonal communications are occurring on a regular basis. Exchanges are open and challenging. The donor wants to be involved in activities that demand more time and talent, such as committee or board membership. The level of giving is substantial and stable. The organization wants the donor's involvement in leadership aspects—as a volunteer fund raiser, advocate, and community representative. The donor receives information that is reserved for insiders, attends events designed for the organization's best friends, and has a personal relationship with the organization's leaders. At this point, the donor is beginning to consider the relationship as long term and may even consider the possibility of a legacy gift in addition to lifetime gifts.

MAJOR, COMMITTED DONOR: INVESTMENT STAGE (Organization and Donor Are Invested)

By now, the organization and donor have a significant investment in each other as partners. Time, talent, and treasure have been received; appreciation, recognition, and stewardship have been given. The exchange has reached an important level; involvement is at its highest. The donor may be involved in decision making that affects not only how the organization delivers services but also where the organization is going in the future. The donor may be a trustee and a leader in a major capital campaign. The organization values the donor's counsel, input, and leadership. Given the high level of investment in the organization's mission, this is the time where tensions may arise around roles, relationships, and directions. Reciprocity is needed, so the relationships can reach its final stage with trust and appreciation.

ACTUALIZED RELATIONSHIP: INSPIRATION STAGE (Organization and Donor Are Partners)

At this stage, the relationship is stable and predictable. Both parties are focused on the mission over the money and are engaged in a true partnership. Given the accomplishments, inspiration takes over, setting the stage for a donor to realize his or her lifetime aspirations and the organization to accomplish goals that were only imagined. Friendship knows no boundaries. Communications focus on what can be done, rather than on what can't be.

Chart is a tool to use in the *case management* of core donors. Case management of donors occurs when specific donors are assigned to specific staff (based on personality cohesion and values orientation) as the primary contact for all interactions with the organization. It is possible for staff to manage a caseload of 50 to 500 donors, depending on the precise situation. The assigned staff member "manages" every activity that involves that donor, be it a tribute gift, a request for information about a program, an invitation to a special event, an address correction, a stock transaction, or a decision to make a bequest. A management plan is developed for each donor case outlining the number/kind of contacts, mailings, and the like.

Stewardship Processes: Accountability for All Things Important

Webster's Dictionary defines stewardship as "the individual's responsibility to manage his life and property with regard to the rights of others." A term long associated with the religious sector, stewardship has become a larger issue in other parts of the nonprofit sector in recent years because of the tremendous growth in contributed dollars, the need for organizations to demonstrate sound fiscal management of those funds, the decline in public trust in nonprofit accountability, and increased competition for funds as government retrenchment occurs. The legal, professional, and ethical definitions of stewardship can be found in a growing number of professional codes, professional literature and articles, and in accounting and financial reporting texts. In his paper on stewardship and public life, Paul Pribbenow asserts that stewardship "is grounded in the belief that all of human life and experience is a gift; a gift that demands a response of faithful service" (1996, 1).

On Financial Responsibility

Unquestionably it is the organization's legal responsibility to monitor the receiving, recording, management, expenditure, and the reporting functions associated with all philanthropic gifts, but it is the fund raiser who is ethically responsible first and foremost for the financial stewardship of donative funds. If financial statements do not make receipts and expenditures clear, it is the fund raiser's responsibility to challenge them.

The best way for organizations to demonstrate to donors that their contributions are used not only as intended but also have meaningful results is to keep records of how each and every gift is expended, not just received. This goes for program activities, as well as fundraising activities. The key is sophisticated financial reporting that provides full disclosure, public reporting, and honest self-evaluation. An objective of financial policies, procedures, processes, and financial statements is to provide information useful for evaluating the effectiveness of the management of resources in achieving the organization's goals. This objective can best be accomplished by using fund accounting. Fund accounting is a system in which separate records are kept for assets donated to an organization that are restricted by donors for certain specified purposes or uses. The financial statements then separate the income and expense for each fund.

Because development directors are the primary contacts with donors, they often bring slightly different perspectives and concerns to the subject of stewardship. Although stewardship requires that a contribution be expended in the way a donor contributes it, there is always room for interpretation—sometimes a donor is unaware of the various options, sometimes a donor makes an informal request, sometimes a donor is led to believe that the organization knows best where to dedicate a gift. The relationship that a fund raiser has with donors can clarify some of these issues—finding out where

> **The best way to demonstrate to donors that their contributions had meaningful results is to keep records of how gifts are expended.**

the donor wants his or her gift allocated is part of the stewardship responsibility.

On Moral and Ethical Responsibility

Stewardship is also the moral and ethical value we place on the philanthropic process—the people who give, the gifts they give, the organizations who receive them, and the recipients who benefit from them. Stewardship is the accountability we assume for all of these assets. Fund raisers and all who participate in the receiving are guardians of "all things important"—people, place, and gifts. Stewardship is our virtuous regard for human and financial resources.

People

- *How are people acknowledged and recognized?* Procedures are needed to ensure that all donors are thanked in a timely and thoughtful way. The process of acknowledging donors should have the same status and be given the same resources as solicitation efforts. People's contributions, whether of time, talent or treasure, desire proper recognition and must never be taken for granted.
- *How are donors treated?* Donors are special—they have given gifts and expected little in return, save appreciation. The way they are referred to when not present is in reality how they will be treated. They are not "hits" or "gets"; they are "us," not "them."
- *How and when are people communicated with?* When people are highly regarded, they are included in all things important. They are informed about changes, advised of activities, and made aware of their gifts' results. They are the first, not the last to know. When people are listened to and can participate in the organization's betterment, communications are functioning at their highest level.

Places

- *How does philanthropy work in the organization?* When philanthropy belongs to everyone, it can reach its full potential. When the ideas for philanthropy are shared, when the responsibility for philanthropy is owned, when the celebration of philanthropy is an everyday occurrence, it works. Fund raising by one or few is not philanthropically centered.
- *How does the organization value philanthropy?* Organizations who receive a high level of philanthropic support have a high regard for the proper role that philanthropy plays in the revenue picture. They see philanthropy as a privilege that must be earned and safeguarded. They do not rely entirely on philanthropy, but seek a diversified revenue base that ensures a vital organization and makes the best use of voluntary funds.
- *What is the community's role?* Philanthropy is the litmus test of an organization's need to exist. When the community gives to a charity, it validates its relevance. When an organization involves citizens in the determination of need, the identification of priorities, and the evaluation of services provided, it remains vital.

Gifts

- *How are gifts solicited?* When fund raising is approached with pride over apology, to advance a cause rather than fund a crisis, people are solicited in a respectful way. Funds are raised, and friends are made. No pressure is exhibited, no exaggerations made. Solicitations are made with full disclosure, information is given about clients and the organizations, and invitations are made to join in the effort. Begging and selling are replaced by donor-focused communications.
- *What kinds of gifts are received?* When everyone is included in the development planning, there are few questions about what is needed and in what order of priority. Funds are raised for the areas of greatest need and likely opportunity. Donors are invited to give to their areas of

interest, improving the potential for future, long-term, mutual relationships.

- *How are gifts protected, invested, and distributed?* Policies are needed to delineate how philanthropic funds are stewarded. The mandate is to restrict them for whatever purpose that was directed, to invest them prudently and wisely, and to ensure they ultimately achieve the outcome intended—next year or 50 years from now.

Policies on Gift Stewardship

Sound management practice mandates written policies and procedures for functions that are deemed important to organizational behavior, and that transcend the coming and going of people. Every organization should have a policy book that dictates how gift stewardship is handled, to safeguard that actions are made in the best interests of all concerned. The following policy categories are recommended:

1. **Gift Acceptance Policies:** Who can accept a gift, with its legal liabilities and moral implications? Who is the contact going forward, to thank and recognize the donors, and steward the gifts?

2. **Gift Type Parameters:** What types of gifts are sought and accepted: in-kind gifts; pledges over time; gifts of tangible value such as property, insurance, real estate, art; gifts of closely held or publicly traded stock. Policies are needed to guide how and when such gifts are sold. What levels of funding are required for trusts and annuities?

3. **Gift Recognition Guidelines:** How are donors recognized, and what distinguishes one group of donors from another? Who receives what recognition items or status, based on what criteria? What are the policies for naming a building, a chair, a program, a fund?

4. **Gift Restriction Policies:** How and when are gifts restricted for program services, endowment purposes, special uses, and for capital improvements? What are the minimum requirements to establish a named fund? How are bequests applied, under what conditions?

5. **Gift Management, Investment, and Distribution Policies and Procedures:** How are funds managed, and by whom? Are investment guidelines in place, and reviewed annually for changes in the marketplace? Who decides, beyond donor designations and restrictions, how and when funds are allocated? How is fund investment and use reported and to whom?

References

Graham, C.P. 1992. *Keep the money coming: A step-by-step guide to annual fundraising.* Sarasota, FL: Pineapple Press.

Greenfield, J.M. 1994. *AHP News* (February): 21–29.

Mixer, J.R. 1993. *Principles of professional fund raising: Useful foundations for successful practice.* San Francisco, CA: Jossey-Bass.

Nichols, J.E. 1995. *Growing from good to great: Positioning your fund-raising efforts for big gains.* Chicago: Bonus Books.

Ostrander, S.A., and P.G. Schervish. 1990. Giving and getting: Philanthropy as a social relation. In *Critical issues in American philanthropy: Strengthening theory and practice,* edited by J. Van Til and Associates. San Francisco, CA: Jossey-Bass.

Pribbenow, P. 1996. *Stewardship and public life: To whom much is given shall much be expected.* Paper presented to Foundation Forum, American Bar Foundation.

Ragsdale, J.D. 1995. Quality communication in achieving fundraising excellence. *New Directions for Philanthropic Fundraising* 10: 17–32.

Chapter 7

Matching Institutional Needs with Donor Interests: Steps 5 and 6 in the Annual Integrated Development Process

The Rationale for Matching: Balancing Idealism with Pragmatism

The fund raiser's role is one of upholding and promoting philanthropic values while managing people, programs, and systems that work by today's *instrumental* standards of cost effectiveness, tangible outcomes, and measurable results. Michael O'Neill writes, "Fund raisers help connect the supply of charitable feelings with

the demand for charitable dollars, balancing the equation of human responsibility" (1993, 35). Granted, it is not easy to balance idealism with pragmatism. Such is the dilemma underlying the matching of people's interests with other people's needs. The variables and variations are limitless. The manner in which matches occur is ideally by plan, but in reality is more prone to circumstance. Given that fund raising tends to be more art than science, there are many paths to the same outcomes. Ambiguities, uncertainties, and judgmental requirements come into play.

As philanthropic agents, we must rely on whatever donor research we have. We must trust our intuition to lead us to the best decisions. We must proceed in spite of risk because of the potential good rewards. We must maintain an optimistic view, no matter what the outcome. And we must embrace the fact that matching takes more effort and creativity than raising funds by playing the mass marketing numbers game.

In pursuing matches, we must also accept that donors are entitled to support causes that interest them and that when appropriate we will tailor our institutional needs to fit those interests. We are ever mindful of the need to assist donors by providing unbiased information that guides them toward a wise decision. Designated giving is integral to the matching concept.

Matching implies trust, entails flexibility, dictates the sharing of power, and accomplishes the philanthropic exchange. Matching goes beyond linking a donor's interest—for example, in homeless children—with an organization's adoption program. It also matches the donor's financial capability with a program's budget, the timing of a donor gift with an organization's fiscal year, the type of gift with the type of solicitation, and the amount of effort put toward the relationship with the anticipated potential.

Matching *is* marketing with four steps:

1. collecting information from the customer (constituency research)
2. developing a mission-driven, customer-focused product (case design)
3. offering the product at the right time, place, and price and by the right person (solicitation strategy selection)
4. ensuring that the product delivers the benefits offered (stewardship practices)

> **In pursuing matches, we must accept that donors are entitled to support causes that interest them.**

Communications theory tells us that a match is viable when perceived as such by those who are matched, rather than by the matchmaker. If both parties believe their needs are addressed, met, or exceeded, the match is achieved (as in transaction communications language when the encoder and decoder send and receive the same messages on the same channels). Simply put, the giver and receiver are then in sync. It should be noted that early perceptions at the beginning of the relationship when satisfaction is high may be different from later ones. However, positive and frequent interactions will nurture the relationship, increasing the perception of satisfaction over time.

The old way of raising funds, the *demand-pull method*, in which the organization appealed for funds on demand and pulled in donors who would support it, is passé. Technology has made it possible for donors to seek and gain access to information about charities on their own. They are creating their own demand, initiating their own pull. Interactivity is the new paradigm. John McIlquham writes, "Nonprofits will no longer have the power to choose when they will prospect, send out mailings and communicate with donors. Instead, donors and prospects will find institutions which match up with their interests via technology" (1996, 13).

There are many implications for the fundraising process as the matching or exchange concept is fully incorporated into the annual giving program as well as the major gifts level. Matching takes more information, more time, and more resources. What is the rationale for expending more efforts on matching? The present-day mood of the donor community seems to justify it.

From the View of the Donor

The concept of matching assumes that people want to have an exchange relationship with others—that civic engagement and social connectedness are a desired state. Oddly enough, the attitude of the American public seems to be going the other way, making philanthropy an even more critical *link* to what is good and right.

Every day, judgments are made about the perceived value of charitable organizations— some are good, others are not. Public opinion about charities varies, as does the amount and accuracy of information available to form those opinions. While the public's philanthropic interest is driven by a combination of internal motivations, the decision to give or not give is based on how donors view the credibility and worthiness of an organization, and those views are derived from the information they receive, what others say and do, how they are treated, and if organizations do what they say they do.

Public Trust, Civic Responsibility, and Social Connectedness Are Declining

There is growing evidence of a shift from communalism to individualism. People are tired of social problems that will not go away, are weary of government intervention and bureaucratic authority, and are disinterested in associations with others. Experts lament the growth of a culture of mistrust, cynicism, and scandal, with a corresponding rise in isolation, boredom, and despair.

In her 1996 Maurice Gurin lecture, Jean Bethke Elstain cited an annual study of civic culture that showed trust in others had reached an all-time low. Public spiritedness is in jeopardy, the social fabric is frayed, and trust in neighbors is low. People are less involved in politics and community; they do not join as much, volunteer as much, or give as much as earlier generations. Elstain contends that the public's "once rough-and-tumble civic attitude" has been replaced with attitudes of "in your face" and "you just don't get it" (1996).

Political scientist James Q. Wilson argues that one reason why Americans are more cynical and less trusting than they used to be is that "government has taken on more and more issues that it is ill equipped to handle well." Social scientists who have researched the sharp decline in citizen participation argue that "the evidence points to nothing less than a crisis in 'social capital formation'—the forging of bonds of social trust and competence" (Elstain 1996, 26–27).

In his article, "Bowling Alone," Robert D. Putnam confirms that civic engagement and social connectedness are diminishing because of a variety of factors: time pressures, economic stresses, increased mobility, suburbanization, women in the workforce, family breakdown, the events of the 1960s, and the electronic revolution, with television as a prime suspect. He suggests that Americans are less inclined to be joiners than they were a quarter-century ago. Even when they do become involved, their commitment extends little further than writing a check for dues or reading a monthly newsletter, rather than engaging directly with matters of common concern. He claims that the most discomfiting bit of evidence of social disengagement is that *more* Americans are bowling today than ever before, but they are bowling *alone*.

At the same time that individuals are cocooning, withdrawing, and isolating themselves from social problems, technology is helping to create a more sterile world. People don't need to be in contact; they can communicate by e-mail, faxes, and the Internet. There is a certain irony in the people's desire to protect themselves from the harsh, unpredictable realities of the outside world while insulating themselves from the very problems that nonprofits are bringing to their attention.

This lack of trust, cynicism in government and authority, and detachment from others have an equally negative effect on the nonprofit sector and on philanthropy.

Skepticism and Criticism of Nonprofits and Fund Raising Are Growing

A 1995 survey on giving by the Independent Sector reports growing distrust among Americans about how charities handle donations. Thirty-one percent said they disagreed with the statement: "Charities are honest and ethical in their use of donated funds." That was the highest level of disagreement since the poll began, 25 percent disagreed two years before, and eight years before 20 percent disagreed (1996, 9).

The same survey also found that the percentage of household giving was down from previous years: 68.5 percent gave in 1995 as compared to 75.1 percent in 1989. The average contribution also dropped from $734 in 1989 (or $902 in 1995 dollars) to $696 in 1995. The percentage of household income donated to charity dropped from 2 percent in 1989 to 1.7 percent in 1996 as well (Independent Sector 1996, 9).

Harvey and McCrohan assert that "there is evidence of declining support for philanthropy by the young, which is exacerbated by a proportional decline in this group in population," and is caused in part by the mistrust of existing institutions and a changed social outlook based on greed and social pressure (1990, 42).

Today's donors increasingly base their giving on enlightened self-interest rather than blind altruism, and, further, they have both a high degree of skepticism and a lack of understanding about the methods and purposes of philanthropy and fund raising (Mixer 1993). "The societal culture has lost a substantial measure of its confidence in the nonprofit sector's integrity. While trust has not been broken completely, scandals and questionable practices large and small have done considerable damage to the sector's perceived integrity" (Hedgepeth 1990, 114).

Public Demands for Accountability and Effectiveness Are Increasing

To assuage their skepticism, to counterbalance the potential abuses, people are asking for more regulations, more accountability, and more results. The public's awareness of abuses and resulting frustration produce a higher demand for proof that organizations and people are doing what they say they do and that it really matters. Two concerns are evidenced: for the *purpose* served by funds raised and for the *temporal efficiency* by which the funds are raised. Harvey and McCrohan (1990) write,

> Having a clear *purpose* gives prospective donors easily understood informa-

tion about the use of their contributions and has a considerable positive effect on donor behavior. . . . The issue of *temporal* efficiency, the proportion of funds raised that actually supports needed services within a reasonable time horizon, also appears to be of considerable importance to donors and industry analysts (55).

Harvey and McCrohan (1990) confirmed in a nationwide sample that perceived fund-raising efficiency did, in fact, lead to higher levels of giving. With minor exceptions, there was a steady increase in the level of donations as the donor's belief in the level of fund-raising efficiency increased. An important threshold level of efficiency was money allocated to programs at and above the 60 percent rating.

Public concern has led to increased interest in nonprofits by regulatory bodies, particularly state attorney's offices and agencies that monitor charitable activities. They are keeping the issues of accountability front and center, cautioning donors not to give unless they have sufficient information about a charity and encouraging them to look more closely at where their money goes. For example, in a 1994 holiday special edition mailing of "Give, but Give Wisely," produced by the Better Business Bureau, an article entitled "Let's Help the Donor Decide" cautions donors about a common practice of nonprofits of allocating their mailing costs to public education rather than fund raising. The concept of letting donors decide is a good one, provided the information they have is accurate, unbiased, and balanced.

Donors Want More Information, Input, and Influence

Increasingly, donors want more control over their money, be it tax dollars that go to government, the consumer purchases they make, or the contributions they make to charity. They are tired of being told where the needs are; they want to decide for themselves. They have developed a "show me" attitude, expecting and wanting to receive evidence that their support is needed, appreciated, and stewarded. Donors want to be understood and valued.

"The era of the uninformed, altruistic donor is waning, replaced by the era of better-educated and demanding contributors" (Harvey and McCrohan 1990, 61). They want specific benefits and demonstrated results from their gifts—at all levels. According to Rebecca Gonzalez-Campoy (1996), donors are more sophisticated and "want to see justification . . . They are looking at their gifts as investments and want to know that an organization plans well for the long term." In many cases they prefer to give their time and money for a particular project, rather than to give it over a long period of time (39).

A 1996 study by the Minnesota Charities Review Council brought light to the kind of information donors want and need to make informed giving decisions. The most-often raised questions needing answers were the following: What difference does my gift make (program use and effectiveness)? How is it spent (for what purposes is it allocated, and what percentage goes to the program)? Who is overseeing its use (are the people entrusted with my gift making wise decisions)?

According to the study, donors want the following types of information:

- *Basic management and fiduciary information:* annual report, financial reports, legal information, management and governance information
- *Solicitation disclosure:* whether the solicitor was paid or a volunteer, employed by the organization, or a telemarketer
- *Empowerment information:* what is the reputation and credibility of the organization, and does it fit with the individual's own ethics and values
- *Accountability, results, and program documentation:* information about how the organization will use its resources to further its mission and the constituents it serves, how effective the organization is at meeting its program goals, what the program does, and where it operates

From the donor's point of view, philanthropy is a choice he or she has to make the world a better place. Donors have precious but limited resources and want to get the most impact for what they have to give. They do not necessarily want to become involved, even in issues they are interested in. However, they do want to be more informed and knowledgeable. The challenge for fund raisers is to understand and appreciate these views and to direct our energies toward rebuilding the trust and confidence that our organizations and philanthropy deserve.

Step 5 in the Annual Integrated Development Process: Match Cases with Constituencies and Set Goals for Each Segment and Each Case/Campaign

As you recall, Step 1 determines institutional readiness and external responsiveness, Step 2 develops strategies for a philanthropic culture, Step 3 identifies and qualifies constituencies and defines market segments, and Step 4 examines and validates the cases and establishes fund-raising priorities. Step 5 brings the results of Step 3 together with the results of Step 4, matching the institution's needs with donors' interests. The outcome is challenging and realistic goals.

The process of matching institutional needs with donors' interests is a balancing act—bringing the *need* together with the *opportunity* and then defining the *ability*. The balancing is important for three reasons:

1. The goals must be *realistic*—if the needs are greater than the opportunity for raising funds, it can be a source of frustration for volunteers and staff.
2. The goals must be *achievable*—if the opportunity seems great, but sufficient funds are not raised, it can be a source of disappointment for volunteers and staff.

3. The goals must be *challenging*—if the opportunity is greater than the need, it can be a disincentive for volunteers and staff.

Fund-raising goals may be set by zero-based budgeting by project or by "plugging" the bottom line. Although the latter approach is never recommended, it may not be possible to start from zero. The fact is that good budgeting is not as difficult as it may appear. The key factors for success are (1) to allocate sufficient time, well ahead of the budget deadline, (2) to not set fund-raising goals until the fund-raising objectives are determined, and (3) to involve as many people as practical in the budgeting and goal-setting process.

There is a lot of emphasis within fund raising on the dollars to the detriment and sometimes the exclusion of relationship building. We know that this focus produces short-term results, but not long-term gains, and this is the reason why goal setting is best done as Step 5, not earlier.

Goals that are balanced—not too high nor too low—ensure a philanthropic process that is rewarding for all concerned, year after year. When goals are realistic, achievable, and challenging, they are not only met but more often they are exceeded. The process of goal setting starts with two simple questions: (1) How much do we need to raise (need)? and (2) How much will people give (opportunity)? Now we ask the third question: (3) How much will we raise (abil-

ity)? The answers translate into our goals (Exhibit 7–1).

Question 1: How Much Do We Need to Raise?

The *needs* are uncovered in the case development process. Individual programs and projects are identified, budgets developed, and the need for philanthropy determined. The cases fall into three general NEED categories: (1) unrestricted operating support, (2) restricted for operations, and (3) restricted for special purposes.

Combined, they represent the *organization's case for support*. Each category has its own case for support, and within each category are mini-cases for support. All cases have detailed budgets, goals, and objectives—and philanthropy needs. The NEED matrix in Exhibit 7–2 is a visual example of the complexity of case categories and philanthropic needs; a children's hospital is used in this example because of the variety of constituent groups and diversity of case types found there.

The NEED matrix (Exhibit 7–2) shows that $4,390,000 is needed from philanthropy in the current year. The objective is to raise funds for all the needs in the budgeted amounts. In the ideal world, donors will support what our organizations need; in the real world, donors support what they think the community needs,

Exhibit 7–1 Goal-Setting Process

add *Need:*	What are our institutional needs?	*How much do we need to raise?*
to *Opportunity:*	What are our donors' interests?	*How much will people give?*
to get *Ability:*	What are our goals?	*How much can we raise?*

Exhibit 7–2 Annual Case Categories and Philanthropic NEED

Case Categories	Case Subcategories	Case Examples	Annual Need for Philanthropy
GROUP A: Unrestricted Operating Costs	1. Organization services	Charitable care for uninsured children	$ 500,000
	2. Discretionary operating needs	As needed for patient emergencies, etc.	200,000
GROUP B: Restricted for Operations	1. Program areas	• Cancer treatment • Emergency services • Surgical & rehab • Neonatal care	1,000,000
	2. Program components	• Medical research • Medical training • Patient education	500,000
	3. Program services	• Child life services • Support groups • Respite care • Home nurse visits	200,000
GROUP C: Restricted for Special Purposes	1. Capital expansion	A new family center	1,000,000
	2. Equipment	Transport units and patient monitors	200,000
	3. New program initiative	Childhood immunization project	250,000 (per year/3 years)
	4. Special focus collaborations	Medical care for foster children	240,000
	5. Endowment purposes	Medical research and fellowships	300,000 (per year/3 years)
			$4,390,000 total

which translates to what the organization "should do." Usually, the needs (the organization/recipients) and the opportunities (the donors support) are compatible, but not always precisely the same. Partnership involves give and take; it entails collaboration, compromise, and commitment to the cause.

Looking closer at Exhibit 7–2, it is evident that some cases will be perceived by donors as more urgent and some less so. Some program cases, because of their nature, already have a donor following. Other cases need to be communicated better, to garner more support. The challenge is to match the constituency segments with the cases that best fit their interests, and vice versa. Gaps will result—there will be programs that are not funded, and some may be over-funded. Cases that appear ambiguous are more difficult to raise money for; the easiest cases are those described with specificity, and the strongest cases usually win out.

Question 2: How Much Will People Give?

How much people will give is estimated based on what they are already giving (renewal and upgrade estimates) and how many new donors will give (acquisition estimates). Each constituency group is assessed individually to determine its interests and potential. Using the same organization as an example, the OPPORTUNITY matrix in Exhibit 7–3 shows that $3,990,000 can be raised in philanthropic support in the current year from new, renewed, and upgraded donors. Some donor groups have a higher average gift than others, and some have higher retention rates. This information is taken into account when estimates are made. The estimates are also based on the linkage, interest, and ability levels of each group as identified earlier. Opportunity estimates must be conservative, but at the same time be made with confidence. Experience proves that an enthusiastic, positive attitude is the stimulus for exceeding even the most aggressive goals. There is no room for pessimism in fund raising.

Question 3: How Much Can We Raise?

The final question is answered by matching the needs and the opportunities in the best possible way. Inevitably, there will be discrepancies between what the organization needs to have funded and what its constituencies want to fund. Two situations can occur: (1) some programs will be under-funded, and (2) some programs will be over-funded. These situations call for creative solutions. For **under-funded programs**, consider doing the following:

> **There is no room for pessimism in fund raising.**

- Find another source of funding to fill the gap.
- Invite loyal "institutional" donors to fund these programs.
- Incorporate these programs into the unrestricted grouping, where discretion is allowed.
- Initiate a new campaign targeted at donors who may have a special interest.
- Cut back the program.

Strategies for **over-funded programs** include

- Expand the program if the need exists.
- Restrict the funds and using them when needed.
- Advise donors of over-funding, pointing out other critical needs.

In the example shown in Exhibit 7–4, the organization's needs totaled $4,390,000 and the constituencies' interests totaled $3,990,000—a shortfall of $400,000 or less than 10 percent. If this were a real-life situation, it would be reasonable to set the goal for each constituency group at 10 percent higher than the opportunity figures, knowing it is a realistic yet challenging stretch given the history and the stability of the donor base. (For this example, assume that the fund-raising costs of $600,000, or 18 percent, are already figured into the $4,390,000 figure. Exhibit 7–5 illustrates such a budget.)

In this example, the annual giving goal is established at $4,390,000, 10 percent above the estimated opportunity figure (in addition to being 9 percent over the previous year). The goal is not just a number, however; it is a challenge. It represents a real need—the actual amount required from philanthropy if the programs are to remain intact. It also represents a significant increase over the previous year, plus an additional stretch of 10 percent.

If a goal is set too low, staff and volunteers will respond with reluctance. They simply will not be motivated to do all that it takes to get the job done. If a goal is set too high, they will work hard, but will be discouraged before they even start, giving up before the end of the campaigns.

Exhibit 7–3 Constituencies and Philanthropic OPPORTUNITY

Constituency Categories	Donor or Source Subcategories	Donor Type and Number	Donor Interest and Potential
Board members	1. Newly recruited	A/2	20,000
	2. Current	R23/10% increase	250,000
	3. Former	R10/10% increase	150,000
		A3	3,000
Employees	1. Current	R300/10% increase	150,000
		A50	1,000
	2. Retired	R25/10% increase	15,000
Physicians	1. Employed status	R150/10% increase	247,000
		A50	50,000
	2. Affiliates	R75/10% increase	75,000
Patient families	1. Emergency room	R400/10% - A75	30,000
	2. Childhood cancer	R300/10% - A50	59,000
	3. Surgical patients	R100/10% - A25	60,000
	4. Neonatal patients	R500/10% - A100	15,000
	5. Other	R250/10% - A50	15,000
Tribute donors	1. Current	R250 - A25	15,000
Special event attendees	1. Current	Event A:$150,000net	500,000
		Event B:$350,000net	
Miscellaneous individual donors	1. Under $1,000	R5,000/10% - A1000	200,000
	2. Over $1,000	R1,000/10% - A150	1,000,000
Private family foundations/trusts		R50/10% - A10	1,000,000
			$3,990,000 total

Note: A, acquisition; R, renewal.

Exhibit 7-4 Constituencies Matched to Cases

Constituency Groups	Case Group A: Unrestricted Gifts for Operating NEED $700,000	Case Group B: Restricted Gifts for Operating NEED $1,700,000	Case Group C: Restricted Gifts for Special Purposes NEED $1,990,000
Board members	$ 2,000	$ 393,000	$ 28,000
Employees		151,000	15,000
Physicians	100,000	147,000	125,000
Patients	50,000	254,000	10,000
Tributes	7,000	8,000	
Special events	150,000	350,000	
Individuals	200,000		1,000,000
Family foundations	200,000	100,000	700,000
Totals Need:	700,000	Need: 1,700,000	Need: 1,990,000
Opportunity:	709,000	Opportunity: 1,403,000	Opportunity: 1,878,000
	+ 9,000	+ 3,000	− 112,000

The right goal will motivate volunteers to do all it takes to meet the need and to work a little harder to achieve success. The joy that comes from such an effort is unparalleled— enough to bring them back again next year.

> There are only three solicitation strategies: personal, impersonal, and participation.

Step 6 in the Annual Integrated Development Process: Select Appropriate Solicitation Methods and Vehicles

By the time the development team reaches Step 6, the choices of which approach to use with each constituency are becoming exceedingly clear. There are only three solicitation strategies: personal, impersonal, and participation (Exhibit 7–6). There are only three basic techniques: in person, by telephone, and by mail. From these come many interpretations and a multitude of combinations. Examples proliferate of unique, creative campaign approaches.

An annual integrated development program includes a series of multiple, continuous, positive asking situations that offer donors repeat opportunities and choices to meet their personal giving objectives. This approach addresses the uniqueness of each individual and acknowledges that donors have different reasons to give, different patterns of giving, and different preferences and reactions to solicitation approaches. Successful development programs seldom use one solicitation strategy or one technique; they use a *combination* of personal, impersonal, and participation strategies that reflects their unique constituencies and organization. This selection is made easier by the work already done in the planning and strategic analysis stages. Four criteria frame the decisions:

1. *Constituency composition:* size, ability, interest, access, and previous support
2. *Organizational capability:* strength of case, leadership, and technology

Exhibit 7–5 Annual Fund Raising Expense Budget

Line Item	199_ Budget	199_ Budget	Budget Variations
1. Salaries and wages			
Development Director (1)	$60,000		
Program director (2)	80,000		
Support Staff (3)	70,000		
Subtotal	210,000		
2. Pension contributions	18,000		
3. Other employee benefits	27,000		
4. Payroll taxes	16,000		
5. Professional fund-raising fees	15,000		
6. Supplies			
cards	3,000		
duplicating supplies	5,000		
stationery	25,000		
Subtotal	33,000		
7. Telephone	7,000		
8. Postage & Shipping			
postage	60,000		
mailing services	15,000		
delivery	2,000		
Subtotal	77,000		
9. Equipment rental	5,000		
10. Printing and publications			
brochures	18,000		
newsletters	50,000		
direct mail materials	100,000		
photos, slides	2,000		
Subtotal	170,000		
11. Travel			
air	2,000		
taxi	500		
mileage	2,000		
hotel	2,000		
Subtotal	6,500		

continues

Exhibit 7–5 continued

Line Item	199_ Budget	199_ Budget	Budget Variations
12. Conferences and meetings			
volunteer donor meeting	3,000		
conference rental	2,500		
Subtotal	5,500		
13. Insurance	2,000		
14. Computer services	5,000		
15. Other expenses	3,000		
Total Expenses	**658,500**		

This format is also used for each fund-raising strategy (donor acquisitions, board campaigns, foundations and corporations) as a method of computing this overall expense budget.

Exhibit 7–6 Annual Giving Techniques Ranked by Effectiveness

PERSONAL STRATEGIES

- Individual solicitation
- Team solicitation
- Solicitation by telephone
- Solicitation by mail

IMPERSONAL STRATEGIES

- Telemarketing
- Direct mail

PARTICIPATION STRATEGIES

- Special events
- Membership

---

3. *Financial and human resources:* cash flow, staffing, and volunteers
4. *Fund-raising goals:* number of prospects, donors, techniques, and activities

Although a combination of solicitation strategies and techniques is advised to maximize the potential reach, nothing is constant—the internal and external environments are always undergoing change. Dynamic functions affect and are affected by changing opinions and attitudes. The approaches used today may remain viable for several years, but will lose their effectiveness over time. New configurations will be necessary.

For instance, when telephone solicitation was first introduced, the public was very receptive. When a volunteer or a student called to ask for support, people were flattered and impressed. With overuse by commercial entities as well as charitable organizations, the public has grown tired of telephone solicitation. They resent the intrusions, growing more resistant even to appeals from their favorite charities. Similarly, when direct mail began, people were highly responsive. They took the time to read the material and were quick to follow instructions to send a check to organizations that made a compelling case. Today, the public is inundated with direct mail offers, creating an annoyance so great that many envelopes are thrown in the trash unopened. Even special events have experienced donor fatigue. A decade ago, walk-a-thons and golf tournaments were novel ideas. Today special events are commonplace—one wonders if there is an original idea for one left.

Too, the donative public has become fickle in its support of nonprofit organizations; they are quick to give and equally as quick to stop giving. Their reasons for not giving are justified when they see money or methodology taking precedence over mission, when they see net proceeds shrinking in comparison to gross receipts, and when they become weary of the impersonal solicitations they receive, even after they make a gift. Evidence shows that donors themselves prefer to be solicited in traditional and personal ways.

The personalized solicitation strategies are basic, fundamental, and effective methods. That does not mean they are simple to implement. Constituency research may indicate that a group of donors will respond well to a **personal solicitation strategy** by peers. The solicitation strategy will begin with a *personal letter* asking for a meeting and explaining its purpose. A peer solicitor will make a *personal telephone call* to a prospect/donor to establish a meeting date and place. *Face-to-face solicitation* will be made during the meeting, after which the solicitor will follow-up with a *personal thank-you note*. In this one example, four different contacts are made to facilitate a personal solicitation—one in person, one by telephone, and two by mail. After the successful completion of each personal solicitation, the organization may solicit the pros-

pects again during the annual *phonathon* campaign and, later in the year, during the seasonal *direct mail* campaign.

For another group of donors, a **telephone solicitation strategy** may be advised. In this case, a *pre-call personal letter* is mailed, a *telephone solicitation* is done, followed by a *mail package* containing additional information to reinforce the request, with a response card and a return envelope.

For yet another group of donors, a **mail solicitation strategy** may be most appropriate. In this case, mail is the only method of communication. The strategy includes a *personalized solicitation letter* followed by a *second reminder*, and when the gift is received, *a personal thank-you letter* is sent. Mail is generally the only standalone or single vehicle approach, which may account for its lower response rates.

Clearly, the most effective solicitation techniques are the most personal—they rely heavily on human resources and minimally on technology. This book advocates the use of individual and team solicitation and personal solicitation by phone and by mail over all other approaches. It does not discount the relative importance or appropriateness of telemarketing, direct mail, benefit events, and membership. These are useful strategies when applied properly—they are simply not as effective as personal solicitation, and their over-promotion encourages fund raisers to resort to them without considering their high cost, low returns, and growing negative implications. The industry's overemphasis on impersonal fund-raising techniques tends to undermine the integrity of the philanthropic process. A great amount of money may be raised through them, but few philanthropists are made. Experience suggests that the further the giver is from the receiver (or donor from the recipient), the weaker the communication and the more fragile the relationship. For fund raisers who must use impersonal techniques because of the magnitude of their prospect base, the geographic distribution of services and donors, or the limited number of staff or volunteers, there are other resources to stay on top of the changing trends and technologies.

Personal Solicitation Strategies

Individual Solicitation

Without question, in-person or face-to-face solicitation is the most effective of all fund-raising techniques, producing the highest rate of positive responses. Individual solicitation is also the most time-consuming and challenging process, whether undertaken by volunteers, staff, or a team. However, when a solicitation is undertaken successfully, it is one of the most rewarding experiences for the solicitor and one of the most satisfying experiences for the donor. An indication of a successful solicitation comes when a donor is at least, if not more, excited about making a gift than the solicitor is in receiving it. The solicitor's real reward comes from observing the satisfaction and pleasure a philanthropic act brings to a donor, knowing that the gift will have an equally positive impact on the lives of the recipients.

Why, then, is there so much resistance on the part of volunteers, especially, to doing personal solicitations? Myths abound, tied to perceptions that personal solicitation is manipulative, demanding, and, worse, a form of begging. The very notion of asking someone for money causes anxiety, discomfort, and even fear in the average person. Since childhood, we have been taught not to ask others for help, much less for *money*. Doing so is seen as presumptuous *and* a sign of weakness, neither of which are widely accepted behaviors in a society that values self-sufficiency and individualism.

One can understand why volunteers resist solicitation assignments, but one would think professional fund raisers should know better. Like volunteers, we fund raisers too have a fear of failure, are embarrassed to ask, and are not fully cognizant or confident of our role in the solicitation process. Check your work list: chances are functional tasks get crossed off by Friday, but relationship contacts get carried over to Monday.

An inexperienced fund raiser might describe face-to-face solicitation as "taking a prospect to lunch." No wonder there is resistance fueled by disappointment. When practitioners complain about the lack of success getting appointments, we need to be reminded that few of us want to have lunch with someone we do not know, much less be solicited by them.

Several conditions must be in place before an individual can be solicited for a contribution. The prospect must be sufficiently *qualified*, there must be a *convincing case*, the prospect has been *properly cultivated*, the solicitor has a *sense of confidence*, and there is a scripted *solicitation strategy* in place.

The best solicitations are those that pair solicitors with prospects based on a pre-existing linkage—friendship creates a natural environment to work in. The comfort in being a solicitor comes from knowing you are not asking for yourself; instead, you are offering the prospect an opportunity to realize his or her own aspirations through a gift to a charitable cause that merits support. As a solicitor, you are doing so much more than asking; you are facilitating an exchange between similar interests and needs with confidence and pride, not hesitation or apology.

The Solicitation Process: Four Steps

The preferred model of individual solicitation uses a four-step process. This process is recommended by a number of experienced practitioners and is practiced by The Fund Raising School. According to Mixer (1993) the process must satisfy the donor's personal motivations, present suitable donor stimuli, and cite potential donor rewards. The parenthetical examples given in the following steps show what a solicitor's role might be; in real life, the donor's responses would influence the solicitor's comments.

Step 1—Introduction: Establish Rapport. The introduction phase is brief, compared to the other three steps. It opens with an exchange of pleasantries, generalities, and mutual interests (could be work, gardening, hunting, mutual friends, family, children, civic activities). The idea is to establish a rapport that is conducive to dialogue. Without avoidance, the purpose of the visit is stated clearly: to discuss how the prospect's interests and the organization's needs can be achieved. The solicitor succinctly points out the pressing social problem (for instance, only 50 percent of today's "baby truants" will finish school), elaborates on the effect (a community of undereducated citizens results in unemployment, poverty, even violence), and expands on the organization's ability to address such problems (the 100-year-old organization has expertise and success helping neglected children and dysfunctional families become healthy and contributing citizens).

Step 2—Exploration: Elicit the Prospect's Input and Seek Areas of Mutual Concern. During the exploration phase, the solicitor attempts to elicit the prospect's concerns, interests, and knowledge about the organization's work in a particular area (in this case, about neglected children who may not develop their potential). Questions are asked to help the solicitor gain a better understanding of the prospect's attitudes, opinions, and values (what are your experiences and concerns related to children, to education?).

Common ground is sought, and mutual views are exchanged. In the process of exploring present-day concerns and future aspirations, the solicitor clarifies what has been said, striving to gain input from the prospect about what might be done and how (how might undereducated parents learn to value education and, in turn, encourage their children to stay in school). Involvement of the prospect to the *solution* is an important goal of this phase, advancing the exchange from awareness to concern to involvement and finally toward action.

The solicitor completes this phase by reinforcing that the organization is well equipped to address the issues and has demonstrated previous success in doing so (93 percent of the children enrolled in the School Success program

have improved attendance, behaviors, and grades; 50 percent of the parents are involved in school activities; several of the parents have returned to school).

Step 3—Clarification: Bring the Interest Together with the Need. During this phase the solicitor clarifies precisely what the organization intends to do with the prospect's help (to counsel, tutor, and mentor families about the importance of a child's education). The solicitor may give several examples of program/project options that will fit with the prospect's personal motivations, experiences, and aspirations. Sensing interest, the solicitor presents the financial needs, refers to others who are supporting the project, gives the qualifications of staff, and points out the benefits that will come from a philanthropic gift.

The donor's benefits may include a sense of personal involvement in the life of a child, civic responsibility and social accomplishment, and increased self-esteem. The tangible benefits may include recognition among peers, an opportunity to become more involved, and increased knowledge about issues that are of importance to him or her.

Finally, the solicitor restates the mutual interests, refers to the program options, and questions the prospect once more about his or her aspirations.

Step 4—Conclusion: Close the Discussion with an Ask. In this phase the solicitor restates the *ask* (Will you join with other Leaders for Learning and underwrite one family's participation in the School Success program?). Assuming the response is positive, the solicitor thanks the prospect graciously and extends an invitation to attend a recognition dinner (to meet some of the families who graduated from last year's program), making note of any necessary follow-up activity.

The solicitation process is designed to be a dynamic, flexible interaction that achieves a mutually beneficial exchange. It is not science and therefore neither predictable nor exact. There are many possibilities during such a process for resistance, disagreement, and even defensiveness. It is a challenge to balance the talking with the listening; the donor and the case must be balanced. Thus, the art comes into play—the solicitor must be respectful, flexible, upbeat, and attentive to the prescribed steps throughout. It is the solicitor's responsibility to offer a prospect the opportunity for involvement; a declination is the prospect's privilege. In that case, thank the prospect for his or her time as you would someone who responded with an affirmative.

Advantages of Individual Solicitation

Individual solicitation has always been the most effective solicitation technique because of the high rates of positive response and the corresponding low cost of implementation. According to Michael P. Scott (1996), "experts estimate that an in-person contact is about 70 percent more effective than one made over the phone" (48). Although its use has declined during the last 15 years with the introduction of new technologies, there is renewed interest in this method today. Many organizations are rethinking their approaches, given growing public resistance to systematic and impersonal solicitations.

Of interest is an article in *The Chronicle of Philanthropy* that reported that giving in the top 400 American charities had increased by 5 percent "due to in part to the emphasis that organizations were placing on raising larger donations from individual donors." According to the article many groups had benefited by abandoning fund-raising techniques that no longer brought in significant returns, such as direct mail and telemarketing. Boys and Girls Clubs of America, which raised $294.9 million in 1995, is reported to be phasing out direct mail solicitation and discouraging their local clubs from running costly special events such as golf tournaments that do not raise much money. "Instead, it is asking its clubs to meet in-person with donors and has been holding special seminars to teach fund raisers how to raise money face to

face" (Blum, Dundjerski, and Marchetti 1996, 58).

Disadvantages of Individual Solicitation

The disadvantages of individual solicitation are related to the high level of expertise needed to facilitate the process and the time associated with it. It is not easy to find already trained and experienced solicitors, so efforts must go toward recruiting, training, maintaining, and replacing volunteers and staff. Personality affinity, or chemistry, between solicitor and prospect can affect the outcome; the solicitor must be the *right* asker. Individual solicitation involves a large commitment of time; one solicitation could involve a half-dozen telephone calls, several letters, and more than one visit.

When to Use Individual Solicitation

The ideal time to use individual solicitation is when volunteers are available, when staff are experienced, when the case is specific, when donor potential is significant, and at the beginning of every campaign (always start your efforts with the best donors and largest gifts).

Team Solicitation

In certain cases, a team of two solicitors will be more effective than one solicitor. In annual giving, teaming is not used often, but is recommended for the important donors at the top. The magnitude of the fund-raising effort and the significance of the donor relationship determine when to involve two solicitors. Team solicitation ordinarily involves a volunteer and a staff member, although two volunteers could accomplish the same goals if they are well informed and experienced. The advantage of using a volunteer and a staff member is to gain a value-added effect of volunteer credibility with staff knowledge, board leadership with program management, and community representation with recipient advocacy.

The four step solicitation process, articulated under individual solicitation, is also used by the team, but the interaction is shared.

Advantages of Team Solicitation

Team solicitation has several advantages over individual solicitation. First, the work is shared, which makes it more attractive to volunteers. Second, the team brings greater expertise and knowledge than a single individual. A team approach results in better communications; the conversation is more focused and interactive. Finally, the possibility of personality conflict is minimized.

Disadvantages of Team Solicitation

It takes more time to train two solicitors, and if used individually, they could solicit twice as many donors. Teaming is not as easy as it appears: two solicitors need to complement each other, they need to be a good fit with the prospect(s), and they need to practice before doing it. The downside, not always anticipated, is the way in which the donor views the team solicitation. The donor may be flattered by the attention or annoyed with what seems like overkill.

When To Use Team Solicitation

Team solicitation is a good technique to use with donors who are already involved with the organization and who have been identified as having both leadership and financial potential. A team approach suggests to the prospect that he or she is important enough to merit the time of two other important people. Teaming is a good technique to use when the request is unusually large and for something special. And team solicitation is a useful technique to use when volunteers or staff are "in training."

Personal Solicitation by Telephone

Because the vast percentage of annual giving prospects will not justify a personal visit, the telephone becomes the method of choice. Organized, personal telephone solicitation is the preferred methodology of volunteers and staff with prospect/donor lists under 1,000. Any larger lists require an organized phonathon, a formalized telemarketing program, a direct mail appeal, or a sophisticated combination of phone and mail.

Small, highly qualified constituent groups, such as board members, employees, designated donors, special fund donors, or friends of board members naturally lend themselves to telephone solicitation, especially if their giving levels are in the mid-range and if they have been loyal supporters. Today's traditional *annual fund campaigns*, such as the YMCA, in which volunteers agree to contact ten qualified prospects/donors by a specified deadline, depend more heavily on telephone solicitation than in previous years when people were more accessible and amenable to personal visits.

Advantages of Personal Telephone Solicitation

Communicating with prospects or donors by telephone has many advantages. First of all, a telephone is easy and quick to use (a little prep time gives you an agenda). Second, a telephone provides an opportunity for two-way communications—questions can be answered, feedback gathered, solicitations made, and gifts pledged. Third, the telephone is less imposing than a personal visit and more effective than a letter; in addition, you can call more than once, leave a message on the answering machine, and follow up with a personal note. Fourth, the telephone is very effective at building donor loyalty, and it is affordable (donors over $100 are the targets). Fifth, the telephone can be used almost 10 hours a day, 365 days a year; good sense dictates when to call, but a portion of every day can be set aside for development staff and volunteers to get maximum use of the telephone. Finally, the telephone has multiple uses: (1) to thank, (2) to gather information, (3) to invite to a special event, (4) to recruit volunteers, and (5) to solicit a gift.

Disadvantages of Personal Telephone Solicitation

The disadvantages are few, aside from the public's growing negative feelings about receiving fund-raising calls in the evening. In the early years of telephone solicitation, people were surprised and even flattered to be called, especially by their favorite charity or alma mater. Since then, telephone marketing companies have virtually inundated the phone waves with electronically generated calls selling everything from home mortgages to storm windows. Nonprofits too have saturated the market, on more than one occasion using the telephone book as their prospect list. Blatant misuse of the telephone as a communications mode has led to a significant decline in its use for fund raising. One can easily understand how annoying it is to receive an unannounced interruption from someone you do not know during what is regarded as personal time.

Nevertheless, the telephone remains an extremely effective method of communicating with donors who "expect" a call (having received a clever postcard or personal note announcing the date and time of the call) and whose choice it is to receive it or decline it. A telephone call unanswered, or even a declination, does not negatively affect a post-call mail solicitation that includes a "sorry to have missed you by phone" or a "hopefully you will consider a gift in the future" note.

When To use Personal Telephone Solicitation

The telephone can be used to *acquire new donors*, provided they are qualified with some prior relationship to the organization (alumni, patients, attendees, or members). The telephone is not as effective for "cold calls," but a pre-mailing will help prepare the donor. With sufficient cultivation and information ahead of time, the telephone *may* be the most effective technique for prospects without a natural connection.

The telephone can be used to *renew donors*, generating a higher response rate than mail so-

licitations to the same group (65 to 85 percent compared to 45 to 60 percent). The renewal response rates from telephone solicitation are particularly high for donors at the higher giving levels (90 percent response rate on average). The telephone is especially effective for renewing *lapsed donors*. And the telephone is the most effective methodology for *upgrading donors* if done in a timely and systematic way (60 to 80 percent response rate).

Volunteer Phonathons

For decades, organizations have used volunteer *phonathons* as an inexpensive way to generate contributions while simultaneously engaging their volunteers in a "painless" form of fund raising. Sometimes they work miraculously; other times they are an exercise in futility.

Organized phonathons work very effectively in conjunction with other solicitation techniques, such as follow-up on prospects who could not be solicited face-to-face or whose giving has lapsed. They are also effective in situations that demand a quick turnaround time and for renewing support that was garnered previously via phone.

Phonathons work best when volunteers are (1) readily available, (2) experienced and enthused about telephoning others, (3) paired with prospects who have close relationships, and (4) motivated by the psychosocial aspects of the activity. The physical environment plays a big role in keeping callers energized and productive throughout the phonathon. The ideal environment is a large room with desks and phones placed so volunteers can challenge and cheer each other on and celebrate successful calls. Volunteers are given cards or computer printouts with information about the prospect and a suggested gift amount. Of course, training is provided, scripts are prepared, and follow-up materials are available to make the calls as easy and efficient as possible, whether they result in a "yes," a "no," or a "maybe." The key is keeping the volunteers motivated and on task.

Three problems can undermine the psychological affect of a phonathon: when only a few volunteers show up, when prospect information is not available or accurate, and when the prospects have not been qualified or cultivated properly.

Personal Solicitation by Mail

Solicitation by mail is the easiest method of the three primary ones. Almost anyone can write a letter asking for support at any time—it just needs to be sincere and direct. A personal mail solicitation can take many forms: a letter, a note, or a postcard that is typed, hand-written, or even faxed. The message can be supported by a brochure, a wish list, a one-page program summary, and even a photo. And it may include a pledge card and a return envelope.

Unlike face-to-face and telephone solicitation, mail as a technique is not interactive. No matter how well written, a letter communicates in only one direction. Therefore, when you use the mail to solicit prospects, you have to *overcommunicate* to be effective. The envelope must first attract someone's attention if they are to open it. For personalized mail, never use a window envelope or label; rather type or hand-address it. Prospects must have prior awareness of the issues/organization; if the letter is not from someone they know or recognize, they will probably discard it. The letter and supporting materials must convey a sense of critical relevance and be interesting enough for prospects to read and comprehend it; a letter should be written as you would write a personal friend, using "I" and "we" language. There must be enough rational information and emotional examples to cause prospects to think about the message; statistics and stories give substance and vivacity. Finally, there must be a sense of urgency to elicit concern sufficient so prospects will act on it; what would happen without their contribution? In sum, a mail solicitation uses many communication principles and is best achieved as if writing a letter to your very best friend.

People are accustomed to being solicited by mail. Many prefer this method, and so it continues to be a popular way to raise money. When letters are personalized, rather than mass pro-

duced, their effectiveness grows immeasurably. Who signs the letter or endorses the campaign effort greatly influences whether the prospect reads the letter and acts on the solicitation. If the solicitor is a friend or a well-known individual, attention is increased, as is the potential for positive response. "We are learning that personal letters do much better than expensive direct-mail letters designed for our agency," said Lee Vriesman, director of annual giving at the Methodist Health Foundation in Indianapolis (Warwick 1993, 43).

Advantages of Personal Mail Solicitation

The advantages of sending personalized mail solicitations are many. There is enormous flexibility with this technique and limitless configurations. Mail solicitations can be tailored to every constituent group. They can be sent 365 days a year and between six to eight times a year to the same prospect (different appeals). Letters can be short or long, accompanied by any number and kind of support materials. They can be printed on agency letterhead or on a specially designed format featuring a campaign theme. Turnaround time for preparation can be a few minutes for one letter to a couple of days if the letter is going to a number of prospects with personalized insertions. Different people can author/sign different letters, as appropriate. Few prospects have negative reactions to receiving mail, though they do complain about too much "direct mail"—the kind that treats them as computer records, rather than live donors.

Disadvantages of Personal Mail Solicitation

There is one major disadvantage to mail solicitation. Mail, even when personalized to the

> **There is enormous flexibility and with personalized mail solicitations, and limitless configurations.**

maximum extent, cannot "talk with" a prospect. Granted, a letter can be written to anticipate a prospect's questions and concerns. It can offer enough information to assuage a prospect's reluctance, it can articulate benefits that a prospect is interested in, and it can communicate opportunities for affiliation. Still it remains static in its presentation.

When To Use Personal Mail Solicitation

Personal solicitation by mail is best used when a prospect or a donor has demonstrated some reluctance to be involved or wishes anonymity. Many donors are quite content to write a check once a year to a charity in which they have developed a sense of confidence. They simply do not want to be more connected. In fact, they prefer relationships to be on their terms. Letters can communicate effectively in these situations and over time may open the door to a more personal interaction.

Personalized letters are also effective in tandem with telephone solicitation and especially for prospects who cannot be reached by telephone. At least 25 percent of the prospect/donor base will need to be solicited by mail; if necessary all of them can be.

Impersonal Solicitation Strategies

Professional Telemarketing

According to Mal Warwick, the preeminent fund-raising counsel on direct response marketing, "Many fund-raising managers dismiss telephone fund raising out-of-hand because of personal bias or resistance from board members. If you're caught in this trap, you may be leaving a great deal of money on the table—and foregoing other valuable benefits as well" (Logan 1993, 41).

The term "professional telemarketing" means that phoning is done by trained paid callers, rather than volunteers. It is highly systematized and uses sophisticated technology, rather than being spontaneous or personal. Telemarket-

ing is more than an occasionally used strategy; most often it is a tactic that is undertaken year-round, year after year. It is unlikely that an organization can implement a telemarketing program without expert counsel, regardless of whether the program is internalized or outsourced—it requires a sophisticated, systematic, organizational approach.

Warwick recommends five key components for a professional telephone fund-raising program:

1. highly motivated callers
2. thorough training and careful supervision of the callers
3. precise selection of the target audiences
4. scrupulous attention to fund-raising ethics
5. compliance with all legal requirements, including registration with state charity regulators

Advantages of Professional Telemarketing

The rationale for using professional telemarketing is from the need to reach a large and growing number of prospects/donors. When numbers begin to exceed 1,000, telephone solicitation is no longer advised as a volunteer activity—there is too much to gain by hiring professional staff and too much to lose by leaving solicitations to chance. Although volunteers may have more influence and impact over the phone than staff, they are not available on an ongoing, consistent basis. At this pivotal point, there are two options: hire staff (maybe on a temporary basis) or out-source the telemarketing.

In-House Professional Telemarketing. Lists in the 1,000 to 5,000 range can be handled by in-house staff as long as sufficient resources are dedicated to their recruitment, training, and management. The most important contributor to success is the capability of the one individual—the coordinator—who has primary responsibility for managing the effort from start to finish. The coordinator is responsible for hiring, training, and supervision; oversight of the night-to-night operations; and the collection and the recording of all receipts. The benefit of an in-house program is the control it gives the organization in hiring and coaching of callers, writing scripts, collections, and evaluation. The down-sides of an in-house program are the constant turnover of callers, the mechanical humdrum of operations, the requirement of working evening hours, and the increasing resistance by prospects to telemarketing: Answering machines screen calls, people are reluctant to make a commitment over the phone, and most want more information sent by mail anyway.

Out-Sourced Professional Telemarketing. Of late, many well-established fund-raising programs have opted for the out-sourcing method of contracting with professional telemarketing firms for services. When the list of prospects/donors exceeds 5,000, out-sourcing is a good choice. Most telemarketing firms provide creative services, telephone hook-up, professional solicitation, daily reporting on results, follow-up direct mail, and collection and processing of pledges. Timothy D. Logan offers tips about how to select the right telemarketing firm in the Fall 1993 issue of *Advancing Philanthropy*. These are the questions to ask (42):

- What is the telemarketing firm's philosophy?
- What is its track record with organizations like yours?
- How much can the firm do, and how fast can they do it?
- Will the salesperson manage your program?
- Who will you be able to call when you need something?
- How often will you receive reports on results?
- What monitoring services do they offer?
- How do they handle feedback and complaints?
- Exactly how is the billing determined?
- What kind of test programs do they offer?
- What about state registration?

- What is their policy regarding ownership of lists?
- Do they work in the for-profit sector too?

Disadvantages of Professional Telemarketing

Telemarketing is an extremely labor-intensive activity and organizationally demanding. Systems, policies, and procedures are needed for every aspect. Failure to manage the human resources, the technological aspects, and the post-acquisition follow-up could render a telemarketing program ineffective. And people are increasingly reluctant to make commitments over the phone.

When To Use Professional Telemarketing

Professional telemarketing is the most effective solicitation technique to use if your organization has a *large number of natural constituents*—alumni, patients, and members—and your image is institutionally well-known, such as an art museum or a hospital. Natural constituents have a *linkage* with the institution that is different from any other potential donor group. They are already familiar with the facility, the staff, and the programs: They have lived on campus, benefited from hospital services, attended performances, or enjoyed the exhibits. Such constituents are described as consumptive donors—they are both givers and beneficiaries. They have a high *interest* in the institution and its programs because they have or will benefit personally from them. Natural constituents do not have the same resistance to telephone solicitations that others do. They recognize the importance of the institution's mission, they are interested in see-

> **Professional telemarketing is the most effective technique to use if your organization has a large number of natural constituents.**

ing it succeed, they are aware that people like themselves already support it, and if treated like a member of the institution's family, they do not resent the call, but in fact may welcome it.

Professional telemarketing is very effective when a *telephone reinstatement program* is in order. When contacted by telephone, lapsed donors, even those who have not given for several years, will respond better than to the most effective letter. Telemarketing also works when an organization is launching a *monthly sustainer program*—upgrading long-term but small donors by offering a monthly pledge plan. It is also effective for donors who have the potential to be *upgraded to higher giving club levels* at $500 or $1,000. A reinstatement program, a monthly sustainer program, or an upgrade giving club program are best accomplished with a combination of pre-mail, telephone, and post-mail packaging that is highly personalized.

Another form of mail/phone combination is the newest technique—the *telefund*. This approach involves a letter or a series of letters mailed in advance of the telephone call to announce the caller's "visit," present the case for support, and suggest a gift level. During the call, the solicitor presents a large amount, working downward as necessary. After the call, other letters are sent to acknowledge and reinforce the pledge and to increase the pledge collection rate.

A word needs to be said about fulfillment of telephone pledges. The industry norm ranges from 70 to 95 percent of the pledged amount. Pledge-to-cash conversion varies widely because of two factors: (1) First-time pledgers have a lower fulfillment rate than repeat pledgers who have become accustomed to pledging by phone, and (2) the number of reminders and timeliness of the collection system itself determine the eventual outcome. Some institutions send invoices every month for up to six months on every outstanding pledge for maximum results. Others "re-call" to determine the reasons behind the unfulfilled pledge.

Exhibit 7–7 is a sample telephone solicitation script.

Direct Mail

Direct mail is the most impersonal and expensive method of solicitation, but is a proven strategy for acquiring new donors. It is the only technique designed to approach large numbers of prospects, particularly those who may not be highly qualified enough to telephone. Direct mail is often referred to as a "numbers game"—the more you mail, the more donors you acquire. The returns can be as little as 0.01 percent depending on the quality of the list and of the mailing package. Advocates of direct mail contend, however, that even a few donors will eventually pay for its high costs. So fund raisers continue to mail direct-response packages to massive numbers of prospects in the hopes that a few will respond and stay around long enough to make direct mail worthwhile. Other advocates point out that direct mail is also a means of informing and educating prospects, building awareness over time that eventually materializes into a response.

Given the numbers, the package complexities, the technology requirements, and the necessary resources, a direct mail program relies heavily on the expertise of specialists and consultants—and on a systems model approach. Successful direct mail must be designed and implemented analogous to a complex set of interrelated parts that function as a whole.

For a practitioner, a direct mail program can be the most exhilarating process to get up and running, the most frustrating to get to run smoothly, and the most rewarding when it delivers results that demonstrably grow over time.

A caution must be exercised here, because in the last year or so, sharp drops in returns have occurred in some of the largest direct mail programs. According to a recent article in the *The*

> **Direct mail is the most impersonal and expensive method, but is a proven strategy for acquiring new donors.**

Exhibit 7–7 Sample Telephone Solicitation Script

INTRODUCTION   *Page One*

Hello, may I speak to _____.
                              (name on card)

       IF NOT AVAILABLE. When is the best time to call back?

I'm _____ calling on behalf of (name of hospital). I'm
calling to ask for your help in meeting a critical need of newborn infants.

Have I reached you at a convenient time? I'll be very brief!

NOT CONVENIENT	When it the best time to call you back? (Be specific: night and time)
NOT INTERESTED	We're hoping that you, like other families with children, will support our efforts to save the lives of children.
NO	Thank you for your time. Have a good evening.
YES	Continue on page two.

Refer patient concerns to Parent Representative
Billing concerns to Customer Service

EXPLAIN AND ASK   *Page Two*

GREAT! Our current need is to purchase new state-of-the-art ventilators for our premature baby
unit. Are you familiar with preemie babies?

(Well then you know that) Often times their lungs are not fully developed and they must rely
on ventilators to keep breathing. The new ventilators ease their breathing and support them as
their lungs mature.

We need 5 ventilators, costing $22,000 each.

So, _____, would you consider making a *tax-deductible* gift of $50.00 to help us buy this
life saving equipment? *PAUSE*

NO	Perhaps $50 is a stretch for you. Would you consider $35? *PAUSE*
NO	Would you consider a $20 gift? (DO NOT GO LOWER!)
NO	Thanks for talking with me. Have a nice evening.
YES	Go to Credit Card Ask.

continues

Exhibit 7–7 continued

END OF CALL: CREDIT CARD   *Page Three*

Thank you for your support. For your convenience, would you be interested in placing your gift on a credit card? (Visa, MasterCard, American Express and Discover). Credit cards gifts minimize our processing costs. *PAUSE*

NO   Go to page four

YES   Great and which card will you be using?

         And the card number please? *REPEAT TO VERIFY*

         And the expiration date? *REPEAT TO VERIFY*
              (If date is expired, do not process, suggest we mail an invoice instead.)

         And how does the signature appear on the card? *REPEAT TO VERIFY*

Thank you for your generous gift of $_____. On your next credit card statement, your gift of $_____ will be listed. Within the next few days, you'll receive a confirmation of this tax-deductible gift.

May I double check the spelling of your last name and confirm your current mailing address? (spell out last name and provide address on card). Thank you.

Again thank you for your generous contribution of $_____. Have a nice evening.

END OF CALL: CASH PLEDGE   *Page Four*

Allow me to confirm your pledge of $_____.

May I also check the spelling of your last name? *VERIFY*

May I confirm your current mailing address? *PROVIDE ADDRESS ON CARD*
Thank you.

You will receive a confirmation of your $_____ pledge in the next few days. Please return your gift in the envelope provided.

Thanks again for your generous gift of $_____. Have a nice evening!

  Courtesy of Children's Health Care. Children's Hospital of St. Paul merged with Minneapolis Children's Medical Center in June 1994 to form Children's Health Care.

Chronicle for Philanthropy, the effectiveness of direct mail is slipping. In 1995, charities sent 12.2 billion pieces of third-class mail, an increase of two billion from a decade ago. However, the rate of response has declined over that time. For example, at the Metropolitan Museum of Art in New York, the response to mailings to attract new members dwindled from 0.9 percent to 0.5

percent in the last three years. When the Disabled Americans Veterans sent an appeal to attract new donors in September 1996, it received contributions from nearly 25 percent fewer people than it did from a similar mailing the previous year. A National Easter Seal Society's 1995 fall mailing to previous supporters generated one-fifth fewer responses than did the 1994 appeal. InnVision, a San Jose, California, shelter for the homeless actually lost money on its 1995 end-of-the-year mailing. According to Michael Stoll, development director for the shelter, "The really disturbing part of our direct mail in the last year is the drop in donors who give $100 or more" (Hall 1996, 23).

The dwindling response is attributed to growing number of charities who are trying to raise money through direct mail, increased frequency of their appeals, higher printing and paper costs, and narrower profit margins.

Key Success Factors in Direct Mail

Direct mail uses the same communication principles as personalized mail solicitations. Success is tied to three factors: (1) the quality of the list, (2) the creativity and readability of the package, and (3) the level of personalization. Direct mail by its nature is expensive and unless the list and the package are tested with a statistically significant group of prospects, the risk of net loss is probably greater than the possibility of net gain. So much is riding on the quality of the list and the package that no recovery plan will replace the lost resources if the direct mail effort is ineffective. Even worse, unless you test, you will not know what went wrong.

The third factor, **personalization**, will distinguish your appeal from others while increasing the chances of a higher response. The *Chronicle of Philanthropy*'s report on seasonal direct mail programs cites the benefits of personalization. When Covenant House in New York switched from sending a traditional three-page Christmas letter to a personalized Christmas card, they increased donations by 20 percent. When the Salvation Army of Metro Atlanta hand-addressed their envelopes, used first-class

stamps, hand-signed the letters, and added a note at the bottom, they tripled the previous year's responses and increased their net proceeds by 198 percent. And when Wheat Ridge Ministries in Itasca, Illinois, started sending two personalized appeals (an initial letter and a follow-up note) several weeks apart, their net revenue doubled (Hall 1996, 31).

Direct mail is a complex technique with many variables. Its components and recommended choices are shown in Exhibit 7–8.

Advantages of Direct Mail

Direct mail is the preferred technique for organizations with large numbers of prospects in wide geographic areas. Direct mail can reach these audiences quickly and systematically. Remember, the primary purpose of direct mail is not to bring in the highest dollar gifts, but to identify and attract new donors. When volunteers are not available, direct mail can be implemented by staff, with the aid of counsel. With advanced technology and good prospect research, it is possible to tailor appeals to different constituencies and to track returns by source and appeal. Direct mail is the best acquisition technique for bringing donors *into* the pyramid of giving.

Disadvantages of Direct Mail

The disadvantages are low response rates, low profit margins, high start-up costs, and increased competition from junk mail.

When to Use Direct Mail

Direct mail is the technique of choice for the acquisition of donors who cannot be reached by others methods and when the large numbers prohibit other approaches. It remains the most effective technique to use during the holiday season, the largest giving time of the year. Although a donor has already given, a direct mail appeal with a holiday theme often generates a second gift. The advantages of a direct mail package during the holiday season lie in its design:

Exhibit 7–8 Direct Mail Components, Choices, and Comments

COMPONENTS	CHOICES	WITH RENEWALS
Mailing Lists	Prior donors Members Prospects Clients/neighbors Rented/leased/purchased	Distinguish between donors • first year • repeat • lapsed Divide renewals by • length • date of last gift • gift size
Outside Envelope	Addressee information Return address Address correction Indicia, stamp, or meter Special message	Use organization's name on front Spell prospect's name correctly Avoid impersonal addressing
Appeal Letter	Stationery Personalized stationery Persuasive wording Request for a gift amount Typed, printed, or computer generated P.S.	Personalize the letter Refer to last gift Cite last year's success Note progress as result Ask for another, larger gift
Enclosures	Brochure, card, or giveaway Photograph and message Reprinted news article or ad Personal note	Summary program report A program brochure

Response Form	Donor name, address, phone
	Gift amount options
	Gift club options
	Information for inquiries (wills,
	  special programs, etc)
		Link levels to recognition and clubs
		Provide information about specific
		  programs

Reply Envelope	Pre-printed address
	Space(lines) for return address
	Postage option (business reply
	  envelope or donor's stamp)
	Combine response form and
	  envelope
		Personalize to someone's attention

Data from NSFRE and Jim Greenfield.

It can be distinctive, creative, and emotional enough to generate a first and sometimes a second annual gift. Direct mail is a technique that will not offend because it is non-invasive—prospects can open it or throw it away without guilt or apology. A direct mail package can always be added to an existing solicitation schedule, offering more variety to the solicitation mix.

Participation Strategies

Special Events

Almost all organizations include special events in their repertoire of fund-raising strategies. Many, in fact, started fund raising with a benefit event. Events range from bake sales to charity balls, golf tournaments to walk-a-thons, auctions to concerts, with each one designed to attract a different constituency.

Special events play a very important role in the fund-raising mix because of the awareness they generate, the opportunities they present for volunteer involvement, and the psychosocial benefits they deliver to prospects and donors alike. In some respects, special events are more of a cultivation than a fund-raising technique. In reality they do not raise a lot of money because of the high costs of site usage, equipment rental, food service, entertainment, prizes, and the like. Although special events have fairly large gross revenues, net proceeds are only in the 50 percent range—making them the least effective way to raise money. Thus, special events are considered a participation strategy.

The success of special event planning and implementation is dependent on a highly organized and systematic approach, one that deserves its own book devoted to tasks, functions, and forms. The intensive amount of labor needed makes them possible only if volunteers are involved.

Although special events are important to the overall development program, this book does not elaborate on them. Because special event management has become a specialty area, see *Successful Special Events* by Barbara R. Levy and Barbara H. Marion, another book in this series.

Membership

A membership program, like a special event, is a solicitation strategy that expands the organization's prospect base. Membership is not a fund raiser; it is a "quid pro quo" program designed to involve people and break even. Membership and annual giving are not synonymous, and the distinctions are very important. Membership is something people belong to; annual giving is something people give to. Members expect tangible benefits in return for their membership fees. Annual donors expect intangible benefits in return for their contributions.

Certain types of organizations are perfectly suited for a membership program. Museums, cultural organizations, public radio and television stations, and community associations all have membership programs. Social service agencies, health care organizations, and educational institutions are not well suited to a membership program, but may have auxiliary groups with a membership or a friends program.

The idea is to have both a membership program and an annual giving program that are related but different. Therein lies the challenge—to communicate clearly about the differences to eliminate confusion of members, donors, and staff. People sometimes join the membership program thinking that they are doing something good for the organization—they are, but they are doing something better for themselves. When organizations fail to separate membership from annual giving—when they offer a basic membership at one price and a sustaining member category at another, in fine print announcing that the difference is a *gift* to the organization—they undermine both efforts. A membership drive must be promoted for what it is: an opportunity to join with others and get something in return, such as invitations to events, gate admission, educational programs, a newsletter, and the like.

> **Membership is something people belong to; annual giving is something people give to.**

A thriving membership program is advantageous to the annual giving program; members are an organization's best prospects for a gift. Members have self-identified themselves as people who are interested in the organization's mission. In many ways, they are more qualified than non-members, because they are already identified, informed, and involved. An effective solicitation strategy for members is not to convert them to annual donors in place of membership, but to encourage them to be both—joiners and givers.

Fundamental strategies: *Put the Emphasis Where It Will Count*

There are only so many fund-raising principles and techniques; experienced practitioners utilize all of them, at different times, with their own adaptations. Regardless of the size, age, or type of annual giving program, yours can certainly benefit from one of the following fundamental strategies, along with a few enhancements or ideas that have come from others.

- Re-energize your annual board campaign.
- Create a new holiday campaign.
- Revitalize your direct mail packages.
- Train your volunteers in personal solicitation techniques.
- Initiate a special purpose major gifts campaign.

Re-energize Your Annual Board Campaign

If board giving to your organization is not meeting your expectations, chances are board members are being asked to give annually simply because they are board members. Being on the board in and of itself is usually not sufficient as a motivator. When seen only as an obligation, giving levels tend to be marginally low. We know from our own experiences, that philanthropic giving by the board should be personally enjoyable and satisfying. Consider these suggestions to improve board giving.

1. **Make an appointment to visit each member of the development committee** (and later with every board member), to discuss their personal reasons for being on the board and what they hope to accomplish during their tenure. Be sure to keep the meetings structured with a series of questions, and to limit them to one hour. Focus on aspects of the organization that relate to philanthropy; not organizational issues that do not relate to fund raising. Your goal is to collect information about each board member's opinions, attitudes, and values. The information you gather is designed to give you a better picture of your board's needs, and their personal and collective interests.

2. **Be sure to ask specific questions about the board campaign itself:** Do they know where the money is going? Do they know why it is needed (what would happen if they didn't contribute)? Are they clear about what level of giving is appropriate for board members, and for them? Chances are, the board members' answers will be a little vague on these points. Experience suggests that most board members are unaware of the real needs, despite the fact that they receive and read financial statements. They may be unclear about where their gift actually goes, except to the bottom line. And, there could be a question in their minds about what they "should" give, as compared to what others do.

3. **Point out the need for a successful board campaign;** explain how foundations, corporation, and major donors measure the size of their grants and gifts by what the organization's board is giving. Show how board giving compares with other constituency categories; has it grown each year at the same rate as the annual operating budget, or less? Ask each board member for his or her opinions, experiences, and expectations. Seek their advice about how to design future board campaigns. No doubt, it has been a very

long time since they were asked for their input on something this important. Use the Board Evaluation Form, Exhibit 7–9, and the Board Member Self-Evaluation Form, Exhibit 7–10.

4. **Collate all the data from these meetings, and prepare a report of your findings.** Discuss your conclusions and impressions with the development team, and involve them in a discussion about what is needed to create a meaningful way to engage the board members more fully. Ask the development team to help evaluate the board's governance responsibilities, and their involvement in fund raising (use one or both of the evaluation instruments included here). Hopefully the evaluations and discussions will lead to a recommendation that a special effort be designed, headed by a team of board members, focused on a "favorite" program or services, with larger and more ambitious goals than any previous year.

5. **Remember—board members, like donors, need to be educated and involved** in order to be interested enough to make your charity one of their favorites. This takes time and engagement.

Create a New Holiday Campaign

The holiday season offers a special opportunity for nonprofits to raise additional philanthropic contributions, in addition to their more typical annual giving campaigns which are often undertaken in the spring of the year. During the holidays the charitable mood seems to surge, and while almost every other charity is sending a holiday appeal, your loyal donors and even some new ones will respond to your mailing—if it is clever, personal, compelling, and unique from the others.

According to a 1995 special report titled "Tis the Season?" published by AAFRC Trust for Philanthropy (Giving USA, 1995) "Both theory and practice support the conventional wisdom that people are more likely to make a charitable gift during the winter holidays." Their survey of a national sample of 100 nonprofits indicated that 31% of their contribution revenue was received between October 1st and December 31st. The last quarter of the year was consistently reported as the period in which contributions were at peak. Contribution receipts were lowest (17.1%) during the summer months of July, August and September. The report listed the following seasonal factors which influenced fund raising consistently from year to year:

1. more fund raising effort,
2. holiday spirit,
3. year-end tax considerations,
4. many organizations' fiscal years end on December 31,
5. media reporting on charitable giving is heightened,
6. certain consumer expenditures.

A holiday campaign is an effective strategy to acquire new donors, and to secure second or third gifts from existing donors. This is one project where it might be better to add more names to your mailing list, rather than to be too selective. The timing is short—only six weeks—with little opportunity for follow-up, so large numbers are important if you want to generate significant dollars. If you are creating your first seasonal campaign, consider the following ideas.

1. **Hire a graphic designer to create a theme and design that is unique** to your organization, and different from all of your other fund raising materials. When you add a second or third campaign to your existing program, you want to set it apart from the other appeals, to minimize donor confusion. A holiday campaign is a strategy designed to ask prospects to give "over and above" their annual gifts, for something special. By creating an entirely different appeal, with a holiday theme and a case that is tied to the season, the campaign will eventually take on an identify of its own—it will become a tradition itself. Consider a theme like *The Little Red Stocking Campaign* or *The Tiny*

Exhibit 7–9 Board Evaluation Form

Board Evaluation Form

Select the answer that best describes how the board members govern your organization.

Suitability as trustees

Trustees fulfill an important role in the organization; they represent a high degree of competence and experience and are in positions to influence others who are critically important to the success of the institution.

☐ all   ☐ most   ☐ half   ☐ few   ☐ none

Composition of the board

Our board as a whole represents our constituencies.

☐ completely   ☐ mostly   ☐ half   ☐ a small portion   ☐ not at all

Our board represents our clients

☐ completely   ☐ mostly   ☐ half   ☐ a small portion   ☐ not at all

Our board as a whole represents a cross section of our community.

☐ completely   ☐ mostly   ☐ half   ☐ a small portion   ☐ not at all

Preparation as trustees

Our trustees brief themselves on our institutions problems and needs; know the agency's history, philosophy, and plans; keep abreast of trends in our organization or which affect our organization; understand the role of a trustee.

☐ all do   ☐ most do   ☐ half do   ☐ few do   ☐ none do

Our trustees prepare themselves for meetings; study and understand reports and background materials; ask probing and insightful questions at meetings; focus on problems; demand and get necessary information for major decisions.

☐ always do   ☐ usually do   ☐ sometimes do   ☐ occasionally do   ☐ never do

Ambassadorship

Our trustees are active spokespersons for our organization, are using their influence with others who can help the organization.

☐ always are   ☐ usually are   ☐ sometimes are   ☐ occasionally are   ☐ never are

continues

Exhibit 7–9 continued

Development activity

Our trustees make financial contributions to our organization, help with the development program, and secure financial support of others for our organization.

☐ all do ☐ most do ☐ half do ☐ few do ☐ none do

Board and committee activity

Our trustees serve on one or more important committees and are active in committee assignment carrying out duties and making useful contributions of ideas and information.

☐ all do ☐ most do ☐ half do ☐ few do ☐ none do

Our trustees attend board meetings regularly and faithfully.

☐ all do ☐ most do ☐ half do ☐ few do ☐ none do

Source: Adapted with permission from Frantzreb and Pray, *Report Card for College Trustee*, pp. 4–8, © 1969.

Tim Fund. The creative theme and design creates a mood and a visual picture that serves as a stimulus for gift-giving. When using a storybook character (such as Tiny Tim), or a person who is legendary (such as Charles Dickens), you are able to use analogies or direct quotes that help articulate how your organization meets the needs of clients, patients, or students during the holiday season.

2. **Offer gift options that are seasonally appropriate, and that are specific and tangible.** For example, offer four or five gift level options (between $25 and $500), listing specific items or services that donors can underwrite: a $25 gift to "give a teddy bear" to a child who is hospitalized, or a "little red stocking" to a child/family who is homeless or in shelter, or a "holiday meal" for a family in need. New prospects may respond only to the $25 level, but loyal donors are more likely to do give at higher levels, and if asked, add an extra $25 for the gift item.

3. **Another successful strategy is to include a "gift" in the appeal, which will capture the prospect's attention,** stimulate a higher response, and if the gift is functional, will help build the campaign's image over time. For instance, include a specially designed bookmark with the organization's name and phone number, or a package of holiday stamps printed with the organization's logo, or a refrigerator magnet with a quote from Charles Dickens, "I will honor Christmas in my heart, and try to keep it all the year long." To keep costs down for the mail package, you can purchase pre-printed holiday-letterhead and envelopes (available through most gift card vendors/printers), selecting a design that is appropriate to your organization's name or mission. The impact of color and design is achieved while greatly reducing your printing expenses.

4. **Personalize the appeal in unique ways.** Offer the donors a gift card or gift tag (which they can personalize) that will be

Exhibit 7–10 Board Member Self-Evaluation

Board Member Self-Evaluation Form on Fund Raising

This is a self-evaluation tool for use by board members. Indicate the degree to which you agree with each statement by check the appropriate number. a score of 1 indicates "This statement does not al all characterize my behavior on this board"; a score of 5 indicates "This statement effectively characterized my behavior on this board".

	1	2	3	4	5
1 I have personally contributed to this organization within my means.	☐	☐	☐	☐	☐
2 I understand the organization well enough to speak for it in the community.	☐	☐	☐	☐	☐
3 I do my share of cultivating prospective donors.	☐	☐	☐	☐	☐
4 I am willing to assist staff in identifying key prospects, help in evaluating their potential, plan the solicitation strategies.	☐	☐	☐	☐	☐
5 I have contacts within the donor community and am wiling to make introductions as appropriate for solicitation by staff and other volunteers.	☐	☐	☐	☐	☐
6 I accompany staff and other volunteers on solicitation visits.	☐	☐	☐	☐	☐
7 I sign letters in support of the organization, as well as letters for follow-up and thank you.	☐	☐	☐	☐	☐
8 I am prepared to make solicitation calls myself.	☐	☐	☐	☐	☐
9 This charity is among the top three in my giving commitments.	☐	☐	☐	☐	☐
10 I intend to, or I have included this organization in my estate plans.	☐	☐	☐	☐	☐

Source: Adapted from a presentation by Robert A. Hutson, Providence Health Foundation, Washington, DC, at Fund Raising Days in Washington, November, 1995, sponsored by the Greater Washington, D.C. Chapter NSFRE.

attached to the teddy bear, the holiday stocking, or the gift of food. In turn, give the recipients a thank you card to fill out, and return it to the donor. Include a photo in the appeal, with information about the how a donor's last gift helped a child/family. And, write a personal note reminding donors about the size of their last gift, urging them to give at a higher level. Remember, it takes only a three hours to handwrite a personal note on 500 appeals.

5. **The timing of a holiday appeal is critical.** Plan ahead to ensure that it is delivered the week of Thanksgiving—no later. This will allow adequate time for a slow delivery by the post office, it will give people at least one month to respond, and it will arrive ahead of the heavy holiday mail—and be right in the middle of the biggest giving season. Examples are shown in Exhibit 7–11.

Revitalize Your Direct Mail Letters and Packages

Recent studies show that "Americans no longer read". One survey indicates that 75 percent of all fund raising letters are thrown away before they are read. Another study says the typical receiver of a solicitation decides in 11 seconds whether to read on; four page letters are "out." Consider the impact of that fact on a fund raisers ability to communicate by mail. If we want people to respond to our packages, we must take this into account by asking "how do they look?" in addition to "how do they read ?" Does the envelope, the theme, the graphic design, and the letter look like something you would want to open, peruse, save or throw, read, consider, perhaps put away, then re-review, consider again, and then respond to? Given the dynamic, multi-stepped decision making process that prospects must go through, it is no wonder direct mail averages are so low.

However, the very same problem presents itself with personalized mail. If the letters you send are not "unique" enough to stand out among all the others, the personal signature on the bottom and the "inserted" personalized message in the body of the letter will be for naught.

Design, color, and tone are extremely influential. They can capture people's attention, create a mood, evoke a response (opening the envelope is the first step), and improve the possibility of getting a look, if not a read. Practitioners and direct mail expects can offer the following tips:

- Use an off-size envelope, with some color.
- Use headlines, bullets, underlines, and lots of white space in your letter.
- Photos and illustrations are a must.
- Improve the design of your reply envelope; throw those 1970 versions out.
- Out-source the graphic design; that is not where fund raisers shine.
- Circulate a "mock-up" before you go to print.

Just Plain Good Letters

Every fund raisers file cabinet is full of letter samples and letter writing tips; entire books are written on just that topic; conference workshops on "how to get prospects to read" are filled to capacity. It would be redundant to offer more, except for the three that have been sitting on the top of my stack of samples and continue to survive my annual "clean." The first one, from Peter Drucker, may not be one to copy, but it certainly is a reminder that sometimes it is best to just plain write.

This letter appeared in the Drucker Foundation News, December 1992. It was titled "The Letter that Produced the Check: a Morality Tale" by Peter F. Drucker. He said, "Every day brings a flood of letters from worthy causes each asking for a donation. I open each letter, always read the first sentence—and then throw it into the wastepaper basket. But a few weeks ago I got a letter I actually read through. It read:*

> There are 2,400 homeless individuals in our suburban area, many of them in families with children. We plan during the coming year to re-settle and re-train 700 of them and to place them in jobs. We know this is a very ambitious goal. But we also know that we have the competence to reach it. For last year we resettled, re-trained and placed 400

Source: Reprinted with permission from P.F. Drucker, The Letter That Produced the Check: A Morality Tale, *Drucker Foundation News*, Vol. 2, No. 2, © 1992.

Exhibit 7–11 Sample Holiday Letters

December 2, 1996

Dear Friend,

This is the season of family traditions—when young and old gather to share a meal, tell stories of bygone days, laugh with delight, sing merrily, and give thanks for our blessings and each other.

> *"Reflect upon your present blessing of which every man has many; not*
> *upon your past misfortunes of which all have some."*
> —Charles Dickens

It has been a good year for our community. A good year for the families we served. **Generous philanthropic support made it possible for The Village to respond to almost every child and family** whose misfortune brought them to our door—more people than any other previous year. Still, more are turning to us:

- Children and their families received crisis counseling and in-home family therapy;
- Children were placed in loving, caring adoptive homes;
- Youngsters were matched with adult mentors in the Big Brothers/Big Sisters Program;
- Families received financial counseling, in an effort to avoid bankruptcy;
- Husbands and wives participated in the marriage counseling program;

Misfortunes come at times when people least expect them and are least able to cope with them. For the families we see, their crisis is too great to handle alone—emotionally and financially. Thank goodness they garner the strength to say they need help. Thanks, too, that people like you have charitable traditions.

Perhaps you already have a family tradition of *"counting your blessings"* this time of the year—by making a year-end gift to your favorite charity. I can assure you, **we would be grateful for such a gift—and so would the many needy children and families who turn to us.**

> *"I will honor Christmas in my heart,*
> *and try to keep it all the year long."*
> —Charles Dickens

Thank you for all you have already done, and all that you will do.

Wishing you and your family a blessed holiday season,

Gary J. Wolsky, President
The Village Family Service Center

Courtesy of The Village Family Service Center, Fargo, North Dakota.

continues

Exhibit 7–11 continued

Holiday Appeal

Tiny Tim Children's Fund

In Tiny Tim, Charles Dickens created a character of indomitable spirit. With every bone in his body, Tiny Tim believed in the hope and joy of the holidays. At Children's Health Care—St. Paul, we see that same strength and courage in children battling formidable diseases and injuries. All they want is to feel better. And all they need is a little help. Your gift can lift them and help us help the children we treat and care for.

$25* Provides a soft, cuddly teddy bear for a child in need of comfort and companionship.

$50 Provides special toys that help to soothe and relax a child during chemotherapy or spinal tap procedures.

$100 Purchases a month's supply of educational coloring books and story books to help children protect themselves from abuse.

$250 Buys a "patient puppet," which staff members use to help a child understand a medical procedure before experiencing it.

$500 Provides an oxygen analyzer, which monitors the amount of oxygen received by a newborn baby who is on a respirator or in an incubator.

As the first general children's hospital in Minnesota, Children's St. Paul has, for more than sixty-five years, dedicated itself to responding to the very special needs of children.

If you donate $25, please write your name on the enclosed Teddy Bear gift tab.

"...*bless us, every one! said Tiny Tim, the last of all.*"

Enclosed is my check for the Tiny Tim Children's Fund.

☐ $25   ☐ $50   ☐ $100
☐ $250 ☐ $500 ☐ $_____

Our Mission

The mission of Children's-St. Paul is to provide comprehensive health care for children, responsive to their special needs, through excellence in clinical care, research and education. In support is mission, Children's-St. Paul:

– Offers care to children of all socio-economic levels.
– Involves families in the child's care.
– Provides health education to the community.
– Provides services in a thoughtful and caring environment.
– Serves as an advocate for children.

Courtesy of Children's Health Care. Children's Hospital of St. Paul merged with Minneapolis Children's Medical Center in June 1994 to form Children's Health Care.

homeless people and their families; and we have learned quite a lot since. And we now have a trained and experienced volunteer force of 80 dedicated men and women. We will get a little money from the county, the State and the Federal Government. But most of the money needed we will have to raise ourselves. And we are determined to raise all the money needed in *our* community and not to accept donations from outside. These are *our* homeless, *our* neighbors, *our* problem, and *our* opportunity. We shall need $650,000, of which no more that 12 percent—a maximum of $78,000—will be spent on administration including the cost of fund raising. We are asking you, Mr. Drucker, for your donation in the amount of $2,500. Please send it to us in the enclosed stamped envelope. We will render you an accounting of the money spent and a progress report every three months. And should we do better than planned and be more successful we are sure that you will welcome us back and will help us celebrate success by making an additional gift.

Mr Drucker concludes: "The letter got my check! And the only sad fact about this little tale is that only the first two sentences are *fact*—the rest is pure fiction. I have yet to received a letter like this."

The second letter offered as a good example is one written by Terese Cain, of the Cabrini House in Minneapolis, MN (Exhibit 7–12). As executive director of the homeless shelter she is able to write about her clients and services in a way that few direct mail writers can; and get it all onto one page and to ask for a "real" gift of $143.94. Now that got my attention.

The third letter arrived just as I was writing this chapter (Exhibit 7–13). It not only got my attention, and a re-read, it was so good it deserved to be added to my "favorite" collection. It emotionally described the problem as "devastating" at the same time it poignantly showed the mother's solution "to regain some stability."

The idea of incorporating a "real" letter into an appeal letter is fundamentally simple—little more needs to be said. Although only the written side of the letter is illustrated here, the reverse side was printed with pictures of four different children, actively engaged in play and a cut line "Our hope is that children grow up in families and communities that cherish them."

Several communication facts from the NSFRE Survey Manual:

- It is estimated that people are exposed to somewhere between 560 to 1800 communication messages daily.
- Different sources say that people need from three to ten reinforcements before they take and action.
- To create effective communications you must:
  1) get **attention**,
  2) stir **interest**,
  3) build **conviction** and **desire**, and
  4) call to **action**.

Train Volunteers in Personal Solicitation Techniques

Volunteers naturally resist the idea of soliciting another for a gift. The very concept is fraught with a myriad of psychological aspects: fear of rejection, perception of begging or selling, uneasiness with money, and/or asking contradicts self-reliance. Just as we are likely to do, volunteers take their assignments very seriously and they want to succeed. Without training and experience their comfort level is too low to effectively to solicit others; with training, they develop the confidence and the skills necessary to achieve success—even when they get a "no" they understand that it is not a rejection of them personally, and that they have given someone the opportunity to give, as well as the privilege of declining.

1. **Consider hiring a consultant** to help you develop a volunteer training program. They will guide you through the process of engaging your development

Exhibit 7–12 Sample Letter

November 29, 1996

John and Jane Doe
444 West 55th Street
Minneapolis, MN 55410

Dear John and Jane,

> *"Dreams are renewable. No matter what our age or condition, there are
> still untapped possibilities within us and new beauty waiting to be born."*
> —Dr. Dale Elmer

Developing untapped potential . . . . . .

Finding the resources within oneself to secure satisfactory employment, reconnect with friends
and family, complete an educational degree, live independently . . . .

Taking charge of their lives, often for the first time . . . .

*These are the things residents of Cabrini House accomplish every day, thanks to people like
you who care about helping homeless individuals turn their lives around.*

For eleven years, adult men and women have come to Cabrini House faced with challenges of
chemical addiction, mental health issues and histories of emotional, psychological and physical abuse. *When residents choose to come to Cabrini House, they are demonstrating tremendous courage, and drawing upon resolve many don't even know they have.* They want to move
forward and take positive steps toward fulfilling their dreams of becoming self-sufficient members in society.

Cabrini provides this opportunity by offering counseling, life skills development, access to volunteer tutors and mentors, connections to community resources, transportation, and assistance with locating affordable housing. After departure, residents are invited to return to the
House anytime for guidance, support or a meal with friends. In return, program participants
work steadily to reach the goals they set for themselves.

Unfortunately, the need for places like Cabrini House continues as housing providers discover home-
lessness is a recurring symptom, rather than a short-term crisis. Over 12,000 Minnesotans sleep
in temporary shelters every night. 97% of Cabrini's residents report barriers of chemical dependency and/or mental health issues. As these other factors take hold in peoples' lives, loss of hous-ing
often follows, and results in a cycle of endless transition. *Cabrini exists to end this cycle.*

During this season of joy and renewal, your gift will continue to make Cabrini's services available to individuals seeking a fresh start. $143.94 will provide services to one resident for one
week. I hope you will consider a gift to Cabrini of this size, or even a little more. Thank you!

Peace to you during this season and always,

Therese Cain
Executive Director

Courtesy of Cabrini House, Minneapolis, Minnesota.

Exhibit 7–13 Sample Letter

Children's Home Society
OF MINNESOTA
1605 Eustis Street
St. Paul, MN 55108

612/ 646-7771

March 1997

Dear Friend:

I want to share this heartfelt letter of thanks with you.

I would like to extend my thanks and gratitude to you and your wonderful staff, the volunteers, the care-givers, and to all those who have made the Children's Home Crisis Nurseries a possibility for families like my own. Without your immediate response and having no family or friends to turn to, I would surely have fallen apart.

Having a spouse leave his family is so devastating, one can only ask many times over, "why?", especially when you believe your life and marriage are stable. If there had been a sign that we would be left behind maybe there could have been some way to prepare for this, but there was none. Instead I am left with fear, anger and sorrow. So many feelings and three small children to protect.

When a mother is faced with the unknown for herself and her children, the mind can go in many directions and the Crisis Nursery helped me through the most difficult challenge of my life.

You helped pull me through my first week by providing my children a safe, stress-free environment with one of your volunteer shelter families. At the same time, your counselors helped me sort through my personal catastrophe and set priorities and goals to regain some stability.

I am thankful for all you have done for me and my children. The care was superior, the support and encouragement you gave me were above and beyond any I have yet received. I will never forget your extended hand of much welcomed relief to me when I needed it most.

A Sincerely Grateful Mother

As I read these words I am reminded of how many children need our help. Each one of us is a vital member of a community of caring for children—a community that reaches out and preserves the dignity of each child. **Children are our community's future.** By working together, we can and do make a difference for families who need us.

Children's Home Society works to fulfill the needs of our community's children through child care, adoption and child abuse prevention services. Children count on us for help. Can we count on your help through a financial contribution?

<u>Show your concern for children</u> by completing the enclosed reply card along with your gift today!

Sincerely,

Fran A. Yoch, President
Board of Directors

P.S. Your contribution **now** really does make a difference.

Courtesy of Children's Home Society, St. Paul, Minnesota.

committee, the board of trustees, the executive director, and your staff. This takes time and expertise. Before your volunteers reach the stage of willingness to learn how to solicit others, they must recognize their own resistance factors, and address them.

2. **Develop a training manual** that includes materials fundamental to a volunteer's knowledge, and skill development. Include the following:
   - The history of philanthropy.
   - Background on the organization.
   - Information about the programs and services.
   - The case for support and fund raising strategies.
   - Volunteer roles and responsibilities in fund raising.
   - Articles about how volunteers can learn to be great fund raisers, such as *Tips for Overcoming Fear*, Exhibit 7–14, and *How to Solicit for Your Favorite Charity*, Exhibit 7–15.

3. **Identify a volunteer leader** who is curious about the solicitation process, is eager to learn, and who will eventually become the chief advocate for fund solicitation among his or her peers. Work closely to help this volunteer be successful, personally and publicly. Review the staged process of solicitation, described in this chapter; give him or her the insights around overcoming fear and resistance, successful tips and techniques, how to handle typical objections, and give him or her plenty of opportunities to role-play the solicitation process, and to experience a real-life team solicitation when you or another expert are involved. De-brief on every solicitation call, giving useful feedback and encouragement, until he or she becomes skilled and confident.

4. **Follow the basic rules to help volunteers succeed** in the "art of solicitation;"
   - Select the right people to solicit—your best prospects.

Exhibit 7–14 Tips for Overcoming Fear

Tips for Overcoming the Fear of Fund Raising in Yourself and Others

1. Make your own contribution first.
2. Focus on one task at a time: making the appointment, studying the materials, making the call.
3. Rehearse the request with a staff member or friend.
4. Do your solicitations when you are at peak energy.
5. Wear something you feel great in.
6. Take a partner.
7. Make the easiest call first.
8. If you have a success, keep moving.
9. Think about the wonderful gains that will happen because of your efforts.
10. Concentrate on the prospect; put yourself in his/her place; imagine how he/she feels; listen to what he/she says.
11. Meet with fellow volunteer fund raisers often, to share good and no so good times.
12. Discuss your fears with friends, joke about them if you can.

Courtesy of Resources and Counseling for the Arts, St. Paul, Minnesota.

Exhibit 7–15 How to Solicit for Your Favorite Charity

How to Solicit a Gift for Your Favorite Charity

1. Set a dollar goal for each prospect before you see him/her.
2. If appropriate, make an appointment. Find a time convenient for the prospect. Be on time.
3. Don't make requests over the phone if you can possible see someone in person.
4. Know your materials; have them arranged so you can find what you want. Give the prospect what he/she needs or asks for. Give printed materials after you're through talking.
5. Talk positively about what your organization wants to do and how it will benefit the prospect.
6. Ask for a specific amount.
7. Let the prospect talk and ask questions. Know when to stop talking, and to "close".
8. Be sympathetic with complaints; offer to get additional information. Never argue.
9. If the prospect says no, thank him/her politely for the time. Leave him/her smiling.
10. If the prospects says maybe, arrange a time to check back. Leave materials, and your name and phone number.
11. If the prospect says yes, make arrangements for how he/she will give/send the gift.
12. Always report results on the same day to the fund raising chair, good or bad.
13. Always send a personal note after the call, even if you didn't receive the gift during the solicitation.
14. Always make the return call if you said you would.

Courtesy of Resources and Counseling for the Arts, St. Paul, Minnesota.

- Limit the number of assigned calls.
- Give them relevant background on the prospects.
- Suggest an amount for them to ask for.
- Give them a few good printed materials to use.
- Give them a deadline—no more than a few weeks out.
- Follow up with them—politely, patiently, and persistently.

Initiate a Special Purpose Major Gifts Campaign

The major gifts campaign is one of the most recent and popular adaptations of the volunteer-driven capital campaign model. This idea comes from:

- increased operational costs, plus a growing need for expanded or new programs

and services (rather than capital improvements)
- a desire to involve or re-involve greater numbers of volunteers in the solicitation of major gifts
- a donor base that is aging, with the ability to make significant financial commitments, for their favorite institutions
- an annual giving program that is experiencing only nominal growth, with a large number of donors who are "stuck" in the middle or the top of the annual giving pyramid
- there is not capital or endowment campaign in sight, and a good number of donors who supported your last campaign(s)

To set the stage for a special-purpose major gifts campaign, follow the same steps used for a large capital or endowment campaign.

1. Determine if your organization is ready for a major gifts campaign by undertaking an organization audit. Is your board ready? Is there strong leadership in place: Is there a solid history of giving? Look at your internal environment: how much money are you raising now? How many annual donors do you have at the middle levels? Are there indications of major gift prospects? Do you have any experience with major gifts solicitations? Then look at your external environment: is your institution well know in your community? Is your case for support well received? Are there any concerns about your organization? Who else is running a major campaign now, or in the future?

2. Determine who your major gift prospects are, and how many there are, and what their potential is. Do this by using the giving pyramid or gift range chart techniques. Understand that most of your major gift campaign prospects will come from your existing current donors base. Those who now give $1,000 a year may have the capacity to give $10,000 if the right person asks, for the reason, at the right time, for the right project. Prospects also include those current on the board of directors, especially those who hold (or have held) leadership positions. An often overlooked group of donors are women, who are now believed to have significant assets themselves, and to have enormous influence over the distribution of joint assets.

3. Initiate a major gifts committee, with roles and responsibilities for approving the concepts, helping to develop the case(s), establishing the campaign strategies, identifying the prospects, and soliciting them. This committee will be involved in what may be a two to three year initiative; each solicitation could include three to twelve contacts between the staff and volunteers. Remember, at the major

gifts level, each solicitation of each prospect is ultimately a mini-campaign in itself The secrets of major gifts solicitation are: prospect research, patience, persistence, and preparedness. (Ted D. Bayley, 1995)

Here are some suggestions from Bruce Flessner of Bentz Whaley Flessner about shifting to a donor-centered major gifts program or campaign:

Start at the top of the donor pyramid and move down:
Focus on big gifts—they are less expensive to raise than small gifts.

Spend time thinking about donors as individuals.
Who are they and where are they coming from? Who have the capacity to give eight-figure, seven-figure, and six-figure gifts? Who are your top five donors or prospects? What's the maximum gift each could make? What area or project would they be interested in? What is their lifetime giving potential? Who will be your five best prospects at the turn of the century?

See your donors and listen to them.
Let them tell you about themselves. Listen. Don't ask specific questions—that's census taking. Engage them, get to know them, and follow through. Be persistent and be patient about results. Thank them and tell them what's happening as a result of their gift.

Forget about the perfect ask—just ask.
People give because they're asked. But too often fund raisers are afraid to ask. Instead, they spend their time preparing and plotting strategies, without ever asking for gift.

Fund raisers need to serve as teachers/ coaches to enable volunteers to be successful. Many volunteers are good for 45 minutes and than they start to mumble.

When you hear that, jump in with "That's why we would like you to consider a $1 million gift."

In Conclusion

To create an environment for philanthropy to flourish in your organization, the idea is to not necessarily to work harder, but to work smarter: Here is a checklist of strategies that might be referred to as "working from the inside out":

☐ Focus more on donors needs, and interests: *do your homework.*

☐ Redefine cases to reflect those needs: *be innovative.*

☐ Move from transfers to transactions: *be on the cutting edge with partnerships.*

☐ Invite people to invest in what they believe in: *walk the talk.*

☐ Reengineer fundraising tactics to communicate more effectively: *be more selective and innovative.*

☐ Move up the pyramid of fund raising: *go where the people and the money are.*

☐ Integrate major gifts into daily activity: *create a seamless fundraising effort.*

☐ Develop a personal solicitation campaign: *invest in the long term for more results.*

☐ Increase involvement of volunteers: *return to the values, the core of philanthropy.*

References

Blum, D.E., M. Dundjerski, and D. Marchetti. 1996. Gifts up 5% at top U.S. charities. *The Chronicle of Philanthropy* (October 31): 58.

Charities Review Council of Minnesota. 1996. *Minnesota donor's jury.* St. Paul, MN: Charities Review Council of Minnesota.

Council of Better Business Bureaus. 1994. *Give but give wisely.* Arlington, VA: Council of Better Business Bureaus.

Elstain, J.B. 1996. Maurice Gurin Lecture presented at the International NSFRE Conference. Los Angeles.

Gonzalez-Campoy, R. 1996. Answering the call for help. *Advancing Philanthropy* (Spring): 39.

Hall, H. 1996. Direct mail: Can it still deliver? *The Chronicle of Philanthropy* (March 7): 23.

Hall, H. 1996. New twists on year-end appeals. *The Chronicle of Philanthropy* (December 12): 31.

Harvey, J.W., and K.F. McCrohan. 1990. Changing conditions for fund raising and philanthropy. In *Critical issues in American philanthropy: Strengthening theory and practice,* edited by J. Van Til and Associates. San Francisco, CA: Jossey-Bass.

Hedgepeth, R.C. 1990. Resource development in the new millenium. *New Directions for Philanthropic Fundraising* 5: 114.

Independent Sector. 1996. 1995 Gallup survey. *The Chronic of Philanthropy* (October 17): 9–12.

Logan, T.D. 1993. Dialing for more than dollars. *Advancing Philanthropy* (Fall): 40–42.

McIlquham, J. 1996. Out on a limb: We are here. *The NonProfit Times* (March): 13.

Mixer, J.R. 1993. *Principles of professional fundraising: Useful foundations for successful practice.* San Francisco, CA: Jossey-Bass.

O'Neill, M. 1993. Fund raising as an ethical act. *Advancing Philanthropy* (Fall): 35.

Putnam, R.D. Bowling alone: America's declining social capital. *Journal of Democracy* 6(1).

Warwick, M. 1993. Can telephone fund raising benefit your organization? *Advancing Philanthropy* (Winter): 43.

Chapter 8

Key Ingredients of the Annual Development Plan: Step 7 in the Annual Integrated Development Process

There are many reasons for writing an annual plan, not the least of which is to ensure that everyone involved is supportive of its goals. More importantly, a written annual plan helps people be clear about *their role* in accomplishing it. Some people are consecutive thinkers, and others are sequential thinkers—a visual product describes this thinking in black and white and produces a document that reduces the possibility of misinterpretation. An annual integrated development plan gives purpose and direction. It serves as a base for approval, periodic review, and assessment of progress by staff and volunteers. Once written, with contributions from all members of the development team, it can still be modified if and when the need arises. A written plan is quite simply a road map, one with ideas shaped by research and intuition—when times change, so will it. Without a plan, there is no reference point to determine the best route when tough choices have to be made.

If the development team has thoughtfully completed the six steps leading up to Step 7, the actual writing of the plan is merely an expression on paper of the challenges already discussed and decisions already made. The writing is done by those having responsibility for project implementation. For instance, if the fund-raising staff is organized by project or methodology, each staff member will write his or her sec-

> **A written plan is quite simply a road map, one with ideas shaped by research and intuition.**

tion of the plan in concert with respective volunteers. Each project section articulates the individual fund-raising project strategies and goals. It is the responsibility of the chief development officer to oversee the writing process and to incorporate each section into a comprehensive whole. The written plan is prepared well in advance of the fiscal year for approval by the organization's development committee or board of directors.

A plan may range in size from 15 to 50 pages, depending on the number of annual fund-raising projects: strategies, campaigns, methodologies, techniques, and the like. Customarily, the plan includes overall objectives, financial projections, timelines, and an organizational chart. Each project section includes six elements: (1) purpose and situation, (2) case, (3) constituency targets, (4) goals-objectives-action steps, (5) roles and responsibilities, and (6) schedule and timelines.

Annual Plan Components

Charitable Mission and Purpose Statement

An organization's mission justifies its place in the philanthropic sector. The act of seeking and receiving philanthropic funds is legitimate when an organization fulfills a need based on the shared values of society. The mission and purpose statement is a critical component of an annual plan, presented first as a reminder that fund raising is but the means to the end.

Case for Support

A *case for support* is a statement that defends the organization's right to raise funds. It is the rationale for philanthropic support and an expression of the cause that inspires and empowers staff and volunteers to facilitate philanthropic exchanges. It is the reason why donors should give. The case statement evolves from an internal and external process that identifies the critical, urgent, and relevant needs of the organization in concert with the preferred needs of the

community. By the time the case statement is crafted and inserted into the annual plan, it has been endorsed by the organization's board and administration. The written case for support does the following:

- identifies and validates needs
- documents the needs
- identifies programs and strategies designed to address the needs
- establishes the competence of the organization and staff
- explains who will benefit from the services that will be made possible by philanthropic support
- identifies the resources that are required to fund the programs
- explains why the prospect should give
- shows how the prospective contributor can give
- responds to the unasked question in the prospect's mind, "What's in it for me?"

The organization's case for support identifies individual programs and services that require philanthropic support in the form of mini-cases, their individual financial requirements and timelines, and their status within the priority list of fund raising.

Philanthropic Values Statement: Guiding Principles

A statement of values is one that guides the philanthropic fund-raising process. It states the cultural values that influence how fund raising is practiced, sets the tone for all communications, establishes ethical principles for organizational behavior, sets boundaries for relationships, and articulates beliefs that translate into action.

Situation Analysis

A summary statement of the strengths, weaknesses, threats, and opportunities of the organization's philanthropic position is a reflection of what has been, is now, and could be. The situation analysis section reminds staff and volunteers of how the organization's history has contributed to its current success. It shows how the organization was shaped by people with vision and courage and was financed by donors whose own aspirations were realized. Given inspiration from the old, an analysis of the present paints a picture of the new future. When staff and volunteers can clearly see where the organization is going, development efforts become their means to getting there. In the annual plan, the situation analysis focuses on the role of philanthropy within the organization for the current and subsequent years. This section may include a list of key assumptions to help set the stage for the strategic goals. The situation analysis formulates the strategic philanthropic goals in a realistic, proactive manner.

Strategic Philanthropic Goals

An integrated development program needs strategic, visionary goals in addition to practical project goals. Strategic goals are written to embrace all other goals; therefore, they are more generic and are long term in scope. They may encompass some of the project goals, but not necessarily all of them; they may set the stage for a future endeavor. Strategic goals may be as broad as "reduce dependency on government support" or "increase awareness of the organization's charitable mission" or "build the case for a future capital/endowment drive." Each strategic goal has objectives and measurable outcomes and is linked to project goals and objectives. Strategic goals can be organized topically by development program management, by fundraising projects, by volunteer leadership and resources, or by constituency building.

Constituency Identification: Current and Potential

The identification of targeted, segmented constituencies gives a picture of the human dimension of philanthropy and promotes the exchange that occurs in the philanthropic process. This section describes the existing base of support in terms that are quantifiable and qualifiable. It celebrates the success of past associations, and it points out the opportunity for expanded support from various constituencies. Constituencies with the greatest immediate potential are identified as high priorities, as are those constituencies who have potential in future years. Constituency interests in program or projects are noted; some projects may be fully subscribed, whereas others need more support from new constituent groups. This section lays out strategies for informing and involving donors to ensure that support is secured for the areas of greatest need.

Financial Projections: Income and Expenses

This section includes a comprehensive revenue and expense budget, with back-up detail. Three budgets are needed: (1) an organizational expense and revenue budget by program, (2) a philanthropic revenue budget by constituency source, and (3) a development expense budget by fund-raising project.

The organization's budget shows all revenue sources, including the amount projected from philanthropy, by program or service (fund accounting practices suggest dividing revenues into restricted or unrestricted revenue for each). The philanthropic budget projects philanthropic support by donor group for each program; by fund-raising project for each program, and cash flow by month. Each project has a subbudget showing net and gross income projections against expenses, as compared to previous years. The development budget shows development department expenses as compared to previous years, with anticipated effectiveness and efficiency rates per fund-raising project.

It may be beneficial also to include an annual giving profile (a pyramid of the previous year's actual giving) and a projected gift range chart (an estimate of the upcoming year's donors based on the number/size of prospects).

Organizational Chart

An organizational chart is a graphic display that clarifies the roles and relationships of staff and volunteers for governance and management purposes. It details staff positions and their primary responsibilities. It explains staff relationships within the development department and with respective volunteer committees. The chart includes all committees, subcommittees, and ancillary support groups and their reporting relationships to the organization's board of directors.

Annual Schedule of Activities

This component provides a visual display of the year's schedule of activities. It shows a calendar year (or longer if useful), month by month. Using bars or another indicator, it points out the time frame of each fund-raising project alongside all other projects.

Individual Project Components

The individual sections within the annual plan describe the diverse strategies and methods for each target audience and each development project. The individual projects are those with unique approaches (such as a holiday campaign), are targeted at a discrete segment (such as a board campaign), are intended to raise funds for a specific program within the organization (such as a special-purpose campaign), or embody an individualized development strategy (such as donor recognition).

Strategies *are the approach;* **goals** *are what is desired;* **objectives** *are what needs to be done;* **methods** *are how it will be done;* **outcomes** *are what happens as a result;* **performance measures** *are an indication of success or shortfall.* Each section has the following components.

Project Purpose, Status, and Strategies

A project is defined as any fund-raising effort that is unique or distinct in its scope, case, or constituency. It may be a campaign or a portion of a campaign (the annual fund campaign or the board campaign); it may be a strategy or a substrategy (the acquisition of new donors or the acquisition of board members as donors); it may be an activity or a component of the activity (a special event or the auction at the event). Each fund-raising project is described in terms of how it came to be, how long or successful it has been, and its primary purpose. The project's status helps define its strengths and weaknesses, whereas the project's strategies identify what to do as a result of them.

Case Description and Funds Needed

This section describes the case for which funds are needed, the amount needed, and the time frame involved. It describes the case in program/service terms, articulating (1) how the program is organized and delivered, (2) who is the intended audience, (3) how many people are/will be served, and (4) what services are provided, by whom and at what cost. This section refers to other sources of revenue for the case, including other fund-raising projects within the plan.

Constituency Targets and Opportunities Identified

This section points out the specific target audiences and the segmentation of those targets, such as acquisition, renewal, upgrade, or recapture. The unique characteristics of the prospects and donors are noted, as are their numbers, their likely responses, and the dollars expected to be raised. This section may show the sequence of solicitation techniques with certain groups and/or the communication steps associated with acknowledgment and recognition (sending newsletters, invitations to events, and the like).

Measurable Goals, Objectives, Methods, and Performance Measures

This section is statistically oriented and written with specific achievements in mind. It focuses on acquiring and increasing contributions by number, size, and kind; strengthening relationships through activities, communications, and interactions; and initiating contacts by constituency segment, number of people, number of visits, number of phone calls, and the like. The goals, objectives, methods, and measures are written in an outline or a pyramid, with each supporting the previous one and together making a whole.

Definition of Roles and Responsibilities

The best way to determine who serves what role, who is responsible for what, and who has a relationship to whom, is to put it on paper. This act in itself reduces tension and misunderstandings before they develop into conflicts. Who directs and executes the plan? How do the staff and volunteers relate? How are volunteers involved? How will they be recruited, trained, supervised, and evaluated?

Activity Timeline and Schedule

Fund raising is a management process that requires strict adherence to realistic schedules in order to succeed. The tasks within fund raising are numerous and sequential. There is little room to retreat, much less to recover if you fall behind schedule—lost opportunities dramatically affect the bottom line, especially at year-end. Deadlines function as both stimuli and con-

sequence to fund raising. This section contains a month-by-month listing of each major activity and a deadline for completion or implementation. The entire schedule may fit on one page, with back-up detail available for use by volunteers.

The annual integrated development plan is a written document that articulates everyone's agreement to stated strategies, goals, and objectives. It is a living document, flexible to changing times and conditions, but still it is a road map that brings order and discipline to the development and nurturing of a philanthropic environment. This document cannot stand alone, however. It is an outgrowth of the organization's strategic and long-range plan, it is a sister document to the marketing plan and the communications plan, and parts of it are used in a multitude of other communications. Most importantly, it is owned—by those who created it and who in the end have the greatest stake in bringing it to fruition. The irony is, that once written and approved, it may go on a shelf until the end of the year, pointing out once more that the process of developing an annual plan is more important than the document's actual use. People may not need to refer to it when they are truly living it.

Several annual plan sections are provided in Appendix 8–A.

Sample Annual Plans

Tribute Giving Program from a Children's Hospital

Philanthropy Goal: $90,000

Description

The Tribute Gift program offers an individual the opportunity to make a personal statement of thoughtfulness to family members, friends and colleagues at the time of a significant life event. It also provides the donor the opportunity to support and show appreciation for Children's Hospital.

Vital hospital programs, such as childhood cancer, neonatal research, child abuse, emergency services, transitional care, child life, pastoral care and pediatric intensive care are supported through the Tribute Gift program. Donors can specify how they would like their gift used.

In 1992, 1,858 tribute gifts were received. This represented a 17.4 percent increase in the number of gifts over 1991 (1,583) and a 29.7 increase over 1990 (1,432). Tribute gift income grew by 48 percent over 1991 ($56,867 to $84,115), due to increased response from the **Philanthropy Update** newsletter, regular communication, follow-up with lapsed donors and memorial informees, increased personalization and communication with current donor/new

donors, and increased use of Tribute call-in service.

The goal for 1993 is $90,000 from 2,200 or more basic tribute gifts. This figure includes Mother's Day and Holiday Tribute giving. This represents an increase of 60 percent over the 1992 goal, and a 3.4 percent increase over actual income for 1992. (This figure allows for unpredictability in the number of single event/large memorial occurrences).

1993 Goals and Objectives

1. Develop and implement strategies to increase the number of gifts by 5 percent from employees, board and medical staff by increasing awareness for benefits of the program.
2. Maximize communication and personalization with all donors.
3. Re-establish tribute giving relationships with a minimum of 150 lapsed tribute donors.
4. Establish tribute giving donor relationship with a minimum of 50 memorial informees.
5. Increase number of individual gifts by 10 percent through continued prospect research cultivation, follow-up with current tribute donor base, distribution of tribute brochure and gift return envelopes, and ongoing promotion of program within the hospital and throughout the community.

Courtesy of Children's Health Care. Children's Hospital of St. Paul merged with Minneapolis Children's Medical Center in June 1994 to form Children's Health Care.

6. Research benefits of adding a tribute giving option to the **Expressions** gift envelope or substituting a tribute envelope during the year. Include tribute giving information in parent welcome packet, and as appropriate on patient units.
7. Redesign tribute gift cards for honor occasions to fully coordinate graphics and to increase giving options.
8. Promote opportunity for donors to designate funds.
9. Implement time-saving acknowledgment procedures.
10. Strategize and initiate appreciation package for parents/family members to recognize physicians and nursing staff, including recognition certificate.

Responsibilities

- Provide assistance to families who have lost a child or family member, determining use of funds and recognition (including commemorative tiles).
- Acknowledge gifts in a timely manner and record names accurately for list purposes in **Expressions** publication.
- Promote tribute giving through ongoing distribution of materials to identified prospects and donor groups.
- Develop and implement an ongoing plan to increase number of donors, dollars received, and average size of gift.

The Tribute Giving Program is made up of two seasonal components: Mother's Day Tribute and Holiday Tribute. They both are designated to meet the needs of donors wishing to express sentiments to loved ones, friends and colleagues.

Mother's Day Tribute

1993 Goal: $4,500

Description

In 1992, the Mother's Day Tribute effort was developed to meet the needs of tribute donors who wished to honor their mothers and loved ones on Mother's Day. This initial effort raised $1,600.

This year the Mother's Day Tribute effort will be included as part of the new Mother's Day annual appeal, benefitting neonatal research and special needs of mothers and children.

With a gift of $25 or more, the donor will have the choice of sending a specially designed Mother's Day card. The card will be hand addressed, stamped and mailed to the honoree or to the donor. (The name and address is written on the card; gift amount is not indicated.)

1993 Goals and Objectives

1. Expand mailing donor/prospect group from 3,729 to 15,000.
2. Obtain a minimum of 150 new tribute gift donors.
3. Provide donors/prospects with a way to honor or memorialize; gift alternative.

Holiday Tribute

1993 Goal: $4,000

Description

The Holiday Tribute card program was developed in 1992 to provide an opportunity for current and lapsed tribute donors, board members, medical staff and employees to convey holiday greetings to family members, friends and colleagues.

With a minimum gift of $15 per card, the hospital hand-addresses, stamps and mails specially designed cards to honorees. Or if preferred, the cards can be sent to the donor for personalization and mailing. (The name and address of the donor is handwritten on the card; and the gift amount is not indicated.) The donor may designate the fund of their choice. The 1992 effort raised $2,947.

1993 Goals and Objectives

1. Provide distinctive and tasteful holiday gift alternative.

2. Strengthen tribute giving relationships with employees, medical staff and regular Tribute donors.
3. Expand mailing prospect group from 6,600 to 10,000.
4. Promote program identity/tradition of holiday giving.

Overall Tribute Giving Program Timelines

January — mailing to memorial informees (October through December)
— new donor letter (October through December)
— fund reports to named tribute fund families
— evaluate 92 Holiday tribute card response/wrap-up
— prepare tribute gift listing for **Expressions** (October through December 92)
— consider redesign of **Expressions** gift envelope

February — strategize Mother's Day Tribute card and envelope
— thank you to 92 donors
— consider redesign of honor tribute cards
— strategize recognition plan for physicians and nursing staff

April — mailing to memorial informees (January through March)
— new donor letter (January through March)
— Mother's Day annual appeal mailing

May — prepare tribute gift listing for **Expressions** (January through April)
— hand address, stamp and mail Mother's Day Tribute cards
— thank yous to Mother's Day Tribute donors
— lapsed 90, 91 & 92 mailing

June — mailing to contract and non-contract employees
— mailing to memorial informees (April through June)
— new donor letter (April through June)

September — lapsed 90, 91 & 92 mailing
— evaluate Holiday Tribute card materials
— prepare Holiday Tribute card mailing list

October — memorial informee mailing (July through September)
— new donor letter (July through September)
— prepare tribute gift listing for **Expression** (May through September)
— finalize Holiday Tribute card materials

November — Holiday Tribute card mailing
— re-evaluate strategies for 94

December — yearend parent/families mailing
— hand address, stamp and mail Holiday Tribute cards
— acknowledgment letter to Holiday Tribute donors
— send holiday cards to selected tribute donors

Fund-Raising Objectives, Strategies, and Performance Measures from an International Religious Organization

Goal #1—FUND RAISING

To be able to provide grants to the most creative and needed ministries of the Church, and to have the resources to make these grants in perpetuity.

Objective #1

To reach 500 members for a total permanent, inviolate endowment of $50 million.

Strategy #1—To educate Board of Trustees on its Fundraising responsibilities so as to raise their level of involvement in the philanthropic process, as well as to give them reason to be involved.

- **Measure**—Associate Director to hold 2-hour seminar on role of Trustees at next Board Meeting
- **Measure**—100% Trustee participation in Fundraising by Conference in May, 1997
- **Measure**—Nominating committee to appoint new trustees each year based on these criteria, especially willingness and ability to help in fundraising, with continued involvement contingent upon the enlistment of new members, e.g., 1 member per year per trustee.

(See Chart 3—Cycle of Fundraising)
(See Chart 5—Board Roles and Responsibilities)
(See Chart 6—Ladder of Effectiveness)

Strategy #2—To obtain accurate prospect list

- **Measure**—Trustees to review current list by next Board Meeting
- **Measure**—Obtain 5:1 ratio of prospects to new members by December 31, 1996

Courtesy of Greek Archdiocese, New York.

(See Chart 7 and 8—Gift Ranges)
(See Charts 9 and 10—Constituency Models)
(See Chart 11—Needed Prospects)

Strategy #3—To make personal visits and phone calls to Trustees to discuss process

- **Measure**—Staff to determine number of visits/phone calls at later date

Strategy #4—Staff members and Trustees to meet with prospects regularly, keeping in mind that development is a *long-term* process

- **Measure**—Number per month to be determined by Staff at later date

(See Charts 12 and 13—Major Gift Development)

Strategy #5—To gain 25 more new members by December 31, 1996; 40 additional members by December 31, 1997; 50 additional members by December 31, 1998; 60 additional members by December 31, 1999; 70 additional members by December 31, 2000

- **Measure**—Individual goals to be determined by Staff at a later date

(See Chart 14—Gift Commitment)
(See Charts 15 and 16—Time/Visit Comparisons)

Objective #2

To reach 100 Associate members, with the promised yield of an additional $10 million for the endowment.

Strategy #1—To involve Associate Officers along with Board for Associate Development

- **Measure**—Educate and implement as above, with the same performance markers

Strategy #2—To gain 25 new members per year until December 31, 2000 (which will rotate as Associates jump into the regular level)

- **Measure**—Individual goals to be determined by Staff at a later date

Objective #3

To institute a planned giving program to take advantage of market potential

Strategy #1—Familiarization with necessary components

- **Measure**—Gather necessary information by December Executive Committee Meeting
- **Measure**—Discuss issues at December meeting
- **Measure**—Introduce and get approval at May, 1997, Board of Trustees Meeting

(See Chart 17—Tripod of Development)

Objective #4

Review ways to improve donor relations that allow them to meet philanthropic goals through a continued relationship with Leadership 100

Strategy #1—Personal contact to be made by Staff with members and lapsed members on a daily basis

- **Measure**—Numbers to be determined at a later date
- **Measure**—Improve 10% drop-out rate every year

Objective #5

Involve grant recipients in process of donor identification

Strategy #1—Meet with grant recipients to discuss potential donors.

- **Measure**—Staff to meet with 1 recipient per month

The Garden Party—Special Event from a Social Service Agency

June 1st, 1997
The Gardens at the St. Vincent and
Sarah Fisher Center

Fundraising Goal:
$207,000 gross/$150,000 net

Event History:
1988
1989
1990
1991
1992
1993 $148,774 gross/$122,309 net
1994 $152,998 gross/$117,983 net
1995 $159,442 gross/$118,020 net
1996 $178,000 gross/$149,700 net

Scope of Event:

This elegant event has a tradition of providing its guests with a tasting of the culinary works of over 55 of Metro Detroit's very best chefs, more than 100 wines from around the world, an incredible rare and collectable wine auction and soothing music from renowned jazz musician Alexander Zonjic and Friends. Each year we have a sell-out crowd of 1,200 community leaders. This event has been dubbed by some in the Metro Detroit area as *"The* event of the year". Also, this year we will be expanding our benefactor and patron package to include valet parking, recognition on invite and program (as was last year), but also, a VIP mingle an hour before with an exclusive wine tasting with our honorary chairs. Tours of the Center will also be available to our guests for the first time ever.

1997 goals and objectives:

1. Research and cultivate repeat attendees to the next giving level

---

Courtesy of Shannon McGuire, Farmington Hills, Michigan.

2. Generate publicity in the community
3. Raise $150,000 for the operating budget (net)
4. Educate committee—via tours, one-on-one conversations, recognition dinners—bringing these donors closer and help move them up the giving ladder.

Responsibilities:

Shannon McGuire—Development Coordinator:

- Manage event & volunteers
- Provide leadership and recognition on behalf of the Center by attending committee meetings—keep committee on track
- Assist committee as needed
- Report status of event to Director of Agency Relations, Executive Director and Development Chair
- Monitor all income/expenses
- Apply for all licenses—ensure all laws are being followed (including SVSFC regulations)
- Educate committee about Center—provide information/tours as needed
- Assist in designing, editing, printing invitation and program—as needed by committee
- Provide event information to Community Relations Coordinator for press release, newsletter, (etc.) publicity
- Build data base

Committee:

- Raise $150,000 for operating budget (net)
- Bring new donors to Center
- Ensure event is in stride with the Daughters mission
- Bring new sponsors to the event

Timeline:

December:

- Begin planning event
- Hold a committee meeting

- Confirm and develop committee
- Have first committee meeting
- Review last year's event
- Set fundraising goals & approve budget
- Assign committee duties

January:

- Hold a committee meeting
- Call target restaurants to confirm chef/owners name(s)
- Send letter (LTR1) asking chefs/owners for participation with response card
- Order all logistical event needs
- Apply for all licensing
- Decide on event entertainment needs
- Send sponsorship proposals
- Schedule Hudson volunteers for mailing
- Reserve rooms for year (including event needs)

February:

- Hold committee meeting
- Meet with Center's maintenance department
- Follow up with any chefs/owners who may not have responded from LTR1
- Draft invite/ticket/posters—choose printer
- Choose printer for program book
- Send ad letters to past and target companies
- Develop target patron/benefactor list with committee
- Send patron/benefactor letter
- Meet with Linda Todd on gardens & decorations
- Confirm sponsors
- Coordinate efforts with Ford Marketing staff

March:

- Hold committee meeting
- Send LTR2 to chefs/owners confirming participation and asking about menu plans and staff attending
- Begin follow-up calls for advertisers

- Compile list of confirmed patrons/benefactors for invite
- Edit, print, and invite/tickets/posters
- DOE volunteers job descriptions written, updated and sent
- Recruit DOE volunteers

April:

- Hold committee meeting
- Send invite
- Distribute PR
- PSA taped
- Go over ticket processing with data base secretary
- Ensure all licensing done in January is sufficient
- Deadline for program entries
- Choose chef incentive
- Check on wine auction status
- Meet with health department

May:

- Final committee meeting
- Hold planting day
- Confirm EVERYTHING
- Submit invoices for payment
- Monitor ticket sales and communicate to committee
- Meet with Federal Mogul
- Have program printed
- Send restaurants reminder letter—distribute parking passes
- Assign staff duties
- Print all thank you letters—volunteers, spanners, etc. & send the first business day after the event
- Location set-up/clean-up

June:

- Distribute survey of event to volunteers and restaurants
- Post event income/expense reports
- Have wrap-up meeting
- Slate date and event chair (co-chairs) for next year

Garden Party 97 Goals

Income	1995	1996	1997 Goal	97 notes
Ticket Sales	$74,380	$57,230	$80,000	800 @ $100
Benefactors	$5,380	$29,600	$30,000	60 @ $500
Patrons	$5,000	$8,200	$12,000	40 @ $300
Sub-Total				
Misc. Donations	$3,185	$4,535	$2,000	
Ad's	$3,300	$13,000	$18,000	
Sponsors	$13,300	$28,000	$30,000	
Wine Auction	$39,210	$34,515	$35,000	
Wine Auction Lot $		$2,000		
Gross Income	*$143,755*	*$177,080*	*$207,000*	
Expenses				
Licensing	$245	$210	$210	
Rental Equipt				
Tent Rental	misc. exp	$5000	$6000	
Golf Cart Rental	$670	$700	$700	
Scotties	$300	$300	$300	
Restaurant equipt	$5,225	$2,294	$2,500	
Linen	$345	$360	$360	
Purchases				
Wine Glasses	$2,751	$996	$2,800	
Paper Products	misc. exp	$1,021	$1,000	
Decorations	$3,465	$2,543	$2,500	
Chef Incentive	$1,907	$1,716	$1,500	
Hirm/Walker/Travel	$8,400	N/A	N/A	
Signage	$377	$501	$500	
Hardware	misc. exp	$1,900	$1,500	
Event needs	misc. exp	$575	$575	
Printing				
Program	$5,815	$3,200	$3,500	
Invite		$1,804	$2,000	
Misc. Printing	$464	$263	$300	
Invite Design	$215	$72	$80	
Misc. Expense				
	$9,652	$50	$200	
Entertainment	$1,500	$2,500	$3,000	
Wine Auction		$5,692	N/A	
Total Expenses	*$41,331*	*$31,697*	*$29,525*	
Total Net Income	**$102,424**	**$145,383**	**$177,475**	
Expense %	71% of all income went back to the kids—29% to expenses	82% of income went back to the kids—18% to expenses	86% of all income goes back to the kids—14% to expenses	

New Strategies for Gift Income from a Small University

I. New strategies for gift income

(The following points address **methods** for achieving some of the goals above, and **strategies for constituency groups**, but, except for non-budgeted items outside the $2.4 million annual fund goal, do not constitute additional funding goals)

A. By **November 1, assign renewal contracts** for all donors of **$1,000 to $24,999** to staff and/or volunteer solicitors.

    1. **Through specific assignments** to trustees, president, or vice president for external relations, **or to development officer indicated by regional contact plan**, ensure **every donor** and qualified prospect is the subject of a **customized contact plan** throughout the fiscal year.

    2. Target for **number of contacts is at least three annually** for each existing donor.

B. **By February 1, identify all currently possible additional prospects** for gifts of $1,000 to $24,999 **and assign** to staff and/or volunteer solicitors.

    1. Similarly, through specific assignments or regional contact plan, **ensure every prospect is the subject of a customized contact plan** throughout the fiscal year.

    2. **Desired number of contacts is at least six annually** for prospective donors.

        a. One personal letter or phone call
        b. One cultivation event
        c. One follow up visit or phone call
        d. One face to face solicitation
        e. One follow up contact
        f. One call or visit for stewardship or updating information

C. By **October 15, complete plan** to **screen, cultivate,** and when appropriate, **solicit all**

Courtesy of North Park College.

possible University **prospects** for gifts over $1,000 **throughout the United States,** as well as potential volunteers and other key constituents

    1. Develop regional assignments for non-leadership prospects. Proposal attached.

    2. Create priority schedule on all constituents in regions—$1,000+ donors, $500+ donors, $1000+ and $500+ lapsed donors, non-donors with potential at $1,000+, potential volunteers, reunion alumni, current parents, etc.

    3. Stay up to date on assignments of all known leadership prospects, working with researcher, campaign director, and appropriate administrators toward a schedule of prospect tracking meetings that will facilitate assignment and implementations of contacts.

D. **By September 16, begin new all-academic-year phonathon,** transferring **all solicitations of LYBUNTS (last year donors) and SYBUNTS (some year donors) up to $999 to phone,** except where this is not possible due to inability to get correct phone numbers or to specific request by donor not to be contacted by phone.

    1. Contact and solicit **all alumni** donors, lapsed donors, reunion alumni, athletic alumni, and seminary alumni by phone prior to end of academic year. **Primary thrust** of these contacts will be **in the fall,** with those not reached in the fall called in the spring. Seminary alumni will be segmented out for calling in the spring.

    2. Contact **all known parents** of current and former students, all friends (non-alum, non-parent), seniors. Friend (non-alum, non-parent) donors will be called in the fall, with those not reached called in the spring.

    3. Never givers and long lapsed donors are prospects for contracted telemarketing group (a la ARIA). **Decision on ARIA** or other company to call never-givers by **November 30.**

4. **Target for phonathon income is $350,000**, and **direct mail $120,000**. These are goals for the primary means of contacting prospects and donors up to $999.

5. A few $1,000 donors will be generated by the phonathon. Credit for these will be given to the strategy that generated them but will be counted in the general goals for gifts at that level.

6. Approach for phonathon solicitations will be designed to result in optimum gift for each donor. Features of the script:

    a. "Ladder" sequence request
    b. Studying profiles prior to call, developing rapport and tailoring conversation to donor
    c. Never requesting less than $25 (the prospect will be asked to suggest a gift that is both comfortable for them and helpful to us if solicitation drops to minimum)
    d. Lots of thanking
    e. Sharing upcoming events of interest
    f. Updating information

7. **Two direct mail pieces** will be sent **to the entire group of prospects from $1 to $999.**

    a. A **year-end letter** will be sent **December 1** as a special gift effort. Suggested focus: institutional scholarships and faculty salaries
    b. **A fiscal year end** mailing will be sent **May 15** as a final push to achieve annual fund goals. Focus: Alumni participation.

        1) Reason for alumni participation focus: Some alumni donors may fall off the low end of the gift spectrum due the new system through the phonathon of a ladder approach request. (We will not ask for gifts lower than $25 as the cost for each pledge is about $14.)
        2) Calendar year end piece should have a festive, holiday attitude
        3) Fiscal year end mailing will be segmented by alumni LYBUNTS, SYBUNTS, non-donors, parent

LYBUNTS, SYBUNTS, and non-donors, and friend LYBUNTS, SYBUNTS, and non-donors.

E. **By fall board meeting**, meet with appropriate board member to **determine dollar goal and details of approach** to trustees for annual giving by the Board of Trustees. **Participation goal is 100%. Complete campaign by end of June.**

    1. Send letter over development committee chair's signature.

    2. Assign board member to president, Vice President for External Relations, and Development Committee members.

F. **Faculty-Staff campaign** will be carried out during **November, segmented by College Staff, College Faculty, Seminary Faculty/ Staff.**

    1. Target for **average gift** will be **$250.**

    2. Target for **participation** will be **100%,** with voluntary second mile giving the focus.

    3. A **letter** signed by faculty-staff co-chairs, mailed **November 1**, will be followed up by **personal contacts in all departments** through an annual fund committee representative.

    4. Recognition could be a program at the faculty-staff Christmas dinner, as well as in the University Magazine.

G. **Reunion giving** targets will be grouped for all reunion classes for the **'1 and '6 classes** and will be implemented primarily through the phonathon during the **fall of 1996.**

    1. **Average gift** will be targeted at **$300,** an increase of **$50 over last year**

    2. **Participation** target will be **73%,** twice last year's level

H. **By January 31, committees** will be **enlisted** for twenty-fifth and fiftieth **reunion** gift efforts for the **class years ending in 2 and 7.**

    1. **By January 15,** Annual giving director, director of development, and alumni direc-

tor will agree on **plan that incorporates both program and gift strategies**

2. Committee should include those interested in program and those who will focus on the class gift (**suggested number on committee—12**).

3. **Gifts** will be **announced** at reunion class **events for '2 and '7 years.**

I. **Senior gift committee** will be recruited with **first meeting** held by **end of fall semester.**

1. Phonathon Assistant, with guidance from Annual Giving Director, will coordinate the effort.

2. **Goal** for senior gift is **$2,500** (nearly double 1995 gift).

3. **Participation goal** remains at **100%**.

4. **Strategy**, to include designation, method of solicitation, and recognition plan, will be **in place by end of February**, with implementation to follow immediately.

5. **Senior gift** will be **announced** at appropriate event during **commencement.**

J. **Parent audience** will be **studied** to determine appropriate fund raising strategies and goals.

1. **By end of October**, write outline of **parent fund raising plan** as part of five-year plan which will be submitted at fall board meeting.

2. Work with computer services to **identify all possible parents**, grandparents, and former parents already in data base, and to **finalize procedure for adding names of new parents** and ensuring they can be segmented for cultivation and solicitation

3. Measure results of parent calling in spring semester to help determine future goals.

4. During Parents' Weekend, hold a **reception for parents of students not receiving financial aid.**

K. **Gift income for Athletic operating funds** will be raised via a **phonathon** that is part of the **paid-student caller all-academic year annual fund phonathon.**

1. We will call **all alumni from athletic programs** and all who have **given to the athletic** program in the past three years

2. **Goal** will be set at **$30,000**. This is twice what was received last year through athletic phonathon and other operations fund raising.

L. In addition to seminary operations, **targets for seminary endowed scholarships will be set by end of October**. Seminary development officer has proposed a $1 million goal for seminary endowed scholarships, as well as a goal for seminary student housing improvements, a capital project.

M. All development officers and other solicitors will seek to **identify all qualified prospects for planned gifts**, and **refer these prospects** to the **Trust Company.**

1. **By November 30**, development department will host **planned giving workshop** led by a representative of the Trust Company

2. **Annual Fund** brochures and all **literature** printed **beginning immediately** will provide **opportunity to be referred to the Trust Company** for a possible planned gift arrangement

3. Heritage Circle members should be invited to make a current gift through a targeted mailing with follow up by staff— Major Gifts Officer and Director of Development or Director of Special Gifts.

N. By **mid-October, a committee** should be formed to **study the precise definition of the Annual Fund**—i.e., which funds actually make up this designation, and **formally establish** any **additional** (non-annual fund) **funding goals for development** outside of the current capital campaign.

O. **Targets for endowment and auxiliary program fund raising will be set and integrated into the five-year plan for development.** Included in this will be any academic or non-academic program that has identified and gained approval of projects for fund raising.

1. **By October 31**, a procedure for **coordinating and centralizing fund raising for auxiliary and other campus programs** will be completed (this will **include a requirement** for **all gifts raised** through other programs to be **processed through development** department gift processing).

2. **One half** of **corporation and foundation goals** will be targeted at **non-budget relieving** projects, many of which will be for auxiliary programs.

3. **By November 30, create prioritized list of budgeted and non-budgeted restricted designations** to equip development officers for prospect contacts with individuals or churches where annual or capital projects are not feasible designations.

P. **Support the Capital Campaign** through screening, cultivation, and solicitation, as appropriate, of campaign prospects **by all development officers.**

1. Director of Development, Major Gifts Officer, Director of Special Gifts, Director of Annual Giving, and Development Associate for Corporations and Foundations will support campaign solicitations and other campaign activities as needed by the Director of the Capital Campaign.

Q. Although a specific target has not been set for annual unrestricted gifts over $25,000, **Major Gifts Officer** will seek to **identify all possible individuals** who may be prospects for **unrestricted gifts at this level** and will **develop** and carry out a **cultivation and solicitation plan for these gifts.**

—Unrestricted gifts received at the major gift level can be redirected when it is deter-

mined annual giving goals through gifts up to $25,000 will be achieved.

R. **By November 30, study** purpose and results of **Golf Tournament** and **make recommendation** on who and which department should be responsible; also how development can best capitalize on the event, given unique prospect group that participates.

1. **Establish volunteer board** and chair for Golf Tournament.

2. **Create list of University suspects** from golf participants and screen, cultivate as appropriate.

II. Prospect identification, tracking, and research

A. **By November 1, finalize and record definitions of all prospect and suspect levels and establish criteria for movement of prospects from level to level**

B. **By October 4, finalize and record regional territories**, relationship criteria, and other rationale for assignment of prospects and constituencies

1. **By October 4, finalize schedule and general objectives of prospect tracking meetings**, including attendees, agendas for October through March, and desired outcomes. (Development of this area will be the shared responsibility of Development Director, Campaign Director, Consultant, Vice President for External Relations, and Researcher).

2. Researcher to spend **40 hours by November 1 toward implementing major prospect tracking module** on Benefactor, and will have one student trained to do basic major prospect data entry on Benefactor; major prospect tracking module will be **fully implemented by June 30.**

3. **By December 1, identify 25 new prospects** at or above the Major Gifts level and

continue to identify **25 new prospects quarterly**

4. **By December 1, identify 25 new suspects** at or above the Major Gifts level and continue to identify **25 new suspects quarterly**

5. **By December 1, make recommendations on assignment** concerning all identified prospects and suspects for Major Gifts level and above.

6. Coordinate tracking process with Directors of Annual Giving and Special Gifts for parallel tracking of high end annual fund gifts.

III. Recognition and appreciation

A. **By October 15, establish recognition strategies for each giving level**, particularly relating to club memberships, to include events, premiums, listings in honor roll, and other public and private recognition venues.

B. **By October 31, schedule annual appreciation event** for donors of $1,000 or more during Spring 1997. Schedule regional appreciation events through Portable University schedule.

C. Respond to **each major gift** (i.e., 25K and above) with an **individualized recognition plan** to be **carried out by June 30, 1997.**

D. Beginning **immediately**, in addition to development officer assigned, **thanking by phone** will be done as follows:

$500—Director of Development or Campaign Director
$1,000—Vice President for External Relations
$5,000—Vice President for External Relations or President
$10,000—President or Board Member

E. Phonathon **pledge letter** signed by director of development. Receipt **letter for all gifts** signed by **director of development**. In addition to receipt letter, monthly acknowledg-

ment letter on letterhead stationery is as follows: $500 donors receive letter on letterhead from director of development, $1,000 and above receive letter from VP for Ext. Rel., and $5,000 and above receive letter from President.

IV. Events

A. As stated above, **one major recognition dinner or reception annually in the Chicago area,** for current donors of $1,000 and above. Determine most viable locations for regional appreciation dinners due to large clumps of donors there and work through Portable University schedule to hold events that can serve both as recognition and as cultivation.

B. **One special, more intimate occasion for recognizing Centennial Society donors.**

1. First class event at unique location with President, Bd Chair, VP, and host

2. Explore nationally-recognized special guest possibilities

C. **Capitalize on program events,** both on campus and throughout the country, which would be good opportunities for cultivation.

D. Proposed: **Fund-raising** or specifically development-oriented cultivation events (number of events, schedule, and location under study):

1. Ask trustees or current donors of $1,000 and above to host and/or sponsor one of **three small gatherings of 12 to 16 people,** with the following format

a. President, VP for External Relations, and host present program
b. Staff, administrators, and host (if willing) make follow up solicitations within two days after event)

2. **Two small,** intimate dinners at president's or trustee's home for two or three couples for campaign and Centennial Society cultivation

3. As stated previously, participate in Golf Tournament and Ravinia events (or others

with similar purposes) once it is determined what role Development staff should play in these events. Events should always be planned with a strategy for follow-up.

4. Consider bringing in top donors to an annual weekend on campus ala "Weekend in the Pines" but instead we call it "Weekend at the Park." Present complete University program and mission. (incorporate into four-year plan)

V. Volunteers

A. During 1996-1997, we will begin recruitment for the following advisory councils which will meet or have members visited up to twice annually to make recommendations about prospects, cultivation, and issues of interest to members and prospective members of their gift club levels.

1. Centennial Society
2. President's Club
3. Friends of North Park
4. Cornerstone Club
5. Friends of the Seminary $1,000 level club
6. Faculty-Staff
7. Parents Fund
8. Tenth, 25th, 35th and fiftieth reunion classes
9. Senior Gift
10. Golf tournament
11. Regional Chapter programs
12. Corp/Fdn advisory board
13. Trustee Development Committee
14. Trustee Campaign Steering Committee

B. We will also use individual volunteers for:

1. Hosting small group events
2. Individual solicitations (i.e. trustees)
3. Corporate or foundation requests

VI. Gift and Pledge Processing

A. Maintain **two day turnaround for processing of gifts** and mailing of receipt.

1. **Write monthly acknowledgment** letter with information about campus activities and issues.

2. Pledge acknowledgment letter written and produced by Annual Fund Director. Director of Development writes gift acknowledgment letters.

B. **Develop** and produce **daily batch reports** from Benefactor; print two copies—one is on file, the other has routing slip attached and is routed to: President's Office, VP for External Relations, Assoc. VP for External Relations, Director of Development, Director of Capital Campaign, Major Gifts Officer, Director of Special Gifts, Development Associate for Corporation and Foundation Relations, and Annual Giving Director.

C. **Develop weekly, monthly, quarterly, annual gift reports** from Benefactor according to current strategies and segmentations.

VII. Centralization

A. **By October 1, notify faculty and administrators** whose programs have funding needs **of procedure to establish funding priorities** for budgeted or non-budgeted designations:

1. **Submit to development director up to five projects,** prioritized

2. **Propose prospects** or suspects to fund projects

3. **Establish monthly meeting to coordinate and assign contacts** of individuals or foundations/corporations/organizations

B. **Write policy and procedure for gift processing to all campus directors** and managers stating **requirement to process all gifts through development department.**

VIII. Constituency-based Initiatives

A. Maintain **upward curve for alumni participation rate.**

—Due to change in phonathon request process, it is less likely we will receive gifts under $10. This may prevent further steep upward curves on participation rate. We will aim to maintain and somewhat increase participation, but rather than continue to inflate this figure by artificial means, to give substance to the University's relationship with its alumni through the means described in the items below:

B. **By end of October**, write **outline for long-range plan to capitalize on constituency based programming** to enhance fund raising opportunities resulting from program initiatives that will thank, connect, inform, and involve alumni, parents, and friends of the University.

1. Work with director of alumni and parent events and director of constituency relations to assist in creating plan which allows us to optimize gift income potential from chapter programs, reunion events, and friend and parent programming.

2. Following Homecoming 1996, recruit committees for reunion giving for 10th, 25th, 35th, and 50th reunion classes of 1997 (i.e., class years ending in 2 and 7), with committees and event plans in place by end of January 1997.

3. Research other institutions who have put alumni and parent relations programs in place in past ten years to learn impact on giving and create appropriate charts and graphs to project potential for the University.

IX. Publications and communications

A. **By end of January, design annual fund brochures** as follows:

1. General annual fund (by end of October)
2. Alumni giving
3. Friends of the University (redesign)
4. Cornerstone Club (new club)

5. President's Club
6. Centennial Society
7. Friends of the Seminary (incorporate new $1,000 club)

—In general these will be tri-fold brochures to fit in a #10 envelope

B. **By end of October, establish regular article in in-house on-campus newsletter regarding development**

1. Focus on achievements
2. Overview of current activities
3. Enlisting all-campus understanding and involvement in development issues, as appropriate, and their help in identifying potential donors to various designations.

C. **By October 31, write first of quarterly "Insiders Memo"** from President to donors of $1,000 and above, and selected major and leadership prospects.

1. Personal style from president
2. Covers academic and co-curricular and "big picture" issues more in-depth and somewhat ahead of their appearance in the University Magazine.
3. Can talk *about* fund raising activities but is not a fund raising piece.
4. Have written by board meeting with certain information "dropped in" at last minute, then printed and mailed quickly thereafter.

D. **By January 31**, establish purpose and goals of an **article on development for parents' newsletter**

E. **By June 30, plan honor roll** for 1996-1997.

F. Develop **donor-friendly financial report** to give out on request after college's full financial report is complete.

X. Data base/computer support

A. **Immediately form computer task force to sort and prioritize needs** relating to computer and data base issues and address systematically. Known issues already:

1. Inconsistency and inaccuracy of giving, club status, source codes, constituency codes, alumni status, phone numbers, employment information

2. Reticence or lack of opportunity to begin utilizing specific modules of Benefactor like the events module, the major prospect tracking module, and need for training to resolve this

3. Need for training on ordering sorts of various kinds

4. Need for data entry—major prospect module and general constituency

B. **Immediately notify campus of procedure and time constraints on requests for information from Benefactor.**

1. **All requests must have a clear date** when information is needed

Chapter 9

Designing the Infrastructure: Steps 8 through 11 in the Annual Integrated Development Process

Strategic Management and Leadership Principles

There are few subjects that have captured the interest of working Americans more than how to be a good manager or a great leader. The subject's popularity is attributed to the competitive marketplace and today's climate of extraordinary change. MBA programs are filled to capacity. Library shelves are heavy with scholarly textbooks on management and leadership theory. Bookstores are overflowing with the latest publications on effective management practices. Workshops, seminars, and videotapes offer shortcuts to being a "five minute manager," or a "fifth dimension thinker," to "getting extraordinary things done" with "seven habits of success."

Disagreement continues over the best approaches; most agree Theory Y is better than Theory X—but what about the human relations model versus the systems contingency model? Is it really possible to *learn* how to be a leader, or are we confined to being good managers?

The idea of management and leadership coming together presents a certain dichotomy; the fundamental purpose of management is to bring order and stability to the organization, while the fundamental purpose of leadership is to challenge and change it.

This remains the ongoing challenge for the contemporary development director.

Fund Raising as Management and Leadership

As a complex, multidisciplinary process, fund raising uses the same basic management principles practiced in other fields: analysis, planning, execution, control, and evaluation. However, the fund raiser has dual management responsibilities: the management of both tasks and relationships. *Task* functions include initiating and coordinating activity; diagnosing and resolving problems; and evaluating accomplishments. *Relationship* functions include maintenance of the group or organization, encouraging individual members, setting standards of behavior, achieving consensus, and reducing tensions. According to The Fund Raising School manual (1993), good management is always based on respect for fellow workers, open communications (up, down, and laterally), confidence in one's own abilities to manage and lead, personal and professional goals that are clear and achievable, and a compelling belief in the organization's goals and the importance of seeing that they are accomplished.

Management skills and principles are fundamental, but they are not enough—*ethical and entrepreneurial leadership is critical to the philan-*

Ethical and entrepreneurial leadership is critical to the philanthropic process.

thropic process. Philanthropic fund raising depends on a value-based orientation, without which our practice will succumb to a merely commercial, business orientation where begging and selling are acceptable. In their book, *The Leadership Challenge*, Kouzes and Posner (1987) propose five leadership practices that are common to successful *leaders*: they challenge the process, inspire a shared vision, enable others to act, model the way, and encourage the heart. As a leader, the fund raiser will evoke expectations and desires of volunteers and staff, search for new approaches and new options, seek to attract commitment and engagement, and take risks.

Most professional fund raisers are comfortable incorporating the principles of management and leadership, leaning more toward one or the other when the occasion calls for it. Nowhere is the need to integrate management and leadership greater than in annual giving. According to Mixer,

The job at hand may require managerial performance such as supervising budget preparation, coordinating schedules of different activities, or hiring personnel. At other times, the task may demand leadership qualities of inspiring volunteers to make extra efforts in a lagging campaign, generating staff and volunteer commitment to achieve a new fund-raising goal, or demonstrating the agency's value to a new constituency (1993, 153).

Issues and Challenges Unique to Fund Raising

Fund raising, as *both* a management function and a leadership dynamic, presents some challenges not found in other professions. First, fund raising is involved extensively in multilevel relationships—with board members, administration, volunteers, staff, vendors, prospects, and donors. Second, fund raising is functionally demanding, and those functions—fund raising, communications, marketing, program development, fiscal administration, and management information systems—must be integrated. Third, fund raising operates in an environment of complexity, change, and potential conflict. The last presents the greatest challenge.

Promote Understanding of Fund Raising

It is widely accepted that fund raising does not get the respect it deserves because it is *not well understood*. This lack of understanding is not limited to the public: fund raising is not always appreciated by those on the inside. Board members, program managers, volunteers, and other staff members are neither cognizant nor entirely comfortable with the role that fund raisers play within and outside the organization. It is imperative for fund raisers to view the internal "public" in the same way as the external public: as a constituency with interests and needs. For instance, thinking about program staff as an important constituent group with whom exchange relationships are desired changes the attitude from "they have their job to do and I have mine" to "when we help each other, *we* can raise more money for *our* programs."

Specific strategies can be used to ease potential tensions, open communications, and promote understanding of the fund-raising function. Kay Sprinkel Grace offers the following strategies for promoting understanding of the development function within the organization (Sprinkel Grace 1991a, 142):

- Present information at board and staff meetings about the functions of the development office.
- Communicate regularly about success in fund raising through mailings and events, including "good news" bulletins about major gifts.
- Let program staff know when the information they provided for a direct mail letter, a proposal, or a brochure had a major impact.
- Invite staff members to a monthly brown bag lunch to let them know what funding sources are available and to generate ideas for specific cases.
- Link program staff with donors who are interested in their work, and invite donors to cultivation activities and events.

Use Engagement and Empowerment Strategies

Fund raising has an unusual position within an organization—it has *wide responsibility, but limited authority.* Look at the functional relationships. The position reports to the CEO, but the fund raiser relates to and is dependent on people at every level—the board members *above* the CEO, as well as the program staff and volunteers *below.* The fund raiser must mentor up and mentor down, follow and lead at the same time. He or she is expected to inform, involve, and include staff and volunteers, both vertically and horizontally. Add the relationship span to the oversight responsibility of functional management tasks, and the fund raiser has a significant challenge, with limited power and decision-making authority. This situation calls for engagement and empowerment competency, a communications proficiency, a change agent capability, and a professional stance. The Fund Raising School (1993) manual advises: "Be persuasive and assertive, but not aggressive; be warm and outgoing, yet keep cool under pressure; allow intuition to kick in when gauging how to rationally manage a difficult situation."

Address Conflicts with Confidence

To make things even more challenging, fund raising is replete with *potential conflicts of interest:* between the donor and the organization, the donor and the fund raiser, the fund raiser and the organization, and among the fund raiser, the donor, and the organization. Mediating between parties is alleged to be the most difficult role a fund raiser must play. Honesty, integrity, and keeping promises are key to resolving conflicts, as is understanding that the organization's and donors' invisible boundaries turn into barbed wire fences when people begin to cross either one of them.

As with other aspects of fund raising, solutions must be addressed by those involved, not solely by the fund raiser. Still it remains the fund raiser's role to serve as the conscience of the charitable mission, to ask the hard questions, and to raise issues when they occur.

Help Lead Change in an Ever-Changing Environment

Fund raisers need to have far more expertise than most managers/leaders, implementing and adapting to fit the circumstances of an *ever-changing environment*. It is not enough to be versed and attentive to the organizational environment (people, plans, systems, tasks, goals); it is crucial that a fund raiser be sensitive to new forces and to circumstances affecting their organizations and have the ability to create and direct change to meet these new conditions. To act as a change agent requires a keen understanding of organizational behavior and group dynamics. Intervention techniques include interpersonal communications, consensus building, teamwork, conflict resolution, and productivity improvement.

Key Strategies

The following strategies are key to building a philanthropic annual program that will flourish in the best of times and the worst of times.

Vision: Taking a New Look

The common definition of a person with vision is someone who can *envision* the future. To envision is to go places where others have not gone nor imagined—to think about what could be, without constraints or barriers. People with vision are able to think "outside the box" or to make paradigms shifts. In the context of

the fund-raising manager/leader, vision means "seeing"—forward, backward, inside, and outside—without getting bogged down in details of everyday matters.

Fund raisers with vision concern themselves with where the organization "fits" within its philanthropic community and where changes will take them both in the future. Fund raisers with vision enable donors to believe the impossible is possible. Most fund raisers are dreamers too; they have the same aspirations that philanthropists do; and the same hopes that program staff do. They serve the same mission and are grounded in the same values.

Take Five. As an exercise to keep a sense of vision alive and well in your organization, invite the development team to take out a piece of paper and pencil, and write for five minutes without stopping about what they want the organization to be in five years. Now ask them to do the same exercise about how *they* personally want to be involved.

Leadership: Doing What Is Not Expected

When leadership is absent, its absence becomes obvious. When present, it seems always to have been there. If visioning is looking forward to what's possible, then leadership is making it so. Leadership is about determined doggedness (transactional leadership) and inspired action (transformative leadership).

In fund raising especially, leadership comes from many sources: the development staff, board members, volunteers, and program staff. As the ascribed "chief" leader of the development program, the fund raiser needs to adapt to each situation, serving whatever role is appropriate while always encouraging others to emerge and excel as leaders too. Remember, it is the followers who give credence to those whose ideas are worth championing.

Put Together a Merger. To help the development team understand and appreciate the value of being both manager and leader, ask them to divide a piece of paper in half by drawing a vertical line from top to bottom. Have them write the word "manager" on one side and the word "leader" on the other side. Ask them to list as many adjectives as possible to describe the obvious characteristics of each and to circle those desirable to fund raising. It will soon be apparent that the line between the two is very thin; one list will seem to be the mirror image of the other, as both sides are needed. Merged, manager and leader attributes make "the ideal whole."

Ethical Action: Doing What Is Right

Making ethical decisions, while never black and white, can best be described as a three-level form of decision making: (1) where laws apply; (2) where the right action is known, but the temptation is to take a different course; and (3) where there are competing options, but there is no clear course for good or evil (Independent Sector 1991).

In fund raising in particular, there seems to be a lot of room for conflict and for ethical examination. The ethical fund raiser will speak out when the situation most warrants it, but least welcomes it. Being the ethical conscience of the charitable mission means rising above the situation, not to it—it means detaching from any personal agendas to make room for everyone else's. We might ask the question, "What do we believe is personally right, but from which we will not benefit personally?"

When faced with ethical issues, the resolution may not be the solution per se, but rather the collection of information and the stimulating discourse that help frame the solution. As Payton said, "There are no ethical answers; there are only ethical questions" (Temple 1993, 1–9).

Elicit a Response. There are many examples to illustrate how diverse opinions and circumstances affect ethical behavior. Present the fol-

> **When faced with ethical issues, the resolution may not be the obvious solution.**

lowing examples at the next development committee meeting to elicit discussion about the importance of ethics in fund raising (Independent Sector 1991):

- Example of an illegal act: The board agrees to sell property to a board member's spouse without competitive bidding and at a price below fair market values
- Example of an unethical behavior: high, dishonest, or inappropriate expenses submitted for travel and meetings
- Example of an ethical dilemma: A board member who heads the best public relations firm in town is the volunteer chair of your publicity committee and has a contract for some of the organization's advertising. Is this relationship acceptable, and if so, under what conditions?

Innovation: Pushing the Edges

Many say that the only constant in life is change. With change comes the necessity of innovation: to sail uncharted waters, to try untested assumptions, to be on the cutting edge. Fund raisers are constantly challenged to innovate: "make an exchange for an equivalent sum" and "to pass from one phase to another" (Webster). Innovation is taking risks, getting in and out, taking things apart and putting them back together, and doing it all with conviction.

Although innovation *is* planned change (it is proactive), change insists on innovation (in this sense it is reactive). The fund raiser needs to demonstrate to others that innovation and change are inevitable and positive, in contrast to change for change's sake.

Move Outside the Box. To help the development team appreciate how innovation leads and manages change, ask them to make a list of the present-day factors influencing the rate of change in fund raising and to identify the extent to which these factors are an opportunity for innovation. Then invite them to brainstorm innovations for each annual fund-raising campaign or project. The rules of brainstorming are to generate ideas without constraints or criticism—no thought is too absurd.

Teamwork: Adding Value

The concept of teamwork as an alternative to individual responsibility is widely accepted but less widely accomplished. In an effort to "team," collaboration may give way to consensus, or worse to compromise. Teamwork works best when respect for diversity is present and when appreciation is given to the unique perspective of each person, which adds value to the mix.

Level the Playing Field. An effective method for building new teams is to help everyone understand the theory of group process, with identified and predictable dynamics. Being aware of the group evolutionary process minimizes confusion, anxiety, and resistance. The first agenda item should be understanding group stages and dynamics.

- Stage I: The ME or Forming Step (checking out the group, agreeing to proceed)
- Stage II: The Conflict or Storming Step (disagreement about issues, and whether to proceed)
- Stage III: The WE or Norming Step (idea generation, growing respect for differences)
- Stage IV: The Work or Performing Step (cohesion results in cooperation, collaboration, and creative decisions)

Successful Manager/Leader "Habits"

Steven Covey (1989) promotes seven "habits" that reflect principles that have been proven successful in countless settings:

1. Exercise strategic choice.
2. Get the mission into individual hearts and minds.
3. Empower people to solve problems at their source.
4. Design win-win systems.
5. Maintain stakeholder information systems.

6. Create synergistic forums.
7. Invest in renewal.

Step 8 in the Annual Integrated Development Process: Establish Roles and Responsibilities for Volunteers and Staff

Consider the original premise for the philanthropic sector: a gathering of people who "by association" would accomplish what one could not. Consider too the voluntary roots of philanthropy. No intimidation was necessary or possible; people voluntarily stepped forward for what they believed in, and their reward was self-satisfaction, not financial remuneration or gain. As such, it seems contradictory to offer an organizational model for the development program that does not bring people together with like interests and beliefs, who will voluntarily set and implement a collaboration agenda. This is to say that the development effort *naturally* involves volunteers, be they board members, committee members, auxiliary members, occasional volunteers, or one-time volunteers. A "philanthropy" program without volunteers contradicts the meaning of the word (voluntary action for the public good).

Volunteers bring expertise, objectivity, advocacy, and credibility to an organization's mission and community position, as they do to the fund-raising program. A development program without volunteers is an endeavor without conscience or soul. No matter how well-meaning we are as professional staff, we are hard pressed to act in an altruistic manner as do volunteers. As paid staff, we may feel called to the fund-raising profession, but it is our *job*.

Over and over again, experience has proven that the most effective and sustainable annual fund-raising programs use the expertise and passion of volunteers alongside the capability and

> **A development program without volunteers is an endeavor without conscience or soul.**

ethical professionalism of trained staff. Team-work, with all its iterations, is the ideal framework for organizational success.

Team Development

The concept of team building is derived from the notion that everyone has something valuable to offer and that a collective effort is more empowering, enabling, effective, and satisfying than individual work that is hierarchically arranged. Teamwork is the key to unlocking the energies and talents within an organization, stimulated by those from outside the organization. The success of sustainable teams comes from a commitment to the value of the team concept, leadership within the team, open communications, and a shared vision. Perhaps the most important benefit of team building comes from the practice of empowerment, making each individual stronger—the whole being greater than the sum of its parts.

A team is an "organized" group of people with defined roles and responsibilities and established goals and schedules. A team shares the decision making, the implementation, the assessment, and the evaluation and changes along the way. A team fosters collaboration, develops cooperative goals, seeks integrative solutions, and builds trusting relationships.

The size of a team ranges from more than one person to a small group. The standard development team is made up of the board chair, the development committee chair, the chief administrator, and the fund raiser. Granted, the development team can include other volunteers and other staff members such as in the case of the development committee. There is no perfect organization model, except that the development team represents the leadership responsible for the philanthropic process: fund raising with all its component and integrative parts.

Organizationally, the development team functions as an executive committee/team, relating to other functional teams (grouped by methodology, such as personal solicitation), project teams (grouped by campaign, such as a board campaign or a special event), representa-tive teams (grouped by constituency, such as physicians), geographic teams (grouped by place, such as a region of the country), and/or operations teams (grouped by tasks and outcomes, such as a donor research or donors relations team).

Regardless of how the development teams are organized, their responsibility is to achieve a culture of organizational effectiveness. Kay Sprinkel Grace offers specific empowerment strategies for the development team(s) (Sprinkel Grace 1991b, 167):

1. Encourage *participation in the planning process* and the setting of fund-raising goals and objectives.
2. Provide *fund raising training* that focuses not only on effective strategies but also on underlying principles, including the importance of substituting pride for apology.
3. *Offer coaching and practice* to reduce anxiety about making the solicitation calls.
4. Invite and *respect their observations and opinions* on development related issues.
5. *Keep them informed* of successes and failures, and ask for their support on key issues.
6. *Team them* with a staff member, experienced volunteers, or other expert witness for solicitation visits.
7. Remind them as much as possible of the *mission of the organization* and of the community needs they are helping meet.

A Few Practical Hints

- Invite anyone and everyone to attend your meetings. A volunteer who assembles mail packages one day a week will welcome the invitation now and then and bring observations that would not be felt by anyone else. Be inclusive rather than exclusive.
- Remove the boxes and the labels from people's jobs. Allow the volunteer or staff member to create his or her own "title"— whatever works for the person, works.

Their own description of their job may be much more accurate than yours.

- Seek expert advice—add even more value by going beyond the team for expertise. Invite others to present and give feedback on issues about which the team is inexperienced. Do not recreate what others have already accomplished without learning from their mistakes and their successes.

Organizational Design

There are innumerable choices of organizational and team design within fund raising. The principal question is which design is the most effective in achieving the organization's mission and goals.

Vertical Model

Most everyone in fund raising is familiar with the traditional organizational structure—a hierarchical arrangement of "boxed" volunteer committees reporting to the board of directors and a list of "staffed" positions reporting through the chief development officer to the executive director. In the case of an institutional foundation as exists in hospitals and educational institutions, a series of dotted lines tie the volunteers and the foundation staff to the organization. An organizational chart has the foundation board or the board development committee at the top, with a dotted line to the chief development officer; the next level of command is a series of volunteer subcommittees, with dotted lines to staff members who have responsibility for such areas as annual fund and major gifts. The third level has the least influence but the greatest amount of "supportive" responsibility—special events may fall into the third level. The top of the organization is where the leadership and decision making take place. The bottom of the organization is where the followership and task functions take place.

This pyramidal structure has been successful for decades, replicated in annual fund campaigns, capital campaigns, and major gifts campaigns, or whenever staff and volunteers work together. In this vertical arrangement, the volunteers far outnumber the staff, and the staff serve as support agents of the volunteer committees.

The *development team* in the vertical, hierarchical model consists of the executive director, development director, board chair, and development committee chair. In some cases, particularly in smaller organizations, the development team consists of only two or three of the above-mentioned positions. Within the hierarchical model, there are two variations (aside from the foundation and non-foundation variations): the volunteer-dominated (Exhibit 9–1) and the staff-dominated hierarchical model (Exhibit 9–2).

In the hierarchical model, role delineation tends to be around functional product lines and responsibility is divided by fund-raising methodology—the annual fund committee, the special events committee, the major gifts committee, and the planned giving committee, with numerous subcommittees, such as the tribute committee, the holiday campaign committee, the board campaign committee, and so on. This arrangement is similar for volunteers and for staff.

Horizontal Model

In a horizontal model, a constituency-focused approach, the development committee and department tend to be more integrated, divided by constituency groups and cases; emphasis is placed on the strategies over the methodologies. The horizontal model is a paradigm shift to better respond to changing attitudes and behavior in the donor marketplace and to train and use volunteer and staff resources more effectively to achieve a higher level of productivity. It is particularly well suited to an annual integrated development program, given its seamless nature. In the horizontal model management is across, not up and down. This model de-emphasizes the typical hierarchical structure and breaks development into its key strategies and creates teams to oversee them. It also breaks down authority-subordinate roles, opens up cre-

Exhibit 9–1 Volunteer-Dominated Hierarchical Model

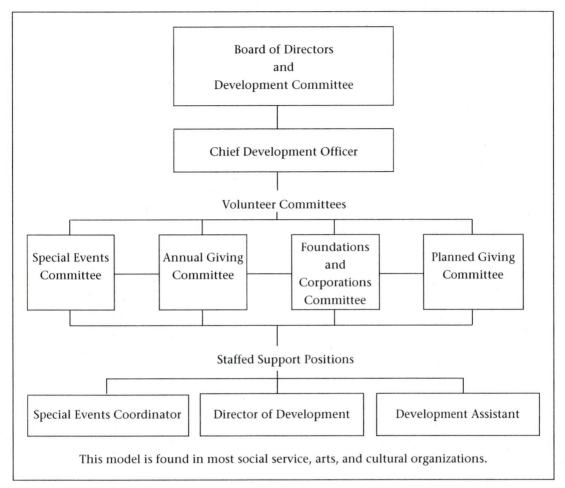

This model is found in most social service, arts, and cultural organizations.

ative and unique partnerships, and helps to reduce the tensions and inequities that tend to develop between volunteers and staff by clarifying responsibilities in a way that is more respectful. It encourages a culture that values the donor/customer first, uses process as a way to involve people and bring added value, and rewards teamwork as well as individual enterprise.

The horizontal model first emerged in the corporate sector and is currently in practice at AT&T, Eastman Chemical, General Electric, Lexmark International, Motorola, and Xerox, among others. It was designed to change the thinking of the corporate specialists who spent their careers climbing a vertical hierarchy to the top of a given function just as fund raisers move from development assistant to special events coordinator to annual fund manager to major gifts officer to chief development officer.

In fund raising, the horizontal model is a relatively new concept, and although there is little evidence of its long-term success, it seems to be more oriented toward donors, volunteers, and staff members (Exhibit 9–3). In other words, it is an organizational dynamic that focuses on the human potential, rather than institutionalized systems.

The team-oriented horizontal model has seven key elements (Byrne 1993).

1. **Organizing around strategy, not task:** Instead of creating a structure around functions or methodologies, the annual giving program is structured around three to five core processes with specific performance goals.

2. **Flattening hierarchy:** A flatter structure reduces supervision of staff and volun-

Exhibit 9–2 Staff-Dominated Hierarchical Model

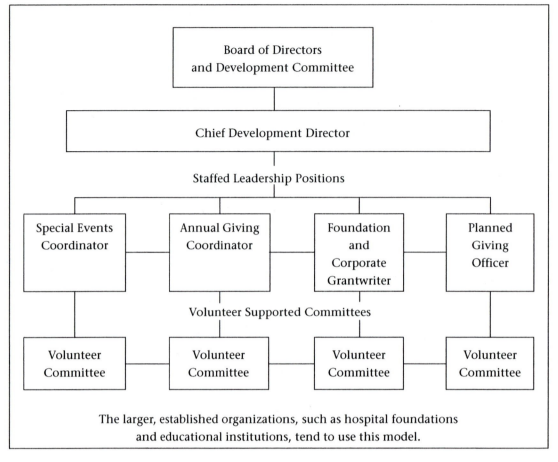

The larger, established organizations, such as hospital foundations
and educational institutions, tend to use this model.

Exhibit 9–3 Team-Oriented Horizontal Model

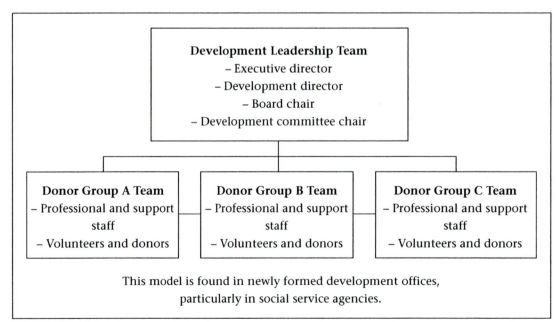

This model is found in newly formed development offices,
particularly in social service agencies.

teers, combines fragmented annual giving tasks, eliminates work that fails to add value, and cuts day-to-day operating activities to a minimum.

3. **Using teams to manage strategies:** A team approach has a common purpose that limits supervisory roles; the team is held accountable for measurable performance goals related to each constituency/case core processes.

4. **Letting donors drive performance:** Donor satisfaction is the primary measure of performance, not profitability. The focus of people's work is on building relationships, rather than technical systems management.

5. **Rewarding team performance:** Staff and volunteers are rewarded for the performance of the entire team, not individual performance.

6. **Maximizing donor contact:** Staff and volunteers have direct, regular contact with donors, increasing the potential for satisfactory matching.

7. **Informing and training all employees:** The amount of information given to all staff and volunteers is increased, teaching them to perform their own analysis and make their own decisions.

The job descriptions in Exhibit 9–4 are provided as a reference tool: they articulate roles and responsibilities for the development team and the development director (titles vary from organization to organization). The functions are applicable to all types of organizations and all sizes of development or annual giving programs.

Step 9 in the Annual Integrated Development Process: Recruit, Train, Empower, and Reward Volunteers and Staff

In fund raising, the principal focus of management/leadership is *not* on tasks, processes, or systems. Rather, it is on maximizing the organization's greatest asset—people. Implicit to this focus is a sufficient commitment to the pro-

vision of support resources (or you will wear people down). It is fundamentally impossible to over-invest in the development of people's potential: first and foremost in their learning and second in their sustenance. According to Brian O'Connell (1985), "The role of staff in a voluntary agency is simple. Your job is to bring about the maximum volunteer involvement, and volunteer satisfaction. You must stimulate, educate, and service. Everything you do must be directly related to the single underlying concept of voluntary action—the promotion of citizen interest in affairs."

To build human capacity within the nonprofit sector is to assert that volunteers are essential for fund raising and that the role of staff is to recruit, train, and enable them—by example. Every staff job description should include responsibility for mobilizing, nurturing, and motivating volunteers. If this sounds more like leadership than management, it is. And the paradox of it is that staff do provide the leadership, whereas volunteers/trustees are actually "in charge"—from a governance position.

Interdependence of Volunteers and Staff

The paradox of "who is in charge here" presents a challenge and a hypothesis that volunteers and staff are really interdependent partners in the philanthropic process. Each brings professional expertise that is different; together, they create a synergistic dual. This does not mean that volunteers or staff could or should do each other's job. There is a fine line where governance and management/leadership come together, and crossing "boundaries" creates tension and conflict. Rather, the notion of interdependence means that volunteers and staff respectfully work to bring their interests, needs, and expertise together, occasionally making up for the shortcom-

> **Volunteers are essential for fund raising, and the role of staff is to recruit, train, and enable them by example.**

Exhibit 9–4 Job Descriptions for The Development Committee/Team

ROLES AND RESPONSIBILITIES OF THE DEVELOPMENT COMMITTEE/TEAM

Purpose

The purpose of the Development Team (or Development Committee) is to, through philanthropy, assure that the (name of organization) has the resources necessary to accomplish its mission. The team oversees the fund development program, its policies, procedures, and activities. The team guides the board of directors in its understanding of and participation in the philanthropic process. The team comprises trustees, development staff, and key volunteers.

Roles and Responsibilities

- **Leadership:** Be knowledgeable about the philanthropic community and the fund-raising process and participate fully to advance the philanthropic position of (name of organization).

- **Oversight:** Provide strategic direction to the development of short- and long-range fund development plans that will address the (name of organization)'s immediate, intermediate, and long-term needs.

- **Fiduciary:** Develop realistic, achievable, and measurable financial goals based on real and anticipated needs with an emphasis on operating projects and program initiatives that advance the (name of organization)'s mission. Assure their realization.

- **Governance:** Ensure that the development policies, procedures, budgets, and program efforts are consistent with (name of organization) and are managed with efficiency and effectiveness.

- **Stewardship:** Ensure that all philanthropic resources are allocated according to donor intent and in the best interest of the recipients served by (name of organization).

- **Advocacy:** Serve as liaison to the community at large, advocating the (name of organization)'s role in (describe organization's purpose).

- **Community Outreach:** Lead the efforts to involve the community in (name of organization) efforts. Identify, cultivate, and enlist other key community leaders in the philanthropic process.

- **Teamwork:** Attend all team/committee meetings and be an active participant in all discussions and activities. Actively support all fund-raising events through attendance, and encourage others to participate and support through volunteerism or/and philanthropic gifts.

- **Philanthropic Leadership:** Demonstrate the importance of philanthropy at (name of organization) by setting an example for others. Make a significant gift to the annual board campaign and other special campaigns, and give serious consideration to gifts for the future.

continues

Exhibit 9–4 continued

POSITION DESCRIPTION FOR THE DIRECTOR OF PHILANTHROPIC AND INSTITUTIONAL DEVELOPMENT

Purpose

The Director of Philanthropic and Institutional Development is responsible for providing dynamic and creative leadership of the development and communications at (name of organization). This position is responsible for planning, designing, and managing all efforts to broaden public awareness of the agency's mission and to generate financial and volunteer support to help underwrite its programs and services. This position requires leadership attributes, strong interpersonal skills, management competencies, communication abilities, and ethical principles. The director serves as a valued member of the administrative team, with accountability to the chief executive officer.

Roles and Responsibilities in Philanthropic Development

- Provide ongoing analysis and assessment of the philanthropic environment, within and outside the organization, to ensure that development strategies and functions are relevant and thriving.

- Work with the board Development Committee to establish short- and long-range development plans and programs that will maximize philanthropic potential. Strategies include annual giving, major gifts, foundation and corporate grant seeking, endowment funding, planned gifts, capital campaigns, and special projects as needed.

- In concert with agency administration and committee members, identify, validate, and prioritize programs that depend on philanthropic support. Prepare case statements, case messages, and case materials to convey effectively a sense of relevance, urgency, and realistic attainment.

- Provide the research necessary to identify and qualify constituent markets. Work with the board committee to establish opportunistic and realistic giving goals and to clarify solicitation roles and responsibilities.

- Develop and implement fund-raising approaches and methodologies that will successfully communicate the organization's needs while matching donors' interests. Oversee prospect identification, donor acquisition, donor renewal, and donor upgrade programs that generate increased financial support.

- Ensure an environment of collaboration between volunteers and staff. Provide information, education, and training so volunteers can be involved actively and successful in fund-raising efforts.

- Initiate and maintain positive exchange relationships with donors, funders, board members, volunteers, program staff, and clientele. Provide opportunities for involvement and engagement.

continues

Exhibit 9–4 continued

- Oversee efforts to acknowledge, recognize, and cultivate donors. Ensure that all philanthropic funds receive the highest level of stewardship.

- Work with the board Communications Committee and agency administration to develop a communications plan that will achieve an increasingly high level of community awareness for and interest in the agency's mission.

- Oversee agency-wide public education and awareness activities, including promotions, brochures, newsletters, media, audiovisuals, tours, presentations, and cause-relating marketing.

Management Functions

- Design an infrastructure that ensures all resources are used wisely, and all strategies are implemented successfully.

- Develop policies and procedures to govern development and communication activities, according to rules, regulations, and approved standard practices.

- Hire, train, manage, and evaluate staff who are responsible for daily operations, general communications, public education projects, donor events and activities, database management, donor research and relations, report generation, and acknowledgments.

- Maintain a work environment that supports teamwork, diversity, and respect for individuals.

- Participate as a member of the administrative team. Help set overall agency priorities and objectives in cooperation with other team members, and participate in the review of agency performance.

Qualifications

- Minimum of a BA degree in management, communications, marketing, or a related field; preferred additional training in philanthropy and development, estate and planned giving, human relations and psychology, organizational development and finance

- A minimum of five years of progressively responsible development experience, with proven achievement in individual donor relations and community partnerships

- Working knowledge of constituency relations, annual and major gift strategies, corporate and foundation grant seeking, volunteer and staff management, and nonprofit marketing

- Strong administrative, management, written, and verbal communication skills

- Experience in planning, budgeting, supervision, and evaluation in a nonprofit setting

- Ability to integrate development and communications theory and practice

- Demonstrated competence in recruitment and motivation of volunteer leadership

- Knowledge of community issues, organizations, and resources

- Demonstrated ability to work with people from diverse cultures and backgrounds

- Commitment to working in a mission-driven organization

ings of each other while never imposing on each other. When the question comes up, "Who is responsible for establishing policy," the answer is the trustees. For the question, "Who is responsible for being knowledgeable about the philanthropic process," the answer is the staff. "Who then is responsible for fund raising"—the answer is both.

To accept the interdependence between board and staff means that each is willing to step forward as leader at one time and to pull back as servant at another. What little research has been done on the relationships between volunteers and staff in fund raising suggests that tensions are both natural (due to status differences and an unclear understanding of roles) and resolvable (when respect and honesty form the prevailing atmosphere).

Then, how do we engage board members successfully in fund raising? In a article on building effective fund-raising teams, Temple and Seiler assert that the key to fostering attitudes of trust and respect between board members and staff on their complementary resources and roles is **training.**

> Staff must be trained to understand the skills and strengths they bring to the trustee-staff team so that they can approach trustees with confidence. Staff training must also focus on the importance of providing leadership by example to trustees other than by managing and directing them tightly. Training for trustees also should include an overview of the support and leadership they can expect from staff, with a focus on the special strengths that trustees bring to the fund-raising process (Seiler and Temple 1994, 77).

The Crucial Role of the Board in Fund Raising: The Need for Training

One measure of a successful organization is the extent to which its board members understand their governance roles and their legal, moral, and ethical responsibilities. Another measure is how involved they are in the organization's fund raising. According to Brian O'Connell (1985), former president of the Independent Sector and author of *The Board Member's Book,* "The fund-raising commitment must begin with the board and must be high on the agenda of a significant number of the trustees. Not only must it be of high priority, it must be high in status and recognition within the organization" (120).

But the familiar cry of "I wasn't recruited to ask people for money" ignores all our good intentions—board members *are* legally responsible for ensuring that the organization has sufficient financial resources to carry out its mission, *but it seems like* they take off their "responsibility hat" when they come on board. In a 1987 study of ten boards in the San Francisco area, 50 percent of those board members responding said that they found fund raising to be distasteful, at least to some degree. On a positive note, 75 percent indicated they would ask for money if they had to, whereas 10 percent would refuse (Wagner 1987, 37).

It is unfair and unrealistic to ask board members to be involved in fund raising without giving them adequate training. According to Lilya Wagner, "Board members become effective fund raisers when they understand the psychological principles of giving and receiving" (1987, 39). She recommends using the five-stage adoption process model presented by Wilcox, Ault, and Agree:

1. **Create awareness:** When communications focus on the organization's mission, board members become aware of the need for fund raising, and consensus about the *rationale* for philanthropy is established. Discussions or training should center on what the organization does, where it is going, what might limit its growth, and the benefit of philanthropic support (financial and community involvement). Strategic thinking and factual knowledge combined will stimulate advocacy for fund raising. A few fund-raising enthusiasts on the board will begin to influence the thinking of others. This is the best

time to establish a new or revitalize an ineffectual development committee/team.

2. **Stimulate interest**: Once the board recognizes there is a reason to pursue philanthropic support as a key organizational strategy, they need to have more information about what it entails. Relevant information provided through committee meetings and training sessions helps build the case for philanthropy. Knowledge about the history, philosophy, and theory of the philanthropic process is essential to their learning. The more the board members know, the more comfortable they become that fund raising is a viable course of action. Because most board members see fund raising as a "tactic," training will allow them to view philanthropic fund raising as a professional endeavor.

As interest builds, board members will begin to indicate preferences for involvement, as well as exhibiting collective synergy. They will begin to see the possibilities, rather than the limitations. And they will begin to recognize the critical importance of building a sustainable program, not one reliant on a quick fix. It seems every board wants their share of the "transfer of wealth," suggesting that a planned giving program be instituted before a fully functional annual giving program is developed.

3. **Encourage evaluation**: Training now turns to evaluating how the fund-raising ideas meet specific needs and wants. Discussions turn to alternative solutions (generating more fees or taking on a cause-related marketing project), the magnitude of the fund-raising program (will we need additional staff, where do we want to be in three years), and the responsibility of the board and volunteers (what will we need to do, to give, and specifically what do I want to contribute in leadership). Collectively and, most important, individually, the board mem-

bers begin to seek feedback from others—they want to validate their involvement and test enthusiasm. By engaging others in discussions, fund raising becomes more acceptable. Anxiety is lessened, the process to build a stronger fund-raising program is validated, and momentum is built. Ideas for cases, constituencies, and campaigns are abundant.

4. **Time to try**: With enthusiasm high and the rationale firmly in place, confidence builds to a point where training can focus on how to ask for a gift. This is the time for solid techniques, practice sessions, reasonable and achievable goals and assignments—and teamwork. This may be the time for the board members to experiment, but success is an imperative if the momentum is to continue. As board members begin to solicit others for support, their enthusiasm and confidence carry them, serving as another motivator for others to participate.

5. **Build on the acceptance**: Training continues, as the development committee and the board become fully immersed in fund raising. The focus shifts to engaging others in accepting that fund raising is the board's role, that participation is rewarding, and that the organizational culture sees it as a the norm rather than the exception. Only as board members continue to be involved in fund raising will they integrate it into their belief system—and influence others to "come on board."

One final recommendation—at the next development team meeting, have a discussion about the various ways that volunteers and trustees can be involved in fund raising *without asking for a gift*. Once the list is completed, ask the volunteers to take it with them, to prioritize the suggestions, and to send it back for staff to compile, print up, and distribute at the next meetings of the development team and board.

Suggestions for volunteer involvement beyond asking others for a contribution include the following:

- Make a contribution; ask your employer to match it.
- Help with the identification of cases and the design of fund-raising projects/programs.
- Suggest names for the prospect list; help research and evaluate them.
- Mail pertinent information to qualified prospects.
- Host an informational event for a group of prospects.
- Invite a prospect/donor to lunch.
- Introduce prospects to the organization's administrators and program staff.
- Participate in a fund-raising event.
- Make personal thank-you calls, and write thank-you letters.
- Talk about being a board member with everyone you meet.

What Board Members and Other Volunteers Expect in Return

In the course of engaging board members in fund raising, it is helpful to have a good perspective of what board and other volunteers expect in return.

The impulse to volunteer is simply a human one. It is the freedom to choose your own work, to pursue a cause or a passion, to innovate and shape, and to grow in the process. The motivations to volunteer remain the same today as in years past. People are motivated by the expectation of need fulfillment, be it recognition from peers, accomplishing something for themselves, achieving psychosocial benefits, or altruistically helping others in need.

Today, more than ever, people are their own initiators of volunteerism—they determine when they can volunteer, what they want to volunteer for, and what they want to accomplish as a result. And they volunteer because of the expectation of need fulfillment in the following areas:

> **Today, more than ever, people are their own initiators of volunteerism.**

- **Recognition:** People are remunerated with money at work; as volunteers they are rewarded with recognition. Volunteers need personal thanks from the people who matter, which is different with each volunteer, and recognition equal to what other volunteers receive.
- **Control:** People often volunteer because they feel in control of the situation; they can say no or yes, they can continue or quit, they can pick the projects they want, and they can do them in the way they want. Only as a volunteer do people have as much "say." They need to be given the ability to control, as long as they perform satisfactorily and "do no harm."
- **Variety:** Many volunteer because the work, the people, the organization are different from everything else in their life. Just as fund raisers resist volunteering as fund raisers, accountants don't always relish being asked to do exactly or only what they do every day of the week. Volunteers will stay motivated too if they have variety in their position appointments and job assignments.
- **Growth:** When asked why people serve on boards, they cite the exposure to information on issues about which they feel strongly, which they would not otherwise receive. Volunteers need to be stimulated, to be challenged, and to grow in knowledge.
- **Affiliation:** Volunteer associations bring people together with common interests, for similar reasons. Meeting others, getting to know them, and having ongoing relationships with them are powerful stimuli. For some, volunteering is their major form of socialization and affiliation. Volunteers need to have many and diverse opportunities to be involved with other volunteers, donors, staff, and the like.
- **Power:** Power and influence go hand in hand for volunteers. When they are involved in something they feel is important, they work hard to help it succeed, especially if they feel empowered. The

more influence and power that come with their involvement, the more satisfying the experience. Volunteers need to be able to influence decisions and have opportunities to guide the program to fruition.

- **Fun:** When volunteering is fun, sometimes that is reward enough. Volunteers need to be with people who do not take themselves too seriously, in social situations that are entertaining and pleasant, and to have a good time while doing good.
- **Uniqueness:** People naturally seek to do what they have not done before: to build a new zoo, to cure a life-threatening disease, to premiere a modern ballet, to help an underprivileged child go to college. Volunteers need the excitement that comes from doing something special and different.

In addition to understanding what are the volunteers' internal motivations, fund raisers will benefit from knowing what will cause them to volunteer *again*. The following actions demonstrate that volunteers are valued:

- Acknowledge and recognize people's valuable time.
- Ensure there is a "fit" between volunteer and organization.
- Clarify and reclarify job responsibilities, roles, and tasks.
- Consider using volunteers in paraprofessional positions.
- Recognize and meet the volunteers' needs.
- Provide professional volunteer management and support.
- Recognize them at the right time by the right person.

The Volunteer Management Plan

Whether yours is a new organization or one with a well-established development program, it would benefit from a written volunteer management plan. A plan helps delineate the specific roles and responsibilities of volunteers at every level and in every capacity. A suggested outline follows:

Step 1. Determine the need for volunteers.
   A. What is the overall purpose?
   B. What are the guiding principles?
   C. What is their purview, by team or committee?

Step 2. Define desired attributes and composition.
   A. What are the desired attributes, experiences, and expertise?
   B. How many volunteers?
   C. Who are the best prospects?
   D. What are the volunteers' expectations and benefits?

Step 3. Establish the recruitment process.
   A. Who is the best person(s) to recruit the prospect(s)?
   B. What materials, background, or information are needed?
   C. What are the timelines, expectations, and desired outcomes?

Step 4. Provide training and orientation.
   A. Who will provide the training?
   B. What materials are needed; what information will be given?
   C. When, how long, and how often will training occur?

Step 5. Make assignments.
   A. What specific assignments or jobs are there?
   B. What are the specific goals, objectives, and timelines?
   C. Who will provide what kind of support services?

Step 6. Evaluate performance and satisfaction.
   A. How is performance measured? How is satisfaction measured?
   B. Who will do the evaluations? What method?
   C. How often does evaluation occur?

Step 7. Provide recognition and rewards.
   A. What kinds of recognition will be provided?
   B. Who will be involved?
   C. When does it take place?

Being a Great Manager of Great People

When discussing the subject of management, most conversations are focused on the management of people, rather than the management of systems. People who are charged with managing human resources may consider it the number one challenge—there are many conflicts inherent in relationships, especially those that are more inclined organizationally or vertically. Too, management consultants and popular authors emphasize building relationships over building algorithms.

If you are already a successful manager, you have not had to worry about the details for a long time. In fact, it's a good possibility that all that "micro stuff" belongs in someone else's job description. People who run the company get there by delegating, engaging, and empowering people.

Some say that great management happens when the typical hierarchical organization chart is turned upside down, implying that the manager's job is not to dictate down, but to hold the organization "up" by hiring the best people, giving them the resources they need, and letting them do their jobs.

Step 10 in the Annual Integrated Development Process: Implement Fund-Raising Approaches and Activities

Key Elements

Step 10 in the Annual Integrated Development Process seems almost anticlimatic if you are process-oriented, and long overdue if you are action-oriented. The implementation step is singularly concerned with control; the development of systems that will ensure that goals and plans are fulfilled. With planning, analysis, and execution strategies and tactics in place, management principles demand systems, policies, and procedures to guide the implementation to a successful conclusion. The following elements are basic to this fund-raising step:

- The Annual Plan: Chapter 7
- Job descriptions for individuals, and committees: Exhibit 9–4
- A solicitation strategy, communications, and acknowledgment schedule by constituency, vehicle, date: Exhibit 9–5
- A task schedule, by campaign and project: Exhibit 9–6
- A gift processing system and procedures: Exhibit 9–7

Implementation Fundamentals for Annual Giving

This implementation step is not entirely dependent on systems; the successful implementation of annual giving strategies also relies on the dynamic interactions that each of us bring to the work we do in different ways. Since organized philanthropy began, we fund raisers have learned from the experiences of those who preceded us, and each generation has added richness to the industry's axioms as time passed. If you were to ask the majority of seasoned professionals to give you a pathway to success, in just a few words, they would undoubtedly give you a similar list of proven implementation fundamentals that have time and again been successful. Mine are

- Plan early, work late.
- Involve volunteers early on.
- Give priority attention to core donors.
- Put your emphasis where it counts and matters.
- Start at the top of the pyramid.
- Raise funds year-round, seamlessly.
- Use diverse methods and creative techniques.
- Use personal solicitation most of the time.
- Cultivate more often than you solicit.
- Write like you talk.
- Sing the organization's praises.
- Give away the praise and the rewards.
- Shoot for the stars; be happy with the moon.
- Love your donors as your friends.
- Help people be all they can be and aspire to do.
- Let your donors give to things they want.

Exhibit 9–5 Solicitation, Communication, and Acknowledgment Schedule

SOLICITATION STRATEGY SCHEDULE

Constituent Campaigns	Personal Visits or Presentation	Personal Phone Calls	Personal Letters	Telemarketing	Holiday Direct Mail
Board Members	X Oct/97	X Nov/97	X Nov/97		X Nov/97X
Employees	X Sept/97	X Oct/97	X Nov/97		X Nov/97X
Prospects Group A		X May/97	X May/97		X Nov/97
Group B			X May/97	X June/97	X Nov/97
Group C			X May/97	X June/97	X Nov/97
Donors Group A	X May/97		X June/97		X Nov/97
Group B		X May/97	X June/97		X Nov/97
Group C			X June/97	X June/97	X Nov/97

CULTIVATION AND COMMUNICATIONS SCHEDULE

Constituent Groups	Call from Dev. Office	Personal Invitation to Tour/Event	Personalized Report from President	Newsletter and Event Invitation	Thank-you Call from a Volunteer
Board Members	X	X	X	X	
Employees			X	X	
Donors Group A	X	X	X	X	X
Group B		X	X	X	X
Group C			X	X	X

ACKNOWLEDGMENT AND RECOGNITION SCHEDULE

Constituent Group	Thank-you Letter from President	Personal Note from Volunteer	Listing in Annual Report	Listing on Donor Wall	Personal Recognition at Annual Event
Board Members	X		X		
Employees	X	X	X		
Donors Group A	X	X	X	X	X
Group B	X	X	X	X	
Group C	X	X	X		

Exhibit 9–6 Schedule of Tasks, Campaigns, and Projects

ACTIVITY BY CASE	JAN	FEB	MAR	APR	MAY	JUNE	JULY	AUG	SEPT	OCT	NOV	DEC
Case 1 — School Success												
Mailing to prospects			�		▧	▧	▧				▧	
Mailing to donors										▧		▧
Mailing to lapsed donors				▧			▧					
Information donor luncheons												
Luncheons to encourage upgrades								▧	▧			
Add names to prospect list		▧	▧			▧		▧	▧			
Plan board campaign 97						▧		▧				
Plan winter campaign 98												
Create book campaign			▧									
Board campaign 97					▧					▧	▧	
Past board luncheons			▧			▧						
New board orientation												
Grant requests to corporations/foundations		▧	▧	▧	▧	▧		▧	▧			▧
Personal meetings with corporations/foundations												

continues

Exhibit 9–6 continued

ACTIVITY	JAN	FEB	MAR	APR	MAY	JUNE	JULY	AUG	SEPT	OCT	NOV	DEC
Case II — Preventing Violence												
Grant request to small businesses			X	X	X							
Grant request to civic clubs				X	X	X	X					
Mailing to churches							X					
Grant requests to corporations/foundations	X	X	X								X	X
Personal meetings with corporations/foundations	X	X	X								X	X
Case III — Community Building												
Planning	X	X										
Grant requests to corporations/foundations	X	X							X	X	X	X
Personal meetings with corporations/foundations	X	X							X	X	X	X

continues

Exhibit 9–6 continued

ACTIVITY	JAN	FEB	MAR	APR	MAY	JUNE	JULY	AUG	SEPT	OCT	NOV	DEC
COMMUNICATIONS												
Newsletter				■	■			■	■			
Annual report		■	■									
Annual meeting				■	■							
Holiday greetings										■	■	
Public awareness planning					■							
Brochures updated					■	■	■	■				
Newsletter updated						■	■					
ADMINISTRATION												
Choose/integrate new software					■	■	■	■				
Integrate new Development Director				■	■							
Meetings with board to determine:						■	■	■				
• LIA												
• Fund-raising interests												
Introductory meetings with foundations						■	■	■	■			
Hire communication specialist												

Courtesy of Family and Children's Service, Minneapolis, Minnesota.

Exhibit 9–7 Gift Processing System and Procedures

Data Processing Staff

- receives the gift
- performs data entry tasks
- updates donor records/files
- prepares daily reports
- prepares transmittal

Business Office Staff

- verifies transmittal
- prepares/makes bank deposit
- receipts as revenue
- issues accounting reports

Development Staff

- reconciles finance reports
- prepares various gift reports
- analyzes data
- reports to Development Committee/Team

Auditor

- reviews financial records
- reviews donor files
- prepares annual audit statement for board review

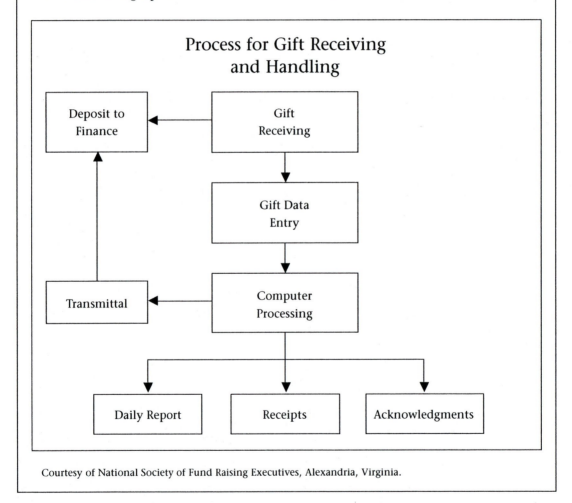

Process for Gift Receiving and Handling

Courtesy of National Society of Fund Raising Executives, Alexandria, Virginia.

Common Mistakes

Besides passing on proven fundamentals, it seems to me that experienced fund raisers ought to make a list of their mistakes and pass them on to newcomes as a way of alerting them to ones they will surely make. It seems inevitable that mistakes will be made, but why they are the same ones over and over again, is a puzzle. Given fund raising's experiential nature, mistake making must be an essential factor in learning. Here are a few that just won't go away.

- no written fund-raising goals
- board members are in name only
- board members who do not give
- inadequate records
- failure to do your homework
- not giving priority to individual donors
- reluctance to ask for gifts
- forgetting to thank donors
- failure to inform, educate, and motivate donors
- failure to seek fund-raising assistance

Step 11 in the Annual Integrated Development Process: Evaluate Strategies and Outcomes; Recommend Improvements and Changes

Accountability, Program Performance, and Profitability

The subject of accountability is on everyone's mind, as competition is growing for limited precious resources, attention is focused on productivity and performance outcomes, and skepticism about effectiveness leads to a demand for more information. What is a nonprofit organization accountable for and to whom? Who are fund raisers accountable to and for what?

Nonprofits, because of their charitable orientation, are held accountable for what they do and how they do it. The public has high expectations of nonprofits—higher than might be imposed on any other sector—because of their

> The public has high expectations of nonprofits—higher than might be imposed on any other sector.

level of esteem for the kind of good work that nonprofits perform. Holding nonprofit organizations accountable for their actions requires some consequences if those actions do not meet expectations, whether they are overly high or not.

Let's say an organization proclaims its mission to be the prevention of teen pregnancy. How would the public hold the organization accountable? What are the criteria for measuring pregnancy counseling services? What are the services measured against? How are the results interpreted? What are the consequences if the organization cannot provide evidence that teen pregnancies were prevented?

Let's say a volunteer agrees to solicit six of his friends who have been identified as high-potential prospects, and he only solicits two of them. How is the volunteer held accountable? By whom? What are the consequences of his inability to fulfill his responsibility?

Let's say a fund raiser implements three different fund-raising projects, but only two of them generate funds while one, a special event, loses money. Does the fund raiser combine the results of the three and report to the board that the overall fund-raising program was a success? Or does he or she let the donors who came to the special event know that their money was "lost"?

Accountability is the public's biggest point of contention with the nonprofit sector—the public's trust literally depends on it. It is the democratic way of exercising respect and compassion for the organization or the individual and of placing responsibility for the impact of one's actions on the community. According to Boris and Odendahl (1990), "In business, profit and the satisfaction of customers may be paramount; in government, public interest and the well-being of the citizen and the state may be the primary objectives; in nonprofits, public interest and the well-being of the clients or those people or ideas served, may be the most important" (190).

The public feels entitled to ask, Are nonprofit organizations and the people who work in them doing what they say they do? Are they wise and prudent users of donated and other resources? In all that they do, do they follow strict guidelines, standards, and procedures? Are there measures and benchmarks of productivity? And are there consequences and penalties if accountability fails? Do they expend each dollar and each hour in the best possible way? Do they have the public's interest and well-being in mind at all times?

Accountability is the way the public measures what philanthropic organizations do in three basic areas: (1) charitable purpose, (2) program performance, and (3) donative resources. State and federal regulatory agencies, national and local charitable governing organizations, and even organizations themselves have policies regarding accountability, governance, use of funds, and fund-raising practices. Step 11 focuses on evaluating only fund-raising practices.

Step 11 is the last step in establishing an annual integrated development program, bringing the process full circle and ready to begin all over again. Remember, this process is an annual one, which will change each year as a result of the evaluation of the outcomes; continued quality improvement is the goal.

Typically, evaluation is a management function that enables the fund raiser, the development department, and the organization to grow. Like Step 10, the activity of evaluation is dependent on systems: performance appraisals, cost analysis instruments, solicitation responses reports, and measurements of outcomes against benchmarks of the organization and the industry. Once collected, the data are evaluated. There are many resources to turn to to obtain examples of fund-raising evaluation tools and measures; entire books are dedicated to them. This section focuses on four areas that require evaluation, noting their respective inputs and outputs: (1) constituency relationships, (2) program produc-

tivity, (3) financial results, and (4) staff/volunteer performance (Exhibit 9–8).

Reports on Annual Sources of Funds, Uses, Programs, and Rate of Growth

Few practitioners have written or presented as extensively on the subject of fund-raising evaluation than James Greenfield. In his book *Fund Raising Fundamentals: A Guide to Annual Giving for Professionals and Volunteers,* he offers many practical evaluation forms.

Exhibit 9–9   Rate of Growth in Giving
Exhibit 9–10   Volunteer Effectiveness Measurement
Exhibit 9–11   Basic Gift Report by Fund-Raising Method
Exhibit 9–12   Cost-per-Dollar Raised Report by Fund-Raising Method
Exhibit 9–13   Forecasting: Results with Program Cost and Performance Measurement

In Conclusion: Accountability of Fund Raising

In recent times there has been a great amount of scholarly inquiry and debate about whether fund raising is a profession, an emerging profession, or just another skill. That debate is unlikely to end as long as there are scholars (and that is good). Were the debate to be decided by mere practitioners, we would say that most assuredly fund raising is an emerging profession—given the magnitude of our practice, the growing body of knowledge, the interest by researchers in our activities and our outcomes, and the growing prestige by which we are held in our nonprofit institutions.

But whether we are in a profession is not for us to determine. The status of the fund-raising profession is determined by others' regard for it. How the public views fund raising— its people and its practices—ultimately determines our level of influence, credibility, and status. Our ability to *account* for, to *evaluate,* and to *improve our practices* comes not from

Exhibit 9–8 Evaluation Elements

EVALUATION ELEMENTS FOR CONSTITUENCY RELATIONS

Donor Records (inputs)
- ☐ Demographics
- ☐ Original source
- ☐ Constituency type
- ☐ Gift dates and methods
- ☐ Solicitation techniques
- ☐ Gift sizes and designations
- ☐ Events attended
- ☐ Visits or tours

Donor Reports (outputs)
- ☐ View of giving pyramid
- ☐ Donor composition
- ☐ Levels of giving
- ☐ Constituency comparisons
- ☐ Technique comparisons
- ☐ Growth rates
- ☐ Responsiveness to events
- ☐ Levels of involvement

EVALUATION ELEMENTS FOR PROGRAM PRODUCTIVITY

Gift Records
- ☐ Gift source/level
- ☐ Campaign type
- ☐ Solicitation technique
- ☐ Date/time of year
- ☐ Case message
- ☐ Level of cultivation

Gift Reports
- ☐ Gift levels
- ☐ Response results
- ☐ Rate of return
- ☐ Calendar comparisons
- ☐ Response comparisons
- ☐ Rate of impact/growth

EVALUATION ELEMENTS FOR FINANCIAL RESULTS

Budgets
- ☐ Overall organization budget
  - • sources of revenue
  - • expense by line item

- ☐ Program budget
  - • sources of revenue
  - • expenses by line item

- ☐ Development operating budget
  - • revenue by fund-raising source
  - • revenue by fund designation
  - • department expense by line item

- ☐ Project budgets
  - • revenue by project
  - • fund-raising expense by project

Financial Reports
- ☐ Balance sheet

- ☐ Operating statement
  - • revenue and expense by month/year

- ☐ Cost comparisons
  - • rate of growth
  - • changes in giving patterns
  - • cost-benefit analysis
  - • cash flow

continues

Exhibit 9–8 continued

EVALUATION ELEMENTS FOR STAFF AND VOLUNTEER PERFORMANCE

Job Descriptions
☐ By position
☐ By team
☐ Roles and responsibilities
☐ Expectation/outcomes
☐ Performance standards

Performance Appraisals
☐ Effectiveness in performance
☐ Measurable outcomes
☐ Interviews with others
☐ Checklists

Exhibit 9–9 Rate of Growth in Giving

	Two Years Ago	Last Year	Annual Rate of Growth %	This Year	Annual Rate of Growth %	Cumula-tive Rate of Growth %
Number of donors						
Number of volunteers						
Number of dollars						
• by source						
• by purpose						
• by program						
Average gift size						
Average cost per gift						
Overall "bottom line" cost percentage						

Source: Reprinted with permission from J. Greenfield, *AHP Spring Journal*, p. 21, © 1994, Association for Healthcare Philanthropy.

forms, or schedules, or financial reports—it comes from asking all the right questions on behalf of the donative public and getting the right answers. Regulation by others, no matter how well intended takes away our right to a profession. It is we who must hold ourselves accountable to a higher standard than others might—with no dual agendas.

Exhibit 9–10 Volunteer Effectiveness Measurement

Number of qualified prospects and trained volunteers available	Low/Medium/High
Number and percent of prospects assigned to volunteers	Low/Medium/High
Number and percent of calls made and percent of gifts received	Low/Medium/High
Number of prior donors renewed and average gift size	Low/Medium/High
Number of upgraded gifts requested, percentage of response, and average gift size	Low/Medium/High
Number and percent of prior donors *not* renewed and the value of their prior gifts not yet renewed	Low/Medium/High

Score: Low =

Medium =

High =

Source: Reprinted with permission from J. Greenfield, *AHP Spring Journal*, p. 24, © 1994, Association for Healthcare Philanthropy.

Exhibit 9–11 Basic Gift Report by Fund-Raising Method (FY94)

Fund-raising Programs	Number of Gifts	Gift Amount	Average Gift Size*
Direct mail acquisition	365	$ 15,500	$ 43
Direct mail renewal	1,005	76,500	76
Membership dues	485	48,500	100
Benefit events	3	59,600	19,867
Personal solicitation	283	102,000	360
TOTALS:	2,141	$ 302,100	$ 141

*Rounded to nearest dollar

Source: Reprinted with permission from J. Greenfield, *AHP Spring Journal*, p. 23, © 1994, Association for Healthcare Philanthropy.

Exhibit 9–12 Cost-Per-Dollar Raised Report by Fund-Raising Method (FY94)

	Gift amount	Budget approved	Budget expended	Cost per dollar raised
Direct mail acquisition	$ 15,500	$ 14,500	$ 14,798	$ 0.96
Direct mail renewal	76,500	1,500	1,620	0.21
Membership dues	48,500	550	585	0.12
Benefit events (3)	59,600	20,000	21,747	0.36
Personal solicitation	102,000	1,200	1,250	0.12
Direct costs	$ 302,100	$ 37,750	$ 38,700	
Indirect costs and overhead		$ 80,000	$ 79,800	
Total costs		$ 117,750	$ 118,500	0.39
Return on investment				155%

Source: Reprinted with permission from J. Greenfield, *AHP Fall Journal*, p. 24, © 1994, Association for Healthcare Philanthropy.

Exhibit 9–13 Forecasting: Results with Program Costs and Performance Measurement

	FY92	FY93	FY94	FY95 (Est.)
Contributions income				
Direct mail acquisition	$ 27,500	$ 31,250	$ 35,500	$ 42,000
Direct mail renewal	55,880	69,500	76,500	85,000
Membership dues	40,400	44,000	48,500	55,000
Benefit events (3)	45,500	53,400	59,600	68,000
Personal solicitation	58,500	65,500	82,000	90,000
Totals:	$227,830	$263,650	$302,100	$340,000
Fund-raising expense				
Labor/payroll	$ 71,500	$ 75,300	$ 79,800	$ 84,000
Nonpayroll costs	32,500	35,600	38,700	40,000
Totals:	$104,000	$110,900	$118,500	$124,000
Net Proceeds	$123,830	$152,750	$183,600	$208,000
Cost-effectiveness percentage	46%	42%	39%	36%
Return on Investment	119%	137%	155%	168%

Source: Reprinted with permission from J. Greenfield, *AHP Fall Journal*, p. 28, © 1994, Association for Healthcare Philanthropy.

References

Boris, E.T., and T.J. Odendahl. 1990. Ethical issues in fund raising and philanthropy. In *Critical issues in American philanthropy*, edited by J. Van Til. San Francisco, CA: Jossey-Bass.

Byrne, J.A. 1993. The horizontal organization. *Business Week* (December 20): 76–81.

Covey, 1989. *Seven Habits of Highly Effective People,* New York: Simon & Schuster.

The Fund Raising School. 1993. *Principles and techniques of fund raising.* Indianapolis, IN: Indiana University Center on Philanthropy.

Independent Sector. 1991. *Ethics and the nation's voluntary and philanthropic community "obedience to the unenforceable."* Washington, DC: Independent Sector.

Kouzes, J.M., and B.Z. Posner. 1987. *The leadership challenge: How to get extraordinary things done in organizations.* San Francisco, CA: Jossey-Bass.

Mixer, J.R. 1993. *Principles of professional fundraising: Useful foundations for successful practice.* San Francisco, CA: Jossey-Bass.

O'Connell, B. 1985. *The board member's book: Making a difference in voluntary organizations.* New York: Foundation Center.

Seiler, T.L., and E.R. Temple. 1994. Trustees and staff: Building effective fundraising teams. *New Directions for Philanthropic Fundraising* (Summer): 77.

Sprinkel Grace, K. 1991. Leadership and team building. In *Achieving excellence in fund raising,* edited by J.A. Rosso. San Francisco, CA: Jossey-Bass.

Sprinkel Grace, K. 1991. Managing for results. In *Achieving excellence in fund raising,* edited by J.A. Rosso. San Francisco, CA: Jossey-Bass.

Temple, E.R. 1993. Fund raising and professional ethics. In *Principles and techniques of fund raising,* edited by the Fund Raising School. Indianapolis, IN: Indiana University Center on Philanthropy.

Wagner, L. 1994. The road least traveled. New *Directions for Philanthropic Fundraising* (Summer): 37, 39.

Bibliography

Broce, T.E. *Fund raising: The guide to raising money from private sources.* Norman, OK: University of Oklahoma Press, 1986.

Burlingame, D.F., and L.J. Hulse. *Taking fund raising seriously: Advancing the profession and practice of raising money.* San Francisco, CA: Jossey-Bass, 1991.

Graham, C.P. *Keep the money coming: A step-by-step guide to annual fundraising.* Sarasota, FL: Pineapple Press, 1992.

Greenfield, J.M. *Fund-raising fundamentals: A guide to annual giving for professionals and volunteers.* New York: John Wiley & Sons, 1994.

Greenfield, J.M. *Fund-raising: Evaluating and managing the fund development process.* New York: John Wiley & Sons, 1991.

Herman, R.D. and associates. *The Jossey-Bass handbook of nonprofit leadership and management.* San Francisco, CA: Jossey-Bass, 1994.

Hodgkinson, V.A., R.W. Lyman, & Associates. *The future of the nonprofit sector.* San Francisco, CA: Jossey-Bass, 1989.

Howe, F. *The board member's guide to fund raising.* San Francisco, CA: Jossey-Bass, 1991.

Ilsey, P.K. *Enhancing the volunteer experience.* San Francisco, CA: Jossey-Bass, 1990.

Krit, R.L. *The fund-raising handbook.* New York: Scott Foresman, 1991.

Kotler, P., and A.R. Andreasen. *Strategic marketing for nonprofit organizations.* (3rd ed.). Englewood Cliffs, NJ: Prentice-Hall, 1987.

Kouzes, J.M., and B.Z. Posner. *The leadership challenge: How to get extraordinary things done in organizations.* San Francisco, CA: Jossey-Bass, 1991.

Mixer, J.R. *Principles of professional fundraising: Useful foundations for successful practice.* San Francisco, CA: Jossey-Bass, 1993.

Nichols, J.E. *Growing from good to great: Repositioning your fund-raising efforts for big gains.* Chicago, IL: Bonus Books, 1995.

Nichols, J.E. *Global demographics: Fund raising for a new world.* Chicago, IL: Bonus Books, 1995.

O'Connell, B., editor. *American's voluntary spirit: A book of readings.* New York: The Foundation Center, 1983.

O'Neill, M. *The third America: The emergence of the nonprofit sector in the United States.* San Francisco, CA: Jossey-Bass, 1989.

Odendahl, T. *Charity begins at home: Generosity and self-interest among the philanthropic elite.* New York: Basic Books, 1990.

Payton, R.L. *Philanthropy: Voluntary action for the public good.* New York and London: American Council on Education, Collier Macmillan Publishers, 1988.

Prince, R.A., and K.M. File. *The seven faces of philanthropy.* San Francisco, CA: Jossey-Bass, 1994.

Rosso, H.A., & Associates. *Achieving excellence in fund raising.* San Francisco, CA: Jossey-Bass, 1991.

Seymour, H.J. *Designs for fund-raising: Principles, patterns, techniques.* Rockville, MD: Fund Raising Institute, A division of Taft Group, 1988.

Shaw, S.C., and M.A. Taylor. *Reinventing fundraising: Realizing the potential of woman's philanthropy.* San Francisco, CA: Jossey-Bass, 1995.

Van Til, J., and Associates. *Critical issues in American philanthropy.* San Francisco, CA: Jossey-Bass, 1990.

Wuthnow, R., and V.A. Hodgkinson. *Faith and philanthropy in America.* San Francisco, CA: Jossey-Bass, 1990.

Index

fund raising, differentiated, 2
historical aspects, 1–7
as institutional process, 3
as sector, 6
skepticism about, 185–186
as spirit, 4–5
as tradition, 3–4
Phonathon, 200–201
Planned giving officer, 17
Power, 262–263
Product orientation, 69
Professional telemarketing,
202–204
advantages, 202–203
disadvantages, 203
in-house professional
telemarketing, 202–203
monthly sustainer, 204
out-sourced professional
telemarketing, 203
sample telephone solicitation
script, 205–206
telephone reinstatement
program, 204
when to use, 203–204
Professionalism, 20–21
Profitability, 270–271, 272
Program evaluation, 52
Program performance, 270–271,
272
Prospect
cultivation, 150–151
donor, differentiated, 151
identification, 150
prospect evaluation grid, 92, 93
prospect research, 17
prospect/donor management
system, 95, 96
solicitation, 151–152
Psychographics, 96
Public information, 13
Public trust, 185
Pyramid of giving, 33, 36, 37

R

Reactive personality, 76–77
Record review, 95–96
Relationship pyramid, 174, 175
Religion
relation to philanthropy, 77
religious affiliation, 4
Repayers, 78
Reward, 167–174
annual giving, 167
Rule of rights, 73

S

Sales orientation, 69–71
Segmentation, 69
Social connectedness, 185
Social exchange relationship, 80
Socialites, 78
Solicitation training session,
41–42
Special event, 209
Special needs list, 167, 168, 169
Special purpose major gifts
campaign, 222–224
Specialization, 20
Staff
annual integrated development
process, 251–256
leadership, 50
roles and responsibilities,
251–256
training, 260–262
Statement of philanthropic values,
57–61
Stewardship
financial responsibility,
179–180
moral and ethical responsibility,
180–181
processes, 179–181
Strategic management, principles,
247–256
Strategic marketing orientation,
71
Sustaining membership drive, 42

T

Targeting, 69
Team solicitation, 198–199
advantages, 199
disadvantages, 199
when to use, 199
Teamwork, 251
team development, 252–253
Technical skills, 19–22
Telefund, 204
Telephone personal solicitation,
199–201
advantages, 199
disadvantages, 200
volunteer phonathon, 200–201
when to use, 200
Telephone pledge, fulfillment, 204
Telephone reinstatement program,
204
Telephone solicitation strategy,
195

Training
board member, 260–262
staff, 260–262
volunteer
consultant, 218–219
personal solicitation
techniques, 218–220
training manual, 219

U

United Way, 43–44

V

Values statement, 57
Vice president of external
relations, 17
Vision, 249
Volunteer, 50–51
annual fund staffed model, 43
annual integrated development
process, 251–256
correlation of volunteering with
philanthropic giving, 80
expectations, 262–263
importance, 50
organization culture, 53
phonathon, 200–201
rating and ranking technique,
92, 94–95
reasons for volunteering, 5
roles and responsibilities,
251–256
training
consultant, 218–219
personal solicitation
techniques, 218–220
training manual, 219
volunteer leadership, 50
volunteer management plan,
263
volunteer partnering, 61, 64
volunteer solicitation pyramid,
annual fund, 41–43

W

Wish list, 169
Women
as fund raisers, 15–16
research on women as
philanthropists, 78–79
Workplace, campaign mode,
43
benefits, 43

About the Author

Karla A. Williams, ACFRE, is an accomplished fund raising executive, with more than 25 years of professional and volunteer experience in the philanthropic field. She is recognized as a leader in the development of innovative fund-raising strategies, and a pioneer in the integration of marketing techniques with fund raising methodologies. She ascribes to a philosophy that places emphasis on donor needs, interests, and values.

Ms. Williams has enjoyed a successful career in four positions: currently as Principal of The Williams Group, with offices in Minnesota and North Carolina; formerly as President of the Children's Hospital Foundation of St. Paul, as Communications and Development Division Director for the Children's Home Society of Minnesota, and prior to that as Executive Director of the Minnesota Zoological Society.

Ms. Williams was in the first class to receive the prestigious designation of Advanced Certified Fund Raising Executive (ACFRE) and currently serves as a board member of the National Society for Fund Raising Executives (NSFRE). She is a frequent lecturer, instructor, and writer on marketing, communications, and development. She serves as faculty for The Fund Raising School at the Indianapolis Center on Philanthropy, the Center for Nonprofit Management at University of St. Thomas in Minnesota, and the NSFRE Survey Course. She has received numerous communications awards through the United Way and other professional organizations. She was awarded the 1993 Major Donor to Philanthropic Education by the Minnesota Foundation Data Center and the 1994 Outstanding Professional Fund Raising Executive from the NSFRE Minnesota Chapter.

As an active volunteer, Ms. Williams has served on many local boards, including the Charities Review Council of Minnesota, the Metropolitan State University Alumni Association Board, the Minnesota International Health Volunteers, and the Family Foundation of America in Milwaukee, Wisconsin. She is active member of the NSFRE Professional Advancement Division and a former president of the NSFRE Minnesota Chapter.

She has a BA from Metropolitan State University with an emphasis in nonprofit management and administration, holds a certificate from the Executive Leadership Institute at Indianapolis Center on Philanthropy and a mini-MBA certificate from the University of St. Thomas, and she has completed her coursework and thesis submission in the Masters of Philanthropy and Development program at St. Mary's University in Minnesota.